Towards Understanding the Qur'ān

Vol. IX

SŪRAHS 33 – 37

English version of

Tafhīm al-Qur'ān

SAYYID ABUL A'LĀ MAWDŪDĪ

Translated and edited by
Zafar Ishaq Ansari

The Islamic Foundation

Published by

THE ISLAMIC FOUNDATION,

Markfield Conference Centre,
Ratby Lane, Markfield,
Leicester LE67 9SY, United Kingdom
Tel: (01530) 244944, Fax: (01530) 244946
E-mail: publications@islamic-foundation.com
Website: www.islamic-foundation.com

Quran House, PO Box 30611, Nairobi, Kenya

PMB 3193, Kano, Nigeria

Distributed by: Kube Publishing Ltd.
Tel: +44(0)1530 249230, Fax: +44(0)1530 249656
E-mail: info@kubepublishing.com

Translated and edited by Zafar Ishaq Ansari

British Library Cataloguing in Publication Data

Mawdudi, Sayyid Abul A'la, 1903–1979
Towards Understanding the Qur'ān
Vol. 9, Surahs 33–37
1. Koran – Commentaries,
I. Title II. Ansari, Zafar Ishaq
III. Islamic Foundation
(Great Britain)
297.1'226-dc22

ISBN–13: 978-0-86037-422-0 *casebound*
ISBN–13: 978-0-86037-427-5 *paperback*

Typeset by: N.A. Qaddoura

بسم الله الرحمن الرحيم

Contents

Editor's Preface – Zafar Ishaq Ansari v

Sūrah* 33: *Al-Aḥzāb (Madīnan Period)
Introduction 1
Text and Explanatory Notes 22
Appendix to *Sūrah Al-Aḥzāb: The Finality of Prophethood* 111

Sūrah* 34: *Saba' (Makkan Period)
Introduction 149
Text and Explanatory Notes 151

Sūrah* 35: *Fāṭir (Makkan Period)
Introduction 205
Text and Explanatory Notes 208

Sūrah* 36: *Yā' Sīn (Makkan Period)
Introduction 239
Text and Explanatory Notes 241

Sūrah* 37: *Al-Ṣāffāt (Makkan Period)
Introduction 277
Text and Explanatory Notes 280

Glossary of Terms 327

Biographical Notes 335

Bibliography 345

Subject Index 351

Name Index 371

Transliteration Table

Arabic Consonants

Initial, unexpressed medial and final:

ء	ʾ	د	d	ض	ḍ	ك	k
ب	b	ذ	dh	ط	ṭ	ل	l
ت	t	ر	r	ظ	ẓ	م	m
ث	th	ز	z	ع	ʿ	ن	n
ج	j	س	s	غ	gh	هـ	h
ح	ḥ	ش	sh	ف	f	و	w
خ	kh	ص	ṣ	ق	q	ي	y

Vowels, diphthongs, etc.

Short:	ـَ	a	ـِ	i	ـُ	u
Long:	ـَا	ā	ـِي	ī	ـُو	ū
Diphthongs:			ـَوْ	aw		
			ـَيْ	ay		

Editor's Preface

The ninth volume of *Towards Understanding the Qur'ān* comprising *sūrahs* 33–37 is being sent to the press. To God are due both praise and thanks for enabling us to accomplish whatever we have been able to. From Him alone we seek succour to continue this work and Him do we beseech to accept this effort as a contribution to a better understanding of His Book.

The present volume, as volumes III through VIII before, has been prepared with the able assistance of Dr. A.R. Kidwai who translated into English *Tafhīm al-Qur'ān*'s explanatory notes to *sūrahs* 33–37. That text served as the basis out of which the explanatory notes of the present volume were given its present shape after a process of careful editing. While Dr. Kidwai's assistance is gratefully acknowledged, the responsibility for the present text – whatever its worth – rests solely with the present writer. The English rendering of the text of the *sūrahs,* however, is entirely mine.

In this volume, as in the previous ones, we have attempted to provide as adequate a documentation as we possibly could. In documenting the *Ḥadīth* we have followed A.J. Wensinck's system in his *Concordance.* However, instead of referring to the number of the *Bāb* of traditions as done by him, we have mentioned the actual titles of the *Kitāb* and *Bāb* of those traditions. It may also be pointed out that while referring to the explanatory notes from various *Tafsīr* works, we have referred to the relevant *sūrahs* and verses rather than to the volumes and pages of any specific editions of those *tafsīrs*. This was done in view of the fact that, as in the case of *Ḥadīth* works, there exist numerous editions of *tafsīrs*, both old and new. Hence, had we referred to any specific editions of *tafsīrs*, it would have been extremely difficult for many of our readers to check the references for it is unlikely that they will have access to the same editions to which reference was made. In our view, the method of referencing adopted by us will make it possible for our readers to locate the cited material without undue difficulty. As for the Bible, all quotations are from its *Revised Standard Edition.*

In preparing the text, I have greatly benefited from the excellent editorial suggestions of Mrs. Susanne Thackray which, I am sure, have enhanced the lucidity of the text. Mr. Naiem Qaddoura of The Islamic Foundation, Leicester did a fine job of setting the English and Arabic material. Likewise, Dr. M. Manazir Ahsan of the Foundation merits ample thanks of this writer. His frequent reminders did not permit him to remain indolent for long. Professor Khurshid Ahmad, my life-long friend, remains as ever, a pillar of strength and an abiding source of inspiration.

This much pertains to the assistance I received from overseas. This does not detract from the fact that my colleagues at the Islamic Research Institute, International Islamic University, Islamabad, assisted me in a variety of ways. Several research scholars of the Institute, particularly Mr. Mubashshir Husain, assiduously culled out for me the information that has gone into Biographical Notes. Mr. Amjad Mahmood, my Personal Secretary, tirelessly typed the text, time after time. A very special mention must be made of the valuable assistance extended by Ms. Madiha Younas (now Mrs. Madiha Sajeel), my Academic Assistant at the Institute. The present volume was a particularly tough one and for about six months she cheerfully immersed herself in all kinds of tasks relating to the volume. This involved extensive research, painstaking identification and checking of relevant material and references, careful editing, and myriad other sundry tasks. Enormous is the gratitude I owe these friends and colleagues.

Over the years my sons and sons-in-law, my daughters and daughters-in-law, and the steadily growing army of my grand-children have been the sunshine of my life. I have no words to thank God enough for this benevolent provision to keep me happy and cheerful in the twilight of my life.

To all those mentioned above, and to many others who assisted, encouraged and inspired me in one way or another, I record my profound sense of gratitude. May Allah bless them all.

Islamabad
Rabi' al-Awwal 1430 H
March 2009

Zafar Ishaq Ansari

N.B. ▶ *referes to the continuation of the paragraph adopted by Mawdūdī in the Urdu translation.*

Sūrah 33

Al-Aḥzāb

(The Confederates)

(Madīnan Period)

Title

The title is taken from verse 20 of the *sūrah* which speaks of the invading confederates.

Period of Revelation

The *sūrah* discusses three important events: (1) the Battle of Aḥzāb also known as the Battle of Khandaq (that is, the Trench) which took place in Shawwāl 5 AH/627 CE; (2) the Battle of Banū Qurayẓah, which took place in Dhū al-Qa'dah 5 AH/627 CE; and (3) the Prophet's marriage to Zaynab, which was also solemnised in Dhū al-Qa'dah 5 AH/627 CE. In view of the above, the *sūrah*'s period of revelation can be established quite accurately.

Historical Background

At the Battle of Uḥud, in Shawwāl 3 AH/625 CE, the Prophet (peace be on him) had posted archers at a certain vantage point.

Due to a lapse on their part the Muslim army suffered a setback. This boosted the morale of the polytheists of Arabia, as well as the Jews and hypocrites. They began to entertain the hope that they would soon be able to obliterate Islam and the Muslims.

Their growing confidence can be gauged from some of the events that took place soon after the Battle of Uḥud. Hardly two months had passed after the battle than the Banū Asad, a tribe of Najd, began to make preparations to invade Madīnah. It was in order to restrain them that the Prophet (peace be on him) launched an expedition known as *Sarīyah* Abū Salamah.* In Ṣafar 4 AH/625 CE, the 'Aḍal and Qārah tribes requested the Prophet (peace be on him) to dispatch some preachers to their region so as to invite people to Islam. Accordingly, he deputed six Companions. However, on reaching Rajī', a location between Jeddah and Rābigh, unbelievers of the Hudhayl tribe attacked these helpless Companions at the instigation of the above-mentioned tribes. Of these, four were killed and two – Khubayb ibn 'Adī and Zayd ibn al-Dathinnah – were sold in Makkah. At the same time in response to the request of Banū 'Āmir's chief, the Prophet (peace be on him) also sent to Najd a preaching mission consisting of 40 (though according to some reports, they were 70 in number) Anṣār youth. They too became targets of treachery. At Bi'r Ma'ūnah, members of the Banū Sulaym tribe, namely those belonging to 'Uṣayyah, Ri'l and Dhakwān, carried out a sudden attack, killing them all.

During the same period, Banū Naḍīr, the Jewish tribe settled in Madīnah, being emboldened by the events related above, persistently violated its pact with the Muslims. In Rabī' al-Awwal 4 AH/625 CE, they even conspired to assassinate the Prophet (peace be on him). In Jamād al-Awwal 4 AH/625 CE, two clans of Banū Ghaṭafān, namely Banū Tha'labah and Banū Muḥārib, planned to attack Madīnah. Thus, the reverse suffered by the Muslims in the Battle of Uḥud and the ensuing loss of their prestige continued to have an impact for some seven or eight months.

---

* *Sarīyah* is the technical term for a military campaign in which the Prophet (peace be on him) did not personally take part. (Distinguished from that, *ghazwah* denotes a battle or military campaign which was led personally by the Prophet (peace be on him).

Thanks, however, to the Prophet's statesmanship and firm resolve and to his Companions' solid allegiance to the cause of Islam, the situation soon changed. For sure, the economic boycott imposed by the Arab tribes made life difficult for the Muslims of Madīnah. Moreover, the unbelieving tribes around the city became increasingly aggressive. Within Madīnah itself the Muslims were constantly exposed to the hostile machinations and conspiracies of the Jews and the hypocrites. However, a handful of true believers, under the Prophet's leadership, successively took a number of steps that restored, and even enhanced, the Muslims' awe and prestige.

Military Campaigns before Aḥzāb

The Muslims took the first decisive step just a day after the Battle of Uḥud. This was the moment when many Muslims lay nursing the wounds they had suffered during the battle and others mourned the loss of their near and dear ones. The Prophet (peace be on him) had himself suffered injuries on the battlefield and his heart lay shattered at the martyrdom of his own uncle, Ḥamzah. At that very juncture, however, the Prophet (peace be on him) directed Islam's devotees to set out in pursuit of the Makkan unbelievers' army that had just invaded Madīnah. This was done lest the enemy decide to turn back and launch another attack. The Prophet (peace be on him) thought that the enemy were returning home without taking full advantage of their victory. In the Prophet's estimation, once the unbelievers had camped for a while during their homeward journey they were bound to feel remorseful at their folly and this realisation would then lead them to mount another offensive. In an effort to thwart this, he decided to pursue the unbelievers' army. His call to arms was instantly greeted by 630 committed Muslims all of whom readily agreed to accompany the Prophet (peace be on him) in chasing the enemy.

While on his way to Makkah, the Prophet (peace be on him) camped for three days at Ḥamrā' al-Asad. There he came to know from a sympathetic non-Muslim that Abū Sufyān, along with his 3,000 strong army, was camped at al-Rawḥā' some 36 miles from Madīnah and that they intended to attack Madīnah again, believing that they had committed a mistake by not reaping the benefit from their victory at Uḥud. On coming to know of the Prophet's hot pursuit, however, they had abandoned their plan. This demoralised the Quraysh as well as the non-Muslim tribes around Madīnah that were hostile to Islam and the Muslims. Not only that, but they also began to recognise that the Muslims were led by an ever-vigilant and resolute leader, one who enjoyed the utmost devotion and loyalty of his followers. (For further details see *Towards Understanding the Qur'ān*, Vol. I, Introduction to *Sūrah Āl 'Imrān*, pp. 229–232.)

Subsequently, no sooner had the tribesmen of Banū Asad begun their preparations to invade Madīnah than the Prophet (peace be on him) came to know of their plan through his informers. Before they could carry out the strike, the Prophet (peace be on him) had dispatched a contingent of 150 Companions led by Abū Salamah (the husband of Umm Salamah before she was married to the Prophet) to ward off their incursion. The Muslim contingent surrounded their enemy suddenly and swiftly. In a fit of panic, the latter beat a hasty retreat leaving behind their provisions, which fell to the Muslims.

Next, it was the turn of Banū al-Naḍīr. The day their conspiracy to assassinate the Prophet (peace be on him) came to light, they were served with a notice to leave Madīnah within ten days. They were warned that those who failed to do so would be put to the sword. 'Abd Allāh ibn Ubayy, the chief of Madīnah's hypocrites, encouraged Banū al-Naḍīr to hold on and not leave Madīnah. Not only did he promise to aid them with his 2,000 strong force, but also told them that the Banū Qurayẓah and Banū Ghaṭafān of Najd might also come to their aid. Encouraged by these false promises, Banū al-Naḍīr sent word to the Prophet (peace be on him) that they would not vacate Madīnah, challenging the Muslims to do whatever they wished. Consequently, no sooner had the period of notice passed than the Prophet (peace be on him) laid siege around their quarters. Ironically, none of their supporters had had the courage to come forward. Eventually, Banū al-Naḍīr laid down their arms on the condition that each group of three people from their tribe would be allowed to carry their belongings with them on one camel, leaving the rest behind in Madīnah. Thus their quarters, in the suburbs of Madīnah, consisting of orchards, fortresses and a considerable quantity of valuables, fell to the Muslims. Thereafter, these treacherous people became scattered far and wide between Khaybar, Wādī al-Qurā and Syria.

The Prophet (peace be on him) then turned his attention to Banū Ghaṭafān who had also drawn up plans to attack Madīnah. He marched out at the head of a 400 strong contingent and seized them unawares at Dhāt al-Riqā'. Stricken by panic, they dispersed into the nearby hills, abandoning their hearths and homes.

In Sha'bān 4 AH/626 CE, the Prophet (peace be on him) went out in response to a challenge thrown down by Abū Sufyān on his way back from the Battle of Uḥud. In this respect, he had warned the Muslims in general, and the Prophet (peace be on him) in particular, that in the following year there would be another encounter between them and the Muslims at Badr. The Prophet (peace be on him) had then asked one of his Companions to convey the following reply to Abū Sufyān: "Yes, that is the tryst between us and you". In accordance with this, the Prophet (peace be on him) set out along with 1,500 Companions and reached Badr on the appointed day. Abū Sufyān, too, set out with a 2,000 strong army for Badr. However, he could not muster sufficient courage to go beyond Marr al-Ẓahrān, currently known as Wādī Fāṭimah. The Prophet (peace be on him) camped at Badr and waited for Abū Sufyān for eight days. During this period, the men constituting the Muslim army engaged in trade and made good money. This incident also helped to reinforce the prestige of the Muslims after their discomfiture at Uḥud. As a result, it became clear to people all across Arabia that the Quraysh were no longer powerful enough to singly take on the Prophet (peace be on him) and his Companions. (For further details see *Towards Understanding the Qur'ān*, Vol. I, *Sūrah Āl 'Imrān*, n. 124, pp. 300–301.)

The Muslims gained further prestige as a result of the following incident. Arab trade caravans *en route* to Iraq, Egypt and Syria used to pass through Dūmat al-Jandal (presently known as al-Jawf).

Map 1: **The Arabian Tribes in the Prophet's Time**

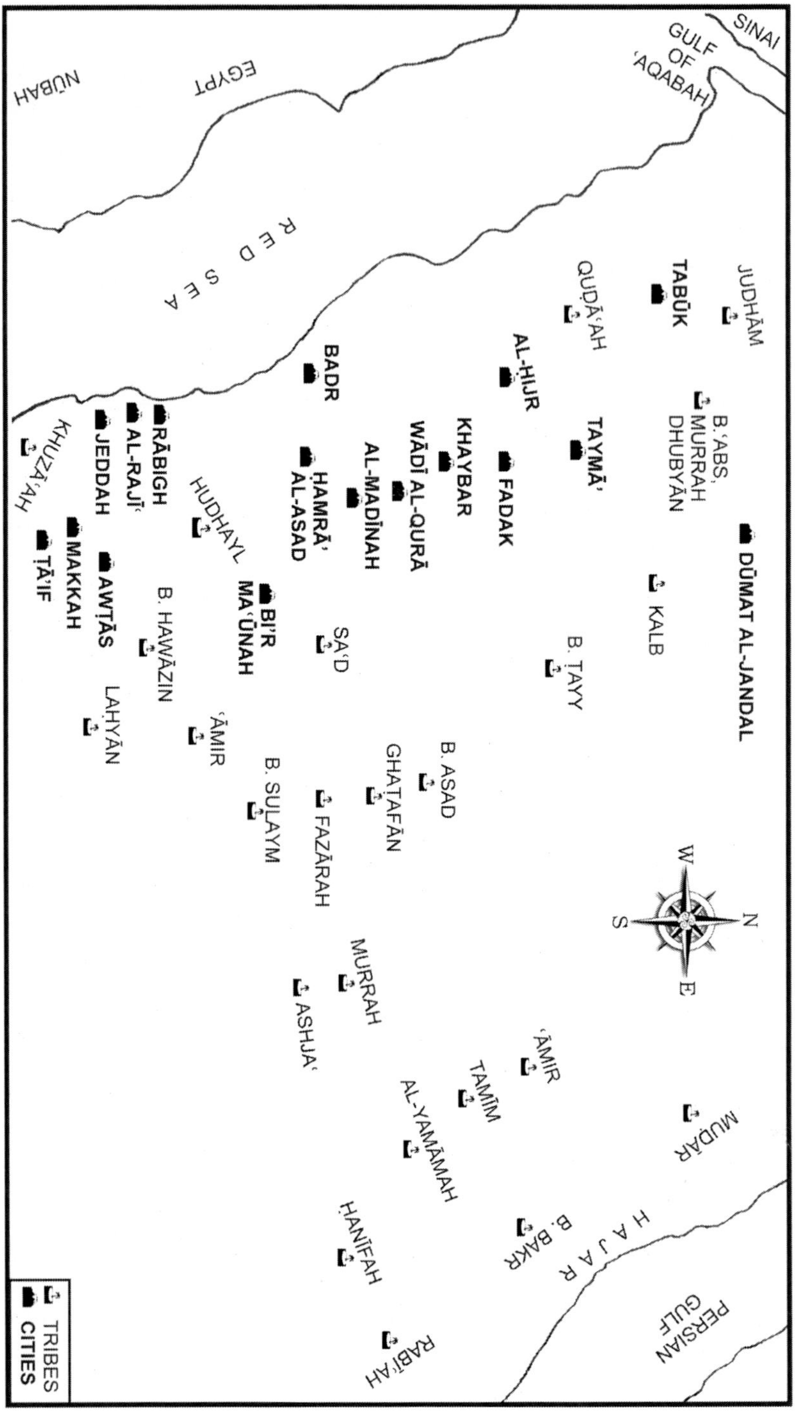

Its inhabitants used to harass and often rob those caravans. In Rabīʿ al-Awwal 5 AH/626 CE, the Prophet (peace be on him) led an expedition with a 1,000 strong army to discipline them. The inhabitants of Dūmat al-Jandal were terror-struck and fled from their homes. This established the supremacy of the Muslims in the whole of north Arabia. Furthermore, the tribesmen living in the vicinity of Madīnah realised that it was beyond the ability of just a tribe or two to confront Islam's rising power. (see Map 1)

The Battle of Aḥzāb

The historical background outlined above also provides the circumstantial setting for the Battle of Aḥzāb. To put it succinctly, the battle represented a joint military venture of a conglomerate of Arab tribes aimed at smashing the base of Muslim power in Madīnah. The venture was initiated by the exiled Banū al-Naḍīr chiefs who had taken refuge in Khaybar. They had toured the entire region persuading the Quraysh, Ghaṭafān, Hudhayl and several other tribes to rally under a single banner and pounce on Madīnah.

Their sustained efforts bore fruit in Shawwāl 5 AH/626 CE. A huge army consisting of many tribes descended on Madīnah. This conglomerate of tribes was itself unprecedented. From the north, the exiled Jews of Madīnah belonging to Banū al-Naḍīr and Banū Qaynuqāʿ, who had settled in Khaybar and the Wādī al-Qurā, made their way to Madīnah. From the east, the following tribes moved forward: Banū Sulaym, Fazārah, Murrah, Ashjaʿ, Saʿd and Asad. From the south, the Quraysh, accompanied by a host of allies, made their advance. In all, a large army numbering between 10,000 and 12,000 set out towards Madīnah.

Had this attack taken the Muslims unawares it would have resulted in a devastating blow to them. However, although the Prophet (peace be on him) lived in Madīnah, he was not unaware of the ominous developments taking place around him. His informers and those who were either favourably impressed by or sympathetic to the Islamic movement – and there were plenty of them in the ranks of various tribes – kept him constantly abreast

Map 2: **The Battlefield of the Trench**

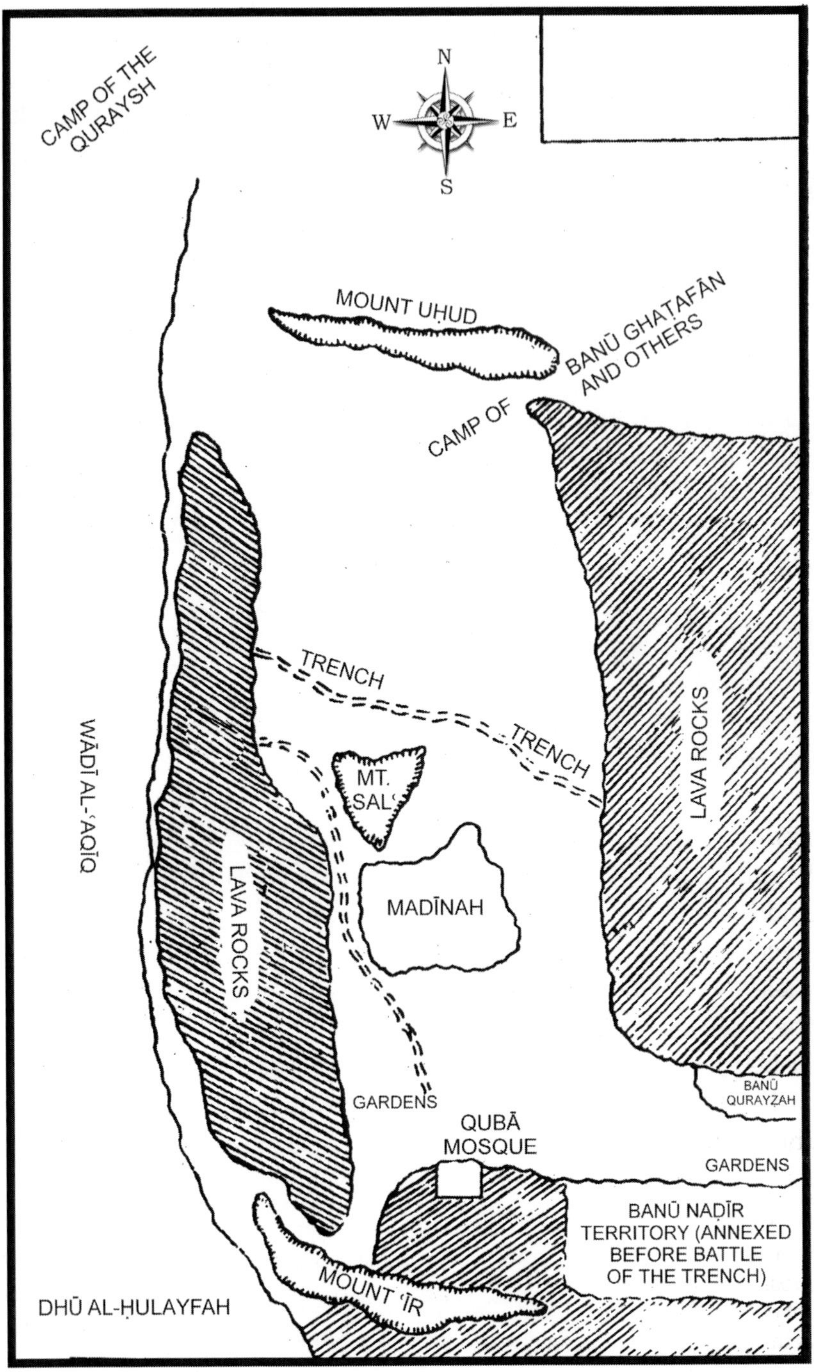

of his enemies' moves.** Hence before this huge army could reach Madīnah, the Prophet (peace be on him) was able to dig a trench on the north-west side of Madīnah in just six days' time. Having done so, the Prophet (peace be on him) then positioned his 3,000 strong army with Mount Sala' to the rear. To the south of Madīnah, there were quite a few dense, impenetrable orchards making it difficult for anyone to launch an offensive from that side. To the east, there stood huge rocks, the result of lava outflows, that ruled out any major attack from that side. The same was true of the western-southern side. Hence, the enemy could only move forward from the eastern and western flanks of Mount Uḥud. It was there that the trench had been dug to protect the city, a strategy the unbelievers had no inkling of. Indeed, it had never occurred to them that they would encounter a trench outside Madīnah; the enemy had simply not taken this possibility into account. In fact, they were altogether unfamiliar with such a defence strategy. Unable to do anything else, they were forced to settle in for a prolonged siege in extremely cold weather conditions, something they had not anticipated. (see Map 2)

One option, however, was left for the invading unbelievers: to incite the Jewish tribe of Banū Qurayẓah, who were then settled in the south-eastern part of Madīnah, to commit perfidy against the Muslims. Thus far Banū Qurayẓah had been the Muslims' allies and were even bound by an agreement to defend Madīnah in the event of an attack upon it. The Muslims, therefore, trusted them and had even moved their family members into their fortresses. Because of this trust, they had also taken no precautionary measures for the defence of that area. Noting this vulnerability, the unbelievers deputed Ḥuyayy ibn Akhṭab, the chief of Banū al-Naḍīr, to Banū Qurayẓah with the mission to persuade them to break their alliance with the Muslims and join the battle against them. Initially, Banū Qurayẓah rejected the suggestion, plainly

** This is an important advantage that an ideological movement has over and against nationalist bands. For nationalists can only count on the support of those belonging to their nation. Conversely, a movement that invites people to a set of principles and an ideology, has the potential to expand in all directions. It is thereby able to extract supporters even from the ranks of its enemies.

telling Ḥuyayy ibn al-Akhṭab that they were bound to the Muslims by an alliance and that they did not nurse any grievance against them. Ibn al-Akhṭab, however, persisted in his plea, arguing with them as follows: "Look! Here is an opportunity. We have mustered the whole of Arabia against Islam. If you let this opportunity go by, you will never have another." Ultimately, the Jews' propensity for hostility towards Islam got the better of them. They, thus, decided to disregard the requirements of morality and breached their pact with the Muslims.

The Prophet (peace be on him) was not unaware of these developments for he had been receiving timely intelligence about them. He directed the Anṣār chiefs – Sa'd ibn 'Ubādah, Sa'd ibn Mu'ādh, 'Abd Allāh ibn Rawāḥah and Khawwāt ibn Jubayr – to meet with the Jewish tribal leaders and dissuade them from violating their pact. As they were about to leave, he instructed them that if Banū Qurayẓah pledged to abide by their pact with the Muslims, then they, the Anṣār chiefs, should come forward and announce the same publicly. If the Jews' decision was otherwise, however, then the Anṣār chiefs were to divulge the news to the Prophet (peace be on him) alone so that the Muslims' morale was not undermined. When the Muslim delegation reached the Jewish quarters, they discovered that the Banū Qurayẓah were bent on mischief. They plainly told the delegation that there was no longer any pact between them and the Prophet (peace be on him). The Muslim delegation returned to the Prophet (peace be on him) and relayed the actual situation by simply uttering: "'Aḍal and Qārah." This meant that Banū Qurayẓah were going to commit the same treachery that had earlier been committed by the 'Aḍal and Qārah tribes who had treacherously killed the Muslim preachers at Rajī'.

The designs of Banū Qurayẓah soon became known throughout Madīnah. Inevitably, this upset the Muslims. For not only were they surrounded by the enemy on both sides, but were now also vulnerable to attack from a part of Madīnah against which they had not erected any defence. Furthermore, their family members had been moved to that same area for safety. It was now clear that the trust the Muslims had given Banū Qurayẓah was misplaced. This situation was further exploited by the hypocrites who launched a psychological offensive to further demoralise the Muslims. For instance, they would say something to the following effect: "Look! We were given to understand that the Roman and Persian Empires would soon be conquered. However, the ground reality is such that we cannot even go out of our own homes to answer a call of nature." Some even launched a whispering campaign suggesting that the Muslims should strike a deal with the besieging enemy, a deal stipulating that the Prophet (peace be on him) would personally be handed over to them. It was indeed a time of great trial in the course of which those who had even an iota of hypocrisy in them were exposed. In this hour of crisis the true believers displayed undaunting resolve and commitment, remaining utterly faithful and steadfast.

At this critical juncture, the Prophet (peace be on him) initiated negotiations with Banū Ghaṭafān, offering them one-third of Madīnah's harvest if they were to dissociate themselves from the siege. The Prophet (peace be on him) consulted the Anṣār chiefs, Sa'd ibn 'Ubādah and Sa'd ibn Mu'ādh, regarding the terms of this truce. These notable Anṣār leaders asked the Prophet (peace be on him) whether they were obliged to accept all this as a directive from God or whether it was a strategy designed to protect Madīnah. The Prophet (peace be on him) affirmed that it was the latter, a policy he himself had designed to protect Madīnah against all the machinations of the Arabian tribes. The Anṣār chiefs then replied to him as follows: "If you want to conclude this truce for our sake, then do away with it. These tribes were not able to extract any levy from us even when we were polytheists. Now we are much stronger by dint of our faith in God and His Messenger (peace be on him). So, how can they now exact any tax from us? Only the sword will settle the issue. God is the Best to decide the matter." So saying, they tore into pieces the draft of the truce which had yet to be signed by the two parties.

In the meantime, Nu'aym ibn Mas'ūd, a member of the Ashja' clan of Banū Ghaṭafān, who had embraced Islam, called on the Prophet (peace be on him). He told him that his acceptance of Islam was not yet known to anyone and, hence, he could be useful in gathering intelligence. Subsequently, the Prophet (peace be on him) directed him to create discord among the enemy ranks.*** As a result, Nu'aym first approached Banū Qurayẓah with whom he had very good relations. He gave them the impression that they (to wit, Banū Qurayẓah) were in a very vulnerable position for it was possible that the Quraysh and Banū Ghaṭafān might withdraw in exasperation, thereby lifting the siege. Banū Qurayẓah, being the Muslims' neighbours, would then have to fend for themselves. He suggested to them that they should take an active part in the battle only if the Quraysh and others sent them some leading members from the various tribes as hostages. This appealed to Banū Qurayẓah and, indeed, they did ask that some people be handed over to them as hostages.

Nu'aym then visited the chiefs of Quraysh and Ghaṭafān, telling them that Banū Qurayẓah did not appear very warm in their commitment to fight alongside them and that it was very likely that they would demand some of their leading members to be handed over as hostages. If this happened, Banū Qurayẓah would then hand over these hostages to the Prophet (peace be on him) in exchange for a deal that they might then strike with him. So doing, he pressed home the point that they should be cautious in their dealings with Banū Qurayẓah.

In this manner, the allies became mutually suspicious. The Quraysh and Ghaṭafān chiefs sent word to Banū Qurayẓah that they were tired of the long, drawn-out siege, that they soon intended to launch a decisive attack and that Banū Qurayẓah should, therefore, also launch their own strike because a two-pronged attack would unsettle the Muslims. To this, Banū Qurayẓah responded by saying that the Quraysh and Ghaṭafān should send them some of their men as hostages, for unless they did so, they would not risk launching an attack on the Muslims. This response went straight to the hearts of the Quraysh and Ghaṭafān. In essence, it confirmed what Nu'aym had told them with regard to Banū Qurayẓah's reservations. They, thus, refused to offer anyone as hostage. This refusal, in turn, convinced Banū Qurayẓah of the

*** On this occasion the Prophet (peace be on him) said: "Resort to artifice to mislead [the enemy] is permissible in warfare."

validity of Nu'aym's apprehension, which he had expressed to them. In sum, Nu'aym's stratagem proved to be a master stroke, one that caused division in the unbelievers' ranks.

The siege had lasted for more than 25 days during a harsh winter. It was also becoming harder by the day to arrange provisions for a huge army that was also demoralised because of internal divisions. Then, came the last straw that broke the confederates' back. One night, a violent hail storm swept through the area, uprooting the tents of the besieging force. In the total darkness of night, they could do nothing to defend themselves against nature's onslaught. Overtaken by panic, they retreated during the night to wherever they had come from. When the Muslims woke the next morning, there was not a single enemy soldier in the vicinity of Madīnah. On noting their desertion the Prophet (peace be on him) exclaimed: "From now on, the Quraysh cannot invade you. Rather, you will attack them." (Bukhārī, *Kitāb al-Maghāzī, Bāb Ghazwat al-Khandaq* – Ed.)

This was indeed an accurate assessment of the situation. The Quraysh, combined with the other tribes opposed to Islam, had made their last concerted effort against the Muslims. They lost this opportunity and no further opportunities to launch another attack would present themselves. The initiative for offensive, therefore, now lay with the Muslims.

Campaign of Banū Qurayẓah

When the Prophet (peace be on him) returned home from the Battle of Aḥzāb (also called the Battle of the Trench), Gabriel came to him at the time of *Ẓuhr* Prayer and asked him not to lay aside his arms. He was told instead that the problem of Banū Qurayẓah should be settled forthwith. On receiving this directive, the Prophet (peace be on him) proclaimed: 'Whoever owes allegiance to me should offer *'Aṣr* Prayer until they reach the quarters inhabited by Banū Qurayẓah.' (Bukhārī, *Kitāb al-Maghāzī, Bāb Marji' al-Nabī min al-Aḥzāb* – Ed.) At the same time, he dispatched a vanguard party under 'Alī's command towards Banū Qurayẓah's quarters.

On his arrival, 'Alī was greeted with a barrage of abuse and obscenity directed at the Prophet (peace be on him) personally and the Muslims generally. This despite the fact that it was Banū Qurayẓah who were guilty of perfidy with the Muslims during the critical days of the siege. They had colluded with the invaders, exposing Madīnah's entire population to the possibility of death and destruction. They could not, therefore, be allowed to escape punishment. Initially, on noting only a small party led by 'Alī, Banū Qurayẓah thought these Muslims had advanced merely to threaten them. Behind 'Alī, however, came the whole Muslim army under the Prophet's own command and in this way the Qurayẓah were surrounded. Totally unnerved and conscious of the fact that they could not sustain a siege for more than two or three weeks, they surrendered on the condition that their case would be adjudged by Sa'd ibn Mu'ādh, the Aws chief. They had selected Sa'd as their arbiter because the Banū Qurayẓah and Aws had been allies for a long time, essentially since the days of *Jāhilīyah*. They, thus, believed that Sa'd ibn Mu'ādh would be influenced by this longstanding relationship. In other words, they expected that like Banū Qaynuqā' and Banū al-Naḍīr, they too would be offered safe passage. Indeed, members of the Aws tribe did urge Sa'd to act leniently towards Banū Qurayẓah.

Sa'd, however, had noted that those Jewish tribes that had been granted safe passage in the past had abused it and had further been instrumental in inciting tribes from all around to attack Madīnah. This, as we know, led to the invasion of Madīnah by an army 10,000 to 12,000 strong. Sa'd was also aware that Banū Qurayẓah had committed a ghastly act of treachery during the Aḥzāb Campaign. So doing, they had exposed all the people of Madīnah to a potentially devastating onslaught. He, therefore, decided that all male members of the Qurayẓah be put to death, their women and children be taken as slaves, and their possessions be distributed among the Muslims. This sentence was duly executed.

Later, when the Muslims entered the Jewish fortresses, they discovered that these traitors had amassed 1,500 swords, 300 body armours, 2,000 daggers and 1,500 shields. Had God not come to the Muslims' aid, these weapons would indeed have been used against them from within Madīnah and the unbelievers and polytheists would have crossed the trench to swoop upon them from that quarter. The haul of these arms removes any doubt about

Sa'd's sagacity in ordering the execution of the male members of the Banū Qurayẓah.

Social Reforms

In the intervening two-year period between the Battle of Uḥud and the Aḥzāb Campaign, the Prophet (peace be on him) and his Companions did not enjoy a moment's peace or tranquillity because of the recurrent troubles and dangers they faced. Nevertheless, the effort to construct a new Muslim society and to bring about reforms in all aspects of life continued apace even during this hectic period. It was also around this time that the promulgation of Islamic laws on marriage, divorce and inheritance were more or less completed. Furthermore, drinking and gambling were forbidden and several new norms were also introduced into the Muslims' social and economic life.

Another related issue that called for reform was the institution of adoption. Up until then the Arabs used to consider their adopted children like their real children, who were, therefore, entitled to a share in inheritance. In turn, the adopted son's mother and his sister by adoption would also share the same close relationship they enjoyed with their real son and brother. As a result, it was not permissible for any adopted son to marry his sisters by adoption, or to marry the divorced or widowed wife of his father by adoption. Such a marriage was considered as outrageous as a person marrying his real sister or mother.

These practices were in flagrant conflict with the Qur'ānic laws of marriage, divorce and inheritance as laid down in *Sūrah*s *al-Baqarah* (*Sūrah* 2) and *al-Nisā'* (*Sūrah* 4). This Arab practice also deprived legitimate heirs of a part of their due share in inheritance and transferred it to those who were not entitled to any share at all. These practices also disallowed marriage between those men and women who were allowed by the Qur'ān to marry. More importantly, these practices contributed to moral corruption which Islamic law sought to forestall. This because the artificial sanctity of ties based on adoption did not and could not have the sanctity characteristic of blood ties. When men and women who are joined in kinship by adoption freely mix with each other, moral lapses are likely to occur.

Hence the dictates of Islamic law on marriage, divorce, inheritance and the sanctity of sexual relations required that treating adopted kin as equivalent with blood kin be abolished once and for all.

The practice of adoption, however, was too deeply entrenched to be scrapped simply by proclaiming that kinship by adoption was not the same as blood kinship. Ideas with deep roots in the past cannot be done away with simply by verbal declarations. Even if people recognised in principle that ties based on adoption do not have the same effect as blood ties, they would nevertheless have continued to be outraged by the idea that a mother by adoption and her adopted son could intermarry. The same applied to marriage between a brother by adoption and his sister by adoption, between a father by adoption and his adopted daughter, and between a father-in-law by adoption and his daughter-in-law by adoption. Moreover, there continued to be a degree of free mixing among people of the above-mentioned categories. It was necessary, therefore, that things be set right and only the Prophet (peace be on him) could take an effective initiative in this regard. For his action, carried out under God's directive, would leave no room for any doubt or reservation in any Muslim's mind. It was for these reasons that a little before the Aḥzāb Campaign God had suggested to the Prophet (peace be on him) that he marry Zaynab, the divorced wife of his adopted son, Zayd ibn Ḥārithah. He complied with this during the siege of Banū Qurayẓah. (This delay in compliance was presumably because Zaynab's waiting period was not then over and the Prophet (peace be on him) himself was preoccupied with matters relating to the impending battle.)

Malicious Propaganda over the Prophet's Marriage with Zaynab

No sooner had the Prophet (peace be on him) married Zaynab than a malicious propaganda campaign of massive proportions was let loose against him. The polytheists, hypocrites and Jews each had an axe to grind. They were jealous of the Prophet's successes on every front. For two years, from the Battle of Uḥud through the Aḥzāb Campaign and the Battle of Qurayẓah, the enemies had successively suffered humiliating defeats. They had, therefore, lost hope that they would ever be able to put up an effective fight against the Prophet (peace be on him) in open warfare, let alone defeat him.

All these disgruntled elements, therefore, tried to destroy the Prophet's high moral ground which lay at the core of his phenomenal success. In this respect, they invented and circulated a malicious story to the effect that the Prophet (peace be on him) had fallen in love with Zaynab, his daughter-in-law by adoption, and that when his adopted son, Zayd, came to know of this, he divorced her. The Prophet (peace be on him) was thus accused of marrying his own daughter-in-law. This was a baseless and sinister allegation. Zaynab was the Prophet's maternal cousin, and he had known her from her childhood. Hence the notion that the Prophet (peace be on him) was charmed by the sight of her, fell in love with her, was simply absurd. In fact, it was he who had suggested, even insisted, that Zayd and Zaynab be married. In so doing, he had even courted the displeasure of his own family members for they could not reconcile themselves with the idea that a girl of such a noble Quraysh family be married to a freed slave. Even Zaynab was not quite happy with this marriage proposal. However, she showed deference to the Prophet's wish on the question of marriage.

The marriage between Zayd and Zaynab sent a loud and clear message throughout Arabia that in Islam a freed slave enjoys the same status as a nobleman of the Quraysh. Had the Prophet (peace be on him) been interested in marrying Zaynab, he need not have arranged her marriage to Zayd in the first place. In other words, there was nothing to prevent him from marrying Zaynab if he had so wanted. Nevertheless, even in the face of these undeniable facts, unashamed enemies invented and then spread malicious stories about the Prophet's 'affair' with Zaynab. So fierce and effectively articulated was this propaganda that it found its way even among the ranks of Muslims.

Initial Injunctions about Ḥijāb

The fact that these sinister stories circulated by enemies penetrated the Muslim community did not reflect well on its moral health. In other words, the incident showed how lavisciousness in society exceeded the limits of moderation. Had this propensity not been there, people would not have countenanced such outrageous allegations against such a pious figure as that of the Prophet (peace be on him), let alone verbally repeat these stories. It was precisely at this juncture that a reform programme under the rubric of *ḥijāb* was introduced in Muslim society. Although these reforms were introduced in the *sūrah* under study, they were given legal shape in *Sūrah al-Nūr* (*Sūrah* 24), one year after slanderous statements were made about 'Ā'ishah. (For details see Introduction to *Sūrah al-Nūr*, *Towards Understanding the Qur'ān*, Vol. VI, pp. 133–147.)

The Prophet's Domestic Life

Two other issues at that time deserved urgent attention. Although these problems were related to the Prophet's domestic life, they were nonetheless significant for they had a bearing on the cause of Islam. The Prophet (peace be on him), as we know, was wholly occupied with striving to promote the true faith. It was imperative, therefore, that he should enjoy the kind of peace and equanimity in his domestic life that would enable him to fully concentrate on his mission. Moreover, it was also necessary that no aspect of his life should give rise to any doubts or misgivings in the minds of people. God, therefore, addresses both these issues in this *sūrah*.

The first issue concerns the financial stringency then facing the Prophet (peace be on him). In fact, during the first four years of his life in Madīnah he did not have any mentionable source of income. It was only in 4 AH/625 CE, after the exile of Banū al-Naḍīr, that a part of the land left behind by them was allocated to him under God's command so as to enable him to meet his expenses. The income so generated, however, did not suffice for his family's subsistence. His mission as God's Messenger kept him exceedingly busy so that he could not spare his physical or mental energy on tasks other than those pertaining to his mission. Hence, when his wives complained of financial stringency the Prophet (peace be on him) inevitably became even more stressed.

Before his marriage with Zaynab, the Prophet (peace be on him) already had four wives – Sawdah, 'Ā'ishah, Ḥafṣah and Umm Salamah. Zaynab was, therefore, his fifth wife. This provided his detractors with a pretext to raise objections against him and even some Muslims were carried away by their malicious propaganda. In particular, they were particularly rankled at the fact that the Prophet (peace be on him) had five wives whereas other Muslims had been restrained from marrying more than four.

Subject Matter and Themes

These are the problems that obtained at the time this *sūrah* was revealed and it naturally addresses these problems.

The *sūrah* consists of several pieces of discourse revealed at different periods of time in the context of the major events then pertaining but which were integrated into one *sūrah*. The major elements of which the *sūrah* is comprised are as follows:

i. The opening verses of the *sūrah* (vv. 1–8) appear to have been revealed a little before the Aḥzāb Campaign. Viewed in its historical setting, it seems that at the time of their revelation, Zayd had indeed divorced Zaynab. The Prophet (peace be on him) felt the need to do away with the concepts, superstitions and practices of pre-Islamic times relating to adoption. Therefore, he considered marrying Zaynab. On the other hand, he was reluctant to do so apprehending that this would trigger a fierce opposition from anti-Islamic forces – especially the hypocrites, Jews, and polytheists.
ii. The next two sections of the *sūrah* (see vv. 9–27) constitute the Qur'ānic critique on the Campaigns of Aḥzāb and Qurayẓah. Obviously, these sections were revealed after the events had taken place.
iii. The discourse from verse 28 through verse 35 makes two important points. First, God served notice on the Prophet's wives to make a choice between worldly life and its allurements on the one hand and the Prophet (peace be on him)

on the other. They were asked to express their preference in clear terms. If they chose this worldly life and its allurements, they would not be held to blame; rather, they would gladly be allowed to exercise their choice. However, if they chose the other option, they would be required to patiently persist in supporting God and His Messenger (peace be on him) even in straitened circumstances. Secondly, some preliminary steps were taken towards the realisation of the contemplated social reform. In fact, those whose mental outlook had been shaped by Islam had already begun to feel the need for it. Nonetheless, initial reform commenced from the Prophet's own household. Accordingly, his wives were asked to speak in a straightforward manner and not be complaisant when speaking to unrelated men, to stay in their homes and not to go about displaying their allurements as in the Time of Ignorance. In this respect, the *sūrah* marks the beginning of the Qur'ānic prescriptions about *ḥijāb* for women.

iv. Verses 36–48 deal with the Prophet's marriage with Zaynab and respond to the objections made by Islam's detractors.

v. Verse 49 lays down an important provision of Islamic law, the provision pertaining to divorce. It is a distinct verse which was presumably revealed in the context of the events obtaining at the time.

vi. Verses 50–52 contain the special rules of marriage exclusively meant for the Prophet (peace be on him). It was, therefore, made clear that the Prophet (peace be on him) was not subject to the several interdictions laid down for common Muslims.

vii. Verses 53–55 represent another major step in the direction of social reform. Specifically, these lay down the following injunctions: restriction on the entry of unrelated men to the Prophet's house; a code of social interaction; outlawing the marriage of the Prophet's wives to all other men, and the injunction that Muslims treat the Prophet's wives as their mothers.

viii. Verses 56–57 (*sic;* read verses 55–58 – Ed.) reproach those who had raised much hue and cry at the Prophet's marriage and family life. The believers were asked to invoke God's blessing and peace upon the Prophet (peace be on him) and to stay clear of fault-finding in the manner of Islam's enemies. They were also directed to leave the Prophet (peace be on him) alone, and to avoid causing hurt even to ordinary believing men and women by making them a target of accusation and slander.

ix. Verse 59 introduces another measure of social reform. It directs all Muslim women to wrap themselves up when they go out and to draw a part of their outer coverings over their bodies.

From here on till the end of the *sūrah,* the whispering campaign mounted by the hypocrites and by people of superficial understanding and low character comes up for strong censure.

In the name of Allah, the Most Merciful, the Most Compassionate.

بِسْمِ ٱللَّهِ ٱلرَّحْمَٰنِ ٱلرَّحِيمِ

(1) O Prophet[1], fear Allah and do not obey the unbelievers and the hypocrites. Verily Allah is All-Knowing, Most Wise.[2] ▶

يَٰٓأَيُّهَا ٱلنَّبِيُّ ٱتَّقِ ٱللَّهَ وَلَا تُطِعِ ٱلْكَٰفِرِينَ
وَٱلْمُنَٰفِقِينَ ۗ إِنَّ ٱللَّهَ كَانَ عَلِيمًا
حَكِيمًا ١

---

1. As we have pointed out in our Introduction to this *sūrah*, these verses were revealed after Zayd had divorced Zaynab. The Prophet (peace be on him) himself felt the need to strike a severe blow at the *jāhilī* practice of adoption and the superstitious notions associated with it. God had also hinted to him that the time had come to do away with that institution and that he should go ahead and marry Zaynab, the divorced wife of his adopted son, Zayd. This would prove to be the final step in eradicating this institution.

The Prophet (peace be on him), however, was reluctant. The unbelievers and hypocrites were already filled with rage and rancour against him because of a succession of accomplishments. He, therefore, felt that his marrying Zaynab might provide them with a scandalous pretext, one which they would use to discredit him. This, in turn, would damage the cause of Islam. The Prophet (peace be on him) was not so much worried about his personal reputation, but rather more concerned about the harm this might do to Islam's cause. He was worried lest the ensuing storm of malicious propaganda might have a negative influence on those who were favourably inclined towards Islam. Furthermore, those whose attitude towards Islam was one of neutrality might also become hostile to Islam. At the same time, the Muslims who had not by then acquired full intellectual maturity might begin to entertain doubts about their faith. In view of all this, the Prophet (peace be on him) felt that it was not expedient to marry Zaynab for this might adversely affect the larger interests of Islam.

2. At the very outset, God removes the Prophet's concerns mentioned above (see n. 1). The purport of what is being said here is to stress that God knows best wherein lie the interests of the faith He had ordained.

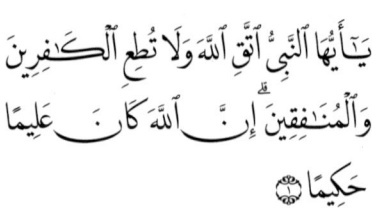

(2) Follow that which is revealed to you from your Lord. Verily Allah is fully aware of all that you do.[3] (3) Put your trust in Allah: Allah is sufficient as Guardian.[4]

وَٱتَّبِعْ مَا يُوحَىٰٓ إِلَيْكَ مِن رَّبِّكَ ۚ إِنَّ ٱللَّهَ كَانَ بِمَا تَعْمَلُونَ خَبِيرًا ۝٢ وَتَوَكَّلْ عَلَى ٱللَّهِ ۚ وَكَفَىٰ بِٱللَّهِ وَكِيلًا ۝٣

Likewise, He knows best when certain steps should be taken and others avoided. The Prophet (peace be on him) should, therefore, not act in any manner that would conform with the wishes of the unbelievers and hypocrites. Rather, he should do what God directs him to do. It is God, not the unbelievers and hypocrites, Who ought to be held in awe.

3. This verse is addressed to the Prophet (peace be on him), to his Companions as well as to Islam's detractors. The fact that the Prophet (peace be on him) is patiently enduring his enemies' assaults on his personal integrity is not hidden from Him. Likewise, God is fully informed about the Muslims who are steadfast in their loyalty and devotion to the Prophet (peace be on him) as well as those who succumb to doubts and suspicions about him. As for the unbelievers and hypocrites, they are told that God is perfectly cognizant of their vicious efforts to malign the Prophet (peace be on him). Indeed, all will be rewarded or punished in accordance with their conduct.

4. This again is addressed to the Prophet (peace be on him) who is directed to discharge the duty entrusted to him and to place his full trust in God. He is also asked not to be intimidated even if all mankind are arrayed against him. Once a person knows for sure that a certain command is from God, he should feel convinced that Islam's best interests will be served by carrying out that command. Once that is clear, it should no longer be his concern to decide about the dictates of wisdom and public interest; rather, he should fully trust God and follow His command. Such is God that one should entrust all one's affairs to Him because He is sufficient both to guide man as well as to come to his aid. It is also reassuring that God guarantees that anyone who acts as directed by Him will not face misfortune.

(4) Allah has never put two hearts within one person's body;[5] nor has He made your wives, whom you compare to your mothers' backs (to divorce them), your true mothers;[6] nor has He made those whom you adopt as sons your own sons.[7] These are only words that you utter with your mouths. But Allah proclaims the Truth and directs you to the Right Path. ▸

مَّا جَعَلَ ٱللَّهُ لِرَجُلٍ مِّن قَلْبَيْنِ فِى جَوْفِهِۦ ۚ
وَمَا جَعَلَ أَزْوَٰجَكُمُ ٱلَّٰٓـِٔى تُظَٰهِرُونَ
مِنْهُنَّ أُمَّهَٰتِكُمْ ۚ وَمَا جَعَلَ أَدْعِيَآءَكُمْ
أَبْنَآءَكُمْ ۚ ذَٰلِكُمْ قَوْلُكُم بِأَفْوَٰهِكُمْ ۖ
وَٱللَّهُ يَقُولُ ٱلْحَقَّ وَهُوَ يَهْدِى ٱلسَّبِيلَ ﴿٤﴾

5. That is, a person cannot be a true believer and a hypocrite, truthful and liar, virtuous and wicked at one and the same time. Obviously no one has been endowed with two hearts: one filled with faithful devotion and the other bereft of Godfearingness. One can either be a true believer or a hypocrite, be a Muslim or an unbeliever. To call a Muslim a hypocrite or a hypocrite a Muslim does not change the reality: a person will either be one or the other.

6. *Ẓihār* was a technical term commonly used by the Arabs. In the time of *Jāhilīyah*, a husband would tell his wife, in a fit of anger, that her back for him was like the back of his own mother. This signified that his wife would henceforth be forbidden to him. God makes it clear that a man's simple utterance about a woman being like his mother does not change his wife into his mother. The man's mother can only be the woman who gave birth to him. In other words, calling one's wife one's mother does not make any difference as regards the real status of the relationship. (It should be noted that the purpose of this verse is not to prescribe detailed laws in regard to *ẓihār*; those laws are laid down in *Sūrah al-Mujādalah*, 58:2–4.)

7. This is the main purpose of the verse. The two things said above are by way of argument to stress that a person does not truly become another person's son merely by his calling him so.

(5) Call your adopted sons after their true fathers; that is more equitable in the sight of Allah.[8] But if you do not know their true fathers, then regard them as your brethren in faith and as allies.[9] You will not be taken to task for your mistaken utterances, but you will be taken to task for what you say deliberately.[10] ▸

ٱدْعُوهُمْ لِءَابَآئِهِمْ هُوَ أَقْسَطُ عِندَ ٱللَّهِ ۚ فَإِن
لَّمْ تَعْلَمُوٓا۟ ءَابَآءَهُمْ فَإِخْوَٰنُكُمْ فِى ٱلدِّينِ
وَمَوَٰلِيكُمْ ۚ وَلَيْسَ عَلَيْكُمْ جُنَاحٌ فِيمَآ
أَخْطَأْتُم بِهِۦ وَلَٰكِن مَّا تَعَمَّدَتْ قُلُوبُكُمْ ۚ

---

8. The first impact of this injunction was that Zayd was no longer called Zayd ibn Muḥammad but rather as Zayd ibn Ḥārithah. (Bukhārī, *Kitāb al-Tafsīr, Bāb Ūd'ūhum li'Ābā'ihim…;* Muslim, *Kitāb al-Faḍā'il, Bāb Faḍā'il Zayd ibn Ḥārithah;* Tirmidhī, *Kitāb al-Tafsīr, Bāb Sūrah al-Aḥzāb* and Nasā'ī, *Kitāb al-Nikāḥ Bāb Tazawwuj al-Mawlā al-'Ārabiyyah* in a tradition on the authority of 'Abd Allāh ibn 'Umar.) In light of this verse, it was forbidden for anyone to ascribe his paternity to anyone other than his father. Bukhārī, Muslim and Abū Dā'ūd narrated the Prophet's following saying as reported by Sa'd ibn Abī Waqqāṣ: "Whoever knowingly calls someone his father other than his own father will be forbidden from entering Paradise." (Bukhārī, *Kitāb al-Farā'iḍ, Bāb man Idda'ā ilā Ghayr Abīhi;* Muslim, *Kitāb al-Īmān, Bāb Ḥāl Īmān man Raghiba…*and Abū Dā'ūd, *Bāb fī Rajul Yantamī ilā Ghayr Mawālīhi.* – Ed.) There are other traditions as well that embody the same principle and declare this act to be a major sin.

9. This forbids false ascription of lineage.

10. There is no harm if someone calls another person his son by way of endearment. Likewise, there is no harm if a person were to affectionately call someone his mother or father, brother or sister. However, it is quite objectionable if he were to say this in the sense that the person concerned has indeed become his mother or father, son or daughter, and that they enjoy the same rights as laid down for blood relatives.

Allah is Most Forgiving, Most Compassionate.[11]

(6) Surely the Prophet has a greater claim over the believers than they have over each other,[12] and his wives are their mothers.[13] ▶

وَكَانَ ٱللَّهُ غَفُورًا رَّحِيمًا ۞ ٱلنَّبِيُّ أَوْلَىٰ بِٱلْمُؤْمِنِينَ مِنْ أَنفُسِهِمْ ۖ وَأَزْوَٰجُهُۥٓ أُمَّهَٰتُهُمْ ۗ

11. One meaning of this is that God has forgiven all their past lapses in this regard and they will not be taken to task for those lapses. The second meaning is that God does not punish people for acts they did not deliberately commit.

12. Muslims' relationship with the Prophet (peace be on him) stands on a higher pedestal than all other relationships. In fact, no relationship bears any comparison with a Muslim's relationship with the Prophet (peace be on him). For his part, the Prophet (peace be on him) is more tender and compassionate towards Muslims than even their own parents. The same is true for his deep, passionate concern for their well-being. It is possible that a person's parents or his own children might harm him, act selfishly towards him, mislead him, or prompt him to commit misdeeds that would push him towards Hell. None of this, however, is conceivable with regard to the Prophet (peace be on him); for he can do only that which is most conducive to every person's best interests. Even though someone might decide to go along the path of self-destruction, the Prophet's advice and guidance will always be that which is most beneficial to him. In view of this, Muslims are obliged to cherish the Prophet (peace be on him) more than everyone else, including themselves, their parents and their children. They should love him more than anything and anyone in the world, and give preference to the Prophet's opinions and judgements rather than to their own. This idea is clearly expressed in the following *ḥadīth*: "None of you can be a true believer unless you hold me dearer than your parents, children and all others." (Bukhārī, *Kitāb al-Īmān, Bāb Ḥub al-Rasūl min al-Īmān* and Muslim, *Kitāb al-Īmān, Bāb Wujūb Maḥabbat al-Rasūl.*) There is some slight variation in the wording of the *ḥadīth* in these two works.

13. While the believers may marry their mothers by adoption, it is forbidden for them to marry the Prophet's wives, for they are mothers for all believers. Marrying them is forbidden to Muslims in the same way

as marrying their own mothers. This was laid down exclusively for the Prophet (peace be on him) and is applicable to no one else.

It is noteworthy that the Prophet's wives are known as the "mothers of the believers" in the sense that it is obligatory for Muslims to hold them in very high esteem; hence, they may not marry them. In all other respects, however, they are not their mothers. For instance, all Muslims, except those who are their kin, will not be reckoned as their *maḥārim* (those with whom marriage is forbidden), and they will be required to observe *ḥijāb* with them. Likewise, the daughters of the Prophet's daughters are not the foster-sisters of all Muslims and, hence, it is not forbidden to marry them. Nor is it forbidden for Muslims to marry the brothers and sisters of the Prophet's wives on the grounds that they are their aunts and uncles. The same applies to shares in their inheritance, which should not go to any Muslim not related to the Prophet's wives by ties of kinship.

It should be noted that this exalted status of the Prophet's wives is a privilege enjoyed by all his wives, including, of course, 'Ā'ishah. This point is significant because a section of people place only 'Alī, Fāṭimah and their children at the centre stage of Islam. These people try to discredit 'Ā'ishah along with numerous other Companions, hurling all sorts of accusations at them. However, they will not be able to make much headway in their maligning campaign for they will be confronted with this Qur'ānic verse, which asks everyone who lays claim to being a believer, to recognise the Prophet's wives as his mothers. To wriggle out of this difficult situation, these people make the bizarre claim that the Prophet (peace be on him) authorised 'Alī to divorce any of his wives after his demise and to let those whom he [that is, 'Alī] liked continue to be his wives. Abū Manṣūr Aḥmad ibn Abī Ṭālib al-Ṭabrasī makes this outrageous claim in his *Kitāb al-Iḥtijāj*, which has been reproduced as follows by Sulaymān ibn 'Abd Allāh al-Baḥrānī: "The Prophet (peace be on him) told 'Alī: 'O Abū al-Ḥasan! This privilege remains as long as we remain obedient to God. So, if any of my wives rises in revolt against you and disobeys God, divorce her and deprive her of the privilege of being 'mother of the believers'".

This report is obviously devoid of any substance according to the accepted canons of *ḥadīth* transmission. Furthermore, in the light of verses 28–29 and 51–52 of this *sūrah*, it even conflicts with the Qur'ān itself. The fact that the Prophet (peace be on him) forfeited the right to divorce any of his wives who had opted for his company is evident from verse 29 of the *sūrah*. (This point is further elaborated in nn. 42 and 93 below.)

Were one to objectively study the above mentioned report, one is bound not only to dismiss it as absurd but also as a sheer fabrication, one that is insulting to the Prophet (peace be on him). This because it depicts

According to the Book of Allah, blood relatives have greater claim over each other than the rest of the believers and the Emigrants (in the cause of Allah), except that you may do some good to your allies[14] (if you so wish). This is inscribed in the Book of Allah.

(7) And call to mind, (O Prophet), when We took ▶

وَأُوْلُوا۟ ٱلْأَرْحَامِ بَعْضُهُمْ أَوْلَىٰ بِبَعْضٍ فِى
كِتَـٰبِ ٱللَّهِ مِنَ ٱلْمُؤْمِنِينَ وَٱلْمُهَـٰجِرِينَ
إِلَّآ أَن تَفْعَلُوٓا۟ إِلَىٰٓ أَوْلِيَآئِكُم مَّعْرُوفًا
كَانَ ذَٰلِكَ فِى ٱلْكِتَـٰبِ مَسْطُورًا ﴿٦﴾
وَإِذْ أَخَذْنَا

him in a very poor light. Not even an ordinary decent person, let alone a Messenger of God, can be expected to consider divorcing his wives after his death or of authorising his son-in-law to divorce them on his behalf if they subsequently have any dispute with him. This lays bare the falsity of such people's claims to have overflowing love and reverence for the Prophet's family and the Prophet (peace be on him) himself. In fact, it also shows the scant respect they have for God's commands.

14. This verse elucidates that with the exception of the Prophet (peace be on him), who holds a unique position in the eyes of Muslims, the mutual relations among Muslims will be based on the principle that one's kith and kin receive priority over all other Muslims in matters such as charity, *Zakāh* and inheritance. It is improper to neglect one's own parents, wives, children and one's brothers and sisters and give charity to others. As regards *Zakāh*, one should first give it to the deserving amongst one's next of kin and then to other needy people. The same principle applies to inheritance. The property left behind by a deceased person is inherited by his closely related kin. A Muslim may help others with gifts, by making *waqf* in their favour, or by specifying something for them in his will. One's heirs, however, cannot be denied their due share of inheritance in order to provide benefit to others.

In effect, this verse puts an end to that special nexus of brotherhood that had been established between the Muhājirūn and the Anṣār after the Prophet's migration to Madīnah. Before the promulgation of this rule,

the covenant from all Prophets; and also from you and Noah and Abraham, Moses, and Jesus the son of Mary. We took from them a solemn covenant[15] ▶	مِنَ ٱلنَّبِيِّـۧنَ مِيثَـٰقَهُمْ وَمِنكَ وَمِن نُّوحٍ وَإِبْرَٰهِيمَ وَمُوسَىٰ وَعِيسَى ٱبْنِ مَرْيَمَ ۖ وَأَخَذْنَا مِنْهُم مِّيثَـٰقًا غَلِيظًا ۝٧

those Muhājirūn and Anṣār who had been bound in this tie of brotherhood inherited each other. God, however, replaced this by promulgating the laws of inheritance, which only take into account blood ties. One may, nonetheless, if one so wants, give any of one's brethren-in-faith whatever one likes as a gift or by means of bequest.

15. God reminds the Prophet (peace be on him) that like other Messengers he had entered into a covenant with God that he must faithfully honour. As to the exact nature of the covenant, it appears from the context that it refers to the Messenger's commitment to obey God's every command and to make others do the same. A Messenger is also charged with the duty to faithfully transmit whatever comes to him from God and to exert his efforts in order that God's commands are put into effect. At other places, too, the Qur'ān speaks of this covenant:

> He has prescribed for you the religion which He enjoined upon Noah and which We revealed to you (O Muḥammad), and which We enjoined on Abraham, Moses and Jesus, commanding: "Establish this religion and do not split up regarding it" (*al-Shūrā* 42:13).
>
> Recall when God took a covenant from those who were given the Book: "You shall explain it to people and not hide it" (*Āl 'Imrān* 3:187).
>
> And recall when We made a covenant with the Children of Israel: "You shall serve none but God ..." (*al-Baqarah* 2:83).
>
> Was not the covenant of the Book taken from them . . . ? "Hold firmly to that which We have given you, and remember what is in it, that you may guard against evil" (*al-A'rāf* 7:169 and 171).
>
> Remember Allah's favour upon you and His covenant which He made with you when you said: "We have heard and we obey" (*al-Mā'idah* 5:7).

What prompts the mention of this covenant in the present context is that the Prophet (peace be on him) was initially somewhat reluctant to put an end to the pre-Islamic custom of adoption because he apprehended severe opposition from Islam's enemies. He felt especially bashful about marrying Zaynab because Islam's enemies would misconstrue this marriage as one motivated by sensuality; further, that they would do so in disregard of the Prophet's utter sincerity in his bid to bring about social reform. He also perceived that his opponents would discredit him as one who wore the cloak of reform, though his real concerns were those of the flesh. Accordingly, God reminds the Prophet (peace be on him) that like His other Messengers, he too is required to carry out God's commands and to ask others to do the same. He should, therefore, disregard the taunts and derisions of his opponents. He should neither be afraid of nor feel shy in the face of his detractors but should rather concentrate on performing the duty assigned to him by God.

Some people construe this to refer to the covenant which was made with earlier Prophets and their respective communities obliging them to believe in and support those Prophets who would come later. (*Āl 'Imrān* 3:81.) In the light of this interpretation, these people subscribe to the notion that even after the Prophet Muḥammad's advent, another Prophet is possible. In other words, they think that since such a covenant was made with the Prophet (peace be on him), his community is bound to follow the Prophet who comes after him!

It is quite clear from the context of the present verse, however, that this is an altogether flawed interpretation. The context does not admit any possibility for the advent of any Prophet after Muḥammad (peace be on him). Nor is the Prophet's community bound to believe in the Prophethood of any such claimant. The content of the verse also reveals that were this interpretation to be accepted, the verse would look altogether odd and incongruous. Besides, its wording also has no suggestion to this effect.

In order to ascertain the nature and meaning of the covenant, the only thing we can do is to refer to those Qur'ānic verses that speak of covenants with Prophets. Had the Qur'ān mentioned only a single covenant, and that too, about the requirement to believe in those Prophets who will appear later, some allowance could have been made for the above interpretation. However, anyone conversant with the Qur'ān recognises that it refers to a number of covenants that were variously made with Prophets and their communities. Therefore, the meaning of the word "covenant" in this verse is determined in keeping with its context, rather than arbitrarily. Such false and tendentious interpretations betray the fact that some people do not turn to the Qur'ān for guidance but instead arbitrarily read their own ideas into it.

(8) so that (their Lord) may question the truthful about their truthfulness.[16] As for the unbelievers, He has kept a painful chastisement in store for them.[17]

(9) Believers,[18] call to mind Allah's favour to you when enemy hosts invaded you. Then We sent against them a wind and hosts that you did not see[19] although Allah was observing all that you were then doing. ▶

لِّيَسْـَٔلَ ٱلصَّـٰدِقِينَ عَن صِدْقِهِمْ ۚ وَأَعَدَّ
لِلْكَـٰفِرِينَ عَذَابًا أَلِيمًا ﴿٨﴾ يَـٰٓأَيُّهَا
ٱلَّذِينَ ءَامَنُوا۟ ٱذْكُرُوا۟ نِعْمَةَ ٱللَّهِ
عَلَيْكُمْ إِذْ جَآءَتْكُمْ جُنُودٌ فَأَرْسَلْنَا
عَلَيْهِمْ رِيحًا وَجُنُودًا لَّمْ تَرَوْهَا ۚ وَكَانَ ٱللَّهُ
بِمَا تَعْمَلُونَ بَصِيرًا ﴿٩﴾

16. That is, God did not simply make a covenant but will also call the people concerned to account and see how true they were to their covenant. Those who fulfilled the requisites of the covenant will be reckoned as God's true servants.

17. For a better appreciation of these verses, one should study them in conjunction with verses 36–41 of this *sūrah*.

18. This marks the beginning of the Qur'ānic critique of the Campaigns of Aḥzāb and Banū Qurayẓah. For a better understanding of these verses one should call to mind the historical background of these battles as outlined in the Introduction to this *sūrah*.

19. This storm of winds did not overtake the unbelievers on the day their army invaded Madīnah. Rather, it befell them about one month after the commencement of their siege. As to the "hosts that you did not see" alluded to in this verse, this refers to those forces which, at God's behest, shape and influence man's affairs even though man does not observe them. In his interpretation of events man is influenced by observable, external factors. He does not take into account any invisible forces at work, though these may often play a decisive role. Since these forces work under the supervision of angels, "hosts that you do not see"

(10) When they came upon you from above you and from below you,[20] when your eyes were stupefied with horror and your hearts leapt to your throats, and you began to entertain diverse thoughts about Allah. (11) The believers were then put to a severe test and were most violently convulsed.[21]

(12) And call to mind when the hypocrites and all those with diseased hearts said: "All that Allah and His Messenger had promised[22] us was nothing but deceit." ▶

إِذۡ جَآءُوكُم مِّن فَوۡقِكُمۡ وَمِنۡ أَسۡفَلَ
مِنكُمۡ وَإِذۡ زَاغَتِ ٱلۡأَبۡصَٰرُ وَبَلَغَتِ
ٱلۡقُلُوبُ ٱلۡحَنَاجِرَ وَتَظُنُّونَ بِٱللَّهِ
ٱلظُّنُونَا۠ ﴿١٠﴾ هُنَالِكَ ٱبۡتُلِيَ ٱلۡمُؤۡمِنُونَ
وَزُلۡزِلُواْ زِلۡزَالٗا شَدِيدٗا ﴿١١﴾ وَإِذۡ يَقُولُ
ٱلۡمُنَٰفِقُونَ وَٱلَّذِينَ فِي قُلُوبِهِم مَّرَضٞ
مَّا وَعَدَنَا ٱللَّهُ وَرَسُولُهُۥٓ إِلَّا غُرُورٗا ﴿١٢﴾

might refer to the angels themselves, though this particular verse does not explicitly mention that an army of angels was sent down.

20. This might also mean that the unbelievers invaded Madīnah from all sides. Alternatively, the expression those who "came upon you from above" might refer to the invaders from Najd and Khaybar whereas those who came "from below you" might refer to those invaders who came from Makkah.

21. The word "believers" here refers to all those who had pledged obedience to the Prophet Muḥammad (peace be on him). These included both true believers and hypocrites. Here, however, God speaks of Muslims in that general sense. In the verses that follow, however, the hypocrites are criticised for their misconduct. The verses which follow this criticism relate to the Prophet (peace be on him) and true believers.

22. In other words, the promise is that the believers will be helped and supported by God and that they will ultimately triumph.

(13) And when a section of them said: "(O people of Yathrib), now there is no place for you to stay, so turn back."[23] (And call to mind) when a section of them was seeking permission from the Prophet to leave, saying: "Our houses are exposed[24] (to attack)," although they were not exposed[25] ▶

وَإِذْ قَالَت طَّآئِفَةٌ مِّنْهُمْ يَـٰٓأَهْلَ يَثْرِبَ لَا مُقَامَ لَكُمْ فَٱرْجِعُوا۟ ۚ وَيَسْتَـْٔذِنُ فَرِيقٌ مِّنْهُمُ ٱلنَّبِىَّ يَقُولُونَ إِنَّ بُيُوتَنَا عَوْرَةٌ وَمَا هِىَ بِعَوْرَةٍ ۖ

23. This verse is open to two meanings. First, that some people argued that it was pointless to take on the unbelievers and hence they should return home. Secondly, that their statement implied that it is pointless to profess and practise Islam; that is, they would be better off reverting to their ancestral faith. If they did so, this would save them from the wrath of all the Arabs which they had incurred by accepting Islam. The hypocrites dropped oblique hints to this effect so that they might intimate their true purpose to those who were taken in by their specious talk. However, when they were faced with someone who was alert and critical, they would shield themselves by saying that they were merely depicting the grave predicament confronting them. By recourse to this stratagem they were able to escape reproach.

24. As Banū Qurayẓah joined hands with the unbelieving invaders, the hypocrites found an opportune moment to desert the Prophet's army. They sought the Prophet's permission to withdraw on the grounds that their homes were vulnerable and that they should be allowed to return in order to defend their families and properties. They said this regardless of the fact that the defence of the Madīnans was the Prophet's responsibility. It was his job, rather than that of each individual, to take the necessary steps to ward off the danger posed by the treacherous Banū Qurayẓah.

25. The Prophet (peace be on him) had already taken precautionary measures as a part of his defence strategy and in his capacity as the supreme commander of the Muslim army. In fact, no immediate threat

(to attack); they only wished to flee (from the battle-front). (14) If the enemy were to enter the town from various directions, and they were summoned to act treacherously,[26] they would have succumbed to it and would have shown little reluctance in doing so. (15) They had earlier covenanted with Allah that they would not turn their backs in flight. And a covenant made with Allah must needs be answered for.[27]

(16) (O Prophet), tell them: "If you run away from death or slaying, ▸

إِن يُرِيدُونَ إِلَّا فِرَارًا ﴿١٣﴾ وَلَوْ دُخِلَتْ
عَلَيْهِم مِّنْ أَقْطَارِهَا ثُمَّ سُئِلُوا۟ ٱلْفِتْنَةَ
لَءَاتَوْهَا وَمَا تَلَبَّثُوا۟ بِهَآ إِلَّا يَسِيرًا ﴿١٤﴾ وَلَقَدْ
كَانُوا۟ عَٰهَدُوا۟ ٱللَّهَ مِن قَبْلُ لَا يُوَلُّونَ
ٱلْأَدْبَٰرَ ۚ وَكَانَ عَهْدُ ٱللَّهِ مَسْـُٔولًا ﴿١٥﴾ قُل
لَّن يَنفَعَكُمُ ٱلْفِرَارُ إِن فَرَرْتُم مِّنَ ٱلْمَوْتِ
أَوِ ٱلْقَتْلِ

confronted them at that precise moment. Hence the pretext that they put forth had no substance.

26. Had the coalition of unbelieving tribes entered their city as victors and had they then invited these hypocrites to cooperate with them in obliterating the Muslims, the hypocrites would have obliged.

27. They had shown weakness during the Battle of Uḥud. However, they had pledged in God's name that they would make up for their lapses whenever the opportunity arose in the future. However, God cannot be deceived by mere words. Whoever makes a pledge to Him is tested so that if he is insincere, his insincerity will be exposed. Therefore, two years after the Battle of Uḥud the hypocrites were put to an even more serious test; through it, they were fully exposed.

this flight will not avail you. You will have little time after that to enjoy[28] (the pleasures of life)." (17) Say (to them): "Who can protect you from Allah if He desires an evil for you? And who can prevent Him if He desires to show mercy to you?" They shall find none other than Allah to be their protector or helper.

(18) Allah knows well those of you who create obstructions (in war efforts) and say to their brethren: "Come and join us."[29] They hardly take any part in battle. (19) They are utterly niggardly[30] ▸

وَإِذًا لَّا تُمَتَّعُونَ إِلَّا قَلِيلًا ١٦ قُلْ مَن ذَا
ٱلَّذِى يَعْصِمُكُم مِّنَ ٱللَّهِ إِنْ أَرَادَ بِكُمْ
سُوٓءًا أَوْ أَرَادَ بِكُمْ رَحْمَةً ۚ وَلَا يَجِدُونَ
لَهُم مِّن دُونِ ٱللَّهِ وَلِيًّا وَلَا نَصِيرًا ١٧
۞ قَدْ يَعْلَمُ ٱللَّهُ ٱلْمُعَوِّقِينَ مِنكُمْ وَٱلْقَآئِلِينَ
لِإِخْوَٰنِهِمْ هَلُمَّ إِلَيْنَا ۖ وَلَا يَأْتُونَ ٱلْبَأْسَ
إِلَّا قَلِيلًا ١٨ أَشِحَّةً عَلَيْكُمْ ۖ

28. Their attempt to run away from death will not help them gain longevity. They will not be able to enjoy life until the Last Day, nor amass the wealth of the whole world. Even if they flee from the battlefield they will live, at the most, for just a few more years. They can enjoy life only as much as has been determined for them by God.

29. Reference is made here to the hypocrites who had no sincere commitment to the Prophet (peace be on him), to faith and to truth. Far from being prepared to imperil their lives and expose themselves to hardships in God's cause, they merely sought a risk-free life of ease and pleasure.

30. The hypocrites were not prepared to devote their energy, time, money or possessions to God's cause. Conversely, the true believers

(in coming to your aid). Whenever there is danger, you will see them looking at you, their eyes rolling as though they were on the verge of fainting at the approach of death. But when the danger passes away, their greed for wealth prompts them to greet you with their sharp, scissor-like tongues.[31] These are the ones who never truly believed, and so Allah has caused their deeds to be reduced to naught.[32] ▶

فَإِذَا جَآءَ ٱلْخَوْفُ رَأَيْتَهُمْ يَنظُرُونَ إِلَيْكَ تَدُورُ أَعْيُنُهُمْ كَٱلَّذِى يُغْشَىٰ عَلَيْهِ مِنَ ٱلْمَوْتِ ۖ فَإِذَا ذَهَبَ ٱلْخَوْفُ سَلَقُوكُم بِأَلْسِنَةٍ حِدَادٍ أَشِحَّةً عَلَى ٱلْخَيْرِ ۚ أُو۟لَـٰٓئِكَ لَمْ يُؤْمِنُوا۟ فَأَحْبَطَ ٱللَّهُ أَعْمَـٰلَهُمْ ۚ

consecrated whatever they had. In fact, the hypocrites were not willing to cooperate with the Muslims in any venture whatsoever, let alone strive and court danger for that cause.

31. This verse is open to the following two meanings:

i. When the believers returned from the battlefield as victors, the hypocrites warmly greeted them and glibly flaunted themselves as sincere believers who had taken an active part in the cause of faith. So doing, they laid claim to the spoils of war.
ii. When the believers were victorious, the hypocrites were eager to be included among the recipients of spoils of war. They vehemently demanded their share, lest they receive nothing.

32. All the good deeds apparently done by them after their outward acceptance of Islam will be reduced to naught by God and they will earn no reward from Him. A point worth noting is that the Qur'ān plainly placed some people outside the fold of Islam even though they verbally claimed to believe in God and His Messenger, offered Prayers, fasted,

That is easy enough for Allah.[33] (20) They think that the invading confederates have not yet gone. But if the confederates were to mount another assault, they would wish to be in the desert among the bedouins and keep themselves informed about you from there. But even if they remained in your midst, hardly would they fight.

وَكَانَ ذَٰلِكَ عَلَى ٱللَّهِ يَسِيرًا ﴿١٩﴾ يَحْسَبُونَ
ٱلْأَحْزَابَ لَمْ يَذْهَبُوا۟ ۖ وَإِن يَأْتِ
ٱلْأَحْزَابُ يَوَدُّوا۟ لَوْ أَنَّهُم بَادُونَ فِى
ٱلْأَعْرَابِ يَسْـَٔلُونَ عَنْ أَنۢبَآئِكُمْ ۖ وَلَوْ
كَانُوا۟ فِيكُم مَّا قَـٰتَلُوٓا۟ إِلَّا قَلِيلًا ﴿٢٠﴾

paid *Zakāh* and joined the Muslims in other good deeds. Notwithstanding this, the Qur'ān declared them as those "who never truly believed". Significantly, this judgement was given on the grounds that in face of the perils attending the encounter between Islam and unbelief, they acted with duplicity. In essence, they preferred their own vested interests to the cause of Islam and shied away from dedicating their lives, money and energy to defend Islam. God, however, does not reward anyone merely for the external appearance of their actions. What He ascertains is whether one's acts are prompted by faith and sincerity or are devoid of them. Rather than the outward appearance of actions, it is one's loyalty to God that brings reward. Whoever is not loyal to God and to His prescribed faith, will find that their outward acceptance of faith and acts of worship and other good deeds are absolutely worthless.

33. Since the acts of the hypocrites were of no worth, there was no reason why God should be reluctant to reduce them to naught. Also, the hypocrites, and for that matter, any power whatsoever, cannot pose any difficulty for God if He decides to reduce them to naught.

(21) Surely there was a good example for you in the Messenger of Allah,[34] ▶	لَّقَدْ كَانَ لَكُمْ فِي رَسُولِ ٱللَّهِ أُسْوَةٌ حَسَنَةٌ

34. The context in which this has been said indicates its purpose. It was to teach a lesson to those who were concerned with their own safety and the furtherance of their own worldly interests on the occasion of the Aḥzāb Campaign. How could they do so when they claimed to believe in and submit to God and to follow the Prophet (peace be on him)? They should have taken into account the example of God's Messenger (peace be on him) among whose followers they were. Had their leader been overly concerned with his personal safety, or was given to a life of ease and comfort, or was someone whose attention was focused on his own interests, or was someone who took to heel at the first sight of danger, then any show of weakness on the part of his followers would have been understandable. In this case, however, their leader, the Prophet Muḥammad (peace be on him) was indeed of quite a different mettle. He did not ask anyone to bear a burden that he himself did not bear. In fact, he was ahead of others in doing so. There was no hardship which he did not share with his followers. He was also among those who dug the trench to protect Madīnah from the onslaught of Islam's enemies. He also equally shared with other Muslims the pangs of hunger and the inclemency of a cold winter. During the siege he was always present on the battlefront and did not shrink even for a moment from taking part in encounters. His own family, too, was exposed to the same perils to which the rest of the Muslims were exposed as a result of Banū Qurayẓah's perfidy. He made no special security arrangements for himself or for his family. Instead, he wed his readiness to sacrifice whatever he had and did so before asking others to do so. He was, therefore, a living role model for his followers, one which they should naturally have followed.

This, then, is the obvious meaning of the verse in its given context. However, the verse is also universal in its import and cannot be restricted only to a particular context. God does not say that the Prophet (peace be on him) is a model only in this particular respect. Rather, he stands out as a role model in the broadest possible sense of the term. Muslims must emulate his example and mould their lives on his exemplary pattern.

for all those who look forward to Allah and the Last Day and remember Allah much.[35] (22) As for the true believers,[36] when they saw the invading confederates, they cried out: "This is what Allah and His Messenger had promised us, and what Allah and His Messenger said was absolutely true."[37] ▸

لِّمَن كَانَ يَرْجُوا۟ ٱللَّهَ وَٱلْيَوْمَ ٱلْـَٔاخِرَ وَذَكَرَ
ٱللَّهَ كَثِيرًا ﴿٢١﴾ وَلَمَّا رَءَا ٱلْمُؤْمِنُونَ
ٱلْأَحْزَابَ قَالُوا۟ هَـٰذَا مَا وَعَدَنَا ٱللَّهُ
وَرَسُولُهُۥ وَصَدَقَ ٱللَّهُ وَرَسُولُهُۥ ۚ

35. For those negligent of God, the Prophet (peace be on him) is obviously not a role model. His example is emulated, however, by all those who remember God much. Likewise, there are those who do not believe and do not look forward to any reward from God. They also do not believe that the Day of Resurrection will ever come. Such a person will fail to discern anything remarkable in the life-example of the Prophet (peace be on him). As for those who look forward to God's grace and favour and are concerned about the Hereafter, they will inevitably draw upon the Prophet's example. The success of such people rests on the extent to which they are able to emulate the Prophet's life-example.

36. After stressing that the Prophet (peace be on him) is the role model, attention is drawn to the exemplary conduct of his Companions. This is done in order to highlight the difference between the wholesome conduct of these true men of faith and the wickedness of false claimants to faith. Outwardly, both seemed alike in so far as both professed to believe, were reckoned to belong to the fold of Islam, and offered Prayers. However, in the hour of crisis each stood apart from the other, making it abundantly clear whose allegiance to God and His Messenger was sincere and whose was not.

37. Here, one should bear in mind verse 12 of this *sūrah* regarding the hypocrites and all those with diseased hearts. When such people witnessed a huge 12,000 strong army attacking from the front and Banū Qurayẓah from the rear, they cried out: "All that Allah and His Messenger had promised was nothing but deceit." They began to contend that the Muslims

This only increased their faith and submission.[38]	وَمَا زَادَهُمْ إِلَّآ إِيمَـٰنًا وَتَسْلِيمًا ﴿٢٢﴾

were promised that were they to believe in God they would receive God's aid, that they would prevail against the Arabs as well as non-Arabs, and the treasures of Caesar and Chosroes would be theirs. However, what happened was quite contrary to this. The whole of Arabia was bent on destroying them and there was no trace of the army of angels that would rescue them from the fierce predicament in which they were caught.

Here, it is pointed out that God's promises to the believers were not uniformly understood. It is made clear that the promises of God and His Messenger (peace be on him) were liable to two different ways of understanding. One way to understand these promises was that of the hypocrites who thought that they had been cheated. True believers, however, understood them differently. When confronted with impending dangers they too recalled those promises. They, however, did not think that they had been promised dominance over the whole world without even raising their little finger in God's cause, or that armies of angels would land on earth to coronate them! They knew well that they themselves would first have to undergo severe tests and trials, endure immense hardships and make enormous sacrifices and only then would they be granted success in this world and the Next. This is what the Qur'ān says on the subject:

> Do you suppose that you will enter Paradise untouched by the suffering endured by the people of faith who passed away before you? They were afflicted by misery and hardship and were so convulsed that the Messenger and the believers with him cried out: "When will Allah's help arrive?" They were assured: "Behold Allah's help is close by", (*al-Baqarah* 2:214).
>
> Do people think that they will be left alone on saying: "We believe", and that they will not be tested? We did test those before them, and God will certainly ascertain those who spoke the truth and those who lied, (*al-'Ankabūt* 29:2–3).

38. Far from feeling threatened, the believers' faith grew and strengthened as they came face to face with this calamitous situation. Also, instead of shirking their obedience to God, they resolved, with even greater faith and mental equanimity, to consecrate to Him their lives and properties.

It is pertinent to note that faith is a state of mind and heart. This is put to the test whenever one is required by one's faith either to do something

(23) Among the believers there are those who have remained true to the covenant they made with Allah. Among those some of them have fulfilled their vow and others await the appointed time.[39] ▸	مِّنَ ٱلْمُؤْمِنِينَ رِجَالٌ صَدَقُوا۟ مَا عَـٰهَدُوا۟ ٱللَّهَ عَلَيْهِ ۖ فَمِنْهُم مَّن قَضَىٰ نَحْبَهُۥ وَمِنْهُم مَّن يَنتَظِرُ ۖ

or refrain from it. On numerous occasions, faith forbids or prescribes something, requiring that one sacrifice one's wealth, time, money, energy and even life. Whoever deviates from the course of obedience will suffer a decline in his faith. By contrast, whoever faithfully carries out the enjoinments of faith will grow in faith and resignation to God. Initially a person becomes a person of faith and submission simply by verbally affirming Islam's basic creed, that is: "There is no deity other than Allah and Muḥammad is His Messenger." But faith is not static. It can grow and decline. A decrease in a person's sincerity and obedience contributes to decline of faith so much so that this process can bring man to the border line of hypocrisy. Conversely, the more sincere a person is in respect of his faith, the more he strives to obey God, and the more devoted and enthusiastic he is to exalt God's religion, the more his faith will correspondingly grow. Such a person can even reach a stage when he becomes an embodiment of utter sincerity and faithfulness (*ṣiddīqīyah*).

This growth and decline in a person's state of faith is, however, known only to God. Hence, when a person affirms his belief in Islam, he becomes a Muslim. He will continue to be considered a Muslim as long as he holds on to that position. No one is in a position to judge another Muslim as half a Muslim, or one quarter of a Muslim, or that someone is twice or thrice as good a Muslim as any other Muslim. As regards their legal rights, all will be considered equal. No one is entitled to a greater or lesser share in rights depending on the state of one's faith. Faith cannot be reckoned in such terms by human beings. Imām Abū Ḥanīfah means exactly this when he says: "Faith neither increases nor decreases". (For details see, *Towards Understanding the Qur'ān, Sūrah al-Anfāl* 8: n.2, Vol. III, pp. 137–138; *Tafhīm al-Qur'ān, Sūrah al-Fatḥ* 48: n. 7.)

39. Some believers have already laid down their lives in God's cause while others are poised to follow in their footsteps, being in a state of utter readiness to sacrifice their lives whenever so required.

They have not changed in the least. (24) (All this is) in order that Allah may reward the truthful for their truthfulness, and either punish the hypocrites or, if He so wills, accept their repentance. Verily Allah is Most Pardoning, Most Compassionate.

(25) Allah sent back the unbelievers empty-handed, their hearts seething with rage. Allah sufficed the believers in their fight. Allah is Most Powerful, Most Mighty. (26) Allah brought down from their fortresses those People of the Book who had supported the invading confederates[40] and cast such terror into their hearts that some of them you kill and some of them you take captive. (27) Allah made you inherit their land, their dwellings, and their goods, and a piece of land on which you had not yet trodden. Verily Allah has power over all things.

وَمَا بَدَّلُوا۟ تَبْدِيلًا ﴿٢٣﴾ لِّيَجْزِىَ ٱللَّهُ
ٱلصَّـٰدِقِينَ بِصِدْقِهِمْ وَيُعَذِّبَ ٱلْمُنَـٰفِقِينَ
إِن شَآءَ أَوْ يَتُوبَ عَلَيْهِمْ ۚ إِنَّ ٱللَّهَ كَانَ
غَفُورًا رَّحِيمًا ﴿٢٤﴾ وَرَدَّ ٱللَّهُ ٱلَّذِينَ كَفَرُوا۟
بِغَيْظِهِمْ لَمْ يَنَالُوا۟ خَيْرًا ۚ وَكَفَى ٱللَّهُ ٱلْمُؤْمِنِينَ
ٱلْقِتَالَ ۚ وَكَانَ ٱللَّهُ قَوِيًّا عَزِيزًا ﴿٢٥﴾ وَأَنزَلَ
ٱلَّذِينَ ظَـٰهَرُوهُم مِّنْ أَهْلِ ٱلْكِتَـٰبِ
مِن صَيَاصِيهِمْ وَقَذَفَ فِى قُلُوبِهِمُ ٱلرُّعْبَ
فَرِيقًا تَقْتُلُونَ وَتَأْسِرُونَ فَرِيقًا ﴿٢٦﴾
وَأَوْرَثَكُمْ أَرْضَهُمْ وَدِيَـٰرَهُمْ وَأَمْوَٰلَهُمْ
وَأَرْضًا لَّمْ تَطَـُٔوهَا ۚ وَكَانَ ٱللَّهُ عَلَىٰ كُلِّ
شَىْءٍ قَدِيرًا ﴿٢٧﴾

40. That is, the Jews of Banū Qurayẓah tribe.

(28) O Prophet,[41] tell your wives: "If you seek the world and its embellishments, then come and I will make some provision for you and release you in an honourable way. (29) But if you seek Allah and His Messenger and the Abode of the Hereafter, then surely Allah has prepared a great reward for those of you who do good."[42]

يَٰٓأَيُّهَا ٱلنَّبِيُّ قُل لِّأَزْوَٰجِكَ إِن كُنتُنَّ
تُرِدْنَ ٱلْحَيَوٰةَ ٱلدُّنْيَا وَزِينَتَهَا فَتَعَالَيْنَ
أُمَتِّعْكُنَّ وَأُسَرِّحْكُنَّ سَرَاحًا جَمِيلًا ﴿٢٨﴾
وَإِن كُنتُنَّ تُرِدْنَ ٱللَّهَ وَرَسُولَهُۥ وَٱلدَّارَ
ٱلْءَاخِرَةَ فَإِنَّ ٱللَّهَ أَعَدَّ لِلْمُحْسِنَٰتِ مِنكُنَّ
أَجْرًا عَظِيمًا ﴿٢٩﴾

---

41. Verses 28–35 of this *sūrah* were revealed during the Campaigns of Aḥzāb and Banū Qurayẓah. Muslim narrates a tradition from Jābir Ibn 'Abd Allāh. It states that one day Abū Bakr and 'Umar called on the Prophet (peace be on him) and saw him sitting in the company of his wives. Addressing 'Umar he said: "They are sitting around me as you see and they are asking for maintenance". Upon hearing this both Abū Bakr and 'Umar scolded their daughters [who were wives of the Prophet], saying that they were harassing the Prophet (peace be on him) and asking him to provide them with something that he did not have. (Muslim, *Kitāb al-Ṭalāq, Bāb Bayān anna Takhyīr Imra'tihi lā Yakūn ...*) One thus learns that the Prophet (peace be on him) was faced with acute financial problems during this period. This demand at a time when his mind was acutely occupied with the battle raging between the forces of unbelief and Islam, irked him all the more.

42. At the time of the revelation of this verse, the Prophet (peace be on him) had four wives – Sawdah, 'Ā'ishah, Ḥafṣah and Umm Salamah. In other words, he had not by then married Zaynab. (Ibn al-'Arabī, *Aḥkām al-Qur'ān*, comments on verses 28–29.) When this verse was revealed, the Prophet (peace be on him) first spoke to 'Ā'ishah saying: "I want to have a word with you. You need not hurry in answering. You may consult your parents and then inform me of your decision". Then he told her the content of the verse revealed to him and then recited this verse to her. She replied: "Do I have to consult my parents in this matter? Without

any hesitation I seek 'Allah and His Messenger and the Abode of the Hereafter'". Then the Prophet (peace be on him) called on his other wives and told them the same. All of them gave the same reply that 'Ā'ishah had given. (Muslim, *Kitāb al-Ṭalāq, Bāb Bayān anna Takhyīr Imra'tihi lā Yakūn ...;* Aḥmad ibn Ḥanbal, *Musnad*, narrated by Jābir ibn 'Abd Allāh and Nasā'ī, *Kitāb al-Ṭalāq, Bāb al-Tawqīt fī al-Janā'iz.*)

The term *takhyīr* signifies a husband authorising his wife to decide unilaterally between continuing to live with or separating from him. Since God had asked the Prophet (peace be on him) to offer this choice to his wives, he accordingly took his wives into his confidence. However, had any of them opted for separation, this would not have been automatic. Rather, the Prophet (peace be on him) would have released them from the bond of wedlock, as is borne out by the text of the verse: "... I will make some provision for you and release you in an honourable way". It was, nonetheless, obligatory for the Prophet (peace be on him) to grant them separation if any of them so desired. For, it was inconsistent with his position as a Prophet not to honour his promise. Moreover, after such separation, that wife would no longer have belonged to the category of "mothers of the believers". It seems that it would not have been unlawful then for any Muslim to marry them, for they would have chosen separation from the Prophet (peace be on him) out of their love for "the world and its embellishments" and this purpose would obviously remain unaccomplished if they were deprived of the opportunity to marry. On the other hand, if any of his wives chose "Allah and His Messenger and the Abode of the Hereafter", the Prophet (peace be on him) would henceforth cease to have the right to divorce those of his wives who had so expressed their preference for God, His Messenger and the Hereafter. The choice offered them inevitably led to one of two logical consequences. Should they prefer this world and its embellishments, they would have to separate; if they expressed their preference for God, His Messenger and the Abode of the Hereafter, they would continue to remain as they were, wives of the Prophet (peace be on him) and "mothers of the believers".

In Islamic law, *takhyīr* is the term used for delegating to one's wife the right to divorce, a right that originally belongs to the husband. A wife, thus, has the choice to remain in wedlock or be separated. The detailed injunctions in this regard, as deduced from the Qur'ān and the *Sunnah*, are as follows:

i. Once a husband grants this right to his wife, he can neither withdraw it nor prevent his wife from exercising it. It is, of course, not mandatory for the wife to necessarily exercise this right. She may choose to continue the marital tie and thus let the right to be separated go by default.

ii. There are two ways to grant this right to a wife. First, by the husband's authorising his wife, in unequivocal terms, that she has the authority to invoke divorce. Secondly, whereby the husband does not clearly specify delegating the right of divorce to his wife, but says something that carries the intention to delegate this right to her. For example, he may say to her: "You have the right", or "Your matter is in your hands". The use of such suggestive expressions without corresponding intention on the husband's part, however, does not amount to delegating to his wife the power to invoke divorce. If she claims to have received such a delegation of power and the claim is contested by the husband under oath, this by the husband saying that he did not intend to divorce his wife, the husband's version will be accepted. An exception can only be made when the wife produces firm evidence to the effect that she was granted this right in the course of a marital quarrel or in the course of their discussion on divorce. For in that context, it would be understood that the husband intended to divorce his wife.

    Another condition pertaining to *takhyīr* is that the delegation of this power is made known to the wife. If the wife is not present when the husband makes such a statement, she must receive definite information about it. If she is present, she should herself hear her husband's statement to this effect. Unless she receives information about his delegation of the right of divorce or directly hears this statement from her husband, she cannot exercise this right.

iii. There is some difference of opinion among jurists regarding the duration of the validity of this right, particularly when the husband grants his wife this right in absolute terms, without specifying any time period for its validity. According to one group of scholars, the wife may exercise this right in the same sitting in which her husband granted this right to her. If she moves away without giving any response or is engaged in something which may indicate that she does not want to make any response, she forfeits her right. This is the opinion of 'Umar, 'Uthmān, 'Abd Allāh ibn Mas'ūd, Jābir ibn 'Abd Allāh, Jābir ibn Zayd, 'Aṭā', Mujāhid, Sha'bī, Nakha'ī, Mālik, Abū Ḥanīfah, Shāfi'ī, Awzā'ī, Sufyān al-Thawrī and Abū Thawr.

    According to another group of scholars, the wife's right is not limited to that particular sitting. She may also exercise it later. This opinion is held by Ḥasan al-Baṣrī, Qatādah, and Zuhrī.

iv. If the husband at the time of delegating the power of divorce to his wife, mentions a specific period of time, say a month or a year, the wife will have this right only during that period. However, if he leaves the timing to her discretion, her right will remain valid for an unlimited period.

v. If the wife seeks separation, she should express it in clear, unmistakable terms. A vague statement in this regard will not be deemed valid.

vi. In terms of legal procedure, the husband may delegate this power to his wife in one of the following three ways: by either saying to her (a) "Your matter is in your hands", or (b) "You have the right", or (c) "You are divorced, if this is what you want". Each of these, however, has different legal implications:

If the husband says to his wife: "Your matter is in your hands", and she responds to this in clear words that indicate her choice of separation, then, according to the Ḥanafī School, this constitutes a single irrevocable (*bā'in*) divorce. (In other words, the husband will forfeit his right to revoke the divorce. After the expiry of the waiting period, however, the spouses may re-marry if they decide to do so.) However, if the husband says at the time while delegating the power of divorce: "Your matter is in your hands to the extent of a single divorce", this amounts to a single revocable divorce. Hence, the husband may take her back as his wife during her waiting period. However, if while making the above statement his intention was to vest her with the right of triple divorce, or if he explicitly said so, this is tantamount to divorce irrespective of whether she explicitly pronounces triple divorce on herself or declares only once that she has separated herself from her husband or that she has divorced herself.

If the husband grants his wife the right of separation by saying to her: "You have the right", and his wife explicitly exercises that right, this will lead, according to the Ḥanafī School, only to a single irrevocable (*bā'in*) divorce, even if the husband intended triple divorce. However, if he explicitly delegates to her the right of triple divorce, her exercise of that right will lead to triple divorce. Shāfi'ī, however, maintains that if the husband's intention was divorce and the wife secures separation, this amounts to a single revocable divorce. According to Mālik, however, this amounts to triple divorce of the wife if the husband had consummated his marriage. However, the husband's claim for a single divorce will be accepted if his marriage with that wife had not been consummated.

If the husband says to his wife: "You are divorced, if that is what you want", and the wife exercises this option, the divorce that will come into effect will be revocable, not *bā'in*.

vii. If, despite the husband's delegation of the divorce right to his wife, she expresses her willingness to continue to be his wife, no

(30) Wives of the Prophet, if any of you commit flagrant indecency, her chastisement shall be doubled.[43] That is easy for Allah.[44] ►

يَـٰنِسَآءَ ٱلنَّبِىِّ مَن يَأْتِ مِنكُنَّ بِفَـٰحِشَةٍ مُّبَيِّنَةٍ يُضَـٰعَفْ لَهَا ٱلْعَذَابُ ضِعْفَيْنِ ۚ وَكَانَ ذَٰلِكَ عَلَى ٱللَّهِ يَسِيرًا ﴿٣٠﴾

divorce will come into force. This is the view of 'Umar, 'Abd Allāh ibn Mas'ūd, 'Ā'ishah, Abū al-Dardā', 'Abd Allāh ibn 'Abbās, and 'Abd Allāh ibn 'Umar. This represents the mainstream view. When Masrūq sought 'Ā'ishah's ruling on the issue, she replied: "The Prophet (peace be on him) delegated this right to his wives, yet they preferred to continue their marital tie with him. It was, therefore, not deemed as divorce". (Bukhārī, *Kitāb al-Ṭalāq, Bāb man Khayyara Azwājahu.*) According to one report, only 'Alī and Zayd ibn Thābit were of the opinion that even in this case a single, revocable divorce will come into force. However, according to another report, both 'Alī and Zayd ibn Thābit held the opinion that no divorce would come into force. (Jaṣṣāṣ, *Aḥkām al-Qur'ān*, comments on verse 28 and Ibn al-'Arabī, *Aḥkām al-Qur'ān*, comments on verses 28–29.)

43. This statement does not mean at all that there was any apprehension that the Prophet's wives would commit "flagrant indecency". The purpose of this statement was to make them realise that the expectations of them were in proportion to their elevated position in Islamic society. Hence, it was expected that their conduct should represent the highest moral standards. The statement made here is similar to the one made in *Sūrah al-Zumar* 39:65: "(Tell them clearly that) it was revealed to you and to all Prophets before you: 'If you associate any others with God in His Divinity, your works will surely come to naught and you will certainly be among the losers?'" This too does not mean that there was any fear that the Prophet (peace be on him), God forbid, would ever be involved in polytheism. The real purpose of the statement was to impress the monstrosity of polytheism on the Prophet (peace be on him) and through him on others, essentially driving home how it is absolutely necessary to stay away from it.

44. Neither their being the Prophet's wives nor their exalted positions could prevent God from His punishment, if He so decided.

(31) But whoever of you is obedient to Allah and His Messenger and does good deeds, Allah will double her reward.[45] We have prepared for her a generous provision.

(32) Wives of the Prophet, you are not like other women.[46] ▶

۞ وَمَن يَقْنُتْ مِنكُنَّ لِلَّهِ وَرَسُولِهِۦ وَتَعْمَلْ
صَـٰلِحًا نُّؤْتِهَآ أَجْرَهَا مَرَّتَيْنِ وَأَعْتَدْنَا لَهَا
رِزْقًا كَرِيمًا ﴿٣١﴾ يَـٰنِسَآءَ ٱلنَّبِىِّ لَسْتُنَّ كَأَحَدٍ
مِّنَ ٱلنِّسَآءِ

45. The Prophet's wives will receive double the punishment for their sins and double the reward for their good deeds. This is on account of their high position in society, for people generally follow in the steps of their leaders, both in good and evil. If they are evil, their misdeeds corrupt the whole nation. Hence such people deserve punishment for their own misdeeds as well as for the misdeeds of those who were prompted to corruption by their example. By the same token, the goodness of their leaders' deeds will not remain confined to them, but will also spread to others. When such people commit evil deeds they receive greater punishment because of the unwholesome impact of their behaviour on others. On the contrary, when they do good, they are rewarded not only for their own deeds but also for the wholesome impact they had on others.

This verse also brings to light the principle that the more sacrosanct something is, the more sacrilegious is its violation, hence entailing a more severe penalty. For example, drinking in a mosque is a much more outrageous sin than doing so within the confines of one's home. Committing unlawful sex with a woman of prohibited degree is a more grave sin than committing it with any other woman, and would naturally entail a more grievous punishment.

46. This marks the beginning of the passage (vv. 32–34) which lays down injunctions pertaining to *ḥijāb*. Although it is addressed to the Prophet's wives, the aim is to introduce the reforms enshrined in these verses to all Muslim households. Once the Prophet's household sets the model of piety and rectitude, that model will be emulated by other Muslim women.

If you fear Allah, do not be too complaisant in your speech lest those with diseased hearts should covet you; but speak in a straight forward manner.[47] ▶	إِنِ ٱتَّقَيْتُنَّ فَلَا تَخْضَعْنَ بِٱلْقَوْلِ فَيَطْمَعَ ٱلَّذِى فِى قَلْبِهِۦ مَرَضٌ وَقُلْنَ قَوْلًا مَّعْرُوفًا ﴿٣٢﴾

Some people express the view that since these verses are addressed to the Prophet's wives, the injunctions enshrined in them are meant only to apply to the Prophet's wives. Just consider, however, what is said in the verses that follow and decide which of the directives mentioned in them is exclusively required for the Prophet's wives and not for other Muslim women. Could it be God's purpose that only the Prophet's wives be free of all uncleanness and that only they should obey God and His Messenger, and that only they offer Prayers and pay *Zakāh*? Now, since this is not the case, how can the Qur'ānic injunction that they stay in their homes and not go about displaying their allurements, as was done in the former Time of Ignorance, and not be complaisant in their speech with men unrelated to them be considered as injunctions specific to the Prophet's wives only and not to other Muslim women? There are no grounds whatsoever for considering some of these injunctions to be of general and others of specific import.

The Qur'ānic statement that the Prophet's wives "are not like other women", obviously does not mean that other women may go out alluringly dressed, that they may speak complaisantly to men unrelated to them whereas the Prophet's wives should not do so. In fact, this statement resembles a refined person's telling his children: "Do not use abusive words; you do not belong to a group of vulgar children". No intelligent person will interpret this statement to mean that the person concerned considers the use of abusive words blameworthy only for his own children but not for others' children; that he does not mind if this habit is found among others.

47. It is not blameworthy for a woman to speak to other men, whenever that is needed. However, a Muslim woman should speak in a straightforward manner so that it leaves no room for anyone to entertain amorous expectations. Her speech should be free from endearing overtones, complaisant tones and affected sweetness that arouses a man's sensual passions and encourage him to make advances. God makes it

(33) And stay in your homes[48] and do not go about displaying your allurements as in the former Time ▸	وَقَرْنَ فِي بُيُوتِكُنَّ وَلَا تَبَرَّجْنَ تَبَرُّجَ ٱلْجَٰهِلِيَّةِ ٱلْأُولَىٰ

plain that this manner of conversation does not behove a God-fearing woman who desires to stay away from immoral conduct. In other words, this manner of conversation with men is characteristic of immoral women, not of pious, believing women.

Let us consider this verse together with the following Qur'ānic directive: "Nor should they stamp their feet on the ground in such a manner that their hidden ornament becomes revealed" (*al-Nūr* 24:31). The message of this Divine directive is loud and clear. Women should not display their charms and allurements to men not related to them. If need arises, and they have to speak to them, they should exercise all necessary precautions when doing so. It is in view of this that women may not make the *adhān*. If a woman is performing Congregational Prayer, unlike men, she may not pronounce the words *Subḥān Allāh* aloud to alert the imām that he has made some mistake. Instead, she may only strike one of her palms against the other.

Considering that Islam does not approve of women's speaking in an alluring manner to men not related to them and, in fact, would rather like them not to speak to such men unless there is need to do so, how can that religion then approve of their appearance on the stage, singing, dancing or walking with dalliance, making a display of their amorous playfulness and behaving, on the whole, coquettishly? How could Islam possibly support women singing melodious love songs, containing lewd stuff, on the radio and other modes of mass media that whip up men's desires? How can it allow her to act in dramas and play the role of someone's wife or beloved? Can it allow women to serve as air hostesses adept at charming passengers? Can it permit their appearing publicly so as to flaunt their attractions in social clubs and other public places in mixed gatherings of men and women? Can it sanction their uninhibited mingling with men and cracking jokes with them? Such practices have no sanction in the Qur'ān. The Qur'ānic directives on such matters are common knowledge. Can anyone point to any evidence in the Qur'ān that legitimises the kind of permissive culture described above?

48. The imperative *qarna* ("stay") used here has been understood variously by lexicographers. In this respect, it is variously considered to

have been derived from the roots *q r r* and *w q r*. If it is considered to be derived from *q r r,* the meaning of the imperative would be: "to be settled down" and "to linger". If, however, it is derived from *w q r,* the meaning would be "stay with serenity" or "stay with grace and dignity". In either case, it signifies that the main sphere of a woman's activity is her home. She should remain in this sphere and focus on discharging her duties. She may go out of this sphere only when there is a need to do so.

This meaning is clearly borne out by the wording of the verse. It is further reinforced by a *ḥadīth.* Abū Bakr al-Bazzār reports on Anas ibn Mālik's authority that women once said to the Prophet (peace be on him): "All acts of merit are for men: they engage in *jihād* and do much else in God's cause. In which acts should we engage so that we may receive a reward equal to that of *mujāhidīn*?" The Prophet (peace be on him) replied: "Whoever of you stays in her home will attain the same degree of merit as *mujāhidīn*". What this means is that a *mujāhid* will devote himself with full equanimity to God's cause because of the security he enjoys at home, knowing that his wife will duly look after his home and children, and that she will not act in a manner that would embarrass him. Since his wife provides him such peace of mind, she will receive an equal share of the reward for her husband's *jihād.* According to another tradition narrated by Bazzār and Tirmidhī on 'Abd Allāh ibn Mas'ūd's authority, the Prophet (peace be on him) remarked: "A woman is an object that ought to be covered. When she goes out, Satan ogles at her. She is closer to God's mercy when she is in the precincts of her home". (Tirmidhī, *Kitāb al-Raḍā'* and Ibn Kathīr, *Tafsīr*, comments on verse 33.) (For further details see *Towards Understanding the Qur'ān, al-Nūr*: 24, Vol. VI, n. 49, pp. 239–242.)

In face of such explicit and emphatic Qur'ānic injunctions there is no justification whatsoever for Muslim women to become members of councils and parliaments, run around in connection with social activities outside their homes, work shoulder to shoulder with men in offices, receive education in co-educational colleges, perform nursing duties in male hospitals, serve as receptionists and hostesses on railways and airlines. Nor is there any good reason to send them to USA or UK for education and training. The only argument for a woman's outdoor role is that 'Ā'ishah took part in the Battle of the Camel. Those who cite this example are perhaps not aware of 'Ā'ishah's own opinion on this matter. The following report has been narrated by 'Abd Allāh ibn Aḥmad ibn Ḥanbal in *Zawā'id al-Zuhd* and by Ibn al-Mundhir, Ibn Abī Shaybah and Ibn Sa'd in their respective works on Masrūq's authority. While reciting this verse of the Qur'ān (see *Sūrah al-Aḥzāb* 33:33), 'Ā'ishah could not control her tears, for it reminded her of her mistake in having taken part in the Battle of the Camel.

of Ignorance.[49] Establish Prayer, give *Zakāh*, and obey Allah and His Messenger. Allah only wishes to remove uncleanness from you, ▸

وَأَقِمْنَ ٱلصَّلَوٰةَ وَءَاتِينَ ٱلزَّكَوٰةَ وَأَطِعْنَ ٱللَّهَ وَرَسُولَهُۥٓ ۚ إِنَّمَا يُرِيدُ ٱللَّهُ لِيُذْهِبَ عَنكُمُ ٱلرِّجْسَ

49. In this verse, two key expressions, *tabarruj* and *jāhilīyah ūlā*, have been used. The connotation of both should be grasped for a better understanding of the verse. *Tabarruj* literally denotes something that is prominent or elevated. *Baraja* is used to denote an object that is manifest and elevated. *Burj* (tower) is one of its derivatives and carries the same connotation. A sailing boat is called a *bārijah* because of its distinct sails which are observable even from a distance.

When the word *tabarruj* is used in the context of women, it carries the following three meanings: (i) displaying the charms of her face and body before others; (ii) displaying her dress and jewellery, (iii) making a show of herself by her coquettish gait and other enticing gestures. Leading lexicographers and Qur'ān-commentators have interpreted *tabarruj* mostly in this sense. Mujāhid, Qatādah and Ibn Abī Nujayḥ define *tabarruj* as walking in an alluring and coquettish manner. According to Muqātil, it denotes a woman's display of her necklace, earrings and neckline. Al-Mubarrad explains *tabarruj* as follows: "A women's revealing her charms which she ought to conceal". Abū 'Ubaydah is of the opinion that it consists in a woman's revealing her charms of [body and dress] in order to allure men. (Ibn Kathīr, *Tafsīr*, comments on verse 33 and Ṭabarī, *Tafsīr*, comments on verse 33.)

As for the word *jāhilīyah*, it occurs in the Qur'ān on three other occasions in addition to its use here. In *Āl 'Imrān* 3:154 it is used with reference to those who flinch from fighting in the cause of God because they entertain false notions about God – "the notions of the Age of Ignorance". In *al-Mā'idah* 5:50 it is said that those who seek the judgement of others than God in their affairs are guilty of desiring "judgement according to the Law of ignorance". In *al-Fatḥ* 48:26 the Makkan unbelievers' attitude is characterised as one of "fierce bigotry – the bigotry of ignorance". This bigotry was responsible for their preventing Muslims from performing *'umrah*. It is recorded in a *ḥadīth* that once during his quarrel with someone Abū al-Dardā' abused him as regards his mother. On observing this, the Prophet (peace be on him) said: "These are vestiges of *jāhilīyah* in you".

O members of the (Prophet's) household, and to purify you completely.[50] ▶	أَهْلَ ٱلْبَيْتِ وَيُطَهِّرَكُمْ تَطْهِيرًا ﴿٣٣﴾

(Bukhārī, *Kitāb al-Adab, Bāb mā Yunhā min al-Sibāb wa al-La'an* – Ed.) According to another *ḥadīth*, the Prophet (peace be on him) observed: "There are three practices of *jāhilīyah*: finding fault with someone's descent, taking divination from the movement of stars, and lamenting and wailing over someone's death". (Bukhārī, *Kitāb al-Manāqib, Bāb al-Qasāmah fī al-Jāhilīyah* – Ed.)

In view of the above uses of the term *jāhilīyah*, it becomes evident that as a technical term in Islam *jāhilīyah* stands for any practice that runs counter to Islamic norms and worldview. As for the expression *jāhilīyah ūlā* which occurs in this verse, it signifies the evil deeds committed by Arabs and others before Islam's advent. It is obvious, therefore, that God forbids women from going about displaying their beauty and charms. God also directs women to stay in their homes. Their main sphere of activity is their home rather than the outside world. If there is any need for them to go out, they may do so but not in the manner of the women of the *jāhilīyah* period. In other words, it is highly unbecoming of Muslim women to go out of their homes bedecked with all possible allurements, displaying their charms by wearing make-up and by using seductive, tight-fitting and revealing dresses. These are the practices of the *jāhilīyah* period, which are not conformable with Islam. It is for anyone to decide whether the culture that is being promoted in our society is derived from the Qur'ān or from *jāhilīyah*. It would be quite a different matter if those who are promoting this *jāhilī* culture have a version of the Qur'ān that is not accessible to ordinary mortals!

50. It is evident from the context that the expression *ahl al-bayt* (members of the Prophet's household) here signifies the Prophet's wives. This is borne out by the fact that a direct reference is made to them: by virtue of the verse opening with the words *yā nisā' al-Nabī* ("O wives of the Prophet") it is clear that it is they who are addressed throughout this passage.

The Qur'ānic expression *ahl al-bayt* is used in Arabic to denote one's family, including one's wife and children. It is patently obvious that a person's wife cannot be excluded from the family. The Qur'ān employs the same expression on two other occasions and in each instance it includes the wife. When the angels gave the good news of the birth of a son to the Prophet Abraham (peace be on him), his wife was astonished to hear this. In amazement she asked: how could they have a son when they were so advanced in age? To this the angels responded: "Do you wonder at Allah's decree? Allah's mercy and His blessings be upon you, O people of the house". (*Hūd* 11:73.) Another instance of the use of *ahl al-bayt* occurs in the context of the Prophet Moses' story. When he arrived at the Pharaoh's palace as a newly-born baby and a search was on to find a wet nurse for him, his sister said: "Shall I direct you to the people of a household (*ahl bayt*) that will rear him?", (*al-Qaṣaṣ* 28:12).

It is plain and clear, both in terms of the Arabic idiom and the Qur'ānic usage of this expression, that the Prophet's wives are obviously included in the term *ahl al-bayt*. Likewise, his children belong to the same category. It is perhaps more appropriate to say that the address is mainly directed to his wives, while his children are implicitly included. Accordingly, Ibn 'Abbās, 'Urwah ibn al-Zubayr and 'Ikrimah maintain that the verse makes a pointed reference to the Prophet's wives. (Ibn Kathīr, *Tafsīr*, comments on verse 33.)

However, were someone to insist that *ahl al-bayt* are restricted to the Prophet's wives alone, this would be erroneous. When we speak of someone's household, we refer to all members of his family. This point was in fact clarified by the Prophet (peace be on him) himself. It is related on Ibn Abī Ḥātim's authority that when he was asked about 'Alī, 'Ā'ishah said: "You are asking me about him who was among those dearest to the Prophet (peace be on him) and whose wife was the Prophet's beloved daughter!" She then recounted how the Prophet (peace be on him) once summoned 'Alī, Fāṭimah, Ḥasan and Ḥusayn and covered all of them with a sheet and prayed: "O Lord! They are of my household. Remove uncleanness from them and purify them". 'Ā'ishah added: "I am also of your household". (In other words, she asked that she, too, be let in under the sheet, and a similar prayer be made for her.) The Prophet (peace be on him), however, told her: "Stay away! Of course, you are one of them". (Tirmidhī, *Kitāb al-Tafsīr, Bāb Sūrah al-Aḥzāb*) Traditions of a similar import are cited by Muslim, Aḥmad, Ibn Jarīr al-Ṭabarī, Ḥākim and Bayhaqī on the authority of Abū Sa'īd al-Khudrī, 'Ā'ishah, Anas, Umm Salamah, Wāthilah ibn Asqa' and other Companions. These reports indicate that the Prophet (peace be on him) pronounced 'Alī, Fāṭimah and their two sons as belonging to his household. In view of these reports, the term *ahl al-bayt* cannot be restricted just to the Prophet's wives.

Equally flawed is the contention that the Prophet's wives do not fall under the category of *ahl al-bayt*. This view is put forward on the grounds of the above-quoted *aḥādīth*. First, what the Qur'ān expressly declares cannot simply be dismissed on the basis of any *ḥadīth*. Secondly, the relevant *aḥādīth* do not mean (portray) what they are claimed to mean. These reports simply indicate that the Prophet (peace be on him) did not cover 'Ā'ishah and Umm Salamah with the sheet with which he had covered 'Alī, Fāṭimah, Ḥasan and Ḥusayn. His action does not signify that he did not consider his wives as part of his household. Rather, the Prophet's wives were already included in his *ahl al-bayt*, for the Qur'ān had addressed them with that title. The Prophet (peace be on him) was concerned about other members of his family (to wit, his daughter, his son-in-law and his grandsons) lest, because of the Qur'ān's wording which specifically addressed his wives, other members of his family were considered outside his household. He, therefore, clarified the point as regards them. No such statement was needed in respect of his wives whom the Qur'ān had already included among the Prophet's *ahl al-Bayt*.

A certain section of people is not only guilty of excluding the Prophet's wives from the category of *ahl al-bayt*, but also insists on restricting its use exclusively to 'Alī, Fāṭimah and their children. Furthermore, it misconstrues the Prophet's prayer for their purification in the sense that like God's Prophets, 'Alī, Fāṭimah and their children are immune from sin. This is deduced from the following words of the verse: "Allah only wishes to remove uncleanness from you, O members of the (Prophet's) household and purify you completely" (verse 33). In their opinion, the word "uncleanness" (used in the verse) stands for sin and God has declared them to be free of sin. This interpretation, however, is not borne out by the wording of the verse under study. Verse 33 does not declare that they have been made free of sin. It simply says that: "Allah only wishes *to remove* uncleanness from you". It is evident from the context that the Qur'ān does not intend to narrate the excellent qualities of the Prophet's household. Rather, it exhorts them to carry out certain deeds and shun others so that God may remove uncleanness from them. In other words, the Qur'ān presents before them a way of life whose observance will enable them to attain purity, implying that if they fail to do so, they will not attain purity. However, if the verse is misinterpreted to mean that the Qur'ān declares the sinlessness of the Prophet's household by saying, "He wants to purify you ...", all those who perform *wuḍū'*, ritual bathing, and *tayammum* should also be taken as sinless. For the Qur'ān uses exactly the same words in *al-Mā'idah* 5:6. "He wants to purify you ...".

(34) Remember the Signs of Allah and the words of wisdom which are rehearsed in your homes.[51] Verily Allah is All-Subtle,[52] All-Aware.

وَٱذْكُرْنَ مَا يُتْلَىٰ فِى بُيُوتِكُنَّ مِنْ
ءَايَٰتِ ٱللَّهِ وَٱلْحِكْمَةِ ۚ إِنَّ ٱللَّهَ كَانَ
لَطِيفًا خَبِيرًا ﴿٣٤﴾

---

51. The imperative *wa yadhkurna* in the verse connotes both "remembrance" and "mention". Taken in the former sense, it directs the Prophet's wives never to forget that they represent a family that is the source of radiating wisdom and good morality for all. They are, therefore, charged with a great responsibility. Let it not happen then that people observe in this pious household patterns of *jāhilī* practices.

If it is taken in its latter sense, the verse directs the Prophet's wives to mention the Prophet's teachings. This because they are privileged to have access to things to which others have no access. This verse makes a pointed reference to the "Signs of Allah and the words of wisdom which are rehearsed in your homes". The former expression "Signs of Allah" obviously refers to the Qur'ānic verses. As for "words of wisdom", this has a broad connotation that covers the totality of wisdom that the Prophet (peace be on him) communicated to people. It may apply, to an equal extent, to the teachings of the Qur'ān. However, there is no good reason to restrict it to the Qur'ān alone. Apart from rehearsing the verses of the Qur'ān, the Prophet (peace be on him) also instructed people by means of his precept and practice.

Some people, however, claim that the word *tilāwah* used in this verse is restricted to reciting Qur'ānic verses. They argue therefore, that both "Signs of Allah" and "wisdom" used in the verse exclusively signify the Qur'ān. This contention is quite faulty. The word *tilāwah* simply meant 'rehearse or recite' at the time this verse was revealed. It was only later on that its use was restricted to rehearsing the Qur'ān alone. Furthermore, the Qur'ān itself does not employ it as a term in the above, restricted sense. For example, in *Sūrah al-Baqarah* 2:102, the same expression is used with regard to the magical chants rehearsed by devils while attributing them to the Prophet Solomon (peace be on him). The Qur'ān, thus, uses the term *tilāwah* in its literal, general sense, and does not specifically confine it to Qur'ānic recitation.

52. To say that "Allah is All-Aware" amounts to saying that He has full knowledge of everything, including the most hidden secrets.

(35) Surely[53] the men who submit (to Allah) and the women who submit[54] (to Allah), the men who have faith and the women who have faith,[55] ▶	إِنَّ ٱلْمُسْلِمِينَ وَٱلْمُسْلِمَـٰتِ وَٱلْمُؤْمِنِينَ وَٱلْمُؤْمِنَـٰتِ

53. Allah is All-Subtle, hence He has access even to the most hidden things; nothing can remain hidden from Him.

54. In other words, those women who have accepted Islam as the code of conduct for their lives and are committed to live in accordance with this code. The reference is, therefore, to those in whom there remains no vestige of any resistance against the Islamic worldview and way of life, those who have adopted the course of obedience and submission to God.

55. The commitment of these people to Islam is not merely a matter of outward conformity. They sincerely believe in Islam and look upon its teachings as their guide. They are firmly convinced that the way prescribed by the Qur'ān and the Prophet Muḥammad (peace be on him) represents the Straight Way and that their success lies in following it. They believe that whatever has been declared by God and His Messenger to be false and wrong is indeed false and wrong. By the same token, they strongly believe that whatever God and His Messenger have declared to be right is indeed so. Their minds and hearts do not feel uncomfortable with any injunctions based on the Qur'ān and the *Sunnah*. Nor do they strain their minds to alter these injunctions so as to mould them according to their own predispositions or in conformity with the ways obtaining in the world, and do so with such skill that none might blame them for distorting the command of the God and His Messenger! The Prophet (peace be on him) has stated the following which represents the true state of faith: "He who is satisfied with Allah as his Lord, with Islam as his faith, and with Muḥammad (peace be on him) as His Messenger has truly savoured the taste of faith". (Muslim, *Kitāb al-Īmān, Bāb al-Dalīl 'alā anna man Raḍiya ...*) Elsewhere, the Prophet (peace be on him) elucidated the same in the following words: "None of you can be a true believer unless his desire is subject to what I have brought". (Al-Baghawī, *Sharḥ al-Sunnah, Bāb Radd al-Bida' wa al-Ahwā'*.)

وَٱلْقَـٰنِتِينَ وَٱلْقَـٰنِتَـٰتِ وَٱلصَّـٰدِقِينَ
وَٱلصَّـٰدِقَـٰتِ وَٱلصَّـٰبِرِينَ وَٱلصَّـٰبِرَٰتِ
وَٱلْخَـٰشِعِينَ وَٱلْخَـٰشِعَـٰتِ

the men who are obedient and the women who are obedient,[56] the men who are truthful and the women who are truthful;[57] the men who are steadfast and the women who are steadfast,[58] the men who humble themselves (to Allah) and the women who humble themselves[59] (to Allah), ▶

56. That is, they do not just pay mere lip service to Islam, but put it into actual practice. They are not such who would, on the one hand, believe in what God and His Messenger have commanded and on the other, act contrary to those commands.

57. That is, they are true and straightforward in their words and deeds. Their conduct is free from lies, deception, cheating, treachery and fraud. They say only what is true and they do only what they regard as right. In essence, they display utter honesty and integrity in their dealings.

58. They are honest in their utterances and straightforward in their relationship with others. Furthermore, they willingly endure the hardships, threats, risks and difficulties that come their way as a result of their observance of Islam. They are not deterred by any loss they might suffer for the cause of Islam. Nor can fear, greed or temptation distract them from the Straight Way.

59. They are absolutely free from pride and arrogance. They recognise well that they are God's servants and that they do not enjoy any position above that of servitude to God. Accordingly, they fully submit themselves to Him. Their hearts and bodies are in a state of submission to God and God's fear permeates their lives. They never betray an attitude that stems from pride or arrogance, which is the wont of those bereft of any God-fearingness. In the context of this verse, the characterisation of believers as those "who humble themselves before God" alludes to observance of

the men who give alms and the women who give alms,[60] the men who fast and the women who fast,[61] the men who guard their chastity and the women who guard their chastity,[62] the men who remember Allah much and the women who remember Allah much:[63] ▶

وَٱلْمُتَصَدِّقِينَ وَٱلْمُتَصَدِّقَـٰتِ وَٱلصَّـٰٓئِمِينَ
وَٱلصَّـٰٓئِمَـٰتِ وَٱلْحَـٰفِظِينَ فُرُوجَهُمْ
وَٱلْحَـٰفِظَـٰتِ وَٱلذَّٰكِرِينَ ٱللَّهَ كَثِيرًا
وَٱلذَّٰكِرَٰتِ

Prayers. This is borne out by the fact that mention of charity and fasting immediately follows Prayer.

60. Apart from paying obligatory *Zakāh*, true believers also voluntarily spend on charity, the emphasis being that they spend generously in God's cause. They try their level best to help their fellow human beings. They do not shrink from supporting any orphan, sick, needy, disabled or poor person who happens to be in the range of their access. Nor do they flinch from spending whatever they have to exalt the religious faith ordained by God.

61. The reference here is to both obligatory and supererogatory fasts.

62. This means that they shun illicit sex and also that they restrain themselves from nudity and obscenity. Nudity and obscenity does not merely consist in appearing before people stripped of all dress. Nudity and obscenity also embraces wearing tight-fitting, revealing or transparent clothes that bring to sharp relief the contours of one's body.

63. That they remember God means that on all occasions and in different matters they mention His Name. Obviously, this emanates from God-consciousness, which is the essence of the Islamic way of life. As the thought of God permeates one's conscious, subconscious and even unconscious states, one becomes fully cognizant of Him. Such a person's actions and utterances are then also marked by God-consciousness. He pronounces God's Name no matter what he does: when he starts eating

for them has Allah prepared forgiveness and a mighty reward.[64]	أَعَدَّ ٱللَّهُ لَهُم مَّغْفِرَةً وَأَجْرًا عَظِيمًا ﴿٣٥﴾

or goes to bed or wakes up. In the course of his conversation too he repeatedly mentions God's Name, referring to His will, His gracious favours and His glory. He invokes God's help in all matters, thanks Him for every bounty he receives, and seeks His succour whenever he encounters any calamity. He fears God whenever he is tempted by sin. Whenever he commits a lapse, he seeks God's pardon. Whenever he needs something, he turns to God and asks for it.

While other acts of worship are performed at their prescribed time, God's remembrance envelopes his life all the time, connecting him to God in servitude in so far as his attention is constantly focused on God and his tongue never tires of mentioning His Name. If man has reached this state, he is like the plant that grows in its ideal environment. His life, his acts of worship, and his religious activities all represent sound growth. In contrast, if one's life is devoid of this constant remembrance of God or if one performs acts of worship only at the appointed hours, one resembles a plant that grows in a hot house, which owes its survival only to the gardener's special care. The Prophet (peace be on him) pressed home this truth in a *ḥadīth*. Mu'ādh ibn Anas al-Juhanī reports that someone asked the Prophet (peace be on him): who will receive the highest reward among those who take part in *jihād*? He replied: "He who remembers God most". He was then asked who will receive the highest reward among those who fast? The Prophet (peace be on him) gave the same reply. He was also asked the same question as regards those devoted to Prayer, *Zakāh*, *Ḥajj* and charity. On each occasion the Prophet's reply was identical: he who remembers God will receive the highest reward. (Aḥmad ibn Ḥanbal, *Musnad,* narrated by Mu'ādh ibn Anas al-Juhanī.)

64. The verse indicates the acts that carry weight in God's sight. In fact they represent the core values of Islam. As far as these values are concerned, no distinction is made between men and women. Each of them, of course, performs different functions in their respective spheres of activity: men work in certain fields and women in others. However, if their acts are permeated with the same values, they will carry the same weight in God's sight and fetch identical reward. Women may devote themselves to domestic chores while men may put into effect

(36) It does not behove a believer,[65] male or female, that when Allah and His Messenger have decided an affair they should exercise their choice. And whoever disobeys Allah and His Messenger has strayed to manifest error.[66]

وَمَا كَانَ لِمُؤْمِنٍ وَلَا مُؤْمِنَةٍ إِذَا قَضَى
ٱللَّهُ وَرَسُولُهُۥٓ أَمْرًا أَن يَكُونَ لَهُمُ ٱلْخِيَرَةُ
مِنْ أَمْرِهِمْ ۗ وَمَن يَعْصِ ٱللَّهَ وَرَسُولَهُۥ فَقَدْ
ضَلَّ ضَلَـٰلًا مُّبِينًا ﴿٣٦﴾

---

the commands of the *Sharī'ah* as God's vicegerents. Likewise, women may bring up children at home while men may stake their lives on the battlefield in the cause of God and His ordained faith. No gender will be treated differently from the other.

65. This marks the beginning of the passage dealing with the Prophet's marriage with Zaynab.

66. According to 'Abd Allāh ibn 'Abbās, this verse was revealed when the Prophet (peace be on him) had sent Zayd's marriage proposal for Zaynab and it was turned down by her and her family. According to 'Abd Allāh ibn 'Abbās, when the Prophet (peace be on him) made the proposal, Zaynab's reaction was: "As regards lineage, I am better than him". According to Ibn Sa'd, she had also said: "I do not feel happy about him for myself for I am of noble Quraysh descent". The same kind of disapproval about the marriage proposal was expressed by her brother, 'Abd Allāh ibn Jaḥsh, the reason being that Zayd was the Prophet's freed slave whereas Zaynab bint Jaḥsh was the daughter of the Prophet's paternal aunt, and his relatives felt grieved that the Prophet (peace be on him) was proposing that a girl of such a prestigious family be married to his freed slave.

It was in this context that the following verse was revealed: "It does not behove a believer, male or female, that when Allah and His Messenger have decided an affair they should exercise their choice". No sooner had this verse been revealed than Zaynab and her family accepted the proposal and the Prophet (peace be on him) personally solemnised the marriage. He also paid the bridal due, amounting to ten dīnārs and sixty dirhams, and gave some clothes and household provisions by way of a gift.

(37) (O Prophet),[67] call to mind when you said to him whom Allah had favoured and you had favoured:[68] ▸

وَإِذْ تَقُولُ لِلَّذِىٓ أَنْعَمَ ٱللَّهُ عَلَيْهِ وَأَنْعَمْتَ عَلَيْهِ

Although this verse was revealed in the context of a particular incident, it lays down the principle that serves as the core of the Islamic way of life embracing every aspect of living. The standing principle is that no Muslim – individual, group, institution, court, legislature or state – is possessed of the authority to decide any matter in contravention of the commands of God and His Messenger. For to be a Muslim means to fully submit oneself to God and His Messenger. No Muslim, whether an individual or a group, can claim the authority to act in violation of God's command and still claim to be obedient of Him and His Messenger. For this would be a contradiction in terms. No sensible person can reconcile these two divergent positions. A Muslim by definition is he who submits unquestioningly to the commands of God and His Messenger. Anyone who refuses to do so must acknowledge that he is not a Muslim. If anyone refuses to submit to God's commands, notwithstanding his tall claims to be a believer, he will be reckoned as a hypocrite both by God and human beings.

67. Verses 36–48 were revealed after the Prophet's marriage with Zaynab. His marriage triggered a fierce and hostile propaganda campaign by the Jews and polytheists. While studying these verses it should be borne in mind that these statements were not meant to clarify and explain things to the Prophet's enemies who were hell bent on maligning him. Instead, these verses were revealed so as to protect Muslims from the pernicious effects of that campaign. Obviously, what these verses said on the issue would not satisfy the unbelievers. It could convince only those who accepted the Qur'ān to be the Word of God. The statements made here are addressed to the believers to ensure they are not swayed by false propaganda. God thus sets the believers' minds at rest and instructs ordinary Muslims as well as the Prophet (peace be on him) as to how they should respond to the situation.

68. This refers to Zayd whose identity is revealed more clearly in the verses that follow. To appreciate what God's favours were to Zayd that are alluded to in this verse and what were His Messenger's favours upon him, one should cast a glance at Zayd's life. Zayd was the son of

Ḥārithah ibn Sharāḥīl, a member of the Kalb tribe. His mother, Su'dā bint Tha'labah, belonged to Banū Ma'ān, a branch of the Ṭayy tribe. When Zayd was a child of eight years his mother took him to her parents' place. People belonging to Banū Qayn ibn Ḥabr raided his camp and carried him away along with others whom they had captured. Zayd was later sold at the 'Ukāẓ Fair in Ṭā'if to Ḥakīm ibn Ḥizām, Khadījah's nephew, who handed him over to his aunt. When the Prophet (peace be on him) married Khadījah, he found Zayd there and was pleased with his character and conduct.

Zayd was then 15 years old. After some time, Zayd's father and uncle came to know that Zayd was living as a slave in Makkah. So they approached the Prophet (peace be on him) and expressed their willingness to pay any amount by way of ransom to secure his freedom. The Prophet (peace be on him) told them that he would like to hear from Zayd himself as to what his own choice was. If Zayd preferred to return to his family, he would not ask for any ransom to set him free. However, if Zayd himself chose to stay where he was, he would not compel him to rejoin his family. Zayd's family members agreed on this solution which met all the requirements of fairness and justice. The Prophet (peace be on him), therefore, summoned Zayd and asked him if he recognised the visitors. He duly identified them as his father and uncle. The Prophet (peace be on him) then said to Zayd: "You know them and also know me. You are free to go with them or continue to live with me". To this Zayd replied: "I do not want to go anywhere, leaving you". His father and uncle probed him further: "Do you prefer slavery to freedom? Do you like to live with strangers rather than with your own family?" Zayd replied: "Having observed (the Prophet's) virtues I do not want to go elsewhere".

On receiving this definite reply, his father and uncle reconciled themselves to the situation, for it was Zayd who had refused to leave the Prophet (peace be on him). It was then that the Prophet (peace be on him) freed him and proclaimed in the assembly of the Quraysh: "I call all of you to be my witnesses. From now on Zayd is my son. He will inherit me and I will inherit him". Accordingly, Zayd came to be known as the son of the Prophet (peace be on him).

This incident took place before Muḥammad's designation as Prophet. Later, Zayd would be one of the first four people to embrace Islam, which he did as soon as the Prophet (peace be on him) proclaimed its message. The other three were Khadījah, 'Alī and Abū Bakr. By then, Zayd was 30 years old and had been in the Prophet's company for 15 years. In 4 AH/625 CE, the Prophet (peace be on him) married Zayd to his cousin, Zaynab, paying the bridal due on his behalf and providing him with essential household items. These are the circumstances to which the Qur'ān alludes by saying: "... whom Allah had favoured and you had favoured".

"Cleave to your wife and fear Allah,"[69] and you concealed within yourself for fear of people what Allah was to reveal, although Allah has greater right that you fear Him.[70] ▶	أَمۡسِكۡ عَلَيۡكَ زَوۡجَكَ وَٱتَّقِ ٱللَّهَ وَتُخۡفِي فِي نَفۡسِكَ مَا ٱللَّهُ مُبۡدِيهِ وَتَخۡشَى ٱلنَّاسَ وَٱللَّهُ أَحَقُّ أَن تَخۡشَىٰهُۖ

69. This refers to the period when marital relations between Zayd and Zaynab had soured. After repeatedly complaining to the Prophet (peace be on him) about Zaynab, Zayd eventually informed him of his decision to divorce her. Although Zaynab had married Zayd in obeisance to the command of God and His Messenger, she could not reconcile herself to the fact that Zayd was a slave who had been freed and brought up by her family. She strongly felt that as a member of the noblest Arab family, she should not have been married to a person of such humble social standing. Accordingly, she never looked upon her husband as her equal, and this inevitably led to marital discord. After only a year of marriage, their marital bond culminated in divorce.

70. Some people misconstrue this to mean that the Prophet (peace be on him) was desirous of marrying Zaynab and wanted Zayd to divorce her. When Zayd informed him of his divorce decision, they argue, the Prophet (peace be on him) made only a pretence, God forbid, of dissuading Zayd from pronouncing divorce. They contend that it was in this context that God said to him: "And you concealed within yourself for fear of people what Allah was to reveal, although Allah has greater right that you fear Him". If one reads this in conjunction with verses 1–3 and 7 of this *sūrah*, it becomes clear that during the period of marital discord between Zayd and Zaynab, God had hinted to the Prophet (peace be on him) that he should marry Zaynab after she was divorced. The Prophet (peace be on him), however, was apprehensive of the scandalous repercussions of marrying his adopted son's wife a situation which would flagrantly violate the hallowed norms of the Arabian society of the time. When Zayd informed the Prophet (peace be on him) of his decision to divorce Zaynab, he asked Zayd to fear God and not to proceed with divorce. The Prophet (peace be on him) did so because if Zayd refrained from divorcing her, he would be spared from marrying Zaynab. However, if Zayd divorced

So when Zayd had accomplished what he would of her,[71] ▶	فَلَمَّا قَضَىٰ زَيْدٌ مِّنْهَا وَطَرًا

her, the Prophet (peace be on him) would have to marry her in keeping with God's directive. The Prophet (peace be on him) was acutely aware of how shocking this act would be considered in the Arabian society of the time. He was, therefore, reluctant to invite a new ordeal upon himself. According to his estimate, this would lead to much mud slinging at him. This needed to be taken into account.

God, however, found the Prophet's stance not quite consistent with his exalted status. God wanted the Prophet (peace be on him) to marry Zaynab for an important reason. Hence, the Prophet (peace be on him) was not in a position to deter Zayd from divorcing his wife just so that he could avoid something that would evoke opposition. It was, therefore, said: "You feared people whereas Allah deserves more to be feared". The text here clearly indicates this. Zayn al-'Ābidīn 'Alī ibn al-Ḥusayn says the same in explanation of this verse: "God had informed the Prophet (peace be on him) of his marriage with Zaynab. When Zayd complained to him against his wife, the Prophet (peace be on him) asked him to fear God and not to divorce her. Thereupon God said that He had already apprised the Prophet (peace be on him) of his marriage with Zaynab. Therefore, by dissuading Zayd, he was trying to conceal what God was to reveal". (Ibn Kathīr, *Tafsīr*, comments on verse 37 and Ṭabarī, *Tafsīr*, comments on verse 37.)

Ālūsī offers the same interpretation in his exegesis, *Rūḥ al-Ma'ānī*. For him, the Prophet (peace be on him) is censured here for not doing what was ideally expected of him. He should either have maintained silence over the whole matter or he should have directed Zayd to do whatever he willed. He should not have tried to deter Zayd from divorcing Zaynab when God had already informed him of his forthcoming marriage to her. (Ālūsī, *Rūḥ al-Ma'ānī*, comments on verse 37.)

71. Zayd went ahead with his intention to divorce Zaynab and, thus, the marital tie between them ended. Zaynab subsequently completed the waiting period and "Zayd had accomplished what he would of her". Divorce alone, however, does not bring about a total end to the marital

زَوَّجْنَـٰكَهَا لِكَىْ لَا يَكُونَ عَلَى ٱلْمُؤْمِنِينَ حَرَجٌ فِىٓ أَزْوَٰجِ أَدْعِيَآئِهِمْ إِذَا قَضَوْا۟ مِنْهُنَّ وَطَرًا ۚ وَكَانَ أَمْرُ ٱللَّهِ مَفْعُولًا ﴿٣٧﴾ مَّا كَانَ عَلَى ٱلنَّبِىِّ مِنْ حَرَجٍ فِيمَا فَرَضَ ٱللَّهُ لَهُۥ ۖ

We gave her in marriage to you[72] so that there should not be any constraint for the believers regarding the wives of their adopted sons after they had accomplished whatever they would of them.[73] And Allah's command was bound to be accomplished. (38) There could be no hindrance to the Prophet regarding what Allah ordained for him.[74] ▶

---

tie. For the husband can take his wife back during the waiting period. Another consideration in this respect is related to any possible conception prior to the divorce. Once the waiting period has expired, however, this concern too becomes redundant.

72. It is evident from the Qur'ānic statement that the Prophet's marriage with Zaynab was not impelled by any personal desire. Rather, he married her in compliance with God's command.

73. It is evident from the verse that God made the Prophet (peace be on him) marry Zaynab for there was no other way of ending *jāhilī* notions about adopted sons and daughters. The Messenger of God (peace be on him) was expected to take the initiative to bring about this social reform. God so directed the Prophet (peace be on him) not because He wanted to make it possible for him to add to the number of his wives. Rather, this directive was in response to an important social need.

74. The text indicates that while it is permissible for other Muslims to contract marriage in this circumstance, the Prophet (peace be on him) was required to do so by God.

Such has been Allah's Way (with the Prophets) who went before. Allah's command is a decree firmly determined.[75] (39) (This is Allah's Way) regarding those who deliver the Messages of Allah and who fear Him, and fear no one else than Allah. Allah is Sufficient as a Reckoner.[76]

(40) Muḥammad is not the father of any of your men, but he is the Messenger of Allah and the seal of the Prophets. Allah has full knowledge of everything.[77]

سُنَّةَ ٱللَّهِ فِى ٱلَّذِينَ خَلَوْا۟ مِن قَبْلُ ۚ وَكَانَ
أَمْرُ ٱللَّهِ قَدَرًا مَّقْدُورًا ﴿٣٨﴾ ٱلَّذِينَ يُبَلِّغُونَ
رِسَـٰلَـٰتِ ٱللَّهِ وَيَخْشَوْنَهُۥ وَلَا يَخْشَوْنَ
أَحَدًا إِلَّا ٱللَّهَ ۗ وَكَفَىٰ بِٱللَّهِ حَسِيبًا ﴿٣٩﴾
مَّا كَانَ مُحَمَّدٌ أَبَآ أَحَدٍ مِّن رِّجَالِكُمْ
وَلَـٰكِن رَّسُولَ ٱللَّهِ وَخَاتَمَ ٱلنَّبِيِّـۧنَ ۗ
وَكَانَ ٱللَّهُ بِكُلِّ شَىْءٍ عَلِيمًا ﴿٤٠﴾

---

75. God has always had a special rule for Prophets. Whenever they receive a command from Him they simply have to carry it out even if the whole world is arrayed in opposition.

76. This phrase is liable to the following two meanings: (i) God suffices for every danger and risk. (ii) God will call everyone to account. One need not fear anyone else than Him.

77. This refutes the baseless objections raised by the Prophet's opponents regarding his marriage with Zaynab.

The first objection raised by the Prophet's detractors was that he had married his own daughter-in-law. The Qur'ān makes it clear that the Prophet (peace be on him) was not Zayd's father. Therefore, his marriage with Zayd's divorced wife should not give rise to such a charge.

The second objection they made was that the Prophet (peace be on him) was not obliged to marry the divorced wife of his adopted son. To this, the Qur'ān responds by asserting that since he is God's Messenger, he is obliged in this capacity to put an end to all false notions concerning what is lawful and unlawful. This is then followed by the following

(41) Believers, remember Allah much (42) and glorify Him morning and evening.[78] (43) It is He Who lavishes His blessings on you and His angels invoke blessings on you that He may lead you out of darkness into light.[79] ▶

يَـٰٓأَيُّهَا ٱلَّذِينَ ءَامَنُوا۟ ٱذْكُرُوا۟ ٱللَّهَ ذِكْرًا
كَثِيرًا ﴿٤١﴾ وَسَبِّحُوهُ بُكْرَةً وَأَصِيلًا ﴿٤٢﴾ هُوَ
ٱلَّذِى يُصَلِّى عَلَيْكُمْ وَمَلَـٰٓئِكَتُهُۥ
لِيُخْرِجَكُم مِّنَ ٱلظُّلُمَـٰتِ إِلَى ٱلنُّورِ ۚ

emphatic statement: "He is the Messenger of Allah and the seal of the Prophets". Since no Messenger will come after him, any gap left in social reform and legislation would never subsequently be filled. Hence, it was necessary for him to eradicate this *jāhilī* practice. This is also followed by yet another forceful statement: "Allah knows everything". In other words, God knows well why it is essential for the Prophet (peace be on him) to put an end to this practice of *jāhilīyah* and what harm could ensue if he did not do so. God knows that no Prophet would be raised after him. Hence, it would not be possible at a later date to extirpate this social evil. If such a radical step were taken by any social reformer in the future, he would not have commanded the same unquestioning acceptance for all times that is attached to the practices of the Prophet (peace be on him). For no one besides him would command the kind of obedience that inspires people to do a thing or deter them from it.

78. The Muslims are instructed about what they should do when the Messenger of God is under fire: they should neither remain silent spectators to the malicious propaganda against him, nor should they be influenced by the false reports circulating about him. Equally important, they should not stoop to the low behaviour of his detractors who hurled abuses at them. Rather, they should remember God all the more. The directive to glorify God morning and evening signifies that we should constantly praise and worship Him. (This is also explained in n. 63 above.) Glorifying God, in any case means constantly declaring God's holiness rather than simply counting the beads of a rosary.

79. The Muslims are told that the unbelievers' hostility and rancour towards them emanate from the fact that God has favoured the Muslims

He is Most Compassionate to the believers. (44) On the Day they meet Him they will be greeted with: "Peace."[80] He has prepared for them a generous reward.

وَكَانَ بِٱلْمُؤْمِنِينَ رَحِيمًا ﴿٤٣﴾ تَحِيَّتُهُمْ يَوْمَ
يَلْقَوْنَهُۥ سَلَٰمٌ ۚ وَأَعَدَّ لَهُمْ أَجْرًا كَرِيمًا ﴿٤٤﴾

---

by raising among them His Messenger (peace be on him) who has brought them out from the darkness of unbelief into the light of faith. Moreover, thanks to him, they have been able to attain moral excellence under his guidance. Thanks, again, to the Messenger's teachings, the treasures of faith and moral excellence were granted to them. They should, therefore, not act in any way that might deprive them of God's mercy.

Coming to the word *ṣalāh*, when it is followed by the preposition *'alā*, its purpose being to signify God's *ṣalāh* on His servants; it denotes His mercy, compassion and benevolence towards them. When it is used with reference to the *ṣalāh* of angels in regard to human beings, it means that the angels pray that God may shower His mercy and favour upon them. When it is said that God invokes *ṣalāh* on the believers it means that God raises their esteem in the sight of others. As a result, they are not only praised by their fellow human beings but also by the angels.

80. The Qur'ānic text here reads: "On the Day they meet Him, they will be greeted with: 'Peace'".

This statement gives rise to the following three meanings: (i) God will greet them, as is stated elsewhere in the Qur'ān, with the word: "Peace". "Peace shall be the word conveyed to them from the Lord Most Merciful". (*Yā' Sīn* 36:58.) (ii) The angels will greet the believers, as is mentioned in *al-Naḥl* 16:32: "Those whose souls the angels seize while they are in a state of purity, saying: 'Peace be upon you. Enter Paradise as a reward for your deeds.'" (iii) The believers will greet one another by invoking peace. This point also features in the following verse:

> Their cry in it will be: "Glory be to You, Our Lord!", and their greeting: "Peace", and their cry will always end with: "All praise be to Allah, the Lord of the universe" (*Yūnus* 10:10).

(45) O Prophet,[81] We have sent you forth as a witness,[82] ▸	يَـٰٓأَيُّهَا ٱلنَّبِىُّ إِنَّآ أَرْسَلْنَـٰكَ شَـٰهِدًا

81. After counselling the Muslims, God now addresses the Prophet (peace be on him) and conveys to him words of solace and assurance. The purpose of these words is to reassure the Prophet (peace be on him) that God has conferred upon him a position of eminence, that his opponents will not be able to cause him any harm by raising a storm of opposition against him. He should, therefore, not let their vile accusations distress him. Instead, he should continue to carry out his duties and let his detractors indulge in their ravings. All men, both believing and unbelieving, should realise that the Prophet (peace be on him) enjoys an exalted status conferred upon him by God.

82. The Qur'ān makes a very significant point in mentioning the Prophet (peace be on him) as a "witness". As to the testimony offered by him, it would be of the following three types:

i. He should bear verbal testimony to those truths and norms which constitute the faith prescribed by God. He is required to publicly proclaim that Islam represents the truth and whatever is contrary to it is falsehood. People may dismiss the Islamic doctrines about God's existence, His Oneness, the existence of angels, Revelation, Life-after-Death, and Paradise and Hell as sheer lies and make the Prophet (peace be on him) the butt of ridicule and mockery. They may also reject them as implausible, thereby dubbing the Messenger (peace be on him) as an enchanted one. God's Prophet (peace be on him) is, nevertheless, obliged to proclaim these doctrines with impunity and brand those who refuse to believe in them to be in error. Likewise, God's Prophet (peace be on him) is required to publicly proclaim the moral concepts, culture and civilisation, and the values, norms and codes that God revealed to him. He is duty-bound to affirm them and dismiss all notions in vogue in the world that are discordant with the Divine scheme of things as false. Likewise, he must uphold as lawful what the *Sharī'ah* pronounces as lawful, regardless of popular beliefs about these matters. By the same token, he must strictly abide by the injunctions of the *Sharī'ah* as regards what is unlawful, even though people may regard these as lawful.

ii. Apart from verbal testimony, he should also bear testimony by his deeds. In other words, he should practice in his own life whatever he preaches. His own conduct should be free from even an iota of what he declares to be evil and sinful. Also, the virtues he preaches should be most gloriously reflected in his own life and character. He should be most eager to carry out whatever he declares to be obligatory. He should be keener than everyone else to shun whatever he declares to be sinful. He should also spare no effort in putting into effect the Law that he declares to be God's Law. His own character and conduct should bear out how very committed and sincere he is to the cause that he espouses. Furthermore, his life should embody the teachings of Islam and serve as a living model for mankind. This, then, will help people to realise what kind of human beings Islam would like to give shape to. It should also give them an idea of the kind of character that Islam cherishes and the way of life that it seeks to establish.

iii. The Prophet (peace be on him) is also required to be a witness in the Hereafter. On the Day of Judgement the Prophet (peace be on him) will testify that he had faithfully conveyed what was revealed to him by God and that he did not shirk from his responsibility. It is on the basis of his testimony that it will be decided who deserves what recompense.

It is clear, therefore, that the Prophet's task as a witness is an onerous one and only a very outstanding personality can accomplish it. It also goes without saying that the Prophet (peace be on him) did not falter even to the slightest extent in discharging his duty as long as he lived. He will, therefore, affirm on the Day of Judgement that he had clearly demonstrated the truth to people. This will constitute God's "persuasive argument against people". Had the Prophet (peace be on him), God forbid, shirked his responsibility even in the least, he would be in no position to act as a witness against people on the Day of Judgement. Nor would a case be proved against the unbelievers who rejected the truth.

Some people twist this Qur'ānic concept of the Prophet's testimony to mean that he will bear testimony to everyone's actions on the Day of Judgement. Going by this logic, the Prophet (peace be on him) is supposed to watch all that people do. For, had it been otherwise, he could not give such testimony. The Qur'ān, however, provides no basis for such an interpretation. According to the Qur'ān, God has put in place an elaborate, independent arrangement for recording all of man's actions. Angels prepare every human being's record of deeds (See *Qāf* 50:17–18 and *al-Kahf* 18:49). Man's limbs too, will testify to his deeds (*Yā Sīn* 36:65, and *Ḥā' Mīm al-Sajdah* 41:20–21). The Prophets are not supposed to bear testimony to man's actions. Rather, their testimony will be to the effect that they conveyed the truth to mankind. The Qur'ān makes this point quite specifically:

> The Day when Allah will gather together the Messengers and say: "What answer were you given?" They will reply: "We have no real knowledge of it. You alone fully know all that lies beyond the reach of perception" (*al-Mā'idah* 5:109).

When the Prophet Jesus (peace be on him) will be asked about the Christians' enmeshment in error, he will say:

> I watched over them as long as I remained among them; and when You did recall me, then You Yourself became the Watcher over them (*al-Mā'idah* 5:117).

These passages clearly state that the Prophets will not bear testimony to men's actions. As to the testimony offered by them, the Qur'ān states this in utterly emphatic terms:

> And it is thus that We appointed you to be the community of the middle way, so that you might be witnesses to all mankind and the Messenger might be a witness to you (*al-Baqarah* 2:143).
>
> (O Muḥammad), warn them of the coming of a Day when We shall bring forth a witness against them from each community and We shall bring you forth as a witness against them all (*al-Naḥl* 16:89).

It is evident from the above that the Prophet's role as a witness on the Day of Judgement will not essentially be any different from that of his community, whereby it too will be a witness against the whole of mankind. Likewise, there will also be witnesses against every community. Had this testimony been related to each and every individual's actions, it would have meant that all of these witnesses and the entire Muslim community are omnipresent, all-hearing and all-seeing, which is clearly out of the question. However, if this testimony is taken in its restricted sense of conveying the message of the Creator to His servants, the Prophet Muḥammad (peace be on him) will, no doubt, be brought forth as a witness on this count.

This view is endorsed and amplified by several *aḥādīth* recorded by Bukhārī, Muslim, Tirmidhī, Ibn Mājah, Aḥmad ibn Ḥanbal and other prominent compilers of *aḥādīth* on the authority of 'Abd Allāh ibn Mas'ūd, 'Abd Allāh ibn 'Abbās, Abū al-Dardā', Anas ibn Mālik and a number of

a bearer of good tidings, and a warner,[83] ▶	وَمُبَشِّرًا وَنَذِيرًا ﴿٤٥﴾

other Companions. Common to all these *aḥādīth* is the point that on the Day of Judgement the Prophet (peace be on him) will see some of his Companions going or being pushed in a direction away from him. Upon observing this he will submit: "O God! They are my Companions". God will, however, tell him that he does not know the deeds they committed afterwards, that is, after his demise. (Bukhārī, *Kitāb al-Anbiyā', Bāb wa Ittakhadha Ibrāhīm Khalīlā*; Muslim, *Kitāb al-Ṭahārah, Bāb Istiḥbāb Iṭālat al-Ghurrah*; Aḥmad ibn Ḥanbal, *Musnad*, narrated by Anas ibn Mālik; Tirmidhī, *Kitāb Ṣifah al-Qiyāmah, Bāb mā jā' fī Sha'n al-Ḥashr* and Ibn Mājah, *Sunan, Kitāb al-Zuhd, Bāb Dhikr al-Ḥawḍ*.)

That this is the case is clarified on the authority of many Companions, and with such an extensive chain of narrators that its authenticity is beyond contest. This conclusively establishes that the Prophet (peace be on him) is not a witness to each and every action of each member of his community.

Coming to the *ḥadīth* that states that the actions of the Prophet's community are presented before him, this too does not run counter to this point. (Tirmidhī, *Kitāb Faḍā'il al-Qur'ān*.) That *ḥadīth* only states that God keeps the Prophet (peace be on him) abreast of the state of his community's condition. It does not suggest in any way that the Prophet (peace be on him) watches at first-hand each and every action taken by the members of his community.

83. One should not lose sight of the difference between the pronouncements of ordinary mortals and Prophets. An ordinary person may give the tiding that sound faith and good deeds will lead to wholesome results. He may also warn people against the evil consequences of unbelief and evil deeds. All this is very different from the tidings and warnings of the person who is sent down by God specifically as the bearer of good tidings and warner. The pronouncements of a Prophet, since he is designated by God, are authoritative and hence binding on people. The good conveyed by a Prophet indicates that a particular action is commendable and merits reward in God's sight, on Whose behalf he declares that act to be so. On the other hand, when he warns against an evil action, then, this is also on God's authority. It must, therefore, be either a sinful and forbidden act and consequently whosoever is guilty of committing it is bound to be punished. This

(46) as one who calls people to Allah[84] by His leave, and as a bright, shining lamp. (47) Announce to the believers the good tidings that Allah has kept bounteous blessings in store for them. (48) Do not yield to the unbelievers and the hypocrites, and disregard the hurt that comes from them, and put your trust in Allah. Allah suffices as the Guardian to entrust one's affairs to.

(49) Believers, when you marry believing women and then divorce them before you have touched them,[85] ▶

وَدَاعِيًا إِلَى ٱللَّهِ بِإِذْنِهِۦ وَسِرَاجًا مُّنِيرًا ﴿٤٦﴾
وَبَشِّرِ ٱلْمُؤْمِنِينَ بِأَنَّ لَهُم مِّنَ ٱللَّهِ فَضْلًا
كَبِيرًا ﴿٤٧﴾ وَلَا تُطِعِ ٱلْكَٰفِرِينَ
وَٱلْمُنَٰفِقِينَ وَدَعْ أَذَىٰهُمْ وَتَوَكَّلْ عَلَى ٱللَّهِ
وَكَفَىٰ بِٱللَّهِ وَكِيلًا ﴿٤٨﴾ يَٰٓأَيُّهَا ٱلَّذِينَ ءَامَنُوٓا۟
إِذَا نَكَحْتُمُ ٱلْمُؤْمِنَٰتِ ثُمَّ طَلَّقْتُمُوهُنَّ مِن
قَبْلِ أَن تَمَسُّوهُنَّ

characteristic is not shared by the warnings and good tidings conveyed by any person other than the Prophets, for the latter are not designated by God to make such pronouncements.

84. Once again, the difference between the preaching of an ordinary person and that of a Prophet is brought out. Anyone may invite people to the truth. However, none other than a Prophet enjoys God's sanction to perform this task. A mission does not simply consist of the mere preaching of the truth. In carrying out this task, he enjoys God's full support. Therefore, opposition to him amounts to waging war against God. This may be better understood in the light of our everyday experience whereby obstructing a government functionary from performing his duty is regarded as an act of rebellion against the state itself.

85. It is patently clear that the expression *nikāḥ* refers to marriage. Lexical authorities define *nikāḥ* in a variety of ways. For some, it carries

you may not require them to observe a waiting period that you might reckon against them. So make provision for them and release them in an honourable manner.[86]	فَمَا لَكُمْ عَلَيْهِنَّ مِنْ عِدَّةٍ تَعْتَدُّونَهَا ۖ فَمَتِّعُوهُنَّ وَسَرِّحُوهُنَّ سَرَاحًا جَمِيلًا ﴿٤٩﴾

the connotations of both copulation and marriage. Some regard it as a metaphorical expression. Others take the opposite view, insisting that it signifies sexual intercourse. Each group seeks to substantiate its view by citing passages from Arabic poetry. Rāghib al-Iṣfahānī, however, emphatically claims that the root meaning of *nikāḥ* is marriage and that it is used only metaphorically for copulation. He, thus, rules out that its literal meaning is copulation. He argues that all expressions for copulation in all languages are regarded as obscene. Hence it is to be taken essentially in the sense of marriage. (See *al-Mufradāt fī Gharīb al-Qur'ān,* q.v., *n k ḥ*) In the light of the Qur'ān and the *Sunnah,* it is a term signifying marriage, or copulation after marriage. Nowhere does the Qur'ān employ this word for copulation outside marriage. The words used for that are *zinā* and *safāḥ*.

86. This is an isolated verse which was presumably revealed with reference to a divorce case that arose at that time. Thus it has been placed between the preceding discourse and the one that follows.

It lays down the following legal provisions:

i. The verse speaks of "believing women". This would imply that the law promulgated here would not apply to women of the People of the Book. *'Ulamā'*, however, are agreed that the same law applies to the women of the People of the Book. If a Muslim marries a woman of the People of the Book, the same laws regarding divorce, bridal-due, waiting period and maintenance that apply to Muslim women apply to women of the People of the Book. That only Muslim women are mentioned in this verse is interpreted by *'ulamā'* to mean that the Qur'ān implies that Muslim women are truly worthy to be marriage partners. It is, however, doubtlessly lawful to marry a Jewish or Christian woman, though it is not preferable. It would appear from the Qur'ānic statement that God expects believing men to marry believing women.

ii. The word *mass*, literally meaning "touching", here figuratively signifies sexual intercourse. Hence, if the husband has been with his wife in privacy and has even physically touched her, his divorcing her should apparently not entail any waiting period if he had actually not had sexual intercourse with her. However, out of precaution, *fuqahā'* have given the ruling that if true privacy takes place – that is, a privacy in which sexual intercourse could take place – then the divorced woman is required to observe the waiting period. The waiting period can only be waived if the husband divorced his wife before having had true privacy with her.

iii. In case divorce is pronounced before the occurrence of privacy, the waiting period is revoked and the husband forfeits the right to take that woman back as his wife, and she instantly becomes free to remarry. It is nonetheless worth reiterating that this is applicable only if she is divorced before privacy takes place. However, if the husband dies before enjoying such privacy, the waiting period is not waived. Instead, the widow has to observe the waiting period of four months and ten days, the same as for a woman whose marriage has been consummated. A widow's remarriage is not valid before the expiry of this waiting period.

iv. "You may not require them to observe a waiting period" underscores the husband's right during the waiting period. Yet he is not privileged with rights, but is rather correspondingly encumbered with the rights he owes his children and the rights he owes God or the *Sharī'ah*. The husband's right proceeds from the fact that during the waiting period he is entitled to take his wife back. Moreover, the paternity of any child is contingent upon the proof of the pregnancy or otherwise of the divorced wife during the waiting period. This right of the child results from the fact that if the child's paternity is established, he will be entitled to certain legal rights. Moreover, his social and moral status will also depend upon his unblemished paternity. As for the rights of God (or of the *Sharī'ah*), it should be noted that even if someone were to neglect his child's rights, the *Sharī'ah* nonetheless provides protection for those same rights. For example, if a husband authorises his wife in writing that he does not require her to observe the waiting period, should he die or divorce her, the *Sharī'ah* will still not allow the waiting period to be waived.

v. The directive: "So make provision for them and release them in an honourable manner", may be followed in either of two ways:

(a) If the bridal due was fixed at the time of contracting the marriage, and then the husband divorces his wife before enjoying true privacy with her, he is obliged to repay half of the bridal due. This point is explicitly made in *al-Baqarah* 2:237. Although one is not obliged to pay anything over and above this, it is nonetheless commendable to make some additional provision for the wife. For instance, it is desirable that apart from returning half the bridal due to his wife, she should also be allowed to retain the bridal garments presented by the husband to her or any other items given to her as gifts at the time of marriage. (b) If the bridal due was not fixed at the time of marriage, the husband is obliged to give some present to his wife. This, however, depends upon his capacity and financial condition, as specified in *al-Baqarah* 2:236. A section of *'ulamā'*, however, insists that divorced women should be given some present, irrespective of whether the bridal due was fixed or not. (As a term of *fiqh*, *mut'at al-ṭalāq* refers to the assets given to the divorced wife at the time when she leaves her husband's place in consequence of divorce.)

vi. "To release them in an honourable manner" does not consist only of graciously bidding farewell to the divorced wife after giving her some present. Rather, the directive means that [even when it is absolutely necessary] to terminate the marital bond, it should be done with good grace. If the husband does not like his wife, for one reason or another, or has some grievance against her, she may still be released gracefully, and the parting of company too should be graceful. The husband for instance, should refrain from publicising her weaknesses which might deter others from marrying her.

It is evident from the verse that to tie up divorce with the permission of a public committee or court is discordant with the underlying spirit and wisdom of God's law on this matter. This because such procedure does not leave any room for honourable separation between the spouses. In such a case, even if the husband does not want it so, things could get out of control, eventually leading to mutual recrimination, defamation, humiliation and embarrassment. This verse, even otherwise, does not admit that the husband's right to divorce should be made contingent on its acceptance by a public committee or court of law, for the verse clearly invests the husband with the right to divorce his wife. It also obliges him to pay half of the bridal due or an amount in keeping with his financial status to his wife if he divorces her before enjoying privacy with her. The thrust of the verse is unmistakable: the husband is put under a financial obligation if he wants to exercise his right to divorce. This is in order that if he wants to divorce his wife, he should exercise this right after due deliberation and not reduce it to a sport. This rule is likely to keep the matters that are vitally related to the two families confined to them alone, thus not providing any opportunity for unrelated outsiders to interfere. This can possibly be achieved if the husband is not obligated to explain to others why he is divorcing his wife.

vii. In view of the wording of the Qur'ānic text, "When you marry ... and then divorce", 'Abd Allāh ibn 'Abbās, Sa'īd ibn al-Musayyib and Aḥmad ibn Ḥanbal contend that divorce is valid only after the marriage has been contracted. Thus, divorce prior to marriage is null and void. For example, if one were to say: "Divorce be upon a woman of such and such tribe or community, if I marry her", such a statement is void. It does not bring about divorce. This ruling is supported by the following *aḥādīth*. The Prophet (peace be on him) said: "The son of Adam does not have the right to divorce [the woman] on whom he has no right". (Tirmidhī, *Kitāb al-Ṭalāq, Bāb fī mā jā'a anna lā Ṭalāq qabl al-Nikāḥ;* Ibn Mājah, *Kitāb al-Ṭalāq, Bāb lā Ṭalāq qabl al-Nikāḥ;* Abū Dā'ūd, *Kitāb al-Ṭalāq, Bāb fī al-Ṭalāq qabl al-Nikāḥ,* and Aḥmad ibn Ḥanbal, *Musnad,* narrated by 'Abd Allāh ibn 'Amr ibn al-'Āṣ.) In a similar vein is the *ḥadīth*: "There can be no divorce before marriage". (Ibn Mājah, *Kitāb al-Ṭalāq, Bāb lā Ṭalāq qabl al-Nikāḥ.*) However, many *Fiqh* scholars maintain that this is applicable only to a case when one divorces a woman one is not married to. Such a divorce is without substance. However, if one were to say: "Divorce be upon you if I marry you", then this statement is not governed by the import of the verse under study and the above-quoted *aḥādīth,* for it amounts to a declaration of divorce as and when one marries a certain woman. This statement is not void. Rather, it leads to instant divorce whenever the man concerned marries that woman. There is, however, some divergence of opinion among jurists regarding the scope of such a divorce.

In the opinion of Abū Ḥanīfah, Muḥammad ibn al-Ḥasan and Zufar, if one specifies a particular woman of a certain community or tribe, such a divorce does come into force. According to Abū Bakr al-Jaṣṣāṣ, 'Umar, 'Abd Allāh ibn Mas'ūd, Ibrāhīm al-Nakha'ī, Mujāhid and 'Umar ibn 'Abd al-'Azīz held the same opinion.

Sufyān al-Thawrī and 'Uthmān al-Battī maintain that divorce comes into force only when a person specifically mentions a particular woman and says that divorce be upon her if he marries her. Ḥasan ibn Ṣāliḥ, Layth ibn Sa'd and 'Āmir al-Sha'bī hold the same view, arguing that this is a general statement that should be qualified (*takhṣīṣ*). In other words, it should be qualified by reference to a specific family, tribe, town, country or people. Ibn Abī Laylā and Mālik, however, disagree with this and state that

(50) O Prophet, We have made lawful for you your wives whose bridal dues you have paid,[87] and the slave-girls you possess from among the prisoners of war, granted to you by Allah, ▶	يَٰٓأَيُّهَا ٱلنَّبِىُّ إِنَّآ أَحْلَلْنَا لَكَ أَزْوَٰجَكَ ٱلَّٰتِىٓ ءَاتَيْتَ أُجُورَهُنَّ وَمَا مَلَكَتْ يَمِينُكَ مِمَّآ أَفَآءَ ٱللَّهُ عَلَيْكَ

along with all this a certain time period should also be specified. For example, if a person says that, if he marries a particular woman or a woman of such and such group or tribe say within ten years then divorce be upon her, divorce will come into force. If such a time period is not mentioned the divorce does not come into force. Mālik further adds that the time period should be a reasonable one. If it is longer than an average life span, divorce will not come into force. (Jaṣṣāṣ, *Aḥkām al-Qur'ān*, comments on verse 49 and Ibn Kathīr, *Tafsīr*, comments on verse 49.)

87. This is a rejoinder to the charge against the Prophet (peace be on him) that while he forbade others from marrying more than four wives at a time, he himself had taken a fifth wife. It may be recalled that the Prophet (peace be on him) had the following four wives at the time of his marriage to Zaynab: 'Ā'ishah, Sawdah, Ḥafṣah and Umm Salamah. He had married Sawdah three years before *Hijrah*. He married 'Ā'ishah in the same year, though she moved into the Prophet's house in Shawwāl 1 AH/623 CE. The Prophet's marriage with Ḥafsah was solemnised in Sha'bān 3 AH/625 CE and with Umm Salamah in Shawwāl 4 AH/626 CE. Thus Zaynab was his fifth wife. The unbelievers and hypocrites used this as a pretext to raise much hue and cry. God, however, declares in the Qur'ān that it was He Who had sanctioned the Prophet's fifth marriage, and that it was He Who had placed the above restriction on all Muslims but had exempted the Prophet (peace be on him) from the same. Since God has the right to lay down a rule, there is no reason why He cannot exempt someone from that rule. It should, however, be noted that the aim of this statement was not to satisfy the unbelievers and hypocrites. Rather, it sought to put the minds of Muslims at rest. Since they believed the Qur'ān to be the infallible Word of God, this verse fully convinced them that the Prophet (peace be on him) had not manoeuvred this exemption for himself. Rather, it is God Who had granted him this privilege.

وَبَنَاتِ عَمِّكَ وَبَنَاتِ عَمَّـٰتِكَ وَبَنَاتِ
خَالِكَ وَبَنَاتِ خَـٰلَـٰتِكَ ٱلَّـٰتِى هَاجَرْنَ
مَعَكَ وَٱمْرَأَةً مُّؤْمِنَةً إِن وَهَبَتْ نَفْسَهَا
لِلنَّبِىِّ إِنْ أَرَادَ ٱلنَّبِىُّ أَن يَسْتَنكِحَهَا

and the daughters of your paternal uncles and paternal aunts, and the daughters of your maternal uncles and maternal aunts who have migrated with you, and a believing woman who gives herself to the Prophet and whom he wants to take in marriage.[88] ▶

88. Apart from granting the Prophet (peace be on him) the right to marry Zaynab, his fifth wife, God also granted the Prophet (peace be on him) permission to marry the following categories of women: (i) Women whom the Prophet (peace be on him) possessed as bondswomen. While availing himself of this permission, the Prophet (peace be on him) chose for himself Rayḥānah from among the prisoners of war taken after the Battle of Banū Qurayẓah, Juwayrīyah from among the prisoners of war taken after the Battle of Banū al-Muṣṭaliq, Ṣafīyah from among the prisoners of war taken after the Battle of Khaybar and Māriyah the Copt who was presented to him by Muqawqis of Egypt. Of these, he set the first three free before marrying them. However, he had had conjugal relations with Māriyah as his bondswoman. It has not been quite established whether he freed her prior to marrying her. (ii) Next come the daughters of his paternal and maternal uncles and aunts who had "migrated with him" in God's cause. The Prophet (peace be on him) was permitted to marry any of them. The expression "who have migrated with him" [to wit, the Prophet] – does not mean that they actually travelled in his company to Madīnah. What is meant here is simply that they too had migrated in Islam's cause just as the Prophet (peace be on him) had done. In conformity with this permission granted by God, the Prophet (peace be on him) married Umm Ḥabībah in 7 AH/628 CE. Also implicit in the verse is the Qur'ānic sanction for marrying both paternal and maternal cousins. In this respect, the Islamic *Sharī'ah* is markedly different from both Judaism and Christianity. A Christian male may not marry any woman whose line of descent joins his anywhere in the last seven generations. At the other end of the scale, a Jew may marry his

(O Prophet), this privilege is yours alone to the exclusion of other believers.[89] ▶	خَالِصَةً لَّكَ مِن دُونِ ٱلْمُؤْمِنِينَ ۗ

own niece (that is, the daughter of his brother or sister.) (iii) A believing woman who was dedicated to the Prophet (peace be on him), that is, one who was prepared to enter into wedlock without claiming any bridal due and was so accepted by the Prophet (peace be on him). In accordance with this provision, the Prophet (peace be on him) married Maymūnah in Shawwāl 7 AH/629 CE. Prior to this, however, he did pay her her bridal due, something that she herself had neither desired nor asked for. This explains the attitude of those Qur'ān-commentators who argue that the Prophet (peace be on him) did not marry anyone who had dedicated herself to him. What this statement means is that he paid the bridal due even in this instance.

89. One possible meaning of the verse is that it is not lawful for any other Muslim to marry a woman without paying her bridal due. Were this verse to be read together with the verses above, it would mean that the permission to have more than four wives is specific to the Prophet (peace be on him) alone, and is not a right enjoyed by any other Muslim. One thus realises that certain commands are specific only to the Prophet (peace be on him) and are not shared by other Muslims. A careful study of the Qur'ān and the *Sunnah* reveals several injunctions of this kind. For example, *Tahajjud* Prayer was made obligatory for the Prophet (peace be on him) whereas it is *nafl* (supererogatory) for all other Muslims. Furthermore, it was forbidden for the Prophet (peace be on him) and his household to accept charity while it is not unlawful for other Muslims. Also, the Prophet's inheritance may not be given to his heirs. All other Muslims are, however, bound by the law of inheritance, as laid down in *Sūrah al-Nisā'* 4:11–12. The Prophet (peace be on him) was also allowed to have more than four wives, but it was not made obligatory for him to render full justice between them. He was also allowed to marry without giving any bridal due to a woman who had dedicated herself to him. Furthermore, the Prophet's wives were not allowed to marry any other Muslim after his demise. These special provisions were exclusively applicable to the Prophet (peace be on him) and were not meant for any other Muslim. Qur'ān-commentators have also identified another feature specific to him: he was not allowed to marry any woman from among the People of the Book, though every Muslim is free to do so.

We know well what restrictions We have imposed upon them as regards their wives and those whom their right hands possess, (and have exempted you from those restrictions) that there may be no constraint upon you.[90] ▶	قَدْ عَلِمْنَا مَا فَرَضْنَا عَلَيْهِمْ فِىٓ أَزْوَٰجِهِمْ وَمَا مَلَكَتْ أَيْمَـٰنُهُمْ لِكَيْلَا يَكُونَ عَلَيْكَ حَرَجٌ ۗ

90. This is the consideration because of which God exempted the Prophet (peace be on him) from the general rule. The Qur'ānic statement, "Let there be no constraint upon you", however, does not imply, God forbid, that he was allowed to have a larger number of wives because of some excessive sexual urge that would not be satisfied by only four, or that restricting him to four wives would have constrained him. Only those blinded by bigotry and prejudice would think so. For only such people can ignore the fact that the Prophet (peace be on him) married a 40 year old lady when he was only 25. Furthermore, for a full 25 years he led a happy, married life with that wife alone. It was only after her death that the Prophet (peace be on him) married again, this time to Sawdah and for four years she was his only wife. No sane and sensible person can, therefore, buy the incredible and mischievous story that the Prophet's sex drive abruptly became so overpowering at the age of 53 that he feverishly began to look around for more wives. Hence, the exemption from the limit of four wives granted to the Prophet (peace be on him) should rather be appreciated in its proper context. One should realise that the Prophet (peace be on him) was charged with an onerous task and allowance had to be made for the milieu in which he was to accomplish this task. Anyone who studies the whole matter objectively will realise why God granted him the freedom to have more than four wives and why limiting it to four would have placed a "constraint" upon him.

The Prophet's task was to reform his crude, uncultivated people not only according to Islamic standards of conduct, but also just from the standpoint of ordinary culture and civilisation. The Prophet (peace be on him) was required to cater for their education and upbringing so that they could develop into a highly civilised and refined nation. It was not enough, therefore, just to educate men, the women's education was just as important. The only way for the Prophet (peace be on him) to do so was to marry several women of different age groups and mental abilities and to personally see to their education so that they could assist him in his effort to bring about the much needed social reform. He was, therefore, assigned the task of educating both rural and urban, young and old women for this purpose.

It was also part of the Prophet's assignment to eradicate the pre-existing order of *jāhilīyah* and put into effect the Islamic way of life. Hence a fierce battle with the leaders and followers of the order of *jāhilīyah* was imminent. Let us recall that this encounter took place in a land known for its tribal mode of life, with all its attendant traditions. It was, therefore, important for the Prophet (peace be on him) to enter into alliances with different families through marital ties, which would subsequently strengthen and broaden the base of friendly relations and put an end to old enmities. In his choice of wives, one of the considerations, in addition to their personal virtues, that the Prophet (peace be on him) took into account, was their tribal affiliation. In marrying 'Ā'ishah and Ḥafṣah, the Prophet (peace be on him) reinforced his friendly relations with Abū Bakr and 'Umar. Umm Salamah came from the family of Abū Jahl and Khālid ibn al-Walīd while Umm Ḥabībah was the daughter of Abū Sufyān. His marriage with them diminished the hostility of these families towards him. After his marriage with Umm Ḥabībah, Abū Sufyān never openly opposed him. Ṣafīyah, Juwayrīyah and Rayḥānah were all of Jewish descent. When he married them after setting them free, the Jews felt obliged to tone down their hostilities against him. According to the custom prevalent in Arabia at that time, when a person married a woman of a tribe he was regarded as the son-in-law of that whole tribe and it was quite unbecoming to be hostile towards him.

As we have noted earlier, social reform and the extirpation of pre-Islamic customs and practices were the tasks the Prophet (peace be on him) was required to accomplish. Realisation of these objectives required that no obstacles should remain in the way of the Prophet marrying women as required by the exigencies of the situation.

This unmasks the error of those who believe that polygamy is permissible only for some specific personal reason and that it cannot be held as justified in any other circumstance. It is patently clear that the Prophet (peace be on him) took several wives not because any of his wives was ill, or barren, or did not give birth to a male issue, or that his concern was to bring up orphans. He did not marry for any of these considerations. Instead, his marriages resulted from the need to convey his message to the maximum number of people, to raise people according to his teachings, to bring about society's reform, as also to serve a number of other social and political objectives. Now, since God has not made plurality of wives contingent upon the existence of some

Allah is Most Forgiving, Most Merciful. (51) Of them you may put off any of them you wish, and you may take any of them whom you wish, and you may call back any of those whom you had (temporarily) set aside: there will be no blame on you (on this account). It is likelier that they will thus be comforted, and will not grieve, and every one of them will be well-pleased with what you give them.[91] ▶

وَكَانَ ٱللَّهُ غَفُورًا رَّحِيمًا ﴿٥٠﴾ ۞ تُرْجِى مَن
تَشَآءُ مِنْهُنَّ وَتُـْٔوِىٓ إِلَيْكَ مَن تَشَآءُ ۖ وَمَنِ
ٱبْتَغَيْتَ مِمَّنْ عَزَلْتَ فَلَا جُنَاحَ عَلَيْكَ ۚ
ذَٰلِكَ أَدْنَىٰٓ أَن تَقَرَّ أَعْيُنُهُنَّ وَلَا يَحْزَنَّ
وَيَرْضَيْنَ بِمَآ ءَاتَيْتَهُنَّ كُلُّهُنَّ ۚ

specific reasons to justify it, previously unheard of reasons are being mentioned in our time. Moreover, God's Messenger (peace be on him) also married many other women and did so for reasons quite different than those presently mentioned. How, then, can there be any justification to limit the permission to have a plurality of wives by making it contingent on arbitrary conditions which were neither laid down by God nor the Prophet (peace be on him)? Not only that, how can it be claimed that these restrictions are in accordance with the *Sharī'ah*?

Underlying all such argumentation is the Western notion that polygamy is inherently evil. Swayed by this notion many people are of the opinion that one can only resort to this otherwise forbidden practice in highly exceptional circumstances. Notwithstanding all the efforts to provide Islamic window-dressing to establish the Islamic credentials of this notion, the fact remains that it is alien to the Qur'ān, the *Sunnah* and the entire religious tradition of Muslims.

91. The objective of the verse was to relieve the Prophet (peace be on him) of tensions in his family life so that he could carry out his duties with full poise and concentration. As God authorised him to treat his wives in the manner he liked, this ruled out the possibility of these believing women bothering him or making his life stressful by engaging in virulent

rivalry among themselves. Notwithstanding the authority granted to him, the Prophet (peace be on him) always treated all his wives with perfect justice and did not prefer one to another. He had fixed turns for each of his wives.

Among *Ḥadīth* scholars, only Abū Razīn expresses the opinion that the Prophet (peace be on him) had fixed turns for only four of his wives, namely, 'Ā'ishah, Ḥafṣah, Zaynab and Umm Salamah and that the others did not have any specific turn. His version, however, is firmly denied by all other Qur'ān-commentators and *Ḥadīth* scholars. They adduce pieces of hard evidence, even after his being given such permission by God, that the Prophet (peace be on him) used to visit all of his wives according to their allocated turns and treated all of them equally well. Bukhārī, Muslim, and Abū Dā'ūd cite the following tradition narrated by 'Ā'ishah: "Even after the revelation of this verse it was the Prophet's practice that if he changed the turn of any of his wives, he obtained permission from the wife whose turn it was to visit another". (Bukhārī, *Kitāb al-Tafsīr, Bāb Qawl Allāh Turjī man Tashā'u...;* Abū Dā'ūd, *Kitāb al-Nikāḥ, Bāb fī al-Qism bayn al-Nisā'* and Nasā'ī, *Kitāb 'Ishrat al-Nisā', Bāb Mayl al-Rajul ilā Ba'ḍ Nisā'ihi.)* Jaṣṣāṣ reports on the authority of 'Urwah ibn al-Zubayr that 'Ā'ishah narrated to him: "In fixing turns for his wives the Prophet (peace be on him) did not prefer one to another. There was hardly a day when he did not visit all of his wives. On a day when it was a particular wife's turn for the Prophet's stay, he did not touch any other wife". (Jaṣṣāṣ, *Aḥkām al-Qur'ān*, comments on verse 51.) 'Ā'ishah also reports that during his last illness which restricted his mobility, he spent his last days at her place after securing permission from his other wives to do so. (Bukhārī, *Kitāb al-Wuḍu', Bāb al-Ghusl wa al-Wuḍu' fī al-Mikhḍab...;* Muslim, *Kitāb al-Ṣalāt, Bāb Istikhlāf al-Imām...*, Ibn Mājah, *Kitāb al-Janā'iz, Bāb mā jā'a fī Dhikr Maraḍ Rasūl Allāh.*) Ibn Abī Ḥāṭim quotes Zuhrī as saying that the Prophet (peace be on him) did not deny a turn to any of his wives. The only exception on this count is Sawdah who had willingly transferred her turn to 'Ā'ishah, as she had grown too old. This should not give rise to the misconception that God granted certain privileges to His Messenger in this respect or that his wives were denied their due rights. Actually, an allowance was made for the Prophet (peace be on him) regarding the number of wives and the same consideration lay behind the bestowal of this authority upon him. In short, this ensured the peace and tranquillity of the Prophet's domestic life. Moreover, it brought an end to distractions. It was indeed a great privilege for his wives to be associated with him as their marriage partner. It also enabled them to assist him in his task of preaching the truth and reforming society. The Prophet (peace be on him) sacrificed all he had in this cause and was joined in this noble task by his male Companions. His wives were directed, in equal measure, to

Allah knows what is in your hearts. Allah is All-Knowing, All-Forbearing.[92] (52) Thereafter women will not be lawful for you, and it will not be lawful for you to take other wives in place of them, even though their beauty might please you,[93] unless they be those whom your right hand owns.[94] Allah is watchful over everything.

وَٱللَّهُ يَعْلَمُ مَا فِى قُلُوبِكُمْ ۚ وَكَانَ ٱللَّهُ عَلِيمًا
حَلِيمًا ﴿٥١﴾ لَّا يَحِلُّ لَكَ ٱلنِّسَآءُ مِنۢ بَعْدُ
وَلَآ أَن تَبَدَّلَ بِهِنَّ مِنْ أَزْوَٰجٍ وَلَوْ أَعْجَبَكَ
حُسْنُهُنَّ إِلَّا مَا مَلَكَتْ يَمِينُكَ ۗ وَكَانَ
ٱللَّهُ عَلَىٰ كُلِّ شَىْءٍ رَّقِيبًا ﴿٥٢﴾

make similar sacrifices. This explains why his wives accepted this Divine judgement willingly. (Ālūsī, *Rūḥ al-Ma'ānī*, comments on verse 51.)

92. This served as a note of warning to his wives and for all others in respect of their attitude towards the Prophet (peace be on him). As for the Prophet's wives, they cannot escape Divine punishment if they nurse any grudge after the promulgation of the Divine command laid down in this verse. Other people are also warned that if they entertain any misgiving about the Prophet's family life, even if it just be in their hearts, then they will be punished. This is followed by the observation that God is Most Forbearing. This underscores the point that if one frees one's mind of insolent misgivings towards the Prophet (peace be on him), one may expect to be pardoned by God.

93. This is open to the following two meanings: (i) it is not lawful for the Prophet (peace be on him) to marry any woman besides those listed in verse 50 of this *sūrah*. (ii) Since his wives have pledged their total commitment to him and preferred the Abode of the Hereafter to this life and are content with their treatment by the Prophet (peace be on him), it is no longer permissible for him to divorce any of them and replace them with others.

94. This makes it quite clear that one may have sexual relations with women whom one's right hand possesses in addition to one's wives. There

is no fixed number of such women. This point is also made in *al-Nisā'* 4:3, *al-Mu'minūn* 23:6 and *al-Ma'ārij* 70:30. In all these instances, such women are placed under an independent category besides wives. These verses allow one to have sexual relations with such women. *Al-Nisā'* 4:3 restricts the number of wives to four. However, God did not place any restriction on the number of other such lawful women. Nor is any suggestion to that effect made in any other verse. However, the Prophet (peace be on him) is told in this verse that it is not lawful for him to marry any more wives from now onwards. Nor may he substitute one wife with another by divorcing one. However, he is free to take those women whom his right hand possesses, meaning that they are lawful to him. That their number has not been fixed is evident from the verse.

This does not, however, mean that the *Sharī'ah* allows the affluent to purchase an unlimited number of slave girls in order to gratify their sexual urges. This is, in fact, an undue advantage that has been derived by those given to self-indulgence by this Qur'ānic provision. The legislation was aimed at facilitating life, rather than to be exploited by those who wanted to indulge in excessive sex. Let us clarify the misuse of this by the following illustration. The *Sharī'ah* allows a man to have up to four wives. It also grants him the right to divorce his wife and replace her with another wife. This law was made in view of the exigencies of human life. However, if one abuses this provision by divorcing one's full quota of four wives after short periods of time and replaces them with new wives, this amounts to abusing and tampering with the spirit of the law. Anyone who is guilty of this is responsible for his own misconduct. The *Sharī'ah* cannot be faulted on this count. Likewise, the *Sharī'ah* allows that women prisoners of war, whom the enemy is not willing to redeem by an exchange of prisoners or ransom, may be taken as slaves. The state may assign them to certain people who are thereby entitled to have sexual relations with them. This is an effective measure to prevent sexual anarchy in society. Now, since the number of prisoners of war cannot be anticipated, the *Sharī'ah* has not fixed a maximum number of male and female slaves whom a person may have.

The buying and selling of slaves has also been made lawful in consideration of the fact that if any slaves, whether male or female, find themselves incompatible with their master, they may then seek a new master. Otherwise, a permanent, irrevocable tie between a master and his slaves would have been a cause of much suffering for both. The laws of the *Sharī'ah* seek to meet and facilitate the needs of people in a whole range of circumstances. If the rich abuse any provision of the *Sharī'ah*, they themselves are to blame rather than the *Sharī'ah*.

(53) Believers, enter not the houses of the Prophet without his permission,[95] nor wait for a meal to be prepared; instead enter when you are invited to eat,[96] and when you have had the meal, disperse. Do not linger in idle talk.[97] That is hurtful to the Prophet ▸

يَـٰٓأَيُّهَا ٱلَّذِينَ ءَامَنُوا۟ لَا تَدْخُلُوا۟ بُيُوتَ
ٱلنَّبِىِّ إِلَّآ أَن يُؤْذَنَ لَكُمْ إِلَىٰ طَعَامٍ
غَيْرَ نَـٰظِرِينَ إِنَىٰهُ وَلَـٰكِنْ إِذَا
دُعِيتُمْ فَٱدْخُلُوا۟ فَإِذَا طَعِمْتُمْ فَٱنتَشِرُوا۟
وَلَا مُسْتَـْٔنِسِينَ لِحَدِيثٍ ۚ إِنَّ ذَٰلِكُمْ كَانَ
يُؤْذِى ٱلنَّبِىَّ

95. This is a prefatory statement regarding the injunction that would be promulgated almost one year later in *al-Nūr* 24:27. It was customary among the Arabs to enter others' houses without seeking their permission. They usually barged straight inside each other's homes and would only then ascertain from women or children whether the male head of the family was at home or not. Inevitably, this *jāhilī* practice bred many social evils and proved to be the precursor of moral lapses. Hence it was laid down that no one, neither close friends nor distant relatives, may enter the Prophet's house without express permission from him. Subsequently in *Sūrah al-Nūr* 24:27 this was made normative for all Muslims.

96. This constitutes another norm relating to social life. Of the ill manners prevalent in Arab social life was that people visited the homes of their friends or relatives at meal times or they prolonged their stay until it was meal time. This put the host to great inconvenience as it was impolite for him to ask his visitors to leave because it was meal time. Were the host to offer them food, this could not always be arranged at such short notice. Moreover, many people did not have the means to offer food to others. God disapproved of this practice and, therefore, directed that they may eat only at the homes of others when they were so invited. This injunction was not meant exclusively for the Prophet's home. It was, however, first introduced in the Prophet's home because it was the model home for all Muslims, the purpose being thereby that this would become a normative element in Muslim culture.

97. This verse seeks to reform another evil practice. Some guests did not leave the host's house even after taking a meal. They would start a never-ending conversation, paying no heed to the inconvenience they

but he does not express it out of shyness; but Allah is not ashamed of speaking out the Truth. And if you were to ask the wives of the Prophet for something, ask from behind a curtain. That is more apt for the cleanness of your hearts and theirs.[98] ▶	فَيَسْتَحْيِۦ مِنكُمْۖ وَٱللَّهُ لَا يَسْتَحْيِۦ مِنَ ٱلْحَقِّۚ وَإِذَا سَأَلْتُمُوهُنَّ مَتَٰعًا فَسْـَٔلُوهُنَّ مِن وَرَآءِ حِجَابٍۚ ذَٰلِكُمْ أَطْهَرُ لِقُلُوبِكُمْ وَقُلُوبِهِنَّۚ

were causing to their host and his family. Some ill-mannered people even put the Prophet (peace be on him) to great inconvenience in this respect. Since he was an exceptionally kind and magnanimous person, he put up with their uncouth manners. On the occasion of his wedding feast to celebrate his marriage to Zaynab, this clumsy behaviour exceeded all limits. As narrated by the Prophet's special attendant, Anas ibn Mālik, the feast was held at night. Most of the guests took their leave after the meal and left, but two or three people continued to chat for quite a while. The Prophet (peace be on him) took their leave and made a round of his wives' homes. On his return, he still found them engrossed in conversation. The Prophet (peace be on him) then went to 'Ā'ishah's apartment. Only after a considerable time, when he was informed of these people's departure, did he go to Zaynab's apartment. God, therefore, made a point of drawing everyone's attention to this objectionable habit. According to Anas ibn Mālik, this was the circumstantial background to this verse's revelation. (Muslim, *Kitāb al-Nikāḥ, Bāb Zawāj Zaynab bint Jaḥsh wa Nuzūl al-Ḥijāb;* Ṭabarī, *Tafsīr*, comments on verse 53.)

98. This is known as the Verse of *Ḥijāb*. Bukhārī cites Anas ibn Mālik's account that before this verse's revelation, 'Umar often submitted to the Prophet (peace be on him): "O Messenger of God! All kinds of people visit you. I wish you had commanded your wives to cover themselves". According to another report, 'Umar once said to the Prophet's wives: "If I had my way, my eyes would not fall upon you". (Bukhārī, *Kitāb al-Tafsīr, Bāb Qawl Allāh: Lā Tadkhulū Buyūt al-Nabī …*) However, since the Prophet (peace be on him) was not free to legislate, he waited for God's command. Finally, God commanded that no male, unless he be a relative of the prohibited degree, should enter the Prophet's home and those who

It is not lawful for you to cause hurt to Allah's Messenger,[99] nor to ever marry his wives after him.[100] Surely that would be an enormous sin in Allah's sight. ▶	وَمَا كَانَ لَكُمْ أَن تُؤْذُوا۟ رَسُولَ ٱللَّهِ وَلَآ أَن تَنكِحُوٓا۟ أَزْوَٰجَهُۥ مِنۢ بَعْدِهِۦٓ أَبَدًا ۚ إِنَّ ذَٰلِكُمْ كَانَ عِندَ ٱللَّهِ عَظِيمًا ﴿٥٣﴾

had some business to conduct should speak to the Prophet's wives from behind a curtain. Consequent upon this command, curtains were hung at the houses of the Prophet's wives. Since his house served as a model, other Muslims took his cue and adopted the same practice. It is evident from the wording of this verse: "That is more apt for the cleanness of your hearts and theirs", that those who seek to maintain purity of heart should follow this practice.

Anyone endowed with common sense will notice that the Qur'ān here stops men from speaking directly to women and further suggests that if they need to speak to each other then they should do so from behind a curtain, this because such behaviour better ensures the purity of their hearts. How can one infer from this directive that mixed gatherings of men and women, co-educational institutions and the unrestrained mingling of men and women at the workplace, women's membership of representative institutions are all fine and that they do not affect the purity of people's hearts? If a person does not want to obey the Qur'ān, the reasonable course for him is that he may do so and say clearly that he is not interested in obeying Qur'ānic injunctions. However, to violate an explicit injunction of the Qur'ān and yet unabashedly claim that this is in accord with the true spirit of Islam, represents sheer degradation. For what is that "spirit" of Islam that exists outside the parameters of the Qur'ān and the *Sunnah*?

99. This alludes to the unbelievers' and hypocrites' allegations against the Prophet (peace be on him) that were being circulated at the time, all as part of a vicious propaganda campaign. Regrettably, even some Muslims of weak faith had begun to contribute to this campaign.

100. This elucidates the point made at the outset of the *sūrah* (verse 6) that the Prophet's wives are the "mothers of the believers".

(54) (It does not matter) whether you disclose something or conceal it, for Allah certainly knows everything.[101]

(55) It will not be blameworthy for the wives of the Prophet if their fathers, their sons, their brothers, their brothers' sons, their sisters'[102] sons, and the women with whom they have social relations,[103] and the persons whom their right hands possess[104] enter their houses. ▶

إِن تُبْدُوا۟ شَيْـًٔا أَوْ تُخْفُوهُ فَإِنَّ ٱللَّهَ كَانَ
بِكُلِّ شَىْءٍ عَلِيمًا ﴿٥٤﴾ لَّا جُنَاحَ عَلَيْهِنَّ فِىٓ
ءَابَآئِهِنَّ وَلَآ أَبْنَآئِهِنَّ وَلَآ إِخْوَٰنِهِنَّ
وَلَآ أَبْنَآءِ إِخْوَٰنِهِنَّ وَلَآ أَبْنَآءِ أَخَوَٰتِهِنَّ
وَلَا نِسَآئِهِنَّ وَلَا مَا مَلَكَتْ أَيْمَٰنُهُنَّ

101. Any person who harbours any ill-feeling towards the Prophet (peace be on him) or his wives will not be able to keep this hidden from God. Those who are guilty of this will be punished by Him.

102. For further details see *al-Nūr* 24: nn. 38–42, *Towards Understanding the Qur'ān*, Vol. VI, pp. 231–233. Ālūsī's comments are also noteworthy: "The command pertaining to brothers, brothers' sons and sisters' sons cover all those relatives, whether by descent or fosterage, whom a woman may not marry. Uncles, paternal as well as maternal, are not mentioned here because they are like a woman's parents. Furthermore, explicit reference to nephews would be redundant, for the underlying reason that granting women relaxation in the observation of *ḥijāb* with their paternal and maternal uncles is the same as exists in the case of paternal and maternal uncles." (Ālūsī, *Rūḥ al-Ma'ānī*, comments on verse 55.)

103. For further details see *al-Nūr* 24: n. 43, *Towards Understanding the Qur'ān*, Vol. VI, pp. 234–235.

104. For further details see *al-Nūr* 24: n. 44, *Towards Understanding the Qur'ān*, Vol. VI, pp. 235–236.

(O women), shun disobeying Allah. Allah is watchful over everything.[105]	وَٱتَّقِينَ ٱللَّهَ ۚ إِنَّ ٱللَّهَ كَانَ عَلَىٰ كُلِّ شَىْءٍ شَهِيدًا ۝
(56) Allah and His angels bless the Prophet.[106] ▶	إِنَّ ٱللَّهَ وَمَلَـٰٓئِكَتَهُۥ يُصَلُّونَ عَلَى ٱلنَّبِىِّ ۚ

105. The promulgation of this explicit injunction meant that anyone who was not covered by the list of relatives enumerated here (see verse 55) was not allowed to enter into anyone's house. Another possible meaning is that women must refrain from the practice of only observing *ḥijāb* before unrelated men when their husbands are present, but not doing so when their husbands are away. Such women might be able to conceal their misconduct from their husbands, but it will not remain hidden from God.

106. God's *ṣalāh* on the Prophet (peace be on him) means that He is exceedingly benevolent and compassionate towards him, lavishes praise on him, blesses his efforts, exalts his renown and showers mercy upon him. As for the angels, their *ṣalāh* on the Prophet (peace be on him) means that they overflow with love for him, they pray to God to exalt his standing, to grant him success in the accomplishment of his mission, and to elevate him to the highest ranks.

The context discloses the purpose of the statement. At that time, the enemies of Islam were engaged in spreading slanderous rumours about the Prophet (peace be on him). In a fit of frustration and an outburst of pent-up malice and rancour, they believed that by engaging in mud-slinging they would be able to undermine the Prophet's moral influence, thanks to which Islam and the Muslims were constantly moving ahead. It was in this context that God revealed this verse. The message that was conveyed through it was as follows: "Notwithstanding the opposition of unbelievers and hypocrites, God is determined to bestow honour and renown upon His Prophet (peace be on him) and his enemies will be humbled. Since God is kind to him, the angels (who administer the whole universe) praise him, his opponents' campaign will eat dust. Their opposition will not matter at all for the Prophet's rank has been exalted by God and he is supported and profusely praised by His angels. In face of such Divine blessings upon him, their hostility will cause him no harm. Angels pray to God day and night to elevate his rank and to strengthen and promote the religious faith he espouses."

Believers, invoke blessings and peace on him.[107]	يَـٰٓأَيُّهَا ٱلَّذِينَ ءَامَنُوا۟ صَلُّوا۟ عَلَيْهِ وَسَلِّمُوا۟ تَسْلِيمًا ﴿٥٦﴾

107. The believers are reminded of the debt they owe the Prophet (peace be on him). Thanks to him, they were guided to the Right Way. They were stumbling in darkness, yet he served as a beacon of light. When they were immersed in moral degradation, he raised them to such heights of moral excellence that they became an object of everyone's envy. They were enmeshed in brutish ways, yet he brought about refinement in their lives. The unbelievers' angst against him was precisely because the Prophet (peace be on him) had abundantly lavished his favours on them rather than because he had caused them any harm. The Muslims' devotion to the Prophet (peace be on him) should match and even surpass the unbelievers' wrath and rancour against him. The Muslims should, therefore, praise him no less than the unbelievers denounce him. Furthermore, they should pray to God for him in the manner that the angels pray for him by day and by night. They pray to God: "O Lord of this world and the Next! Lavish upon Your Prophet boundless mercy in measure to his endless favours upon us and crown him with glory in this world and exalt him in the Hereafter by granting him the most favoured position".

This verse directs Muslims towards two things: *ṣallū 'ālayhi* (to invoke blessings upon him) and *sallimū taslīmā* (to invoke peace on him). When the word *ṣalāh* is used in conjunction with the preposition *'alā*, it carries the following three meanings: (i) to incline towards someone, turn towards someone, or lean towards someone with love; (ii) to praise someone, and (iii) to pray for someone. When the phrase is used with respect to God, the third meaning is rendered redundant, for God cannot pray to anyone. In this instance, the meaning is restricted to either of the first two. However, when the expression occurs in the context of God's servants, be they angels or humans, it can embrace all three meanings. Implicit in such invocations is love, praise, glorification and prayer for God's mercy. The directive to Muslims to make such an invocation thus entails their developing a deep attachment to the Prophet (peace be on him) whereby they praise and glorify him and make supplications for him.

As for *salām*, it admits two meanings: (i) to remain secure from every affliction and impairment, and (ii) to enjoy a state of peace and security from active hostility. Saying *sallimū taslīmā* for the Prophet (peace be on him), in keeping with the first meaning of the term, signifies that the Muslims should pray that God may grant him absolute peace and tranquillity. Moreover, it is an exhortation to Muslims that they help and support the Prophet (peace be on him) with their hearts and souls, that they abstain from whatever entails opposition to him and should faithfully follow and obey him.

When this injunction was revealed, several Companions said to the Prophet (peace be on him): "O Messenger of God! You have instructed us how to greet you when we meet you (by saying *al-salāmu 'alayka yā Rasūl Allāh*) and also how to pronounce *salām* on you during Prayer (by saying *al-Salāmu 'alayka ayyuhā al-Nabī wa Raḥmat Allāh wa Barakātuh*). How, then, should we invoke *ṣalāh* for you?" In response, the Prophet (peace be on him) taught his Companions many versions of *ṣalāh*, an account of which follows:

> Ka'b ibn 'Ujrah: *Allāhumma Ṣalli 'alā Muḥammad wa 'alā Āl Muḥammad kamā Ṣallayta 'alā Ibrāhīm wa 'alā Āl Ibrāhīm innaka Ḥamīd-un Majīd; wa Bārik 'alā Muḥammad wa 'alā Āl Muḥammad kamā Bārakta 'alā Ibrāhīm wa 'alā Āl Ibrāhīm innaka Ḥamīd-un Majīd.* (O God, exalt Muḥammad and the people of Muḥammad as You exalted Abraham and the people of Abraham. Surely, You are Immensely Praiseworthy, Enormously Magnified. O God, bless Muḥammad and the people of Muḥammad as You blessed Abraham and the people of Abraham. Surely You are Immensely Praiseworthy, Enormously Magnified.) This version, with slight verbal variations, is cited on the authority of Ka'b ibn 'Ujrah by Bukhārī, Muslim, Abū Dā'ūd, Tirmidhī, Nasā'ī, Ibn Mājah, Aḥmad ibn Ḥanbal, Ibn Abī Shaybah, 'Abd al-Razzāq, Ibn Abī Ḥātim and Muḥammad ibn Jarīr al-Ṭabarī. (Bukhārī, *Kitāb al-Tafsīr, Bāb anna Allāh wa Malā'ikatahu ...*; Muslim, *Kitāb al-Ṣalāh, Bāb al-Ṣalāh 'alā al-Nabī...*; Ibn Mājah, *Kitāb Iqāmah al-Ṣalāh wa al-Sunnah fīhā, Bāb al-Ṣalāh 'alā al-Nabī*; Abū Dā'ūd, *Kitāb al-Rukū', Bāb al-Ṣalāh 'alā al-Nabī...*; Tirmidhī, *Kitāb al-Witr, Bāb mā jā'a fī Ṣifat al-Ṣalāh*; Nasā'ī, *Kitāb al-Sahw* and Aḥmad ibn Ḥanbal, *Musnad*, narrated by Ka'b ibn 'Ujrah.)

The version quoted above is also narrated by 'Abd Allāh ibn 'Abbās, with minor variations, (Ṭabarī, *Tafsīr*, comments on verse 59).

> Abū Ḥumayd al-Sā'idī's version is as follows: *Allāhumma Ṣalli 'alā Muḥammad wa Azwājihi wa Dhurrīyatihi kamā Ṣallayta 'alā Ibrāhīm wa Bārik 'alā Muḥammad wa Azwājihi wa Dhurrīyatihi kamā Bārakta 'alā Āl Ibrāhīm Innaka Ḥamīd-un Majīd.* (O God, exalt Muḥammad and his wives and his children as You exalted Abraham, and bless Muḥammad and his wives and children as You blessed

the people of Abraham. Surely You are Immensely Praiseworthy, Enormously Magnified.) (Bukhārī, *Kitāb al-Tafsīr, Bāb anna Allāh wa Malā'ikatahu…*; Muslim, *Kitāb al-Ṣalāh, Bāb al-Ṣalāh 'alā al-Nabī…*; Ibn Mājah, *Kitāb Iqāmah al-Ṣalāh wa al-Sunnah fīhā, Bāb al-Ṣalāh 'alā al-Nabī*; Abū Dā'ūd, *Kitāb al-Rukū', Bāb al-Ṣalāh 'alā al-Nabī…*; Mālik, *Muwaṭṭā', Kitāb al-Ṭahārah, Bāb mā jā'a fī al-Ṣalāh'alā al-Nabī*; Nasā'ī, *Kitāb al-Sahw* and Aḥmad ibn Ḥanbal, *Musnad*, narrated by Abū Ḥumayd al-Sā'idī.)

Abū Sa'īd al-Khudrī's version: *Allāhumma Ṣalli 'alā Muḥammad 'Abdika wa Rasūlika kamā Ṣallayta 'alā Ibrāhīm wa Bārik 'alā Muḥammad wa 'alā Āl Muḥammad kamā Bārakta 'alā Ibrāhīm.* (O God, exalt Muḥammad, Your servant and Your Messenger as You exalted Abraham, and bless Muḥammad and the people of Muḥammad as You blessed Abraham.) (Bukhārī, *Kitāb al-Tafsīr, Bāb anna Allāh wa Malā'ikatahu…*; Nasā'ī, *Kitāb al-Sahw* and Aḥmad ibn Ḥanbal, *Musnad*, narrated by Abū Sa'īd al-Khudrī.)

Buraydah al-Khuzā'ī's version: *Allāhumma Ij'al Ṣalātaka wa Raḥmataka wa Barakataka 'alā Muḥammad wa 'alā Āl Muḥammad kamā Jā'a ltahā 'alā Ibrāhīm. Innaka Ḥamīd-un Majīd.* (O God, lavish Your exaltation, mercy and blessing on Muḥammad and the people of Muḥammad as You lavished them on Abraham. Surely You are Immensely Praiseworthy, Enormously Magnified.) (Aḥmad ibn Ḥanbal, *Musnad*, narrated by Buraydah al-Khuzā'ī.)

Abū Hurayrah's version: *Allāhumma Ṣalli 'alā Muḥammad wa 'alā Āl Muḥammad wa Bārik 'alā Muḥammad wa 'alā Āl Muḥammad kamā Ṣallayta wa Bārakta 'alā Ibrāhīm fī al-'Ālamīn. Innaka Ḥamīd-un Majīd.* (O God, exalt Muḥammad and the people of Muḥammad and bless Muḥammad and the people of Muḥammad as You blessed Abraham in the worlds. Surely You are Immensely Praiseworthy, Enormously Magnified.)

Ṭalḥah's version: *Allāhumma Ṣalli 'alā Muḥammad wa 'alā Āl Muḥammad kamā Ṣallayta 'alā Ibrāhīm Innaka Ḥamīd-un Majīd wa Bārik 'alā Muḥammad wa 'alā Āl Muḥammad kamā Bārakta 'alā Ibrāhīm. Innaka Ḥamīd-un Majīd.* (O God, exalt Muḥammad and the people of Muḥammad as You exalted Abraham. Surely You are Immensely Praiseworthy, Enormously Magnified; and bless Muḥammad and the people of Muḥammad as You blessed Abraham. Surely, You are Immensely Praiseworthy, Enormously Magnified.) (Ṭabarī, *Tafsīr*, comments on verse 59.)

Notwithstanding slight verbal variations, all the above versions of *ṣalāḥ* and *salām* on the Prophet (peace be on him) mean substantively the same. Let us, therefore, recapitulate the important points emerging from the above discussion:

i. The Prophet (peace be on him) apprises the Muslims that the best way to send benedictions upon him is to pray to God that He may send His *ṣalāh* and *salām* on him. Those who are unaware of what is meant by God's *ṣalāh* and *salām* on the Prophet (peace be on him) express their sense of bewilderment at this. They say: "God asks us to send our *ṣalāh* and *salām* on the Prophet (peace be on him) but, strangely enough, we are being required to ask God to send His *ṣalāh* and *salām* on the Prophet (peace be on him)".

   By directing the Muslims to do so, the Prophet (peace be on him) implicitly indicated that human beings cannot fully acquit themselves of the responsibility of sending *ṣalāh* and *salām* on him, no matter how keen they might be to do so. Hence they should turn only to God, supplicating for His *ṣalāh* and *salām* for him. For we cannot enhance the Prophet's status, only God can do so. We cannot fully repay our debt of gratitude to the Prophet (peace be on him), only God can recompense him. Despite all our efforts to enhance his renown, and to promote the religious faith taught by him, we cannot achieve any success without God's support and succour. Again, even our having love and reverence for the Prophet (peace be on him) also depends on God's help. This because Satan constantly seeks to mislead us by his promptings against which we seek God's refuge. The only way to invoke *ṣalāh* on the Prophet (peace be on him) is to pray to God that He may lavish His *ṣalāh* upon him. Whoever recites *ṣalāḥ* and *salām* on the Prophet (peace be on him) acknowledges before God his inability to adequately send benedictions upon him, an inability that drives him to solicit God to send His *ṣalāh* and *salām* on him.

ii. Out of grace and magnanimity, the Prophet (peace be on him) did not limit *ṣalāh* and *salām* just to himself; instead, he also included his wives (*azwāj*) and children (*dhurrīyah*). Moreover, he included his *āl*, meaning that the *ṣalāh* and *salām* for the Prophet (peace be on him) was not limited to only the Prophet's immediate family, but also included all his followers and all adherents of his way. In Arabic lexicon, two words are used: *āl* and *ahl*. The difference between the two is as follows: a person's *āl* encompass all his associates, supporters and followers, regardless of whether they are his kin or not. In contrast, a person's *ahl* are his kith and kin, regardless of whether they are his followers or helpers in his cause or not. The

Qur'ān employs the expression *Āl Fir'awn* (the people of Pharaoh) on 14 occasions. In all these instances, it refers to all those who were on Pharaoh's side in his encounter against the Prophet Moses (peace be on him). Nowhere is it used specifically for Pharaoh's family. (See *al-Baqarah* 2:49–50; *Āl 'Imrān* 3:11; *al-A'rāf* 7:130 and *al-Mu'min* 40:46.) Therefore, the expression *Āl Muḥammad* does not include in its ambit anyone who does not follow the Prophet's way, even if he be a member of his family. On the other hand, it denotes all those who follow his way, disregarding whether they enjoy his kinship or not. Those members of the Prophet's family who follow him, beyond doubt, are a part of *Āl Muḥammad*.

iii. It is noteworthy that in every version of *ṣalāh* and *salām* on the Prophet (peace be on him) taught by him reference is made to the Prophet Abraham (peace be on him) and [in most to] his *āl*. This denotes the prayer that the Prophet Muḥammad (peace be on him) and his people enjoy the same blessings and peace that were conferred upon the Prophet Abraham (peace be on him) and his people. Many people have found this difficult to comprehend and *'ulamā'* have offered a wide range of opinions though none of them are fully convincing. In my opinion – and true knowledge rests only with God – reference is made to the Prophet Abraham (peace be on him) on account of the unique distinction that God bestowed on him. His distinction consists in being the patriarch of the Jews, Christians and Muslims alike; in sum, of all those who recognise Prophethood, Revelation and Scripture as the source of guidance. As God made him the leader of all believers, the prayer in regard to the Prophet Muḥammad (peace be on him) is that he be granted the same exalted position as Abraham so that all those who believe in Prophethood have faith in his being the Prophet.

There is a consensus among scholars that invoking *ṣalāh* on the Prophet (peace be on him) is a *sunnah* in Islam, and it is *mustaḥabb* (recommended) to recite it whenever his name is mentioned. There is also a consensus that it is *sunnah* during the Prayer. All *'ulamā'* are agreed on the point that every Muslim is obliged to invoke *ṣalāh* upon the Prophet (peace be on him) at least once during their lifetime. The Qur'ānic command with regard to this issue is unmistakable. However, there are disagreements among *'ulamā'* regarding the details of the *ṣalāh*. Shafi'ī, for instance, insists that *ṣalāh* on the Prophet (peace be on him) is *farḍ* (obligatory); the Prayer of anyone who fails to do so is void. The Companions 'Abd Allāh ibn Mas'ūd, Abū Mas'ūd al-Anṣārī, 'Abd Allāh ibn 'Umar and Jābir ibn 'Abd Allāh and Sha'abī, Muḥammad Bāqir, Muḥammad ibn Ka'b al-Quraẓī and Muqātil ibn Ḥayyān among the Successors, and Isḥāq ibn Rāhwayah among the *fuqahā'* subscribe to this opinion. In the later days of his life, Aḥmad ibn Ḥanbal, too, held this opinion. However, Abū Ḥanīfah, Mālik and the majority of *'ulamā'* are of the view that it is obligatory (*farḍ*) to invoke *ṣalāh* on the Prophet (peace be on him) once in a Muslim's lifetime. This is similar to the *shahādah*: when a person pronounces the *shahādah*, affirming God's Godhead and the Prophet Muḥammad's Messengership, just once he fulfils the obligation of embracing faith. By the same token, if one recites *shahādah* or *ṣalāh* on the Prophet (peace be on him) once in a lifetime then it is no longer *obligatory* to repeat it.

Another group of scholars regards the recitation of *ṣalāh* on the Prophet (peace be on him) as a compulsory component of Prayer. However, they only insist on its recitation in the *tashahhud*. According to another group, it is *wājib* to recite it while praying without tying it with *tashahhud*. Some are of the view that it is *wājib* to recite *ṣalāh* on the Prophet (peace be on him) whenever his name is mentioned. Others maintain that it must be recited only once in a sitting, no matter how many times the Prophet's name is mentioned.

At the end of the day, all such differences of opinion are only about whether *ṣalāh* on the Prophet (peace be on him) is obligatory or not. However, there is absolute agreement that reciting *ṣalāh* on the Prophet (peace be on him) is an act of great merit and excellence and is worthy of reward from God. No one who has been blessed with faith can have any dissenting opinion on the matter. *Ṣalāh* on the Prophet (peace be on him) is the natural outpouring of gratitude on the part of every Muslim who is aware that he is his greatest benefactor after God. The more one values the bounty of one's faith and of Islam, the greater will one value God's bounties – faith in, and submission to God – the more he will value the beneficence of the Prophet (peace be on him), and the more he values this beneficence the more he will recite *ṣalāh* on him. Its recitation is an index of a person's attachment to the Prophet (peace be on him) and of the value he attaches to his faith. The Prophet (peace be on him) said: "Angels continue to recite *ṣalāh* on a person as long as he recites *ṣalāh* on me". (Ibn Mājah, *Kitāb Iqāmah al-Ṣalāh wa al-Sunnah fīhā, Bāb al-Ṣalāh 'alā al-Nabī*.) Of similar import are his other observations. "He who recites *ṣalāh* on me once receives *ṣalāh* ten times from God", (Muslim, *Kitāb al-Ṣalāh, Bāb al-Ṣalāh 'alā al-Nabī*...). "One who regularly sends *ṣalāh* upon me is more entitled to enjoy proximity with me on the Day of Judgement", (Tirmidhī, *Bāb mā jā'a fī Faḍl al-Ṣalāh 'alā al-Nabī* – Ed.), and "He is a miser who fails to send *ṣalāh* on me when my name is mentioned before him", (Tirmidhī, *Kitāb al-Da'wāt 'an Rasūl* ...).

On the question of whether sending *ṣalāh* with the words, *Allāhuma ṣalli 'alā fulān* (on such a person) the words: *"ṣalla Allāh 'alayh wa sallam"* upon anyone other than the Prophet (peace be on him) is lawful or not, the *'ulamā'* have divergent views. According to one group of scholars, the most prominent among whom is Qāḍī 'Iyāḍ, it is absolutely legitimate to recite *ṣalāh* also on persons other than the Prophet (peace be on him). These *'ulamā'* substantiate their opinion by referring to the following Qur'ānic verses which speak of *ṣalāh* with regard to others than the Prophet (peace be on him):

> Upon them (the believers) will be the blessings (*ṣalawāt*) and mercy of their Lord (*al-Baqarah* 2:157).
>
> (O Prophet!) Take alms out of their riches and thereby cleanse them (the believers) and bring about their growth (in righteousness), and pray (*ṣalli*) for them (*al-Tawbah* 9:103).
>
> It is He Who lavishes His blessings (*yuṣallī 'alaykum*) on you and His angels invoke blessings on you (*al-Aḥzāb* 33:43).

Moreover, on several occasions the Prophet (peace be on him) employed the expression *ṣalāh* as praying for people other than Prophets. For example, he prayed thus for one of his Companions: *Allāhumma ṣalli 'alā Āl Abī Awfā.*

At the request of Jābir ibn 'Abd Allāh's wife, he said: *Ṣallā Allāh 'alayka wa 'alā zawjika* (may Allah endow His blessings upon you and your husband). When people came to the Prophet (peace be on him) with *Zakāh*, he would pray for them as follows: *Allāhumma Ṣalli 'alayhim* (O God, endow Your blessings on them). While praying to God for Sa'd ibn 'Ubādah, the Prophet (peace be on him) said: *Alāhumma Ij'al Ṣalātaka wa Raḥmataka 'alā Āl Sa'd ibn 'Ubādah* (O God, let Your blessing and mercy be on the *āl* of Sa'd ibn 'Ubādah). Regarding the souls of believers, the Prophet (peace be on him) gave the tiding that angels make the following supplication: *Ṣallā Allāh 'alāyka wa 'alā jasadika* (May God bless you [i.e. your soul] and your body).

Nonetheless, the mainstream view is that while the Prophet (peace be on him) could invoke *ṣalāh* for others, it is inappropriate for Muslims to do so for anyone other than the Prophet (peace be on him). It is customary, therefore, for Muslims to use the word *ṣalāh* exclusively with respect to Prophets. Its use for others should, therefore, thus be avoided. Prompted by the same consideration, 'Umar ibn 'Abd al-'Azīz wrote to one of his officials: 'I have come to know that some preachers use the term *ṣalāh* for their patrons. The use of this term is specific to the Prophet (peace be on him). Upon receiving this letter of mine you should stop them from doing so and ask them to use it exclusively for the Prophet (peace be on him). They should rest content with making supplications for other Muslims'. (Ālūsī, *Ruḥ al-Ma'ānī,* comments on verse 56.) The majority is also of the

(57) Verily those who cause annoyance to Allah and His Messenger – Allah has cursed them in this world and in the Hereafter and has prepared for them a humiliating chastisement.[108] (58) Those who cause hurt to believing men and to believing women have invited upon themselves a calumny[109] and a manifest sin.

إِنَّ ٱلَّذِينَ يُؤْذُونَ ٱللَّهَ وَرَسُولَهُۥ لَعَنَهُمُ ٱللَّهُ
فِى ٱلدُّنْيَا وَٱلْـَٔاخِرَةِ وَأَعَدَّ لَهُمْ عَذَابًا
مُّهِينًا ﴿٥٧﴾ وَٱلَّذِينَ يُؤْذُونَ ٱلْمُؤْمِنِينَ
وَٱلْمُؤْمِنَٰتِ بِغَيْرِ مَا ٱكْتَسَبُوا۟ فَقَدِ
ٱحْتَمَلُوا۟ بُهْتَٰنًا وَإِثْمًا مُّبِينًا ﴿٥٨﴾

---

view that *ṣalāh* is specific to the Prophet Muḥammad (peace be on him) and should not be used even for other Prophets.

108. The expression "those who cause annoyance to Allah" refers to disobeying God, to those who are unbelievers, polytheists and atheists, and to those who tamper with God's commands regarding what is lawful and what is not; God's annoyance is also incurred when anyone causes annoyance to the Prophet (peace be on him). As we know, obedience to the Prophet (peace be on him) is tantamount to obeying God. In like view, taunting, opposing, and disobeying the Prophet (peace be on him) is tantamount to taunting, opposing and disobeying God Himself.

109. This constitutes the definition of *buhtān* (calumny). If one charges someone with a fault that he does not have, this amounts to calumny. The same holds for ascribing a misdeed to someone that he has not committed. The Prophet (peace be on him) defined *buhtān* (calumny) along the above lines. Both Abū Dā'ūd and Tirmidhī cite the following tradition: Someone asked the Prophet (peace be on him) to define *ghībah* (backbiting). To this he responded: "Speaking of your brother in a manner that would displease him". They further asked him whether this also applied when such a fault was indeed found in that person. He replied: "If someone has a certain fault and you mention it, this amounts to backbiting him. However, if that person does not have that fault and you ascribe it to him, you have committed *buhtān* (calumny) against him". (Abū Dā'ūd, *Kitāb al-Adab,*

(59) O Prophet, enjoin your wives and your daughters and the believing women, to draw a part of their outer coverings around them.[110] ▶

يَـٰٓأَيُّهَا ٱلنَّبِيُّ قُل لِّأَزْوَٰجِكَ وَبَنَاتِكَ
وَنِسَآءِ ٱلْمُؤْمِنِينَ يُدْنِينَ عَلَيْهِنَّ مِن
جَلَـٰبِيبِهِنَّ

Bāb fī al-Ghībah; and Tirmidhī, *Kitāb al-Birr, Bāb mā jā'a fī al-Ghībah.*) Obviously, *buhtān* (calumny) is a moral vice and those guilty of it will be punished in the Hereafter. It also becomes clear from the above verse that an Islamic state should declare calumny a cognizable offence.

110. This verse lays down the injunction: ويدنين عليهن من جلابيبهن (to draw a part of their outer coverings around them). Here two important words have been used: *jalābīb* sing. *(jilbāb)* and *idnā'*. Now *jilbāb* is the Arabic word that denotes a large sheet used to wrap around the body. As for *idnā'*, it denotes bringing something close and wrapping it around. However, when the preposition *'alā* is affixed to *idnā'*, it denotes letting something down from above. Some modern translators and Qur'ān-commentators, under the influence of Western predilections, have translated this injunction to simply denote "to wrap up". They do so in order to circumvent the requirement to cover the face. Had this, however, been the purpose of the Qur'ānic verse, the words would have been *yudnīna ilayhinna*. Anyone who knows the Arabic language will never accept that *yudnīna ilayhinna* can mean simply to wrap a sheet around. The words *min jalābībihinna* also prevent one from accepting this as the meaning of the relevant words. For the preposition *min* here indicates that what is meant is a part of the sheet, rather than the whole of it. It is also obvious that if a sheet is wrapped around the body it will have to be the whole sheet rather than a part of it. Thus the clear meaning of the injunction is that women should wrap themselves in a sheet and throw a part of it over themselves. This is what is known in Urdu usage as *ghūnghat dālnā* (drawing the veil).

In fact, this is how this injunction was understood by people closest to the Prophet's time. According to Ibn Jarīr al-Ṭabarī and Ibn al-Mundhir, Muḥammad ibn Sīrīn requested 'Ubaydah al-Salmānī to explain the verse under discussion. (Let us clarify that 'Ubaydah embraced Islam during the Prophet's time but he could not meet him. It was only during the Caliphate of 'Umar that he came to Madīnah and spent the rest of his life there. He enjoyed the same fame and position as the jurist Qāḍī Shurayḥ did.) In answering what this query means, he picked up his sheet and wrapped it around himself, covering his head, forehead, and the whole of his face, leaving open only the area for one of the eyes. This is how he illustrated the thrust of the verse. 'Abd Allāh ibn 'Abbās also subscribed to almost the same interpretation. On the authority of Ibn Jarīr al-Ṭabarī, Ibn Abī Ḥātim and Ibn Marduwayh, he said: "God has asked women that when they go out of their homes, they should wrap themselves in their over-garments and cover their faces, leaving open only the eyes". The same interpretation of the verse is ascribed to Qatādah and Suddī. (Jaṣṣās, *Aḥkām al-Qur'ān*, comments on verse 59.)

All prominent Qur'ān-commentators in the age of the Companions and Successors were unanimously of the same opinion. In explicating the thrust of the Qur'ānic command directed at Muslim women "to draw a part of their outer coverings around them", Ibn Jarīr al-Ṭabarī points out that decent ladies should not resemble slave girls in their dress. Their faces and hair should not be uncovered. Rather, they should wear an over-garment so that no wicked person might molest them, (*Jāmi' al-Bayān*, 22:33). In the words of Abū Bakr al-Jaṣṣās: "This verse indicates that young women are obliged to keep their faces covered before men unrelated to them. When going out, they should cover themselves and display modesty so as not to arouse any expectations in the hearts of immoral men", (Jaṣṣās, *Aḥkām al-Qur'ān*, comments on verse 59). Likewise, Zamakhsharī reiterates the same by insisting that women should put on their over-garments on themselves, thus covering their head and face with them, (Zamakhsharī, *al-Kashshāf*, comments on verse 59). According to Niẓām al-Dīn al-Nīsābūrī, the verse commands women to cover their heads and faces by throwing a part of their over-garments on themselves, (Nīsābūrī, *Gharā'ib al-Qur'ān*, comments on verse 59). Rāzī suggests the following rationale of the command: "Since these women will be dressed in this manner, people will realise that they are not women of loose character. For a woman who keeps her face covered, though it is not one of those parts of the body which must be kept covered, she cannot be expected to uncover other parts of her body that are required to be kept covered. People will recognise them as modest women and with whom they cannot indulge in illicit sex", (Rāzī, *al-Tafsīr al-Kabīr*, comments on verse 59).

There is another point implicit in the verse: that the Prophet (peace be on him) had more than one daughter, for the Qur'ān says: "O Prophet, enjoin *your wives* and *your daughters* ..." (emphasis added), the address clearly being in the plural. The verse, thus, exposes the falsity of the stand of those people, who without any fear of God, contend that Fāṭimah was the Prophet's only daughter from his own loins, while the rest were his step daughters. Swayed by prejudice, such people fail to realise the

It is likelier that they will be recognised and not molested.[111] ▶	ذَٰلِكَ أَدْنَىٰٓ أَن يُعْرَفْنَ فَلَا يُؤْذَيْنَ ۗ

enormity of their guilt in denying the Prophet's other daughters his paternity: these people will be subjected to stringent interrogation on the Day of Judgement for their iniquity. All reports unanimously state that the Prophet's wife Khadījah gave birth to four daughters rather than just one. The Prophet's earliest biographer, Ibn Iṣḥāq in his account of the Prophet's marriage with Khadījah, records: "Except Ibrāhīm, Khadījah gave birth to all the children of the Prophet (peace be on him). The names of his children are: Qāsim, Ṭāhir, Ṭayyib, Zaynab, Ruqayyah, Umm Kulthūm and Fāṭimah", (*Sīrat Ibn Hishām*, Vol. 1, p. 174). Hishām ibn Muḥammad al-Sa'īd al-Kalbī, an authority on genealogy, maintains: "Prior to his designation as Prophet, Qāsim was the first child born to the Prophet (peace be on him), followed by Zaynab, Ruqayyah, and Umm Kulthūm in that order" (Ibn Sa'd, *Ṭabaqāt*, Vol. 1, p. 133). Ibn Ḥazm affirms in his *Jawāmi' al-Sīrah* that Khadījah gave birth to four daughters. Of them, Zaynab was the eldest, followed by Ruqayyah, Fāṭimah and Umm Kulthūm, (*Jawāmi' al-Sīrah,* pp. 38–39). Ṭabarī, Ibn Sa'd, Abū Ja'far Muḥammad ibn al-Ḥabīb, author of *Kitāb al-Muḥabbar,* and Ibn 'Abd al-Barr, author of *Kitāb al-Istī'āb*, state on the authority of authentic sources that before marrying the Prophet (peace be on him), Khadījah had two husbands. Of them, one was Abū Hālah al-Tamīmī, whose offspring was Hind ibn Abī Hālah. Her other husband was 'Atīq ibn 'Ā'idh al-Makhzūmī, whose daughter was also called Hind. After the death of her husband, Khadījah married the Prophet (peace be on him). The unanimous view of all the genealogists of the time is that Khadījah gave birth to the Prophet's four daughters, whose names have been given above (Ṭabarī, *Ta'rīkh*, Vol. 2, p. 411; Ibn Sa'd, *Ṭabaqāt*, Vol. 8, pp. 14–15; Ibn al-Ḥabīb, *Kitāb al-Muḥabbar*, pp. 78–79 and *al-Istī'āb*, Vol. 2, p. 718). These reports re-echo the Qur'ānic assertion that the Prophet (peace be on him) had several daughters rather than just one.

111. The simple and modest dress of those women will help them to be recognised as decent and chaste women, rather than as dissolute playgirls with regard to whom sexually corrupt men will entertain the expectation of a positive response to their amorous overtones. Furthermore, reference is made to the fact that their demeanour will prevent them from being molested.

Let us reflect a little on the spirit of this injunction. The way it has been expressed speaks volumes for the purpose of the injunction and represents the spirit of Islamic social law. We have already taken note of the Qur'ānic command enshrined in *Sūrah al-Nur*, 24:31 that believing women should not reveal their adornments except to certain categories of people enumerated in the verse. They are also asked not to stamp their feet on the ground in such a way that their hidden ornaments are revealed. Were we to consider the above injunction in conjunction with the present verse, it becomes evident that the Qur'ānic directive is aimed at ensuring that women conceal their charms from men not related to them. Evidently this objective can be realised only when women cover themselves by plain, simple over-garments. For, were they to use any attractive and colourful outer covering, it would undermine the very purpose of the injunction. Furthermore, the Qur'ānic command is not confined simply to using an outer covering; rather, it directs women to let down a part of their outer coverings.

The intent of the command is unmistakable: women should keep their faces covered in addition to covering the adornments of their bodies and garments. Moreover, God indicates the rationale underlying this command: that believing women should stand out for their chastity and moral rectitude and thus be spared molestation. Needless to add, this directive is addressed to those women who are subjected to the molestation and amorous overtures of corrupt men, and who are outraged if they are taken as women of dissolute character. Their preference is to live as chaste housewives. Addressing such decent and respectable women, God instructs them that they should not go out attractively dressed, displaying charms that are relished by lustful men. The best way for them is to go out after fully covering themselves by their over-garments, and this includes their faces. They should also walk modestly and quietly so that even the tinkling of their ornaments should not draw men's attention to them. This purpose will be defeated, however, if women dress coquettishly, exposing their charms to men and attracting their lusty gaze. The purpose can be realised though if they cover themselves with a plain, simple outer garment and if they cover their faces with its edge and not let there be any tinkling of ornaments that would attract people. However, there are women who dress up most attractively and put on full make up before they step out of their threshold. What can be the purpose of all this except to expose their ravishing charms to men, and to invite their attention towards themselves.

One is free to have one's viewpoint on any issue, and this may or may not be in harmony with the Qur'ānic teaching on that issue. In like manner, one has a choice in accepting or rejecting the Qur'ān as a code of conduct. However, unless one is bent upon mutilating the message

Allah is Most Forgiving, Most Merciful.[112]

(60) If the hypocrites and those in whose hearts there is a sickness,[113] and the scandal mongers in Madīnah[114] do not desist from their vile acts, We shall urge you to take action against them, and then they will hardly be able to stay in the city with you. ▶

وَكَانَ ٱللَّهُ غَفُورًا رَّحِيمًا ﴿٥٩﴾ ۞ لَّئِن لَّمْ يَنتَهِ ٱلْمُنَٰفِقُونَ وَٱلَّذِينَ فِى قُلُوبِهِم مَّرَضٌ وَٱلْمُرْجِفُونَ فِى ٱلْمَدِينَةِ لَنُغْرِيَنَّكَ بِهِمْ ثُمَّ لَا يُجَاوِرُونَكَ فِيهَآ إِلَّا قَلِيلًا ﴿٦٠﴾

---

of the Qur'ān by deliberately misinterpreting its intent, every forthright person will plainly recognize that what has been said above represents the teaching of the Qur'ān. Anyone who acts contrary to this should either concede that his action is contrary to the Qur'ānic teaching or that he regards the Qur'ānic guidance as flawed.

112. God will forgive the misdeeds of the pre-Islamic period providing people reform their attitude after the communication of His Guidance to them in very clear terms and providing they refrain from wilfully flouting His directives.

113. The word "sickness" in the verse refers to the two serious flaws of those who suffer from such sickness. One, they claim to be Muslims but nurse ill-will towards Islam and Muslims. Two, they suffer from malintent, licentiousness and a criminal mindset.

114. This refers to those who, from time to time, circulated vile rumours in Madīnah in order to create a scare among the Muslims as well as to demoralise them. They also spread reports to the effect that the Muslims had suffered a disgraceful defeat at one place or another, or that a huge army was on its way to crush the Muslims, or that Madīnah was about to be invaded. Furthermore, they circulated scandalous stories about the Prophet's family and other Muslims with a view to poisoning the public mind and weakening the Muslims' moral influence.

(61) They shall be cursed from all around and they shall be ruthlessly killed wherever they are seized. (62) This has been Allah's Way with those who have gone before, and you shall find no change in Allah's Way.[115]

(63) People ask you concerning the Hour[116] (of Resurrection). Say: "Allah alone has knowledge of it. What do you know? Perhaps the Hour is nigh." ▶

مَّلْعُونِينَ ۖ أَيْنَمَا ثُقِفُوٓا۟ أُخِذُوا۟ وَقُتِّلُوا۟
تَقْتِيلًا ﴿٦١﴾ سُنَّةَ ٱللَّهِ فِى ٱلَّذِينَ خَلَوْا۟
مِن قَبْلُ ۖ وَلَن تَجِدَ لِسُنَّةِ ٱللَّهِ تَبْدِيلًا ﴿٦٢﴾
يَسْـَٔلُكَ ٱلنَّاسُ عَنِ ٱلسَّاعَةِ ۖ قُلْ
إِنَّمَا عِلْمُهَا عِندَ ٱللَّهِ ۚ وَمَا يُدْرِيكَ لَعَلَّ
ٱلسَّاعَةَ تَكُونُ قَرِيبًا ﴿٦٣﴾

---

115. It is an abiding principle of God's Law that those who seek to corrupt people are not given the chance to flourish in an Islamic state and society. As the state adheres to the Islamic code of life, it pre-warns all wicked elements to mend their ways. If they fail thereafter in giving up their corrupt ways, they are treated with great severity.

116. Unbelievers and hypocrites often asked the Prophet (peace be on him) when the Day of Reckoning will come to pass. The purpose of their query was not to find out the truth of the matter. Rather, they raised the question as a part of their campaign to ridicule and mock the Prophet (peace be on him). They did not believe in the Hereafter and looked at its whole concept as nothing else than an empty threat. They did not ask about the time of the Hour of Reckoning because they sincerely wanted to mend their behaviour out of fear of that awesome Day. Far from it, instead, they wanted to tell the Prophet (peace be on him) that even though they had fiercely opposed him, they had still not been struck by God's scourge. Hence they mockingly asked the Prophet (peace be on him) to tell them when the Resurrection would take place and when they would be taken to task.

(64) Allah has cursed the unbelievers and has prepared for them a Blazing Fire; (65) therein they shall abide for ever. They shall find none to protect or help them. (66) On that Day when their faces shall be turned around in the Fire, they will say: "Would that we had obeyed Allah and obeyed the Messenger." (67) They will say: "Our Lord, we obeyed our chiefs and our great ones, and they turned us away from the Right Way. (68) Our Lord, mete out to them a double chastisement and lay upon them a mighty curse."[117]

(69) Believers,[118] do not be like those who distressed Moses ▸

إِنَّ ٱللَّهَ لَعَنَ ٱلْكَـٰفِرِينَ وَأَعَدَّ لَهُمْ
سَعِيرًا ﴿٦٤﴾ خَـٰلِدِينَ فِيهَآ أَبَدًا ۖ لَّا يَجِدُونَ
وَلِيًّا وَلَا نَصِيرًا ﴿٦٥﴾ يَوْمَ تُقَلَّبُ وُجُوهُهُمْ
فِى ٱلنَّارِ يَقُولُونَ يَـٰلَيْتَنَآ أَطَعْنَا ٱللَّهَ وَأَطَعْنَا
ٱلرَّسُولَا۠ ﴿٦٦﴾ وَقَالُوا۟ رَبَّنَآ إِنَّآ أَطَعْنَا سَادَتَنَا
وَكُبَرَآءَنَا فَأَضَلُّونَا ٱلسَّبِيلَا۠ ﴿٦٧﴾ رَبَّنَآ ءَاتِهِمْ
ضِعْفَيْنِ مِنَ ٱلْعَذَابِ وَٱلْعَنْهُمْ لَعْنًا
كَبِيرًا ﴿٦٨﴾ يَـٰٓأَيُّهَا ٱلَّذِينَ ءَامَنُوا۟ لَا تَكُونُوا۟
كَٱلَّذِينَ ءَاذَوْا۟ مُوسَىٰ

---

117. For other instances in point see *al-A'rāf* 7:187, *al-Nāzi'āt* 79:42–46; *Saba'* 34:3–5, *al-Mulk* 67:24–27; *al-Muṭaffifīn* 83:10–17; *al-Ḥijr* 15:2–3; *al-Furqān* 25:27–29 and *Ḥā' Mīm al-Sajdah* 41:46–49.

118. We should bear in mind that the Qur'ānic expression "O believers" denotes at places those who truly believe while at other places it denotes the community of Muslims as a whole. In the latter instance, the word "believers" comprehends both true believers and hypocrites. Moreover, the Qur'ān occasionally addresses the hypocrites directly. When hypocrites and people of infirm faith are addressed as "believers", the purpose is to put them to shame for their misdeeds despite their claim

and then Allah declared him quit of the ill they spoke about him; and he had a high standing with Allah.[119] (70) Believers, fear Allah and speak the truth: (71) Allah will set your deeds right for you and will forgive you your sins. Whoever obeys Allah and His Messenger has achieved a great triumph.

(72) We offered the trust to the heavens and the earth ▶

فَبَرَّأَهُ ٱللَّهُ مِمَّا قَالُوا۟ ۚ وَكَانَ عِندَ ٱللَّهِ
وَجِيهًا ﴿٦٩﴾ يَٰٓأَيُّهَا ٱلَّذِينَ ءَامَنُوا۟ ٱتَّقُوا۟ ٱللَّهَ
وَقُولُوا۟ قَوْلًا سَدِيدًا ﴿٧٠﴾ يُصْلِحْ لَكُمْ
أَعْمَٰلَكُمْ وَيَغْفِرْ لَكُمْ ذُنُوبَكُمْ ۗ
وَمَن يُطِعِ ٱللَّهَ وَرَسُولَهُۥ فَقَدْ فَازَ
فَوْزًا عَظِيمًا ﴿٧١﴾ إِنَّا عَرَضْنَا ٱلْأَمَانَةَ عَلَى
ٱلسَّمَٰوَٰتِ وَٱلْأَرْضِ

---

to have faith. One can easily ascertain from the context what kind of people are meant when the expression "O you believers" is used. In the verse under study, it is the Muslims as a whole who are addressed.

119. Muslims are asked not to behave like Jews. They should not act towards the Prophet (peace be on him) in the manner the Jews did *vis-à-vis* the Prophet Moses (peace be on him). Although the Jews look upon the Prophet Moses (peace be on him) as their great benefactor, their actual conduct towards him is recorded in the following Biblical passages: *Exodus* 5:20–21, 14:11–12, 16:2–3 and 17:3–5; and *Numbers* 11:1–15 and 14:1–10.

The Qur'ān draws attention to the Jews' ingratitude towards the Prophet Moses (peace be on him) and warns the Muslims not to do the same in relation to the Prophet Muḥammad (peace be on him). They are warned that if they do so, they will face the same end that befell the Jews. On several occasions the Prophet (peace be on him) drew attention to this. For example, he once distributed the booty among Muslims. When they left the scene, someone said: "Today Muḥammad (peace be on him) did not fear God or the Hereafter in his distribution of booty". This was overheard by 'Abd Allāh ibn Mas'ūd who reported it to the Prophet (peace be on him). In reply, however, he said to him: "May God's mercy be upon Moses. He was subjected to even greater suffering (*adhā*) and yet he remained patient". (Tirmidhī, *Bāb Faḍl Azwāj al-Nabī;* Abū Dā'ūd, *Kitāb al-Ādāb* and Aḥmad ibn Ḥanbal, *Musnad,* narrated by 'Abd Allāh ibn Mas'ūd.)

and the mountains, but they refused to carry it and were afraid of doing so; but man carried it. Surely he is wrong-doing, ignorant.[120] (73) (The consequence of man's carrying the trust is) that Allah may chastise hypocritical men and hypocritical women and accept the repentance of believing men and believing women. He is Most Forgiving, Most Merciful.

وَٱلْجِبَالِ فَأَبَيْنَ أَن يَحْمِلْنَهَا وَأَشْفَقْنَ مِنْهَا
وَحَمَلَهَا ٱلْإِنسَٰنُ ۖ إِنَّهُۥ كَانَ ظَلُومًا
جَهُولًا ﴿٧٢﴾ لِّيُعَذِّبَ ٱللَّهُ ٱلْمُنَٰفِقِينَ
وَٱلْمُنَٰفِقَٰتِ وَٱلْمُشْرِكِينَ وَٱلْمُشْرِكَٰتِ
وَيَتُوبَ ٱللَّهُ عَلَى ٱلْمُؤْمِنِينَ وَٱلْمُؤْمِنَٰتِ ۗ
وَكَانَ ٱللَّهُ غَفُورًا رَّحِيمًا ﴿٧٣﴾

---

120. Concluding the discussion on this question, God draws man's attention to his true position in this world. If he behaves irresponsibly, treating life in the world as though it were a mere play and sport, and follows a wrong path, he will court destruction. The word "trust" used here denotes man's vicegerency, with which he was invested on earth. What the Qur'ān calls "trust" is referred to in *al-Baqarah* 2:30 as *khilāfah* (vicegerency), which has been conferred upon man. God has granted man the freedom to obey or to defy Him. He has also granted man the power and authority which he exercises in harnessing to use God's numerous creatures in exercise of the freedom so granted him. The inevitable and logical consequence of this is that man will be held responsible for his actions and will be recompensed for both his good and evil deeds. Man does not enjoy power and authority of his own. Rather, God has conferred it on him. Accordingly, he is accountable to God for his exercise of that power and authority. In view of these considerations, the Qur'ān employs the expression "trust" and "vicegerency" for describing man's position in the world's scheme of things.

The idea that the task of vicegerency is crushingly heavy is conveyed through the description of the heavens and earth which, notwithstanding their massiveness, shrank from accepting it. It was man who shouldered this burdensome task in spite of his infirmities and weaknesses. That the heavens and the earth declined to shoulder this responsibility may be meant literally or be a metaphorical representation of the truth. We can neither accurately know or comprehend the true state of God's relationship with His creatures. For us, the earth, the sun, the moon and the mountains appear to be deaf and dumb. That may, however, not be the case in their relationship with God. It is, therefore, likely that when God asked them to bear this great responsibility, they trembled with fear and expressed their inability to do so. They may even have petitioned God that they would prefer to remain His subservient creatures, unencumbered with free will and choice. Alternatively, they may have declined the offer of free will fearing that they might not be able to acquit themselves of the responsibilities flowing from it. Likewise, another possibility is that before the present phase of existence, God had granted a particular form to the entire human species and they expressed their willingness to undertake this responsibility. There is no valid reason to rule this out as a possibility. Only he who suffers from illusions about his intellectual calibre might dismiss this out of hand. Equally tenable is the view that the whole description is allegorical and is simply aimed at emphasising the extraordinary nature of the situation. God Himself describes the scene as though the massive earth, the heavens and the mountains stood on one side and man, of five or six feet, on the other. God asked all those present as to who would take up the role of His vicegerent. He made it clear that the creature taking up this role would be free to affirm God's supremacy and obey His command out of choice or he may refuse to do so, rising in revolt against Him. After having granted this authority, God would retire from the scene as if He were no longer there. Vast power and immense potential would be conferred upon man, along with the ability for him who took up the role to lord it over other creatures. However, at an appointed hour, this creature would be taken to task. Those who had misused the freedom granted by God would be subjected to a punishment that had not been inflicted upon anyone before. Conversely, those who faithfully obeyed God and refrained from disobeying Him, although they could have done so, will be granted unprecedented reward. All were then asked: who of you is ready to shoulder this task?

This offer left all awe-struck, with one creature after another expressing their inability to shoulder this responsibility. After others had declined the offer, man expressed his readiness to accept it. He accepted this offer in the hope of attaining the highest position in God's dominion. He was willing to face all the risks to which he was exposed in the hope of winning great rewards.

The whole scenario brings to mind the onerousness of man's responsibility. It is a great pity that man does not realise the greatness of his role. God, therefore, brands man as "ignorant" and "wrong-doing". He is "ignorant" in so far as he is not cognizant of the immense responsibility he is carrying. He is also "wrong-doing" in so far as he is inviting destruction upon himself and numerous other creatures by his misdeeds.

Appendix to *Sūrah al-Aḥzāb*[1]

The Finality of Prophethood

Some people in our time have come up with the mischievous notion of a new Prophethood.[2] They have done so by implanting an altogether novel interpretation to the expression *'khātam al-nabīyīn'* that occurs in verse 40 of *Sūrah al-Aḥzāb*. They thereby claim that the implication of the verse is that all Prophets who will be raised in the future will bear the stamp of the "seal of the Prophets" (that is, Muḥammad – peace be on him). To put it differently, their contention is that there will appear no Prophet in the future who does not bear the Prophet Muḥammad's stamp.

The context in which this verse occurs, however, does not permit any such interpretation. Not only that, this interpretation is quite discordant with the main thrust of the Qur'ānic passage.[3] The discourse here consists of refuting the objections made about the Prophet's marriage with Zaynab and removing the misgivings created by Islam's enemies. Against this backdrop, does it make sense to assert – and that too quite abruptly in the middle of the

---

1. The text of the Appendix has been slightly abridged. It should be studied in conjunction with n. 77 to *Sūrah al-Aḥzāb* – Ed.

2. This refers to Mirzā Ghulām Aḥmad of Qādiyān, who claimed to be God's Prophet, as well as to his followers who are generally known as Qādiyānīs or Aḥmadīs. Since the finality of the last of all Prophets Muḥammad (peace be on him) was vigorously denied by Mirzā Ghulām Aḥmad and his followers, the Appendix is devoted to a discussion of their religious doctrines and their ramifications – Ed.

3. In order to appreciate the thrust of the discourse, see nn. 67–79 to this *sūrah*.

verse – that the Prophet Muḥammad (peace be on him) is the seal of those Prophets who will appear in the future, that all such Prophets will carry his seal? By no stretch of the imagination does this contention fit with the context. If at all, such a statement could only weaken the impact of the argument directed at the Prophet's detractors. These detractors could have exploited such a statement for their own ends, claiming that the Prophet (peace be on him) did not have any pressing reason to marry Zaynab; that had it really been important to extirpate the custom of adoption, this could also be accomplished by some future Prophet who would bear the Prophet Muḥammad's seal!

These people further explain the expression '*khātam al-nabīyīn*' to mean that Muḥammad (peace be on him) was the most superior Prophet. According to their opinion, although the Prophet Muḥammad (peace be on him) represents Prophethood *par excellence*, the door of Prophethood is still open and other Prophets will keep coming after him though they will not be of the same stature. This interpretation also carries the same flaw we noted above; that it is incongruous with the context. Not only that, in fact it negates the import of the Qur'ānic passage altogether. For the unbelievers and hypocrites could have easily argued that the Prophets of the future, though less distinguished than the Prophet Muḥammad (peace be on him), could still accomplish the tasks that he might have left unfinished. Since the advent of other Prophets was anticipated, it was not at all necessary for the Prophet Muḥammad (peace be on him) himself to put an end to the institution of adoption.

The Literal Meaning of *Khātam al-Nabīyīn*

The context requires that the Qur'ānic appellation *khātam al-nabīyīn* be interpreted in no other sense than that of the finality of Prophethood: namely, that no Prophet will ever appear after the Prophet Muḥammad (peace be on him). This, however, is not only the requirement of the text but also accords with the meaning of the word *khātam* in Arabic. For both the literal meaning and idiomatic usage of the word mean "to seal, to close, to reach the end, and to finish a task". Consider the following by way of illustration:

khatam al-'amal means *faragha min al-'amal*: "he finished the task";

khatam al-inā': "he closed the mouth of the utensil and sealed it [so that nothing should go out of or enter it]";

khatam al-kitāb: "he closed the letter and sealed it [to make it secure]";

khatama al-qalb: "he sealed the heart [so that it neither comprehends anything new nor forgets anything already learnt]";

khitāmu mashrūbin: "the taste left behind by a drink after it has been drunk";

khātamatu kulli shay'in: *'āqibatuhu wa ākhiratuhu*: the final result and end of everything;

khatam al-shay': meaning that something has reached its end. In this very sense is understood the expression *khatm al-Qur'ān* (completion of the reading of the Qur'ān till its end), and it is the same sense that the last verses of a *sūrah* are known as its *khawātīm*; and

khātam al-qawm: meaning the last person of the tribe. (See *Lisān al-'Arab, Qāmūs, Aqrab al-Mawārid*).[4]

---

4. We have referred here only to three standard Arabic lexicons. This point, however, has not only been made in these three, but in all standard Arabic lexicons. All provide the same definition of *khātam*. However, those who do not believe in the finality of Muḥammad's Prophethood resort to interpreting the word *khātam* in a figurative sense. For them, the conferment of the title *khātam al-shu'arā'* or *khātam al-fuqahā'* or *khātam al-mufassirīn* on someone does not mean that no poet or jurist or *mufassir* will ever be born after him. Rather, these titles emphasise the paramount standing of a person in his field.

In any case, it should be noted that the use of the word *khātam* in a figurative sense, meaning "perfect" or "most superior", does not imply that that would become the literal meaning of the word and its use in the sense of "last" would therefore be flawed. In fact such a position can only be taken by those who are not aware of the basics of linguistics. In no language can the occasionally used figurative meaning of a word become its real meaning. If one says to an Arab *jā'a khātam al-qawm*, he will take it to mean that the whole tribe has arrived, including the last member of that tribe. He will not consider it to mean that the most perfect or the most accomplished member of the tribe has arrived.

Let us also note that titles such as *khātam al-shu'arā'*, *khātam al-fuqahā'*, *khātam al-muḥaddithīn* are conferred by fellow human beings. Now, no human being is

In view of this Arabic usage, all lexicographers and *Tafsīr* scholars are agreed that *khātam al-nabīyīn* means "the last of the Prophets". In Arabic idiom, *khātam* does not carry the connotation of a seal used in the post office for marking letters. Rather, it refers to the seal put on an envelope in order to make it firmly secure.

Aḥādīth on the Finality of Prophethood

This meaning of *khātam al-nabīyīn*, as derived from the Qur'ānic context and Arabic lexicon, is reinforced by the following authentic *aḥādīth*, all of which affirm the doctrine of the finality of Prophethood:

i. The Prophet (peace be on him) said: "The Prophets used to lead the Israelites. When a Prophet passed away, another Prophet replaced him as his successor. However, there will be no Prophet after me; rather, there will only be caliphs". (Bukhārī, *Kitāb al-Manāqib, Bāb mā Dhukira 'an Banī Isrā'īl.*)
ii. The Prophet (peace be on him) said: "The likeliness of the parable to illustrate the relationship between me and the Prophets who preceded me is this: Someone erected a beautiful, magnificent mansion. However, a brick was missing in a corner. People visited and admired the mansion, yet they asked: 'Why was the missing brick not put in its place?' I am that missing brick – I am *khātam al-nabīyīn*". In other words, Muḥammad's Prophethood marks the culmination of the institution of Prophethood. No gap is left after it for anyone to fill. (Bukhārī, *Kitāb al-Manāqib, Bāb Khātam al-Nabīyīn.*)

---

capable of knowing whether a person with the same degree of excellence will be born in the future or not. Hence, in human usage, these titles convey, at most, an emphatic and exaggerated tribute to a person in recognition of his excellence in some field. However, when a person says about someone that a certain quality ends with him, this can only be taken in a figurative sense. The case of God, however, is different. Had God called someone *khātam al-shua'arā'*, no poet could have been born after him. By the same token, since God designates the Prophet Muḥammad (peace be on him) as *khātam al-nabīyīn*, there cannot be any Prophet after him in the future, for God knows the Unseen that lies beyond man's perception. The use of the word *khātam* by God and man do not and cannot have the same meaning.

Four *aḥādīth* of a similar import occur in Muslim under the chapter *Kitāb al-Faḍā'il, Bāb Khātam al-Nabīyīn*. The last *ḥadīth* on this subject contains the following words: "So I appeared and I have brought to an end the chain of Prophets". The same *ḥadīth* is included in Tirmidhī's collection. (See *Kitāb al-Manāqib, Bāb Faḍl al-Nabī* and *Kitāb al-Ādāb, Bāb al-Amthāl*.)

In the *Musnad* of Abū Dā'ūd al-Ṭayālisī, this *ḥadīth* is bracketed with the *aḥādīth* narrated by Jābir ibn 'Abd Allāh. It ends with these words: "With me the Prophets come to an end". In the *Musnad* of Aḥmad ibn Ḥanbal, a variant of the same *ḥadīth* features on the authority of Ubayy ibn Ka'b, Abū Sa'īd al-Khudrī and Abū Hurayrah.

iii. The Prophet (peace be on him) said: "I have been granted excellence over [other] Prophets on the following six counts: (a) I have been granted the ability to make pithy statements. (b) I have been reinforced with the ability to inspire awe. (c) Spoils of war have been made lawful for me. (d) The earth has been made for me both a place of worship and a means for gaining purity. [This refers to the fact that Islam permits offering Prayers anywhere on earth, not necessarily just inside a mosque. Likewise, if water is not available for *wuḍū'* or for taking a bath, clay may be used for making *tayammum* in its place.] (e) I have been sent as a Prophet to the whole world, and (f) With me the Prophets come to an end". (Muslim, *Kitāb al-Masājid wa Mawāḍi' al-Ṣalāh*, and Tirmidhī, *Kitāb al-Siyar, Bāb mā jā'a fī al-Ghanīmah* ...)

iv. The Prophet (peace be on him) observed: "Prophethood and Messengership have come to an end. So there will be no Messenger after me, nor any Prophet". (Tirmidhī, *Kitāb al-Ru'yā, Bāb Dhahāb al-Nubūwah*, and Aḥmad ibn Ḥanbal, *Musnad*, narrated by Anas ibn Mālik.)

v. The Prophet (peace be on him) said: "I am Muḥammad. I am Aḥmad. I am Māḥī in so far as unbelief will be obliterated at my hands. I am Ḥāshir, for after my departure, people will be mustered [on the Day of Judgement to the Grand Assembly]. [In other words, the Last Day is imminent after my demise.] I am 'Āqib who will not be followed by any Prophet". (Bukhārī and Muslim, *Kitāb al-Faḍā'il, Bāb Asmā' al-Nabī*; Tirmidhī, *Kitāb al-Ādāb, Bāb Asmā' al-Nabī;* Mālik ibn Anas, *Muwaṭṭa', Kitāb Asmā' al-Nabī*, and al-Ḥākim, *al-Mustadrak, Kitāb Tawarīkh al-Anbiyā', Bāb Dhikr Nabī Allāh wa Rūḥihi 'Īsā.*)

vi. The Prophet (peace be on him) came out of his home and said: "God did not send any Prophet but that he warned his community against Dajjāl. [However, Dajjāl did not appear during their time.] I am the Last Prophet and you are the last community. Inevitably, Dajjāl will appear in your time". (Ibn Mājah, *Kitāb al-Fitan, Bāb al-Dajjāl.*)

vii. 'Abd al-Raḥmān ibn Jubayr reports that he heard 'Abd Allāh ibn 'Amr ibn al-'Āṣ say: "One day the Prophet (peace be on him) got out of his home and came to us. It appeared from his gestures that he was bidding farewell to us. He said thrice: 'I am Muḥammad, the unlettered Prophet'. He added: 'There is no Prophet after me' ". (Aḥmad ibn Ḥanbal, *Musnad*, narrated by 'Abd Allāh ibn 'Amr ibn al-'Āṣ.)

viii. The Prophet (peace be on him) said: "There is no Prophethood after me. There will only be *mubashshirāt* (good tidings)". He was asked to clarify what he meant by *mubashshirāt*. He replied: "A true or righteous vision". [In other words, the sending down of any further revelation is out of the question. At most, someone may be granted a directive by means of a true or righteous vision.] (Aḥmad ibn Ḥanbal, *Musnad*, narrated by Abū al-Ṭufayl; *Aḥādīth* of a similar import are mentioned in Abū Dā'ūd, *Kitāb al-Rukū' wa al-Sujūd, Bāb fī al-Du'ā' fī al-Rukū'* and Nasā'ī, *Kitāb al-Taṭbīq, Bāb Ta'ẓīm al-Rabb fī al-Rukū'.*)

ix. The Prophet (peace be on him) said: "Had there been a Prophet after me, he would be 'Umar ibn al-Khaṭṭāb". (Tirmidhī, *Kitāb al-Manāqib, Bāb fī Manāqib 'Umar ibn al-Khaṭṭāb.*)

x. The Prophet (peace be on him) told 'Alī: "You are to me like Aaron to Moses (peace be on them). However, there is no Prophet after me." (Muslim, *Kitāb Faḍā'il al-Ṣaḥābah, Bāb min Faḍā'il 'Alī ibn abī Ṭālib.*)

The above *ḥadīth* has also been reported by Bukhārī in the context of the Expedition of Tabūk. Two *aḥādīth* of similar import also feature in the *Musnad* of Aḥmad ibn Ḥanbal on the authority of Sa'd ibn Abī Waqqāṣ. The concluding statement of these *aḥādīth* is: "There is no Prophethood after me". Abū Dā'ūd al-Ṭayālisī, Aḥmad ibn Ḥanbal and Muḥammad ibn Isḥāq have related extensive reports on this subject. After reading them, it becomes clear that the Prophet (peace be on him) had decided at the time of his departure on the Expedition of Tabūk to leave 'Alī behind to oversee the safety and security of Madīnah. On learning this, the hypocrites began passing derogatory remarks against him. 'Alī went to the Prophet (peace be on him) and asked him: "Are you leaving me in the midst of women and children?" The Prophet (peace be on him) comforted him by saying: "Your relationship with me is the same as that of Aaron with Moses (peace be on them)". What he meant to say was that in the same way that the Prophet Moses (peace be on him) had placed the Children of Israel in the Prophet Aaron's care when he left for Mount Sinai, so had the Prophet (peace be on him) entrusted the defence of Madīnah to 'Alī. Fearing that portraying him as someone similar to the Prophet Aaron (peace be on him) might subsequently give rise to any dangerous misgiving, he immediately clarified that no Prophet would ever appear after him.

xi. Thawbān narrates that the Prophet (peace be on him) said: "Thirty big liars will appear in my community, each of whom will claim to be a Prophet. However, I am the last of the Prophets. There is no Prophet after me". (Abū Dā'ūd, *Kitāb al-Fitan wa al-Malāḥim, Bāb Dhikr al-Fitan wa Dalā'ilihā.*)

xii. The Prophet (peace be on him) said: "Among the Children of Israel, who preceded you, there were some who were spoken to (*yukallamūn*) [by God], even though they were not God's Prophets. If there will be any such person in my community, it will be 'Umar". (Bukhārī, *Kitāb Faḍā'il al-Ṣaḥābah, Bāb Manāqib 'Umar bin al-Khaṭṭāb.*)

In its variant version recorded by Muslim, the expression *muḥaddathūn* is used in place of *yukallamūn*. However, the two mean the same, and refer to those who have had the privilege of being spoken to by God, or being spoken to from the Unseen. It is thus clear from this *ḥadīth* that if any one Muslim were to be granted this privilege, it would have been 'Umar.

xiii. The Prophet (peace be on him) proclaimed: "There will be no Prophet after me. Nor will there be any *ummah* after my *ummah*". (Bayhaqī, *Kitāb al-Ru'yā*, and Ṭabarānī, *al-Mu'jam al-Kabīr*.)

xiv. The Prophet (peace be on him) said: "I am the Last Prophet and mine is the last mosque (of any Prophet)".[5] (Muslim, *Kitāb al-Ḥajj, Bāb Faḍā'il al-Ṣalāh bi Masjid Makkah wa al-Madīnah.*)

---

5. Those who deny the finality of Muḥammad's Prophethood cite this *ḥadīth* in support of their position, pointing out that the expression *ākhir al-masājid* (last of the mosques) was used for the Prophet's Mosque in Madīnah by the Prophet (peace be on him) himself. They contend that it is called the last of the mosques even though numerous mosques were built after it. Going by the same analogy, they maintain that despite the Prophet's title of being *khātam al-nabīyīn*, other Prophets will keep appearing. They affirm that he is, nonetheless, the last Prophet in terms of his excellence and his mosque will be the last mosque.

Such far-fetched and preposterous contentions betray the total inability of these people to comprehend the words of God and His Messenger (peace be on him). The expression *ākhir al-masājid* occurs in a *ḥadīth* in Muslim's *Ṣaḥīḥ*. On studying it along with the other *aḥādīth* on the same subject, one can easily grasp the sense in which the Prophet (peace be on him) spoke of his mosque as the last of the mosques. According to the traditions on the authority by Abū Hurayrah, 'Abd Allāh ibn 'Umar and Maymūnah in Muslim's *Ṣaḥīḥ*, the Prophet (peace be on him) declared three mosques to be higher in rank than all others and anyone who prays in them receives one thousand times the reward for praying elsewhere. It is, therefore, permissible to undertake a journey to these mosques to offer Prayer in them. On the contrary, it is not permissible to travel to any other mosque specifically for the purpose of praying in it. Of these three, the first one is Masjid al-Ḥarām built by the Prophet Abraham (peace be on him); the second is the Aqṣā Mosque, built by the Prophet Solomon (peace be on him), and the third is the Prophet's Mosque in Madīnah. The purport of the above *ḥadīth* is that since no Prophet will come after the Prophet Muḥammad (peace be on him), there will not be any other mosque after the Prophet's Mosque in Madīnah which will have the distinction that praying in it will fetch a higher reward (than praying in ordinary mosques) and for which it would be permissible to undertake a journey.

A large number of Companions narrated these *aḥādīth* from the Prophet (peace be on him) and many *Ḥadīth* scholars have cited them with strong chains of narrators. After studying them it becomes evident that on several occasions, in a variety of ways, and using a variety of expressions, the Prophet (peace be on him) stressed that he was the last Prophet and that no Prophet would appear after him. He made it absolutely clear that with him Prophethood came to an end. Those who would lay claim to be Prophets or Messengers after him would be liars and impostors.[6]

This is the evident and authentic meaning and implication of the Qur'ānic expression *khātam al-nabīyīn*. The Prophet's statements represent the clinching argument and final word on the issue. In this instance, he is elucidating a Qur'ānic text which makes his elucidation all the more authoritative and binding. Who can be better placed than the Prophet (peace be on him) to comprehend and explain the Qur'ānic teaching on the finality of Prophethood?

The Companions' Consensus

Next in rank to the Qur'ān and the *Sunnah* comes the consensus of the Companions. History bears out that soon after the Prophet's demise the Companions waged war against all false claimants to Prophethood as well as against their followers.

In this connection particular mention should be made of the incident of Musaylimah (d. 12 AH/633 CE) generally called

---

6. Those rejecting the finality of Muḥammad's Prophethood are able to cite, at most, the following report from 'Ā'ishah in which she says: "Say that he (the Prophet Muḥammad, peace be on him) is *khātam al-anbīyā'* but do not say that there is no Prophet after him". First, it is the height of audacity to cite anyone's saying to refute the Prophet's own categorical statement. Furthermore, this particular report ascribed to 'Ā'ishah is quite unreliable. No notable *Ḥadīth* scholar has recorded it. It is found only in a single work of *tafsīr*, *al-Durr al-Manthūr,* and in a single dictionary on *Ḥadīth*, *Takmilat Majma' al-Biḥār*. This tradition, however, is devoid of any chain of narrators. This is an absolutely weak tradition which is the statement of a Companion [rather than that of the Prophet, peace be on him]. Strangely, this tradition is presented as against the Prophet's own authentic statements which have been narrated by all the leading *Ḥadīth* scholars and are supported by reliable chains of narrators.

Musaylimah the Liar. Although he did not deny that Muḥammad (peace be on him) was a Prophet, he nevertheless claimed to be his associate in Prophethood. In this respect, he once wrote the following to the Prophet Muḥammad (peace be on him): "From Musaylimah the Messenger of God to Muḥammad, the Messenger of God. Peace be upon you. You should know that I have been made your associate in your mission [of Prophethood]". (Ṭabarī, *Ta'rīkh*, Vol. 2, p. 399.) Ṭabarī also informs us that the *adhān* pronounced under Musaylimah included the usual declaration: "I bear witness that Muḥammad is the Messenger of God". Notwithstanding Musaylimah's categorical affirmation of Muḥammad's Prophethood, he was declared to be an unbeliever and outside the fold of the Muslim community and a war was waged against him. It is on record that the members of the Ḥanīfah tribe had professed belief in Musaylimah in good faith; they had been misled into believing that the Prophet Muḥammad (peace be on him) had himself taken Musaylimah as his associate in his Prophetic mission. Furthermore, a person who had studied the Qur'ān in Madīnah gave them the false impression that the Qur'ānic verses had been revealed to Musaylimah. (Ibn Kathīr, *al-Bidāyah wa al-Nihāyah*, Cairo, Dār Iḥyā' al-Turāth al-'Arabī, 1988, 1st ed., Vol. 5, p. 62.)

Notwithstanding this, the Companions refused to accept Banū Ḥanīfah [who had accepted Musaylimah's claim to Prophethood] to be Muslims and fought against them. There is no basis for the contention that the fighting against them was on account of their rebellion rather than apostasy. For, according to Islamic law, rebel Muslims who are taken prisoners of war cannot be enslaved. Even rebellious *dhimmīs* cannot be held as slaves. However, when an attack was launched against Musaylimah and his followers, Caliph Abū Bakr proclaimed that their women and children would be enslaved and that is what happened. One of the female slaves fell to 'Alī's share and later gave birth to a leading Islamic personality, Muḥammad ibn al-Ḥanafīyah.[7] (Ibid., Vol. 6, p. 358.) It is evident

7. The word al-Ḥanafīyah refers to a lady of the Banū Ḥanīfah tribe, which is reflected in the name of this son of 'Ālī.

from this account that the Companions fought against Banū Ḥanīfah not because they had risen in revolt, but because they had accepted Musaylimah's claim to Prophethood after the Prophet's demise. This action was immediately taken up after the Prophet's demise under Caliph Abū Bakr's leadership and was endorsed by the entire body of Companions. This is a clear instance of the Companions' consensus.

The Consensus of *'Ulamā'*

Another clinching argument in matters of faith is the consensus of the *'ulamā'* down the ages. Now, from the very early days of Islam the unanimous opinion of the *'ulamā'* of every time and place has been that there can be no Prophet after the Prophet Muḥammad (peace be on him) and, hence, whoever lays claim to Prophethood or believes in any such claimant is an unbeliever and so outside the fold of Islam. Here are various pieces of evidence that substantiate this:

i. In the days of Imām Abū Ḥanīfah (al-Nu'mān ibn Thābit, d. 150 AH/765 CE), someone laid claim to be a Prophet and requested that he be provided an opportunity to present the signs of his Prophethood. Upon learning this, Abū Ḥanīfah remarked: "Whoever asks such a person to present the signs of his Prophethood will also become an unbeliever. For the Prophet Muḥammad (peace be on him) has already declared: 'There is no Prophet after me' ". (Ibn Aḥmad al-Makkī, *Manāqib al-Imām al-A'ẓam Abī Ḥanīfah*, Hyderabad, India, 1321 AH, Vol. 1, p. 161.)
ii. While explaining verse 40 of *Sūrah al-Aḥzāb*, Ibn Jarīr al-Ṭabarī (d. 310 AH/920 CE) says: "The Prophet Muḥammad's advent marked an end of Prophethood. This door will not be opened for anyone till the Last Day". (Ṭabarī, *Tafsīr*, comments on verse 40, *Sūrah al-Aḥzāb*.)
iii. In his *al-'Aqīdah al-Salafīyah*, Imām Abū Ja'far Aḥmad ibn Muḥammad al-Azdī al-Ṭaḥāwī (321 AH/935 CE) while mentioning the doctrines of the pious forbears,

especially of Imām Abū Ḥanīfah, Imām Abū Yūsuf and Imām Muḥammad ibn al-Ḥasan, says the following about Prophethood: "The Prophet Muḥammad (peace be on him) is God's exalted servant, His choicest Prophet, His favourite Messenger, the last of all Prophets, the leader of the pious, the chief of the Messengers, and the beloved of the Lord of the worlds. Every claim to Prophethood after him amounts to error and slavery of the carnal self" (Abī al-'Izz al-Hanafī, *Sharḥ al-Ṭaḥāwīyah fī al-'Aqīdah al-Salafīyah*, Riyadh, Wakālat al-Ṭibā'ah wa al-Tarjamah, 1413 AH, pp. 108, 118, 119, 123 and 124.)

iv. Abū Muḥammad 'Alī ibn Aḥmad Ibn Ḥazm al-Andalusī (d. 456 AH/1064 CE) says: "It is certain that Divine revelation ended with the Prophet Muḥammad's demise. Its self-evident proof is that revelation is sent only to a Prophet. And God has specified that the Prophet Muḥammad (peace be on him) is the last of the Prophets". (*Sūrah al-Aḥzāb* 33:40.) (Ibn Ḥazm, *Al-Muḥallā, Kitāb Masā'il al-Tawḥīd, Faṣl al-Waḥy qad Inqaṭa'a...*)

v. Imām Abū Ḥāmid Muḥammad ibn Muḥammad al-Ghazzālī[8] (d. 505 AH/1111 CE) maintains: "If this door is opened (that is, the door of rejecting consensus as a decisive proof), this would lead to many an outrage. For example, if one were to contend that the advent of a Messenger is possible even after our Prophet Muḥammad (peace be on him), there should be no reluctance in declaring such a person to be an unbeliever. However, when this matter comes up for discussion, anyone who wants to prove that there should be no reluctance in refuting the possibility of Prophethood, he is bound to have recourse to consensus. This because reason as such does not exclude this possibility. As for the saying narrated from the Prophet: 'There will be no Prophet after me', or God's declaration that the Prophet is *khātam*

8. We are reproducing this opinion of Imām Ghazzālī (*sic*) *in extenso* since his affirmation of the finality of Muḥammad's Prophethood has been vigorously contested by those who do not believe in that doctrine.

al-nabīyīn, these will not prevent people from trying to explain this away. Such people are likely to contend that the expression *khātam al-nabīyīn* (in *al-Aḥzāb* 33:40) means only "the Messengers of great resolve" (*ulū al-'Azm min al-Rusūl*). If they point out that the word *nabīyīn* is of general import, it will not be difficult for them to qualify.

As to the Prophet Muḥammad's proclamation that there will be no Prophet (*Nabī*) after him, the exponent of the false view might insist that the door is still open for the appearance of a Messenger (*Rusūl*) after him on the grounds that the word that occurs in the tradition is "Prophet" rather than "Messenger". He can also put forward the claim that there is a distinction between Prophets and Messengers and that Prophets have a rank above that of Messengers, and so he can keep putting forward silly points such as these and others in order to vindicate his false position. It is not, of course, hard to keep quibbling about words which are amenable to even more fantastic interpretations. Anyone engaged in this kind of nonsense cannot be dismissed as utterly inadmissible on verbal grounds for we have come across even more unusual interpretations and have yet not declared such people guilty of nullifying the texts. Such people will be refuted by pointing out that the consensus of the Muslim community's understanding of this statement ["there will be no Prophet after me"] and its related context has been that there will never appear any Prophet nor any Messenger after the Prophet himself". It is also a unanimously held doctrine of the Muslim community that this matter is not open to any other interpretation or qualification. Anyone subscribing to a divergent view on this issue is guilty of rejecting the consensus view of the community. (Ghazzālī (*sic*), *al-Iqtiṣād fī al-I'tiqād, al-Quṭb al-Rābi': Ithbāt Nabūwat Nabīyinā Muḥammad... , Bāb Bayān man Yajib Takfīrihi min al-Firaq*.)

vi. Abū Muḥammad Ḥusayn ibn Mas'ūd al-Baghawī (d. 510 AH/1122 CE) who is celebrated for his distinguished services to the *Sunnah*, states in his exegesis *Ma'ālim al-Tanzīl*: "God terminated Prophethood with the Prophet Muḥammad (peace be on him). He is thus the last of the Prophets... Ibn 'Abbās maintains that in this verse (*al-Aḥzāb* 33:40), God has declared that no Prophet will appear after him". (Al-Baghawī, *Ma'ālim al-Tanzīl,* comments *Sūrah al-Aḥzāb* 33:40).

vii. Abū al-Qāsim Maḥmūd ibn 'Umar ibn Muḥammad al-Zamakhsharī, (d. 538 AH/1143 CE) expressed the following opinion in his *tafsīr, al-Kashshāf*: "Let us take up the question of how the Prophet Muḥammad (peace be on him) can be regarded as the last Prophet in face of reports of the advent of the Prophet Jesus (peace be on him) towards the end of time. He [that is, Muḥammad] is the last Prophet in the sense that no one will be designated a Prophet after him. The Prophet Jesus (peace be on him) had been designated a Prophet before him. When he will return, he will return as an adherent of the Prophet Muḥammad's *Sharī'ah*, and will offer Prayer facing the *qiblah* prescribed for the Prophet (peace be on him), as though he were a member of the Prophet's *ummah*". (Zamakhsharī, *al-Kashshāf,* comments on verse 40, *Sūrah al-Aḥzāb* 33:40.)

viii. Qāḍī 'Iyāḍ, Abū al-Faḍl 'Iyāḍ ibn Mūsā ibn 'Iyāḍ ibn 'Amr (d. 544 AH/1149 CE) writes: "Anyone who claims to be a Prophet or believes that someone may acquire Prophethood by his efforts, that by purifying his heart he can attain the level of Prophethood as some philosophers and extravagant Sufis claim, or anyone who claims to receive revelation even though he does not declare himself to be a Prophet ... all such people are unbelievers and are guilty of rejecting the Prophet Muḥammad (peace be on him) for falsehood. This because he [that is, the Prophet] has informed us that he is the last of the Prophets and that no Prophet will come after him. He has conveyed to us God's message that Prophethood will end with him and that he is God's Messenger for all human beings. The entire Muslim community accepts the above statements literally and does not admit that any other interpretation is possible regarding this matter. In view of this consensus as well as on grounds of transmitted information there is no doubt that all such people are unbelievers." (*Al-Shifā', al-Qism al-Rābi' fī Ta'rīf Wujūh al-Aḥkām..., al-Bāb al-Thālith.*)

ix. In his celebrated work, *al-Milal wa al-Niḥal*, Tāj al-Dīn Abū al-Fatḥ Muḥammad ibn 'Abd al-Karīm al-Shahrastānī (d. 548 AH/1153 CE), writes: "Anyone who contends that there will appear a Prophet after the Prophet Muḥammad (peace be on him), except that it be for the second coming of the Prophet Jesus (peace be on him), is definitely an unbeliever and there is no difference of opinion on this question". (*Al-Milal wa al-Niḥal*, Vol. 3, p. 249.)

x. Fakhr al-Dīn al-Rāzī (606 AH/1210 CE), while elucidating the verse under discussion in his *al-Tafsīr al-Kabīr*, says: "The Qur'ān proclaims that the Prophet Muḥammad (peace be on him) is *khātam al-nabīyīn* in order to stress that had it been possible for some other Prophet to appear after him, he would have taken care of any gaps that remained in performance of his tasks of exhortation and elucidation. However, since no Prophet is to come after Muḥammad (peace be on him), he is exceedingly compassionate with his *ummah* and provides clear guidance. In so doing, he is akin to the father who realises that after he dies his child will have no guardian to look after him". (Rāzī, *al-Tafsīr al-Kabīr,* comments on verse 40, *Sūrah al-Aḥzāb* 33:40.)

xi. In like manner, 'Abd Allāh ibn 'Umar al-Bayḍāwī (d. 685 AH/1286 CE) says the following in his exegesis *Anwār al-Tanzīl*: "The Prophet Muḥammad (peace be on him) is the final Prophet, marking an end to the chain of Prophets, the whole institution thus having been sealed. The reappearance of the Prophet Jesus (peace be on him) after Muḥammad (peace be on him) is not in conflict with this. For, after his second coming, Jesus will follow the Prophet Muḥammad's faith". (Bayḍāwī, *Anwār al-Tanzīl*, comments on verse *Sūrah al-Aḥzāb* 33:40.)

xii. 'Abd Allāh ibn Aḥmad ibn Maḥmūd al-Nasafī (d. 710 AH/ 1310 CE) states in his *Madārik al-Tanzīl*: "He [the Prophet] is *khātam al-nabīyīn*, that is, he is the very last of all Prophets. No one will be appointed a Prophet after him. As for the Prophet Jesus (peace be on him), he was appointed to this office before the time of Muḥammad (peace be on him), and his descent (in the future), will be in his capacity as one of the followers of the *Sharī'ah* of the Muslim community", (Nasafī, *Madārik al-Tanzīl*, comments on verse 40, *Sūrah al-Aḥzāb*).

xiii. In his *Tafsīr al-Khāzin*, 'Alā' al-Dīn al-Baghdādī (d. 741 AH/1341 CE) says: "God concluded Prophethood with the Prophet Muḥammad (peace be on him). There is no Prophethood after him. Nor does he have any associate in his Prophethood. It is in God's knowledge that no Prophet will appear after him". (Baghdādī, *al-Khāzin*, comments on *Sūrah al-Aḥzāb* 33:40.)

xiv. The same truth is reiterated more emphatically in Ibn Kathīr's (d. 774 AH/1373 CE) influential *Tafsīr* as follows: "The verse categorically declares that there will be no Prophet after the Prophet Muḥammad (peace be on him). This being so, it is all the more evident that there cannot be any Messenger after him. For Messengership is more specific as compared to the office of Prophethood, which is of a more general nature. Every Messenger is a Prophet whereas every Prophet is not a Messenger. Anyone who lays claim to Prophethood after the Prophet Muḥammad's time is a liar, an impostor, is immersed in error, seeks to misguide others, and this is notwithstanding any supernatural spells and magical tricks he may have contrived. This ruling applies to every false claimant [to Prophethood] until the Last Day". (Ibn Kathīr, *Tafsīr*, comments on verse 40, *Sūrah al-Aḥzāb* 33:40.)

xv. In *al-Jalālayn*, Jalāl al-Dīn al-Suyūṭī (d. 911 AH/1505 CE) remarks: "The words *Wa kān Allāh bi kulli Shay'in 'Alīmā* (Allah has full knowledge of everything) means that God knows that there will be no Prophet after Muḥammad (peace be on him) and when Jesus (peace be on him) comes down to earth he will follow the *Sharī'ah* of the Prophet (peace be on him)". (Suyūṭī, *Jalālayn*, comments on *Sūrah al-Aḥzāb* 33:40.)

xvi. Aḥmad Ibn al-Nujaym (d. 970 AH/1563 CE) says: "If one does not believe that the Prophet Muḥammad (peace be on him) is the last of the Prophets, he is not a Muslim. This is so because it is one of the essential articles of faith which everyone ought to know and believe in", (Ibn al-Nujaym, *al-Ashbāh wa al-Naẓā'ir, Kitāb al-Siyar, Bāb al-Riddah*).

xvii. Mullā 'Alī ibn Sulṭān al-Qārī (d. 1016 AH/1605 CE) writes in his *Sharḥ al-Fiqh al-Akbar*: "According to consensus, any person's declaration of his Prophethood after Muḥammad (peace be on him) amounts to unbelief", (Mullā 'Alī al-Qārī, *Sharḥ al-Fiqh al-Akbar, Bāb Baḥth fī Ithbāt Nabūwat Muḥammad*).

xviii. Ismā'īl Ḥaqqī (d. 1137 AH/1725 CE) while explaining the verse under study in his *tafsīr*, *Rūḥ al-Bayān*, points out: "'Āṣim recited the word (i.e. *khātam*) with a *fatḥah,* which is a word that denotes an instrument used to seal something. What it thus meant is that the Prophet Muḥammad (peace be on him) is the last in the series of Prophets; that is, with him the door of Prophethood was sealed. Others recite the word with *kasrah* after *t*, that is, they read it as *khātim*, meaning thereby that the Prophet (peace be on him) was the one who sealed the door of Prophethood. This makes the word substantially an equivalent of the word *khātam*. Whatever be the recitation, [whether with *fatḥah* or *kasrah*] the two have the same meaning.

After the Prophet (peace be on him) the *'ulamā'* of the *ummah* will inherit from Muḥammad (peace be on him) only *wilāyāh* (sainthood) rather than Prophethood, for Prophethood ended with him. The descent of the Prophet Jesus (peace be on him) after the Prophet Muḥammad (peace be on him) does not pose any difficulty in grasping the above mentioned article of faith. Since the Prophet Muḥammad (peace be on him) was *khātam al-nabīyīn*, no Prophet will be raised after him. The Prophet Jesus (peace be on him) was appointed a Prophet before him. However, when he makes his reappearance, he will be like any other adherent of the *Sharī'ah* sent down to the Prophet Muḥammad (peace be on him). When he [that is, Jesus] will offer his Prayers, he will face the same *qiblah* prescribed in Islam for offering Prayers. He will be like any other member of the Muslim community. [After his second coming] he will not receive revelation. Nor will he prescribe any new commands on God's behalf. Rather, he will be the Prophet Muḥammad's *khalīfah*. *Ahl al-Sunnah wa al-Jamā'h* firmly believe that no Prophet will appear after the Prophet Muḥammad (peace be on him). This because God has proclaimed that he is *khātam al-nabīyīn*.

The Prophet (peace be on him) amplified this by asserting that there is no Prophet after him. If someone believes, on the contrary, in the advent of any Prophet after Muḥammad (peace be on him), he will be regarded as an unbeliever, for he is guilty of rejecting a categorical Islamic text. Likewise, anyone who harbours any doubt regarding this will also be declared an unbeliever for, thanks to overwhelming proof on the question, the truth stands distinct from falsehood. Whoever claims to be a Prophet after the Prophet Muḥammad (peace be on him) makes a patently false claim", (Ḥaqqī, *Rūḥ al-Bayān*, comments on *Sūrah al-Aḥzāb* 33:40).

xix. The following ruling is recorded in *Fatāwā-'i 'Ālamgīrī*, a collection of *fatāwā* compiled by the leading *'ulamā'* of the twelfth/eighteenth century at the behest of the Indian Muslim ruler, Aurangzeb 'Ālamgīr: "If someone does not accept the Prophet Muḥammad (peace be on him) as the Final Prophet, he is not a Muslim, and were someone to claim to be a Messenger or Prophet [after him], he will be declared an unbeliever". (*Fatāwā-'i 'Ālamgīrī, Kitāb al-Siyar, Bāb fī Aḥkām al-Murtaddīn*.)

xx. Muḥammad ibn 'Alī al-Shawkānī (d. 1250 AH/1834 CE) states in his exegesis, *Fatḥ al-Qāḍīr*: "The recitation which has gained wider currency is *khātim* while 'Āṣim's preference is for *khātam*. Taken in the former sense, the meaning is that the Prophet Muḥammad (peace be on him) marks the end of the chain of Prophets, that he appeared at the end of the series. In the latter sense, it signifies that he is like a seal for the Prophets in so far as he put an end to Prophethood and his inclusion adorned the whole series of Prophethood". (Shawkānī, *Fatḥ al-Qadīr*, comments on *Sūrah al-Aḥzāb* 33:40.)

xxi. Maḥmūd ibn 'Abd Allāh al-Ālūsī (d. 1270 AH/1854 CE) explained thus in his *Rūḥ al-Ma'ānī*: "A Prophet, in comparison to a Messenger, has a more general connotation. The Prophet Muḥammad (peace be on him), being *khātam al-nabīyīn*, is also *khātam al-mursalīn*. His advent in this capacity indicates that there will not be any Prophet for men nor for *jinn* after him... Whoever claims after the Prophet Muḥammad (peace be on him) that he receives Divine Revelation meant for the Prophets will be declared an unbeliever. There is no difference of opinion in the *ummah* on this question". (Ālūsī, *Rūḥ al-Ma'ānī*, comments on verse 40, *Sūrah al-Aḥzāb* 33:40.)

"That the Prophet Muḥammad (peace be on him) is *khātam al-nabīyīn* has been stated in the Qur'ān. What is meant by it has been clearly elucidated by *aḥādīth*. Over and above that, the entire Muslim community is totally agreed on this issue. Therefore, anyone who lays a claim contrary to that will be branded an unbeliever". (Ālūsī, *Rūḥ al-Ma'ānī*, comments on verse 40, *Sūrah al-Aḥzāb* 33:40.)

We have recounted above the agreed view of the leading Muslim *'ulamā'*, Qur'ān-commentators and jurists of all times and places, ranging from India, Morocco, Andalus and Turkey to Yemen. We have also highlighted the efforts of these authorities to drive home the fact that this agreed view has been there since the early days of Islam all the way up to our own time. We have deliberately refrained from citing the views of the *'ulamā'* of the present century [that is, the twentieth century] lest it be contended that their views represent a negative reaction to the views expressed by a recent false claimant to Prophethood. The opinions of earlier authorities, however, cannot be dismissed on the grounds of lack of impartiality. What comes out very clearly from all the above quotations is that throughout the centuries, since the early days of Islam, the Prophet Muḥammad (peace be on him) has consistently and unanimously been recognised as the last of all Prophets. Muslims have all along believed that the door of Prophethood was closed forever after his time. Likewise, it has been universally held by them that whoever claims to be a Prophet or Messenger after the Prophet Muḥammad (peace be on him) or who endorses such a claim made by anyone else, falls outside the fold of Islam.

It is up to every intelligent person to explore the meaning of *khātam al-nabīyīn* in the light of its established meaning in Arabic lexicography, the context of the Qur'ānic verse, the Prophet's own elucidation, and the Companions' and Muslim community's unanimous view on the subject. Alternatively, he might opt for a different interpretation that leaves the door wide open for new claimants to Prophethood. Yet, how can those people who not only admit the possibility of the advent of new Prophets, who in fact have themselves even claimed to be Prophets and whose claim to Prophethood was actually endorsed by others, be regarded as Muslims?

The following three points regarding this issue are worthy of serious consideration.

Is God Hostile to Our Having Faith?

It must be recognised, to begin with, that the issue of Prophethood is essential to faith. According to the Qur'ān, it ranks as one of the three fundamental articles on which one's acceptance or rejection of faith rests. If someone does not accept a genuine Prophet to be so, he will be considered an unbeliever. By the same token, if a person recognises someone as a Prophet when in fact he is not a Prophet, in that case too he will be considered an unbeliever. God could not leave human beings unguided on such a crucial issue. Had there been the possibility for any Prophet to appear after the Prophet Muḥammad (peace be on him), God would have clearly spelled that out and the Prophet himself would have categorically proclaimed it. Also, before his demise, he would have repeatedly impressed this point on his followers so that they might believe in the Prophets who would appear at a later date. God and His Prophet (peace be on him), after all, are not hostile to our having faith, hence it is unthinkable that they would keep us in the dark about the Prophets of the future. The fact, on the contrary, is that both God and His Prophet (peace be on him) have categorically affirmed that no Prophet will appear in the future. This has been an integral part of the Muslims' belief from the very beginning of Islam up to this day.

Were a person to appear now claiming Prophethood, we Muslims would unhesitatingly reject his claim. For this rejection, only God can call us to account. If that happens, we will be able to produce the textual evidence needed to prove that we had been asked by the Book of God and His Prophet's *Sunnah* not to believe in any Prophet after the Prophet Muḥammad (peace be on him). We are fully confident that God will not punish us for our rejection of any claimant to Prophethood. However, since the door of Prophethood has been closed and the advent of a new Prophet is out of the question, all claimants to Prophethood should think of the evidence they can produce before God to refute the charge of unbelief against them. Should they rely on flimsy reasons for such a claim and risk a grievous punishment by God for unbelief? They would be well-advised to examine the evidence they have and which they might put forth before God for their acquittal. They should indeed properly weigh the supporting evidence for their acquittal and consider it in comparison with the evidence we are presenting below.

Is There Any Need for Another Prophet?

Another point worth considering is that Prophethood is not a property that is developed in a person by worship and good deeds. Nor is it a reward for anyone's services. Rather, it is an exalted office to which God appoints a person, in keeping with a special need He has for him. Whenever that need arises, God raises a Prophet. In case there is no such need or if that need has already been met, no Prophet is raised. It becomes evident from reading the Qur'ān that a Prophet is needed only in the following four circumstances:

i. If there are a people among whom no Prophet was raised earlier and that the message of the Prophets who had been raised among others did not reach them.
ii. That the teachings of the preceding Prophet had either been forgotten or distorted so that it was no longer possible to follow in the footsteps of that Prophet.
iii. That the teaching and guidance communicated by the preceding Prophet were incomplete. In such a case, a Prophet is required to bring about the completion of God's prescribed faith.
iv. Another Prophet is raised when there is the need to reinforce and assist a Prophet in the accomplishment of his mission.

Now, it is quite obvious that none of these circumstances exist after the advent of the Prophet Muḥammad (peace be on him).

The Qur'ān itself states that his message is for the whole of mankind. It is also evident from history that his message had reached all nations of the world. Therefore, there is no longer any need to raise Prophets among the nations of the world. Both the Qur'ān and the corpus of *Ḥadīth* and *Sīrah* establish that the Prophet's teachings have been preserved in their pristine purity. The Prophet's message has not been tampered with. The Book revealed to him is available in its original form, unmarred by alteration or distortion and will remain so till the end of time. Furthermore, the guidance imparted by the Prophet (peace be on him) has been recorded so graphically and faithfully that one can even today re-live the ambience of his day.

The Qur'ān also asserts that through the Prophet (peace be on him) God's ordained faith was completed, (see *al-Mā'idah* 5:3). Hence, no fresh Prophet is needed to complete the Prophet's mission. As for the need for another Prophet as a helper, this could only have been during Muḥammad's own time. Since no other Prophet was designated as his associate, this too is now a closed chapter.

If there were to be a Prophet after Muḥammad (peace be on him), the need for that should indeed be a pressing one. Even if one were to say that a Prophet is needed in order to reform the Muslims, it should be noted that no Prophet was ever raised in the past for this purpose. Hence, no Prophet will appear for this purpose now. When a Prophet is appointed, he either receives revelation that represents a new message from God for mankind, or through him the earlier message is amplified, or it is purged of accretions and interpolations. Since the Qur'ān and the Prophet's *Sunnah* are fully recorded and have been well preserved and Islam is a faith characterised by completion and perfection, there is no need whatsoever for any fresh revelation. Hence, only reformers, not Prophets, are needed in our time and in the future.

A New Prophethood: Will it be a Blessing or a Curse?

If a new Prophet were to appear now this would naturally raise the question: who is a believer and who is not? Those who pledged their allegiance to this new claimant to Prophethood would become a separate community and those who rejected him would be in the opposite camp. The difference between the two would relate to basic rather than to secondary issues. There would possibly be no common ground between the two camps unless either of them abandons its position for the two would also have different sources of guidance and law. Each would insist on following its respective sources and contest the other's credibility. They neither could, nor would, coalesce into a well-knit, harmonious social body.

Bearing the above points in mind, one readily realises why the doctrine of the finality of Prophethood is a great blessing from God for the Muslim *ummah*. Thanks to it, Muslims have grown into a universal fraternity and this doctrine has been securing them against divisive forces which could otherwise have caused serious dissensions in their ranks. Whoever recognises the Prophet Muḥammad (peace be on him) as his guide and leader and is not committed to draw upon any other source of guidance than the Prophet (peace be on him) is a member of the Muslim fraternity. One may join this fraternity at any time and anywhere. Had the door of Prophethood not been sealed, the Muslim community could not have achieved such unity and cohesion. Instead, it would have been fragmented as a result of the advent of ever new Prophets.

Sheer common sense requires that the door of Prophethood be closed since a Prophet has already been raised for all mankind, his mission accomplished and his teachings fully preserved. This ensures the rallying of all believers into a united community whose solidarity is preserved by the finality of Prophethood. Even if a new Prophet were to be the "reincarnation" of some previous Prophet, and regardless of whether he claims to be the follower of a previous Prophet or has an independent status on account of being vested with a new *Sharī'ah* and a new Scripture, the mere fact of his advent as a Prophet would inevitably culminate in the division of the Muslim community into believers and unbelievers. In fact, even if there was any genuine need to raise a new Prophet, this division would be inevitable. However, in the absence of any reason for his advent, it is not at all in sync with God's Wisdom and Mercy to unnecessarily test His servants' faith and thwart their growth into an integrated collectivity. The Qur'ānic teaching on the finality of Muḥammad's Prophethood, as amplified by the *Sunnah* and endorsed by the consensus of the Muslim community down the ages, is a perfectly reasonable development. What the Muslims need now and will also need in the future are reformers who help them live up to the requirements of their faith.

The Truth Relating to the Promised Messiah

Those who urge gullible Muslims to believe in a new Prophet tell them that there are *aḥādīth* that contain tidings about the appearance of the Promised Messiah. Now, since this Messiah was a former Prophet, his advent does not run counter to the doctrine of the finality of Muḥammad's Prophethood. In other words, both beliefs – the finality of Prophethood and the advent of the promised Messiah – are equally valid and are not at all mutually contradictory. Intriguingly, however, those people who do not believe in the finality of Muḥammad's Prophethood do not take the Prophet Jesus, son of Mary (peace be on him), to be the promised Messiah. They contend that he is dead. They claim that *aḥādīth* inform us of the advent of someone *like* Jesus, the Messiah, and that this person had already appeared in our midst! Therefore, pledging allegiance to him is, so they claim, not discordant with belief in the finality of Prophethood.

Cited below are authentic *aḥādīth* on the subject with full bibliographic references. A glance at them will disclose the content of what the Prophet (peace be on him) actually said and how those pronouncements are being tendentiously interpreted today.

Aḥādīth on the Second Coming of the Prophet Jesus

i. Abū Hurayrah narrates that the Prophet (peace be on him) said: "By Him in Whose Hand is my life! The son of Mary will descend amongst you as a just ruler. He will break the cross and kill the swine,[9] and bring an end to war. (In a variant tradition the word *jizyah* is used in place of war, signifying an end to *jizyah*.)[10] There will be such abundance of wealth that no one will [even] be willing to take money. (Things will come to such a pass that for people) one prostration before God will be better than this world and all that it contains". (Bukhārī, *Kitāb al-Anbiyā', Bāb Nuzūl 'Īsā ibn Maryam*; Muslim, *Kitāb al-Īmān, Bāb Nuzūl 'Īsā ibn Maryam*; Tirmidhī, *Kitāb al-Fitan, Bāb mā jā'a fī Nuzūl 'Īsā* and Aḥmad ibn Ḥanbal, *Musnad*, narrated by Abū Hurayrah.)

---

9. Jesus' breaking the cross and killing the swine signify that Christianity will, thus, lose its status as an independent religious faith. The superstructure of Christianity rests on the dogma that God caused His only son Jesus to die an 'accursed' death on the cross, a death to expiate for man's sins.

Among the followers of God's Prophets, it is only Christians who have this unenviable distinction of embracing dogma and abandoning Law. They even consider swine lawful although it has invariably been considered unlawful in God's Law as promulgated by all of God's Prophets. So, when the Prophet Jesus (peace be on him) reappears and proclaims that he is not the son of God, that he did not die on the cross to expiate for man's sins, this will demolish the whole structure of Christian dogma. Likewise, he will state that he did not declare swine to be lawful for his adherents, nor grant them any licence to live independently of God's Law. These declarations will deal a final blow to the second major characteristic of Christianity, its independence of Law.

10. In other words, all communities will overcome their mutual differences and merge into the broader Islamic community. Hence there will be no warfare and *jizyah* will not be imposed on anyone. These points are made explicitly in *aḥādīth* nos. v and xv below.

ii. In another variant tradition with the same content cited on Abū Hurayrah's authority, these additional words also occur: "Until the descent of 'Īsā ibn Maryam, the Last Day will not occur". (Bukhārī, *Kitāb al-Maẓālim, Bāb Kasr al-Ṣalīb....* and Ibn Mājah, *Kitāb al-Fitan, Bāb Fitnat al-Dajjāl . . .*)

iii. Abū Hurayrah narrates that the Prophet (peace be on him) said: "How will you fare when Ibn Maryam will descend amongst you and at that time your *imām* (leader) will be from among yourselves".[11] (Bukhārī, *Kitāb al-Anbiyā', Bāb Nuzūl 'Īsā ibn Maryam*; Muslim, *Kitāb al-Īmān, Bāb Nuzūl 'Īsā ibn Maryam* and Aḥmad ibn Ḥanbal, *Musnad,* narrated by Abū Hurayrah.)

iv. According to Abū Hurayrah, the Prophet (peace be on him) said: "Jesus son of Mary will appear and then he will kill the swine and blot out the cross, and Prayer will be combined for him. He will distribute so much money that no one will be willing to take it. He will abolish *kharāj* (tribute). He will descend in Rawḥā'[12] and will proceed from there for *Ḥajj* or *'Umrah* or both". (The narrator is unsure whether the Prophet (peace be on him) specified *Ḥajj* or *'Umrah,* or mentioned both.)[13] (Aḥmad ibn Ḥanbal, *Musnad,* narrated by Abū Hurayrah.)

v. Abū Hurayrah narrates that, after relating an account of Dajjāl's appearance, the Prophet (peace be on him) said: "While Muslims will be preparing themselves to take on Dajjāl and will be standing in rows for Prayer, and the *iqāmah* will already have been pronounced when Jesus son of Mary will appear and lead the Muslims' Prayer. On spotting him, God's enemy [that is, Dajjāl] will dissolve as salt dissolves into water. Were Jesus (peace be on him) to spare him, he would dissolve to death on his own. However, God will make Jesus kill him with his own hand and he

11. The Prophet Jesus (peace be on him) will not lead the Prayer. Rather, he will pray behind the *imām* of the Muslim community.

12. This is located at a distance of some 35 miles from Madīnah.

13. It is worth noting that the person who claimed to be like the Promised Messiah neither performed *Ḥajj* nor *'Umrah* throughout his life.

will show to the Muslims the stains of Dajjāl's blood on his spear". (Al-Tabrayzī, *Mishkāt al-Maṣābīḥ, Kitāb al-Fitan, Bāb al-Malāḥim.*)

vi. Abū Hurayrah reports that the Prophet (peace be on him) said: "There will be no Prophet during the period between me and him [that is, Jesus] (peace be on him). He will appear; so recognise him when he appears. He is a person of average height, with reddish and whitish complexion. He will be dressed in two yellow garments. His hair will look as if water will trickle down from it, though it will not be wet. He will wage war in the cause of Islam, break the cross to pieces, kill the swine and waive *jizyah*. During his time, God will cause all religious communities other than Islam to vanish. He will kill Dajjāl. His stay on earth will be for forty years. Then he will die and Muslims will offer his funeral Prayer". (Abū Dā'ūd, *Kitāb al-Malāḥim, Bāb Khurūj al-Dajjāl,* and Aḥmad ibn Ḥanbal, *Musnad,* narrated by Abū Hurayrah.)

vii. Jābir ibn 'Abd Allāh says that he heard the Prophet (peace be on him) say: "Then Jesus, son of Mary, will appear. The leader of the Muslims will invite him to lead the Prayer. However, he will decline, saying that their leader should be from among themselves.[14] He will say so in recognition of the honour bestowed by God upon the Muslim community". (Muslim, *Kitāb al-Īmān, Bāb Nuzūl 'Īsā ibn Maryam* and Aḥmad ibn Ḥanbal, *Musnad,* narrated by Jābir ibn 'Abd Allāh.)

viii. In the context of the report about Ibn Ṣayyād, Jābir ibn 'Abd Allāh says: "Then 'Umar ibn al-Khaṭṭāb said: 'O Messenger of God! Grant me the permission to kill him'. The Prophet (peace be on him) replied: 'If he is that person (Dajjāl), you are not to kill him; Jesus, son of Mary, will kill him. If he is not that person (Dajjāl), you have no authority to kill a *dhimmī* (those with whom you have a covenant)'".

---

14. In other words, he who leads the Muslims should be from their own ranks.

(Al-Tabrayzī, *Mishkāt al-Maṣābīḥ, Kitāb al-Fitan, Bāb Qiṣṣat Ibn Ṣayyād.*)

ix. In connection with the story of Dajjāl, Jābir ibn 'Abd Allāh narrates that the Prophet (peace be on him) said: "Then suddenly Jesus, son of Mary (peace be on him), will appear in the midst of them [that is, the Muslims]. It will then be the time for Congregational Prayer and it will be said to him: 'O Spirit of God! Come forward to lead the Prayer'. However, he will say: 'No! Your *imām* should come forward and lead the Prayer'. After performing the *Fajr* Prayer, the Muslims will advance to take on Dajjāl. When that liar spots the Prophet Jesus (peace be on him), he will start to dissolve as salt dissolves into water. The Prophet Jesus (peace be on him) will advance towards him and kill him. Things will come to such a pass that even trees and stones will call out: 'O Spirit of God! Here is a Jew [hiding behind me]'. He will not spare any follower of Dajjāl; he will kill all of them". (Aḥmad ibn Ḥanbal, *Musnad*, narrated by Jābir ibn 'Abd Allāh.)

x. Relating the account of Dajjāl, Nawwās ibn Sam'ān al-Kilābī states that while Dajjāl is engaged in the toils of his work, God will send down Jesus, son of Mary (peace be on him). He will descend in the eastern part of Damascus, next to the white minaret, and will be dressed in two yellow garments, his hands resting on the arms of two angels. Whenever he will incline his head, it will seem as though drops are trickling down and when he raises his head, these drops will appear trickling down like pearls. Every unbeliever whom the air of his breath reaches will be killed. Then he will pursue Dajjāl, seize him at the gate of Ludd[15] and kill him. (Muslim, *Kitāb al-Fitan, Bāb Dhikr al-Dajjāl*...; Abū Dā'ūd, *Kitāb al-Malāḥim, Bāb Khurūj al-Dajjāl;* Tirmidhī, *Kitāb al-Fitan, Bāb mā jā'a fī Fitnat al-Dajjāl*, and Ibn Mājah, *Kitāb al-Fitan, Bāb Fitan al-Dajjāl* . . .)

---

15. Ludd, the Biblical Lydda, a town in Palestine (now known as Lod), is only a few miles away from Tel Aviv, the capital of Israel. The Israelis have built a big airbase there.

xi. It is stated on the authority of 'Abd Allāh ibn 'Amr ibn al-'Āṣ that the Messenger of God (peace be on him) said: "Dajjāl will appear in my *ummah* and will remain for forty. (I am not sure, forty days, or forty months or forty years).[16] Then God will send Jesus son of Mary (peace be on him) who will look as though he is 'Urwah ibn Mas'ūd. He will pursue Dajjāl and kill him and then remain for seventy years. During this period there will not be any enmity between any two people". (Muslim, *Kitāb al-Fitan, Bāb fī Khurūj al-Dajjāl . . .*)

xii. Ḥudhayfah ibn Asīd al-Ghifārī reports: "Once the Prophet (peace be on him) joined us while we were chatting. He enquired as to what we were talking about. When we told him that we were discussing about the Last Hour, he said: 'It will not strike before the appearance of these ten signs. Then he spelled out the following ten signs: (a) smoke, (b) Dajjāl, (c) the beast of the earth, (d) the sun's rise in the West, (e) the appearance of Jesus son of Mary, (f) Gog and Magog, (g) three major landslides:[17] one in the east, (h) one in the west, (i) and one in the Arabian Peninsula, and (j) finally, the devastating fire, originating from Yemen that will drive people to the Grand Assembly". (Muslim, *Kitāb al-Fitan, Bāb fī al-Āyāt*... and Abū Dā'ūd, *Kitāb al-Malāḥim, Bāb Amārāt al-Sā'ah.*)

xiii. Thawbān, the Prophet's freed slave, reports that the Prophet (peace be on him) said: "God has secured two armies of my community from the Hellfire – one that will carry out a military expedition in India and the other that will be with Jesus, son of Mary". (Nasā'i, *Kitāb al-Jihād, Bāb Ghazwat al-Hind* and Aḥmad ibn Ḥanbal, *Musnad*, narrated by Thawbān.)

xiv. Mujammi' ibn Jāriyah al-Anṣārī states that he heard the Prophet (peace be on him) say: "Ibn Maryam will kill Dajjāl at the gate of Ludd". (Aḥmad ibn Ḥanbal, *Musnad*, narrated

---

16. This statement about forty days, forty months, or forty years is by 'Abd Allāh ibn 'Amr ibn al-'Āṣ.

17. The three major incidents of "sinking" or "caving in" mentioned in this tradition signify landslides.

by Mujammi' ibn Jāriyah al-Anṣārī and Tirmidhī, *Kitāb al-Fitan, Bāb mā jā'a fī Qatl 'Īsā ibn Maryam al-Dajjāl.*)

xv. In a lengthy *ḥadīth* on Dajjāl, Abū Umāmah al-Bāhillī says: "While the *imām* will have moved forward to lead the *Fajr* Prayer, then suddenly Jesus, son of Mary, will descend among them. The *imām* will then move backwards to the front row so that he [that is, Jesus] may come forward [to lead the Prayer]. Jesus will put his hand between the two shoulders of the *imām* and ask him to lead the Prayer for the call for Prayer was made for him [that is, for the *imām* to lead it]. Accordingly, the *imām* will lead the Prayer. After the Prayer is over, Jesus will ask that the gate be opened. Outside the gate, Dajjāl will be positioned along with 70,000 armed Jews. As soon as Dajjāl spots him [that is, Jesus] he will start dissolving, as salt dissolves in water. He will then take to flight. However, Jesus will say to him: 'You cannot escape my blow'. He will seize Dajjāl at the eastern gate of Ludd and then God will inflict defeat upon the Jews…The earth will abound with Muslims, like a pot full to the brim with water. The whole of mankind will profess the same faith and no one besides God will be worshipped". (Ibn Mājah, *Kitāb al-Fitan, Bāb Fitnat al-Dajjāl wa Khurūj 'Īsā.*)

xvi. 'Uthmān ibn Abī al-'Āṣ said that he heard the Prophet (peace be on him) say: "Jesus son of Mary will descend at the time of *Fajr* Prayer. The leader of the Muslims will request him: 'O Spirit of God! Lead the Prayer'. Then he [Jesus] will say: 'The leaders [of Prayer] are in the ranks of Muslims'. Then the leader of the Muslims will lead the Prayer. After the Prayer, Jesus (peace be on him) will advance towards Dajjāl, with his spear. On spotting him, Dajjāl will melt like lead. Jesus (peace be on him) will kill him with his spear and his followers will flee after suffering defeat. However, they will not find any refuge anywhere. Even trees and stones will call out: 'O believer! Here is an unbeliever'". (Aḥmad ibn Ḥanbal, *Musnad*, narrated by 'Uthmān ibn Abī al-'Āṣ; also Ṭabarānī, *al-Mu'jam al-Kabīr* and al-Ḥākim, *al-Mustadrak, Kitāb al-Fitan wa al-Malāḥim.*)

xvii. In a lengthy tradition, Samurah ibn Jundub narrates on the Prophet's authority: "Jesus son of Mary will descend among the Muslims at the time of *Fajr* Prayer and God will inflict defeat upon Dajjāl and his army. Even walls and the roots of trees will cry out: 'O believer! Come and kill the unbeliever hiding behind me' ". (Aḥmad ibn Ḥanbal, *Musnad* narrated by Samurah ibn Jundub and al-Ḥākim, *al-Mustadrak, Kitāb al-Fitan wa al-Malāḥim*.)

xviii. 'Imrān ibn Ḥaṣīn reports that the Prophet (peace be on him) said: "There will always be a group in my community that will adhere to the truth and prevail over the enemy until God delivers His judgement and Jesus son of Mary (peace be on him) comes down [to earth]". (Aḥmad ibn Ḥanbal, *Musnad*, narrated by 'Imrān ibn Ḥaṣīn.)

xix. In connection with the story of Dajjāl, 'Ā'ishah narrates that: "Jesus (peace be on him) will descend and kill Dajjāl. Then he will remain on earth for forty years as a just *imām* and an equitable ruler". (Aḥmad ibn Ḥanbal, *Musnad*, narrated by 'Ā'ishah bint Abū Bakr.)

xx. Safīnah, the Prophet's freed slave, reports: "The Prophet Jesus (peace be on him) will descend and God will cause the death of Dajjāl near the steep track of Afīq Valley".[18] (Aḥmad ibn Ḥanbal, *Musnad*, narrated by Safīnah.)

These *aḥādīth* are narrated on the authority of as many as 14 Companions with sound chains of narration and form part of the most authentic works of *Ḥadīth*. Although there are several other *aḥādīth* which mention these matters, we have refrained from citing them here lest this session becomes overly lengthy. Furthermore, we have only listed those *aḥādīth* that are supported by a strong chain of narrators.

---

18. Afīq, presently known as Fīq, is currently under Israeli occupation and has a kibbutz named Afik and is the last town in Syria along its border with Israel. Lake Ṭabarīyā (Tiberias) lies ahead of it a few miles to the west and is the source of the River Jordan. On its south-western side, in the midst of mountains there is a steep track which descends some 2,000 feet at the spot which is the source of the River Jordan. This is known as 'Aqabat Afīq (the steep track of Afīq).

The Upshot of the above *Aḥādīth*

It becomes clear by reading the above quoted *aḥādīth* that the one who is mentioned in the traditions is the Messiah himself rather than the "incarnation" or "shadow" of the Messiah, or even of the Promised Messiah. Instead, these *aḥādīth*, categorical as they are, leave no room to entertain the notion that someone in our own time, born out of his mother's womb and his father's sperm, can claim to be the Messiah, whose advent was foretold by the Prophet Muḥammad (peace be on him). Rather, these *aḥādīth* pointedly and categorically declare the second coming of Jesus (peace be on him) who was born to Mary without a father around two thousand years ago. Here it is besides the point to discuss whether Jesus is presently dead or alive somewhere. Even if he is dead, God has the power to raise him to life.[19] Nor is it beyond God's power to let someone survive for several thousand years in His universe and then stage his return whenever He so wills.

Anyone who believes in *Ḥadīth* is bound to have the distinct impression from the above that it is only Jesus, son of Mary, who will descend. As for those who reject *Ḥadīth* as a source of knowledge, they simply do not believe in anyone's return to earth. For the doctrine of Jesus' second coming rests entirely on *Ḥadīth*. What we come across in some present-day writings, however, sounds like a joke. In one breath these people derive from the relevant *aḥādīth* the idea of the second coming of Jesus, son of Mary, and in the next breath they totally disregard the explicit information contained in the very same *aḥādīth* and claim that he who will come will not be Jesus, son of Mary, but someone like him!

Another point evident from these *aḥādīth* is that the second coming of Jesus, son of Mary, will not be his coming as a Prophet. He will not receive any fresh revelation. Nor will he be sent down with any new message or command from God. Nor will he add anything to, or take away anything from, the Prophet Muḥammad's *Sharī'ah*. Nor will he be assigned the task to renew the true faith.

---

19. Those denying this phenomenon should better study *Sūrah al-Baqarah* 2:259, which explicitly states: "Allah then caused him to remain dead for a hundred years and then raised him to life…".

Upon his appearance, Jesus will not ask mankind to believe in him. Nor will he raise a community of those who believe in him.[20] Instead, he will be sent with the specific assignment to obliterate the mischief caused by Dajjāl. For this particular purpose, he will appear in the midst of Muslims in such a way that they will have no doubt as regards his identity. They will readily recognise him as Jesus, son of Mary, whose descent on earth will be at an appointed hour exactly as the Prophet Muḥammad (peace be on him) had predicted. He will join the Muslim Congregational Prayer and pray behind the leader of the Muslims.[21] He will insist that the leader of the Muslims lead the Prayer; this in order that people do not mistakenly think that he has returned in his former capacity as a

---

20. Muslim scholars have duly clarified this point. For example, Sa'd al-Dīn Mas'ūd ibn 'Umar Taftāzānī (d. 793 AH/1390 CE) says the following in his *Sharḥ 'Aqā'id al-Nasafī:* "It is certain that the Prophet Muḥammad (peace be on him) is the last Prophet...Were someone to point out that *aḥādīth* speak of the descent of the Prophet Jesus (peace be on him) after him, we will say 'Yes, but [in this second coming] Jesus will follow the Prophet Muḥammad (peace be on him), for his [that is, Jesus'] *Sharī'ah* stands abrogated.' Accordingly, neither Revelation will be made to him, nor will he prescribe any religious command; rather, he will serve as the Prophet Muḥammad's deputy", (*Majmū'ah al-Ḥawāshī al-Bahīyah 'ala Sharḥ 'Aqā'id al-Nasafīyah,* Cairo, Maṭba'ah al-Kurdistān al-'Ilmīyah, 1329 AH, pp. 189–190).

Almost the same point is pressed home by Ālūsī in his *tafsīr*, *Rūḥ al-Ma'ānī*: "After his second coming, the Prophet Jesus (peace be on him) will maintain his earlier Prophethood. While he will not be removed from his Prophetic status, yet he will no longer adhere to his former *Sharī'ah* which will stand abolished for him and his followers. Instead, he will be bound to the Islamic *Sharī'ah* both in its broad principles and its details. He will not receive any fresh Revelation. Nor will he be authorised to lay down any law; rather, he will serve as the Prophet's deputy and as a ruler among the rulers of the Muslim community" (Ālūsī, *Rūḥ al-Ma'ānī*, comments on *Sūrah al-Aḥzāb* 33:40.)

Imām Rāzī elucidates the point further: "The era of the Prophets lasted until the day of the Prophet Muḥammad (peace be on him). His advent marks the end of the chain of Prophets. It is not odd, therefore, that after his second coming the Prophet Jesus (peace be on him) will be a follower of the Prophet Muḥammad (peace be on him)", (Rāzī, *al-Tafsīr al-Kabīr,* comments on *Sūrah al-Nisā'* 4:159).

21. Although one *ḥadīth* (v) mentions that the Prophet Jesus (peace be on him) will lead the Prayer after his descent, the more authentic *aḥādīth* (iii, vii, ix, xv and xvi) indicate that he will decline the request to lead the Prayer. Rather, he will ask the imām of the Muslims to step forward and lead the Prayer. This is a consensus view of Qur'ān-commentators and scholars of *Ḥadīth*.

Prophet. It goes without saying that in the presence of a Prophet, no one else can lead the Prayer or be the leader of the community. As Jesus (peace be on him) will join the Muslim community as its member, this will amount to his proclaiming that his return is not in the capacity of a Prophet. Thus, Jesus' second coming will not conflict with the doctrine of the finality of the Prophet Muḥammad's Prophethood.

This second coming of Jesus may be likened to the visit of a former head of state during the reign of another head of state to perform a specific assignment under the latter's authority. Such a return does not lead to the abrogation of the existing constitution. A constitutional crisis would arise only if the former head of state attempts to resume his former office or refuses to acknowledge the existing authority, for this would amount to his challenging the legality of the existing order. If he does not resort to any of the above-stated courses, the mere assignment of a task to a former head of state will not cause any disruption.

The above analogy applies fully to the Prophet Jesus' second coming. His appearance will not be a negation of the finality of Muḥammad's Prophethood. Were Jesus to assume the office of a Prophet again and carry out his Prophetic mission or were someone to reject his former status as a Prophet, this would be taken as defiance of the Divine scheme of Prophethood. However, the above quoted *aḥādīth* rule out all such possibilities, for they stress that there is no Prophethood after Muḥammad (peace be on him). Furthermore, they also constitute the tidings about the second coming of the Prophet Jesus (peace be on him). It is perfectly clear, then, that his second coming will not be meant to carry out any Prophetic duty.

Likewise, Jesus' second coming will not raise any new questions among Muslims as to who is a believer and who is not. Even today, if a Muslim does not accept Jesus (peace be on him) to be a Prophet, he will be regarded as an unbeliever. The Prophet Muḥammad also believed Jesus was a Prophet of God. The entire body of Muslims, accordingly, holds on to this belief. The same position will apply at the time of Jesus' second coming. Muslims will not affirm their belief in him as a new Prophet; rather, they will maintain their belief in his former status as a Prophet. This belief does not contradict the Muslims' doctrine of the finality of Muḥammad's Prophethood. It does not contradict it today, nor will it do so after Jesus' second coming.

The last salient point brought home by the *aḥādīth* quoted above is that Dajjāl will rise from among the Jews. The Prophet Jesus, son of Mary, will be sent again in order to put an end to the great mischief unleashed by Dajjāl. The latter will present himself as the Messiah. The full significance of this incident can only be grasped after studying Jewish history and Jewish beliefs. The Israelites have constantly suffered ever since the Prophet Solomon's demise for they were enslaved and dispersed throughout the Babylonian and Assyrian Empires. Their Prophets tried to comfort and console them by giving them the good tidings of the Messiah's advent, of someone who would deliver them from their unenviable plight. In view of these predictions, the Jews have looked forward to the advent of this Messiah who will be a king and will fight his way through, conquering one land after another, and who will gather the Israelites from all parts of the world and settle them in Palestine, thereby setting up a vast empire for them. However, when the Prophet Jesus, son of Mary, was sent down by God as the Messiah, and they saw that he was without an army, they refused to recognise him as the Messiah. Rather, they were hostile to him and contrived ways and means to kill him. From then on to this day, the Jews have eagerly awaited the promised Messiah's advent. Their literature abundantly reflects this utopia. Both the Talmud and Rabbinical writings paint a rosy picture of the glorious days of this promised Messiah, sustaining their dreams for centuries. They dream that the Messiah, being a colossal military and political leader, will conquer for them the entire region lying between the River Nile and River Euphrates, and that this entire region will become their homeland. They also cherish the hope that he will attract Jews from all parts of the world and reassemble them in their homeland.

Anyone who considers the conditions obtaining in the Middle East in the backdrop of the Prophet Muḥammad's predictions will realise that the stage is now set for the emergence of the Great

Dajjāl. Not only did the Prophet Muḥammad (peace be on him) predict the appearance of the Great Dajjāl, but he also alerted the Muslims to the calamities that will then befall them. They will be under such strain and stress that a single day will weigh upon them as though it were one full year (al-Ḥākim, *al-Mustadrak, Kitāb al-Fitan wa al-Malāḥim*). The Prophet (peace be on him), therefore, sought God's refuge against this and also exhorted his *ummah* to do the same.

At this critical juncture, God will not raise someone *like* the Messiah to confront the Dajjāl, but will send the Messiah himself, whom the Jews had once refused to accept as such and who, in their view, they crucified. Moreover, let it be clear that this true Messiah will not descend in India, Africa or America. The site of his descent will also be the site of the decisive encounter. It will be Damascus, hardly 50 or 60 miles from Israel's borders.

All these truths are clearly borne out by the above quoted *aḥādīth*. Furthermore, they prove beyond any shadow of doubt that the fraud perpetrated in our land [that is, India and Pakistan] regarding the promised Messiah is nothing but an act of blatant deceit and fabrication.

The most ludicrous part of this fabrication is the following version of the matter offered by the person claiming to be the one foretold of in the above *aḥādīth*. This is how he explains why he should be considered Jesus, son of Mary:

> God named me Maryam (Mary) in the third part of *Barāhīn-i Aḥmadīyah*. As is evident from *Barāhīn-i-Aḥmadīyah*, I was nurtured for two years as "Mary"…Then, as in the case of Mary, the spirit of Jesus was infused into me and I was metaphorically pregnant with it. After a few months, not exceeding ten, I was transformed from Mary to Jesus, as is clear from the inspiration cited in the fourth part of *Barāhīn-i Aḥmadīyah*. This is how I stand as the son of Mary. (*Kashtī-'i Nūḥ*, pp. 87, 88 and 89.)

So, this person first became Mary, then on his own he became impregnated, and eventually gave birth to himself as Jesus, son of Mary! There remained, however, a difficulty even after having become Jesus. According to *aḥādīth*, Jesus, son of Mary, would descend in Damascus, a famous historical city in Syria that has been in existence for long and exists even today. (see Map 3) Just see how this hard nut was cracked:

> Let the interpretation of the word Damascus be clear. God revealed to me that in this case a town in which wicked people live, and who have Yazīd's disposition and follow the ideas and habits of Yazīd ... Since this town of Qādiyān is inhabited by a majority of such people who have Yazīd's disposition, it bears a degree of resemblance and relationship with Damascus. (Note on *Izālāh-'i Awhām*, Lahore: Anjuman-i Aḥmadīyah, pp. 63–73.)

However, there remained yet another obstacle. The relevant *aḥādīth* specify that the son of Mary will descend near the white minaret. This was also overcome by ingenuity. The so-called Messiah had a minaret constructed in Qādiyān! According to *aḥādīth*, this should have been in existence before the appearance of the Messiah, whereas in this case it was built after the appearance of this so-called Messiah.

There remained still another serious problem to resolve. According to the *aḥādīth*, Jesus, son of Mary, should have killed Dajjāl at the gate of Ludd. Many fantastic excuses were proffered on this count. Initially, the self-proclaimed Messiah conceded that Ludd is a small township in Jerusalem. (*Izālah-'i Awhām*, p. 220.) Later on, it was contended that: "Ludd is an appellation used of such people who pick up quarrels... As and when Dajjāl's mischief reaches its peak, the promised Messiah will appear to put an end to this mischief", (ibid., p. 30). However, since this interpretation was usually regarded as untenable, it was claimed that Ludd actually refers to Ludhiana (a town near Qādiyān), and the killing of Dajjāl at its gate only signifies that despite the opposition from the evil ones, the oath of fealty to Mirzā Ghulām Aḥmad was first pledged in Ludhiana, (*al-Hudā*, p. 91).

Anyone who critically considers these far-fetched interpretations is bound to discover that Mirzā Ghulām Aḥmad, who laid claim to being the Messiah, was guilty of nothing less than a blatant, wilful act of impersonation.

Map 3: **The Site of the Messiah's Descent**

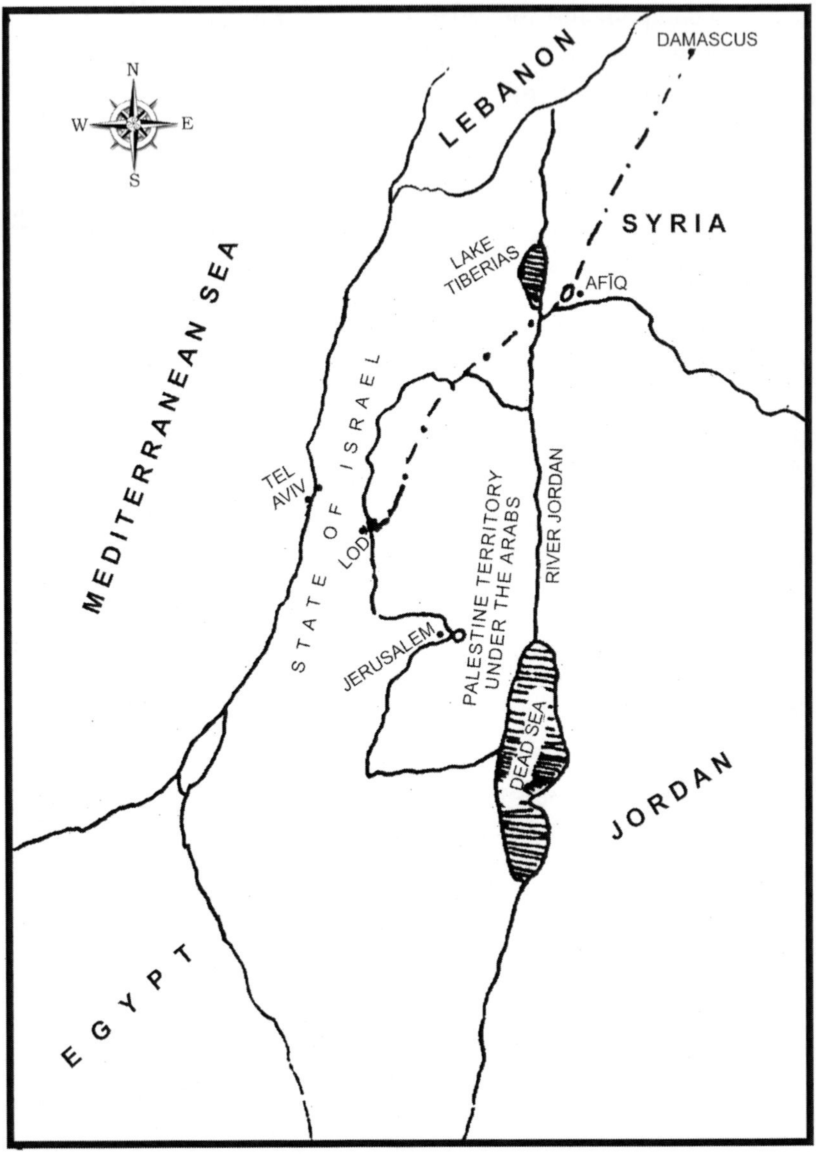

Sūrah 34

Saba'

(Makkan Period)

Title

The *sūrah*'s title is taken from verse 15 in which the word Saba' occurs. (This signifies that the *sūrah* contains an account of the people of Saba'.)

Period of Revelation

There are no authentic traditions to indicate the exact period of this *sūrah*'s revelation. However, it appears from its contents that it must have been revealed either during the early or middle phase of the Prophet's Makkan life. Now, if the *sūrah* was revealed during this middle phase, then it was possibly during the beginning of it when the persecution of the Muslims had not yet reached extreme heights. Opposition to Islam at that time was largely confined to mocking, ridiculing, defaming, slandering and other such means so as to sow doubt and suspicion among people about Islam and the Prophet (peace be on him). All this was part of the unbelievers' campaign to nip Islam in the bud.

Subject Matter and Theme

The *sūrah* consists of responses to the Makkan unbelievers' hostile criticism of the Prophet's teachings relating to monotheism, the Hereafter and his own Prophethood. Their criticisms and objections were usually couched in the form of sarcastic innuendos, mocking remarks and vile accusations. The *sūrah* explicitly identifies their criticisms before going on to respond to them. On other occasions, the Qur'ānic responses themselves indicate the criticisms they specifically addressed. Such responses are mostly expressed in the form of elucidation, admonition and persuasive evidence. At times, however, the opponents are warned of the dire consequences of their adamant rejection of the Truth. It is in this context that the stories of the Prophets David and Solomon (peace be on them) and of the people of Saba' are recounted. These stories are meant to drive home the fact that history provides two distinct examples from which people can learn a lesson. One is that of these two great Prophets – David and Solomon – who, notwithstanding their unrivalled might and glory, did not succumb to arrogance and vanity. Rather than act rebelliously towards God, they continued to be His grateful servants. By contrast, the people of Saba' were swayed by pride and arrogance for the simple reason that God had blessed them with His bounties. As a result, they were punished so severely that no trace of them remains besides legendary tales.

After citing these examples, the unbelievers are told to consider these two opposing models of conduct and to decide for themselves which of the two is better: a life anchored in affirmation of monotheism and the Hereafter and characterised by thankfulness to God, or one rooted in unbelief, polytheism, rejection of the Hereafter, and immersion in worldliness.

In the name of Allah, the Most Merciful, the Most Compassionate.

بِسْمِ ٱللَّهِ ٱلرَّحْمَٰنِ ٱلرَّحِيمِ

(1) All praise be to Allah to Whom belongs all that is in the heavens and all that is in the earth,[1] and all praise be to Him in the World to Come.[2] He is Most Wise, All-Aware.[3] (2) He knows what penetrates into the earth and what goes forth from it, ▶

ٱلْحَمْدُ لِلَّهِ ٱلَّذِى لَهُۥ مَا فِى ٱلسَّمَٰوَٰتِ
وَمَا فِى ٱلْأَرْضِ وَلَهُ ٱلْحَمْدُ فِى ٱلْءَاخِرَةِ
وَهُوَ ٱلْحَكِيمُ ٱلْخَبِيرُ ۝١ يَعْلَمُ مَا يَلِجُ فِى
ٱلْأَرْضِ وَمَا يَخْرُجُ مِنْهَا

---

1. *Ḥamd* signifies both praise and gratitude, and both these meanings are intended in this verse. Since the entire universe belongs to God, He deserves to be praised for all the glorious manifestations of beauty and excellence, of wisdom and creative power, of consummate workmanship and artistry that we see around us and throughout the universe. Hence anyone who derives any benefit, amusement or pleasure from anything should offer thanks to God. Now, since all that exists in the universe is exclusively God's, only He deserves to be praised and thanked.

2. All bounties in this world have been bestowed upon their recipients by God alone. The same will happen in the World-to-Come: there too, the source of all good that one receives will be God alone. Evidently, therefore, it is God alone Who deserves praise and gratitude in this world and in the Next.

3. That is, all what God does bespeaks of the highest degree of wisdom and benevolence, of perfection and excellence. He knows everything about all His creatures. He knows well the whereabouts of each of them, of their actual conditions, of their needs and requirements. He also fully knows what is conducive to their well-being, what they have done thus far, and what they will do in the future. He has full knowledge of every atom of the universe He has created.

what descends from the heaven and what ascends to it. He is the Most Merciful, the Most Forgiving.[4]

(3) The unbelievers say: "How come the Hour is not coming upon us!"[5] Say to them: "Yes indeed, by my Lord, by Him Who fully knows the realm beyond the ken of perception, that the Hour shall inevitably come upon you.[6] ▶

وَمَا يَنزِلُ مِنَ ٱلسَّمَآءِ وَمَا يَعۡرُجُ فِيهَاۚ وَهُوَ
ٱلرَّحِيمُ ٱلۡغَفُورُ ۝٢ وَقَالَ ٱلَّذِينَ كَفَرُواْ
لَا تَأۡتِينَا ٱلسَّاعَةُۖ قُلۡ بَلَىٰ وَرَبِّي لَتَأۡتِيَنَّكُمۡ
عَٰلِمِ ٱلۡغَيۡبِۖ

4. If an individual or group has not been hit by a scourge despite their defiance of God's commands that does not mean that this world is a banana republic governed by a foolish sovereign. Rather, the Mercy so shown results from the fact that God is Most Compassionate and Most Forbearing; in essence, He overlooks man's misdeeds. He also has full power to instantly punish all culprits and deny them their sustenance. He can paralyse them and even destroy them in an instant. However, this is not His way. Thanks to His immense mercy – and this despite His being All-Powerful – He grants respite and reprieve to those that are disobedient so that they may mend their ways. Moreover, if and when they give up their misconduct, God readily pardons them.

5. The unbelievers, feigning ignorance, made this comment by way of jest and sarcasm. The purpose in so doing was to emphasise the fact that the Prophet (peace be on him) had constantly warned them that the Day of Judgement was just around the corner. No one knew, however, what prevented its coming though it was supposedly on its way. In this way, the unbelievers sought to show that though they had repeatedly rejected and mocked the Prophet (peace be on him) and demonstrated their utter disrespect towards him, God's scourge had still not visited them.

6. Here, while swearing by God, mention is made of His attribute of fully knowing "the realm beyond the ken of perception". This suggests that while the Last Day is bound to come, the exact time of

Nothing escapes Him, not even the smallest particle in the heavens or the earth; nor is anything smaller or bigger than that but is in a Manifest Book."[7] (4) (The Hour shall come) that He may reward those who believe and do righteous deeds. Theirs shall be forgiveness and a generous provision. (5) As for those who worked against Our Signs in order to frustrate them, they shall suffer a painful chastisement.[8] ▶

لَا يَعْزُبُ عَنْهُ مِثْقَالُ ذَرَّةٍ فِى ٱلسَّمَٰوَٰتِ
وَلَا فِى ٱلْأَرْضِ وَلَآ أَصْغَرُ مِن ذَٰلِكَ
وَلَآ أَكْبَرُ إِلَّا فِى كِتَٰبٍ مُّبِينٍ ۝٣
لِّيَجْزِىَ ٱلَّذِينَ ءَامَنُوا۟ وَعَمِلُوا۟
ٱلصَّٰلِحَٰتِ ۚ أُو۟لَٰٓئِكَ لَهُم مَّغْفِرَةٌ وَرِزْقٌ
كَرِيمٌ ۝٤ وَٱلَّذِينَ سَعَوْ فِىٓ ءَايَٰتِنَا مُعَٰجِزِينَ
أُو۟لَٰٓئِكَ لَهُمْ عَذَابٌ مِّن رِّجْزٍ أَلِيمٌ ۝٥

---

its coming is known only to God. This truth is variously and frequently stated in the Qur'ān. See *al-A'rāf* 7:187; *Ṭā Hā* 20:15; *Luqmān* 31:34; *al-Aḥzāb* 33:63; *al-Mulk* 67:25–26 and *al-Nāzi'āt* 79:42–44.

7. This is among the arguments adduced in the Qur'ān to establish that the Life-to-Come lies well within the realm of the possible. This argument was occasioned by the unbelievers' rejection of the Hereafter on the grounds that after human beings have been reduced to dust, and the elements of which they were composed have been widely dispersed they cannot be brought together again so as to bring them back to life, (see verse 7 below). In other words, the unbelievers thought that disintegrated and decomposed human bodies could not be brought together again. This misconception is removed by the Qur'ān's assertion that every particle in the farthest stretches of the universe is in God's record and He knows its whereabouts. Hence, whenever God decides to resurrect human beings, He will have no difficulty in re-assembling all the component parts of which each individual body was comprised.

8. The upshot of what has been said (see verse 4 above) is that the World-to-Come is within the range of the possible. What is now

(6) (O Prophet), those who have knowledge see clearly that what has been revealed to you from your Lord is the Truth and directs to the Way of the Most Mighty, the Immensely Praiseworthy Lord.[9]	وَيَرَى ٱلَّذِينَ أُوتُواْ ٱلْعِلْمَ ٱلَّذِىٓ أُنزِلَ إِلَيْكَ مِن رَّبِّكَ هُوَ ٱلْحَقَّ وَيَهْدِىٓ إِلَىٰ صِرَٰطِ ٱلْعَزِيزِ ٱلْحَمِيدِ ۝٦

being said goes a step further. It affirms that the Next World is not simply possible; it is imminent. A time will surely come when God will punish the wrong-doers for their erroneous actions and reward the righteous for their good deeds. Reason as well as justice require that the guilty should be punished and the upright rewarded. We, however, know that all people are not necessarily recompensed in this life for their good and bad deeds; in fact, many a time we observe that what happens is quite contrary to what one would reasonably expect. Hence a time must come when these essential requirements of justice are met. This will happen on the Day of Judgement. Should there be no Afterlife, it would be tantamount to injustice.

Another point is also evident from what has been said above: that faith and righteous deeds lead to God's "forgiveness and generous provision" (see verse 4 above). On the contrary, "a painful chastisement" awaits those who engage in hostile efforts to frustrate God's true religion and bring about its degradation. This implies that those who sincerely believe but whose deeds are somewhat flawed will receive forgiveness even if they do not receive "generous provision". As for the unbelievers who are not actively opposed to the true faith, their situation is somewhat different from the unbelievers engaged in active opposition. While such people will not escape chastisement, they will nonetheless be spared the kind of pain and grievous punishment earmarked for actively hostile unbelievers.

9. The unbelievers may go to any length they wish to falsify the truth expounded by the Prophet (peace be on him) but their efforts will not meet with success. Their efforts can, at most, deceive those who are ignorant. As for those endowed with knowledge, they will not be misled by them.

(7) The unbelievers say: "Shall we direct you to the man who tells you that when you have been utterly broken to pieces, you will be raised to life again? (8) Has he forged a lie against Allah, or is he afflicted with madness?"[10]

Nay, but those who do not believe in the Hereafter are doomed to be chastised and are far gone in error.[11] ▶

وَقَالَ ٱلَّذِينَ كَفَرُوا۟ هَلْ نَدُلُّكُمْ عَلَىٰ
رَجُلٍ يُنَبِّئُكُمْ إِذَا مُزِّقْتُمْ كُلَّ مُمَزَّقٍ
إِنَّكُمْ لَفِى خَلْقٍ جَدِيدٍ ﴿٧﴾ أَفْتَرَىٰ عَلَى
ٱللَّهِ كَذِبًا أَم بِهِۦ جِنَّةٌۢ ۗ بَلِ ٱلَّذِينَ لَا يُؤْمِنُونَ
بِٱلْـَٔاخِرَةِ فِى ٱلْعَذَابِ وَٱلضَّلَـٰلِ ٱلْبَعِيدِ ﴿٨﴾

---

10. The Quraysh chiefs knew well that it was difficult for common people to consider the Prophet (peace be on him) as unveracious. This because the whole community positively knew him to be truthful. Indeed, throughout his life, they had never heard a false word from him. Therefore, the unbelieving chiefs had to launch an attack on some of the Prophet's doctrines, claiming for instance, that he expounded absolutely fantastic notions, not least life after death. This, according to them, indicated quite simply that he was either a liar or a madman. Their portrayal of the Prophet (peace be on him) as a madman, however, was as baseless as their contention that he was a liar. This because it was impossible for any rational being to believe that a person so distinctively intelligent and conspicuously wise could be a maniac. How could any person in his proper senses stomach this kind of nonsense? God, therefore, does not advance any argument to refute this foolish and vile statement. Instead, He addresses their sense of wonder at the idea of the Afterlife.

11. This constitutes the first part of the Qur'ānic rejoinder to their contention. The unbelievers are emphatically told that while the Prophet (peace be on him) was acquainting them with the truth, they persisted in paying no heed to him. They had chosen, instead, to blindly pursue the path that would lead them straight onto Hell. Such was the extent of their pitiful folly that they dismissed the Prophet (peace be on him), who was virtually consuming himself with concern to save them, as a madman.

(9) Do they not see how the heavens and the earth encompass them from the front and the rear? We could, if We so wished, cause the earth to swallow them or let fragments of the sky fall upon them.[12] ▶

أَفَلَمْ يَرَوْا۟ إِلَىٰ مَا بَيْنَ أَيْدِيهِمْ وَمَا خَلْفَهُم مِّنَ ٱلسَّمَآءِ وَٱلْأَرْضِ ۚ إِن نَّشَأْ نَخْسِفْ بِهِمُ ٱلْأَرْضَ أَوْ نُسْقِطْ عَلَيْهِمْ كِسَفًا مِّنَ ٱلسَّمَآءِ ۚ

12. This is yet another rejoinder to the unbelievers' contention. To better appreciate this one needs to recall that the Makkan unbelievers mainly rejected the Hereafter on the following grounds: (i) They were not inclined to believe in Divine reckoning and judgement for this would place curbs on their unbridled freedom. (ii) They were totally opposed to the idea of Resurrection and the Day of Judgement. They were not at all prepared to believe that a day would come when the present order of existence would come to an end, giving way to an altogether new one. (iii) They also found it hard to believe in resurrection of the dead. It seemed impossible to them that those who had long since been dead, whose bodies had disintegrated, and whose tiny fragments, from which they had been composed, that were now lost in earth, water or air could ever be brought back to life. The response enshrined in this verse is relevant to all three objections raised by the unbelievers. Additionally, it also embodies a severe warning to such unbelievers in these words: "We could, if We so wished, cause the earth to swallow them or let fragments of the sky fall upon them".

The verse also succinctly brings out the following points: (i) A careful observation of the universe testifies that it is neither a plaything nor the product of any accident. It has been created by the Omnipotent Lord in perfect wisdom. It is absurd, therefore, to think that in such a well-ordered universe, man, who is endowed with rational faculty, discernment, and choice, will not be called to account. (ii) Anyone who studies the workings of the universe is bound to realise that there is no reason at all why it should be difficult for the Afterlife to happen. Even a slight alteration in the laws that hold together the order of the heavens and the earth can instantly lead to Doomsday. The entire system of the universe is indicative of the fact that God,

Verily there is a Sign in this for every servant (of Allah) who penitently turns to Him.[13]	إِنَّ فِي ذَٰلِكَ لَآيَةً لِّكُلِّ عَبْدٍ مُّنِيبٍ ۝٩

Who has created the universe, is certainly possessed of the power to create another one should He choose to do so. For, obviously, had its re-creation been difficult He could not have created it in the first place. (iii) The unbelievers entertain a very fallacious concept of the Creator of the heavens and the earth. They think that it is beyond Him to resurrect anything. Notwithstanding the decomposition and disintegration of human bodies, every part of those bodies will still remain within the confines of the heavens and the earth. Now, since God is the Lord of the heavens and the earth, it is pretty easy for Him to retrieve all the fragments of which those bodies were comprised. It is He Who brought them into being, and provided them with all that their bodies were composed of. Since He created human beings in the first instance and gave shape to their bodies, He can easily re-create them.

Implicit in this argument is the warning that the unbelievers are surrounded by God and that they will find no refuge against Him. He has the power to afflict them with any calamity whenever He so wants: they may, for example, be overtaken by a scourge that strikes them from on high or one from beneath their feet. People take this planet earth as their home and build their houses on it. At any moment, the earth can be violently shaken by an earthquake, causing innumerable human beings to be buried under it. Likewise, the sky presently appears to people as a safe canopy. However, lightning, torrential rain, or other such calamities can easily destroy them. In such a condition, their heedlessness of God and the Hereafter and their prattle against their sincere well-wisher, the Prophet (peace be on him), simply amounts to courting self-destruction.

13. An unbiased seeker after truth and guidance can learn many lessons from the system operating in the heavens and the earth. However, those averse to God are simply incapable of perceiving any Divine signs in natural phenomena.

(10) We bestowed Our favour upon David.[14] (We commanded): "O mountains, sing Allah's praises with him"; (and so did We command) the birds.[15] We softened the iron for him, (saying): (11) "Fashion coats of mail and measure their links with care and act righteously.[16] I am watching over whatever you do."

(12) And We subdued the wind to Solomon: ▶

۞ وَلَقَدْ ءَاتَيْنَا دَاوُۥدَ مِنَّا فَضْلًا ۖ يَٰجِبَالُ
أَوِّبِى مَعَهُۥ وَٱلطَّيْرَ ۖ وَأَلَنَّا لَهُ ٱلْحَدِيدَ ﴿١٠﴾ أَنِ
ٱعْمَلْ سَٰبِغَٰتٍ وَقَدِّرْ فِى ٱلسَّرْدِ ۖ وَٱعْمَلُوا۟
صَٰلِحًا ۖ إِنِّى بِمَا تَعْمَلُونَ بَصِيرٌ ﴿١١﴾
وَلِسُلَيْمَٰنَ ٱلرِّيحَ

14. Reference here is made to the many favours God bestowed upon the Prophet David (peace be on him). He was an ordinary young man who hailed from the tribe of Judah and who lived in Bethlehem. He was brought into the limelight following his slaying of the mighty Goliath in the battle against the Philistines. His heroism endeared him to all Israelites. This marked his rise to eminence and power. Subsequent upon the death of Saul, David was first made the ruler of Judah at Hebron (present-day al-Khalīl). He then conquered Jerusalem and made it his capital. Under his dynamic leadership a vast kingdom, stretching from the Gulf of Aqaba to the western banks of the Euphrates, was established, a kingdom whose hallmark was faith in God. In addition to this, David was endowed with exceptional knowledge, wisdom, justice, integrity and devotion to God. (For further details see *Towards Understanding the Qur'ān, al-Baqarah* 2:251, n. 273, Vol. I, p. 193; *Banī Isrā'īl* 17:5 n. 7, Vol. V, pp. 12–16.) (For the Bible see *Samuel* 1:16–17, *Samuel* 2:2–5, *Kings* 1:2, *Chronicles* 1:3–12 – Ed.)

15. Verse 79 of *Sūrah al-Anbiyā'* states the same truth. (See *Towards Understanding the Qur'ān, al-Anbiyā'* 21:79, n. 71, Vol. V, p. 284.)

16. This occurs in *Sūrah al-Anbiyā'* 21: 80. (See also *Towards Understanding the Qur'ān, al-Anbiyā'* 21:80, n. 72, Vol. V, pp. 284–5.)

its morning course was a month's journey and its evening course was a month's journey.[17] We gave him a spring flowing with molten brass,[18] and We subdued for him *jinn* who, by his Lord's permission, worked before him.[19] Such of them as swerved from Our commandment, We let them taste the chastisement of the Blazing Fire. (13) They made for him whatever he would desire: ▶

غُدُوُّهَا شَهْرٌ وَرَوَاحُهَا شَهْرٌ ۖ وَأَسَلْنَا لَهُۥ عَيْنَ
ٱلْقِطْرِ ۖ وَمِنَ ٱلْجِنِّ مَن يَعْمَلُ بَيْنَ يَدَيْهِ بِإِذْنِ
رَبِّهِۦ ۖ وَمَن يَزِغْ مِنْهُمْ عَنْ أَمْرِنَا نُذِقْهُ مِنْ
عَذَابِ ٱلسَّعِيرِ ﴿١٢﴾ يَعْمَلُونَ لَهُۥ مَا يَشَآءُ

17. See *Towards Understanding the Qur'ān, Sūrah al-Anbiyā'* 21:81 and nn. 74–75, Vol. V, pp. 285–7.

18. Some earlier Qur'ān-commentators interpret this to mean that God caused a spring to flow from the earth for Solomon (peace be on him). What actually sprang forth from the spring, however, was molten copper. This statement can also be interpreted to mean that the melting of copper and the manufacture of numerous items made from that metal became so common and widely spread during the Prophet Solomon's time that one felt as though springs of molten copper flowed there. (For further details see *Towards Understanding the Qur'ān, Sūrah al-Anbiyā'* 21: n. 74, Vol. V, pp. 285–6.)

19. We have already discussed whether those made subservient to the Prophet Solomon (peace be on him) were human beings of agricultural and mountainous regions or actual *jinn*, known across the world as an invisible species. (For a detailed discussion see *Towards Understanding the Qur'ān, Sūrah al-Anbiyā'* 21: n. 75, Vol. V, pp. 286–7, and *Sūrah al-Naml* 27: nn. 23, 45 and 52, Vol. VII, pp. 146, 158 and 161.) (See also Sir Sayyid Aḥmad Khān, *Tafsīr al-Qur'ān wa Huwa al-Hudā wa al-Furqān*, Patna: Khuda Bakhsh Oriental Public Library, 1995, Vol. 3, pp. 57–72, see esp. p. 67 – Ed.)

stately buildings, images,[20] basins like water-troughs and ▸	مِن مَّحَـٰرِيبَ وَتَمَـٰثِيلَ وَجِفَانٍ كَٱلْجَوَابِ

20. The word *tamāthīl* (sing. *timthāl*) here stands for replicas of natural objects, be they men, animals, trees, flowers, rivers, or any other inanimate objects. According to *Lisān al-'Arab*:

التمثال إسم للشئ المصنوع مشبها بخلق من خلق الله

"*Timthāl* signifies a replica of something created by God", (Q.v. *timthāl, Lisān al-'Arab*). According to al-Zamakhsharī's famous exegesis, *al-Kashshāf*:

التمثال كل ما صور على صورة غيره من حيوان وغير حيوان

"*Timthāl* signifies all that has been made after the shape (*sūrah*) of any other object, be it animate or inanimate." (Zamakhsharī, *al-Kashshāf*, comments on verse 13.) Therefore, the Qur'ānic account does not necessarily mean that the images made by the *jinn* for the Prophet Solomon (peace be on him) necessarily consisted of statues or images of human beings and animals. Images might equally be those of plants and flowers, natural scenery, and other beautiful designs used by the Prophet Solomon (peace be on him) to decorate his buildings.

Misconception has also arisen because some Qur'ān-commentators have stated that Solomon (peace be on him) had images made of Prophets and angels. These statements were based on Israeli traditions. In the light of those traditions such scholars argued that the making of such images was not prohibited in the Law of earlier religious communities. Our scholars, when they cited these traditions, did so without critically appraising their authenticity; in fact they failed to recognise that the Prophet Solomon (peace be on him) was a follower of Mosaic Law, which forbade the drawing of images and the making of statues of human beings and animals.

Mosaic Law in this regard is like the *Sharī'ah* of the Prophet Muḥammad (peace be on him) which forbids it. These Qur'ān-commentators also ignored the fact that a group of Israelites maligned the Prophet Solomon (peace be on him) out of spite. In fact, they went so far as to hurl vile accusations of polytheism, idolatry, magic and illicit sex at him. Therefore, no Israeli tradition regarding such a distinguished Messenger of God should be accepted if it is discordant with the Law ordained by God. It is common knowledge that all Prophets raised among the Israelites from the time of the Prophet Moses (peace be on him) through the time of the Prophet Jesus (peace be on him) were followers of the Torah. This because none of them was granted any other Scripture which would abrogate the Torah. That it is categorically forbidden in the Torah to make images and statues of humans and animals is evident from the following passages:

> You shall not make for yourself a graven image, or any likeness of anything that is in heaven above, or that is in earth beneath or that is in the water under the earth, (*Exodus* 20:4.)
>
> You shall make for yourselves no idols and erect no graven image on pillars, and you shall not set up a figured stone in your land, to bow down to, (*Leviticus* 26:1.)
>
> Beware lest you act corruptly by making a graven image for yourselves, in the form of any figure, the likeness of male or female, the likeness of any beast that is on the earth, the likeness of any winged bird that flies in the air, the likeness of anything that creeps on the ground, the likeness of any fish that is in the water under the earth, (*Deuteronomy* 4:16–18.)
>
> Cursed be the man who makes a graven or molten image, an abomination to the Lord, a thing made by the hands of a craftsman, and sets it up in secret, (*Deuteronomy* 27:15.)

In the face of these explicit commands how can anyone accept the claim that the Prophet Solomon (peace be on him) directed the *jinn* to make images or statues of Prophets and angels? How can one trust the traditions of the Israelites who had stooped so low as to accuse him of idolatry out of infatuation for his polytheistic wives? (See *Kings* 7:15.)

In any case, as far as the above-mentioned Qur'ān-commentators are concerned, one important point is worth noting. Alongside recounting the Israelite tradition, they explicitly stated that making images and statues was forbidden in the *Sharī'ah* of Muḥammad (peace be on him), and hence, no one may do so on the grounds of following the example of the Prophet Solomon (peace be on him). On the contrary, some of our contemporaries, who have a penchant to follow in the footsteps of Westerners, refer to this verse to legitimise image-making and idol-carving. They claim that since images and statues were made at the bidding of a Messenger of God, and that the

Qur'ān mentions this without expressing any disapproval of his act, shows that it has, necessarily, to be considered as lawful.

The contention of these uncritical followers of the West suffers from two basic flaws: (i) The Qur'ānic expression *tamāthīl* does not necessarily mean human or animal representations. The word can also be used to signify images of inanimate objects. It is wrong, therefore, to infer on the basis of this that the Qur'ān sanctions human and animal representation. (ii) It is established by several authentic *aḥādīth* that the Prophet (peace be on him) forbade, in quite categorical terms, the drawing and keeping of living beings' images. Of these the following *aḥādīth* are noteworthy:

a. 'Ā'ishah relates that Umm Ḥabībah and Umm Salamah had seen images in a church in Abyssinia and they narrated that to the Prophet (peace be on him). He told them: "Such was the state of those people that when some righteous member of their community died, they erected a shrine at his grave and made images in it. On the Day of Judgement they will be declared the worst creatures in God's sight". (Bukhārī, *Kitāb al-Ṣalāh, Bāb Hal Tunbashu Qubūr Mushrikī al-Jāhilīyyah wa Yuttakhadhu Makānuhā Masājid;* Muslim, *Kitāb al-Masājid, Bāb al-Nahy 'an Binā' al-Masājid 'alā al-Qubūr wa Ittikhādh al-Ṣuwar fīhā …;* and al-Nasā'ī, *Kitāb al-Masājid, Bāb al-Nahy 'an Ittikhādh al-Qubūr Masājid.*)
b. Abū Juḥayfah relates that the Prophet (peace be on him) cursed those who made images. (Bukhārī, *Kitāb al-Buyū', Bāb Mu'kil al-Ribā; Kitāb al-Ṭalāq, Bāb Mahr al-Baghīy wa al-Nikāḥ al-Fāsid,* and *Kitāb al-Libās, Bāb Man La'ana al-Muṣawwir.*)
c. Abū Zur'ah relates: "Once I entered a house in Madīnah with Abū Hurayrah and saw an image-maker at the top of the house, making images". On observing this, Abū Hurayrah said: "I have heard the Prophet (peace be on him) say that God says: 'Who can be a greater wrong-doer than he who imitates Me in My [act of] creation. Let them just create a grain or an ant' ". (Bukhārī, *Kitāb al-Libās, Bāb Naqḍ al-Ṣuwar;* Aḥmad ibn Ḥanbal *Musnad,* narrated by Abī Hurayrah; Muslim, *Kitāb al-Libās, Bāb Taḥrīm Taṣwīr Ṣūrat al-Ḥaywān….* The traditions in Muslim and Aḥmad ibn Ḥanbal, *Musnad,* identify this house to be Marwān's.)
d. Abū Muḥammad al-Hudhalī relates on the authority of 'Alī that once he was with the Prophet (peace be on him) attending a funeral. [On that occasion] the Prophet (peace be on him) said: "Who of you will go to Madīnah and then leave no idol

but shatter it, no grave but level it down, and no image but destroy it?" A person said: "I will go, O Messenger of God". He then went but returned home without (accomplishing these tasks) for fear (of reprisal from) the people of Madīnah. Then 'Alī said: "I will go there, O Messenger of God". The Prophet (peace be on him) said: "Then go". He went there and returned and said: "O God's Messenger, there is no idol which I have not shattered, nor any grave which I have not levelled down, nor any image which I have not destroyed". Then the Prophet (peace be on him) said: "Anyone who hereafter makes any of these things has rejected what was revealed to me". (Aḥmad, *Musnad,* narrated by 'Alī ibn Abī Ṭālib; Muslim, *Kitāb al-Janā'iz, Bāb al-Amr bi Taswiyat al-Qabr;* Nasā'ī, *Kitāb al-Janā'iz, Bāb Taswiyat al-Qubūr idhā Rufi'at.*)

e. 'Abd Allāh ibn 'Abbās narrates from the Prophet (peace be on him): ". . . [W]hoever makes any image will be punished and will be tasked to breathe a soul into it. And he will not be able to breathe a soul into it". (Bukhāri, *Kitāb al-Ta'bīr, Bāb Man Kadhiba fī Ḥulumihi;* al-Tirmidhī, *Abwāb al-Libās, Bāb mā jā'a fī al-Muṣawwirīn;* al-Nasā'ī, *Kitāb al-Zīnah, Bāb Dhikr mā Yukallafu Aṣḥāb al-Ṣuwar Yawm al-Qiyāmah;* Aḥmad ibn Ḥanbal, *Musnad,* narrated by 'Abd Allāh ibn 'Abbās.)

f. Sa'īd ibn Abī al-Ḥasan narrates that one day he was with 'Abd Allāh ibn 'Abbās when someone came to him. He said that he was a person who made his living by his hand, by making images. 'Abd Allāh ibn 'Abbās said to him: "I will narrate to you only what I heard the Prophet (peace be on him) say. And I heard him say: 'Whoever makes an image God will chastise him until he breathes a soul into it and he will never be able to do so'. Upon hearing this, the person was greatly enraged and his face turned pale. Ibn 'Abbās told him: 'If you insist on making images, then make images of trees, but don't make the image of an object with a soul'". (Bukhārī, *Kitāb al-Buyū', Bāb Bay' al-Taṣāwīr allatī laysa fīhā Rūḥ wa mā Yukrahu min Dhālik;* Muslim, *Kitāb al-Libās, Bāb Taḥrīm Taṣwīr Ṣūrat al-Ḥaywān...;* Nasā'ī, *Kitāb al-Zīnah, Bāb Dhikr mā Yukallafu Aṣḥāb al-Ṣuwar Yawm al-Qiyāmah;* Aḥmad ibn Ḥanbal, *Musnad,* narrated by 'Abd Allāh ibn 'Abbās.)

g. 'Abd Allāh ibn Mas'ūd relates that the Prophet (peace be on him) said: "On the Day of Judgement those who make images will be given the severest punishment". (Bukhārī, *Kitāb al-Libās, Bāb 'Adhāb al-Muṣawwirīn Yawm al-Qiyāmah;* Muslim, *Kitāb al-Libās, Bāb Taḥrīm Taṣwīr Ṣūrat al-Ḥaywān...;* and Nasā'ī, *Kitāb al-Zīnah, Bāb Dhikr Ashadd al-Nās 'Adhāban*; Aḥmad ibn Ḥanbal, *Musnad*, narrated by 'Abd Allāh ibn Mas'ūd.)

h. According to 'Abd Allāh ibn 'Umar, the Prophet (peace be on him) said: "Those who make images will be punished on the Day of Judgement. They will be asked to breathe life into what they have made". (Bukhārī, *Kitāb al-Libās, Bāb 'Adhāb al-Muṣawwirīn Yawm al-Qiyāmah;* Muslim, *Kitāb al-Libās, Bāb Taḥrīm Taṣwīr Ṣūrat al-Ḥaywān...;* Nasā'ī, *Kitāb al-Zīnah, Bāb Dhikr mā Yukallafu Aṣḥāb al-Ṣuwar Yawm al-Qiyāmah*; Aḥmad ibn Ḥanbal, *Musnad*, narrated by 'Abd Allāh ibn 'Umar.)

i. 'Ā'ishah narrates: "I bought a pillow with images on it. When the Prophet (peace be on him) arrived, he kept standing at the door but did not step inside. I said: 'I turn in repentance to God for the sin that I might have committed'. He asked me about the pillow. I explained that it was for his comfort so that he might recline. However, he told me that those who make such images will be chastised on the Day of Judgement. They will be asked to imbue with life all that they have made. Angels of mercy do not enter a house wherein there are images". (Bukhārī, *Kitāb al-Libās, Bāb man Kariha al-Qu'ūd 'alā al-Ṣuwar;* Muslim, *Kitāb al-Libās, Bāb Taḥrīm Taṣwīr Ṣūrat al-Ḥaywān...;* Nasā'ī, *Kitāb al-Zīnah, Bāb al-Taṣāwīr;* Ibn Mājah, *Kitāb al-Libās, Bāb al-Ṣuwar fī al-Bayt*; Mālik, *Muwaṭṭa', Kitab al-Isti'dhān, Bāb mā jā'a fī al-Ṣuwar wa al-Tamāthīl.*)

j. 'Ā'ishah relates: "Once the Prophet (peace be on him) came to me. I had hung in my room a curtain with images on it. On spotting it, his complexion changed. He tore the curtain to pieces, saying: 'On the Day of Judgement the severest punishment will be given to those who try to make the like of God's creation' ". (Muslim, *Kitāb al-Libās, Bāb Taḥrīm Taṣwīr Ṣūrat al-Ḥaywān...;* Bukhārī, *Kitāb al-Libās, Bāb mā Wuṭi'a min al-Taṣāwīr;* Nasā'ī, *Kitāb al-Zīnah, Bāb Dhikr Ashadd al-Nās 'Adhāban.*)

k. 'Ā'ishah narrates: "Once when the Prophet (peace be on him) returned from a journey, a curtain with images of winged horses was hanging at my door. He asked me to take that curtain off, and I took it off". (Muslim, *Kitāb al-Libās, Bāb Taḥrīm Taṣwīr Ṣūrat al-Ḥaywān...;* Nasā'ī, *Kitāb al-Zīnah, Bāb al-Taṣāwīr.*)

l. Jābir ibn 'Abd Allāh relates that the Prophet (peace be on him) forbade keeping images in the house and also forbade making them. (Tirmidhī, *Abwāb al-Libās, Bāb mā jā'a fī al-Ṣūrah.*)

m. 'Abd Allāh ibn 'Abbās narrates from Abū Ṭalḥah al-Anṣārī that the Prophet (peace be on him) said: "Angels of mercy do not enter a house which has a dog or an image". (Bukhārī, *Kitāb al-Libās, Bāb man Kariha al-Qu'ūd 'alā al-Ṣuwar.*)

n. 'Abd Allāh ibn 'Umar said: "Once Gabriel promised [to visit] the Prophet (peace be on him) but delayed [in coming] for quite a while, so much so that he was distressed and went out of his house. There the Prophet (peace be on him) met Gabriel and complained to him about the incident. Gabriel told him: "We do not enter a house which has a dog or an image in it." (Bukhārī, *Kitāb al-Libās, Bāb lā Tadkhul al-Malā'ikah Baytan fīhi Ṣūrah.*)

Several *aḥādīth* with the same import are recorded by Bukhārī, Muslim, *Kitāb al-Libās, Bāb Taḥrīm Taṣwīr Ṣūrat al-Ḥaywān...;* Abū Dā'ūd, *Kitāb al-Libās, Bāb fī al-Ṣuwar;* Tirmidhī, *Kitāb al-Isti'dhān wa al-Ādāb, Bāb mā jā'a fī ann al-Malā'ikah lā Tadkhul Baytan fīhi Ṣūrah wa lā Kalb;* Nasā'ī, *Kitāb al-Zīnah, Bāb Dhikr Ashadd al-Nās 'Adhāban;* Ibn Mājah, *Kitāb al-Libās, Bāb al-Ṣuwar fī al-Bayt;* Mālik, *Muwwaṭṭā', Kitāb al-Isti'dhān, Bāb Mā jā'a fī al-Ṣuwar wa al-Tamāthīl;* Aḥmad ibn Ḥanbal, *Musnad,* narrated by 'Alī ibn Abī Ṭālib, on the authority of several Companions.

As opposed to these *aḥādīth,* some other *aḥādīth* are also put forward. These appear to make some allowance for images. For example, Abū Ṭalḥah al-Anṣārī maintains that one is allowed to use a curtain where the material has an image embroidered on it, (Bukhārī, *Kitāb al-Libās, Bāb Lā Tadkhul al-Malā'ikah Baytan fīhi Ṣūrah.)* Of similar import is 'Ā'ishah's report that when she tore off the material with images on it for making a mattress, the Prophet (peace be on him) did not object to it. (Muslim, *Kitāb al-Libās, Bāb Taḥrīm Taṣwīr Ṣūrat al-Ḥaywān....*) Likewise, Sālim ibn 'Abd Allāh maintains that the prohibition is directed only against those images that are displayed prominently, but not against those that are spread on the floor. (Aḥmad ibn Ḥanbal, *Musnad,* narrated by 'Abd Allāh ibn 'Umar.)

However, none of these traditions contradicts the fourteen *aḥādīth* quoted above. Moreover, as far as the making of images is concerned, no tradition declares it to be lawful. The traditions which are cited to legitimise image-making are related to the images that had already been made. In this connection the tradition narrated by Abū Ṭalḥah al-Anṣārī that it is allowed to use a curtain with an image embroidered on it is patently unacceptable for it runs counter to many authentic *aḥādīth* that state that the Prophet (peace be on him) not only expressed interdiction of hanging curtains with images on them, but also had them torn down. Furthermore, Tirmidhī and Mālik state that Abū Ṭalḥah al-Anṣārī's own practice was that he felt uneasy about using any cloth that had images on it. This was his attitude as regards carpets, let alone curtains. (Tirmidhī, *Kitāb al-Libās, Bāb mā jā'a fī al-Ṣūrah;* Mālik, *Muwwaṭṭa', Kitāb al-Isti'dhān, Bāb mā jā'a fī al-Ṣuwar wa al-Tamāthīl.)* As for the above-mentioned reports narrated by 'Ā'ishah and Sālim ibn 'Abd Allāh, at the most they suggest the lawfulness of using fabrics with images on them provided they are not an object of esteem. They may be tolerated if they are so placed on the floor that they are trodden over by people's feet. These *aḥādīth*, however, cannot be stretched so far as to legitimise the cultivation of a whole culture that regards making images and statues a proud achievement of human civilisation and which seeks to promote it among Muslims.

The ultimate rule bequeathed by the Prophet (peace be on him) with regard to images is evident from the practice of his Companions. It is a standing principle of Islamic law that the authentic Islamic position is that which was promulgated by the Prophet (peace be on him) in the later years of his life after a gradual unfolding of legal injunctions and the grant of temporary allowances. The fact that the more distinguished Companions adhered to a particular practice after the Prophet's time further proves that that was his final ruling. Let us, therefore, examine the Companions' attitude on the question of images:

i. 'Umar ibn al-Khaṭṭāb told the Christians: "We do not enter your churches because of statues with images." (Bukhārī, *Kitāb al-Ṣalāh, Bāb al-Ṣalāh fī al-Bī'ah.*)
ii. 'Abd Allāh ibn 'Abbās used to offer Prayer in churches except in those that had images. (Bukhārī, *Kitāb al-Ṣalāh, Bāb al-Ṣalāh fī al-Bī'ah.*)
iii. Abū al-Hiyāj al-Asadī relates that 'Alī told him: "Shall I not send you to accomplish the same mission for which the Prophet (peace be on him) had once sent me: leave no statue until you have destroyed it, and leave no elevated grave until you have levelled it down, and leave no image until you have erased it." (Muslim, *Kitāb al-Janā'iz, Bāb al-Amr bi Taswiyat al-Qabr;* Nasā'ī, *Kitāb al-Janā'iz, Bāb Taswiyat al-Qubūr idhā Rufi'at.*)
iv. Ḥanash al-Kinānī relates from 'Alī that he deputed his security chief on a mission and said: "Are you aware of the nature of your mission? It is the same mission that the Prophet (peace be on him) assigned to me. It consists in destroying all images

and levelling down all graves". (Aḥmad ibn Ḥanbal, *Musnad,* narrated by 'Alī ibn Abī Ṭālib.)

This well-proven rule has been recognised by Muslim jurists to be the authoritative Islamic position. Referring to an authoritative legal text, *al-Tawḍīḥ,* Badr al-Dīn al-'Aynī maintains:

> Our [i.e. Ḥanafī] and other jurists consider the making of images of any animate object not only forbidden, but do so quite vehemently and consider it a major sin, regardless of whether one makes them to show disrespect or for any other purpose. Making images is forbidden in all circumstances for it amounts to imitating God's act of creation. Every image is forbidden, be it on a piece of cloth, or on dinars, dirhams or on coins of small value, or on pots or walls. However, making images of inanimate objects, for example trees, etc., is not forbidden. It is immaterial whether the image casts a shadow or not. This is the position of Mālik, Sufyān al-Thawrī, Abū Ḥanīfah and other jurists. According to Qāḍī 'Iyāḍ, dolls are the only exception to the above rule. Mālik even disapproves of the purchase of dolls. (Badr al-Dīn al-'Aynī, *'Umdat al-Qārī, Bāb 'Adhāb al-Muṣawwirīn Yawm al-Qiyāmah.* Nawawī amplifies this viewpoint in his *Sharḥ Muslim, Kitāb al-Libās wa al-Zīnah, Bāb Taḥrīm Taṣwīr Ṣūrat al-Ḥaywān*...)

This, therefore, is the Islamic position as regards *making* images. As for *using* images made by others, the Islamic ruling as held by jurists has been expressed in the following words by Ibn Ḥajar al-'Asqalānī:

> The Mālikī jurist Ibn al-'Arabī says that the unlawfulness of an image which casts a shadow is unanimously recognised as forbidden, regardless of whether it is an object of respect or of disrespect. Dolls for girls are exempt from the above ruling which enjoys consensus. Ibn al-'Arabī is also of the opinion that if there is an image which casts no shadow and remains in its actual state, [that is, it is unlike the reflection in a mirror but is unchanging like printed images], that too is forbidden. It is immaterial whether such an image evokes respect or disrespect. However, if its head is cut off or if some of its parts are dismembered, it may be used ... Imām al-Ḥaramayn al-Juwayanī is of the opinion that one may use a curtain or pillow

> with an image on it. No image may, however, be hung on a wall or ceiling, for this amounts to showing respect to it. However, if it is on a curtain or a pillow, it does not evoke respect... Ibn Abī Shaybah holds this opinion on the authority of 'Ikrimah that the *'ulamā'* in the age of the Successors were of the opinion that an image on [the sheet of] a floor or on a pillow, will be an object of disrespect [and hence will not be forbidden]. They were of the opinion that if an image was placed on an elevated spot it is forbidden, but is permissible if it is trampled by feet. This position is also ascribed to Ibn Sīrīn, Sālim ibn 'Abd Allāh, 'Ikrimah ibn Khālid and Sa'īd ibn Jubayr. (*Fatḥ al-Bāri, Kitāb al-Libās, Bāb mā Wuṭi'a min al-Taṣāwīr.*)

All this makes it clear that the prohibition of images in Islam is far from being an issue admitting doubt or disagreement. Rather, in view of the Prophet's explicit commands, the Companions' practice, and the unanimous ruling of Muslim jurists down the ages, the prohibition of images is an accepted rule. It cannot be altered simply in deference to the strained, hair-splitting interpretations of those who have evidently been swayed by alien, un-Islamic cultures.

Let us now also take note of the following relevant points so that there remains no basis for any misunderstanding about the matter.

Some people try to make a distinction between a photograph and an image that is drawn by hand. It is, however, noteworthy that the *Sharī'ah* prohibits images as such rather than a particular way of making them. An image is an image, irrespective of whether it is made by a camera or by a human hand. The *Sharī'ah* makes no distinction in its ruling in consideration of the mode or mechanism involved in the making of the image.

Some people argue that the Islamic prohibition against images was only a transient measure, aimed at extirpating polytheism and idolatry. Now, since pictures no longer pose that danger, this prohibition need not be maintained. This line of argument, however, is quite fallacious. First, at no point do the relevant *aḥādīth* specify the above to be the underlying reason of the Islamic prohibition of images. Moreover, there is no substance in the claim that polytheism and idolatry have by now been altogether abandoned. In the Indo-Pakistan subcontinent itself there are millions of polytheists who are still given to idolatry. Likewise, a range of polytheistic practices is in vogue in many other parts of the world. Even Christians, who are the People of the Book, worship statues of the Prophet Jesus (peace be on him) and Mary and a number of Christian saints. Even a large number of Muslims have been unable to resist succumbing in one way or another to the worship of God's creatures.

There are others who contend that only images with a polytheistic drift should be prohibited. In other words, such people would only like the images or statues of people who are already objects of worship to be prohibited while they see no reason why the pictures and statues of others should be considered forbidden. Those who articulate such views are evidently not content with deducing legal rulings from God's commands and directives. They go further and arrogate to themselves the authority to prescribe the *Sharī'ah* on God's behalf. Such people hardly appreciate that images, apart from promoting polytheism and idolatry, are also a source of many other evils. They are, for example, a means for promoting and reinforcing personality cults. They are especially a potent means to create a false halo around dictators, monarchs and political leaders. They have also been extensively used to arouse lust and lasciviousness which has reached its zenith in our time. Moreover, images are manipulated in our time on a wide scale to serve propaganda purposes, to sow hatred and hostility between nations, to arouse discord and dissension and to mislead the common man. It is wrong, therefore, to say that the Islamic prohibition against making images is based solely on the premise that there is a necessary nexus between them and idolatry. The *Sharī'ah* forbids making images of living beings, and we have no authority to abrogate or amend that rule. If we do not claim to be the promulgators of the Islamic *Sharī'ah*, and consider ourselves simply to be its followers, then we must totally give up the practice of dealing in images. It does not behove us to first assume something to be the reason underlying an Islamic injunction and then follow up this arbitrary assumption and end up legitimising some kinds of images and prohibiting others.

There are also some others who claim that there are some innocuous kinds of images that do not pose any danger and are not conducive to any evil. For them, such images as are bereft of political propaganda, the promotion of hatred and discord, the arousal of lasciviousness or other evils of the kind need not be prohibited. However, this is flawed logic. Those who make this point succumb to the error we have already identified. They first venture to determine, of their own accord, the underlying reason of an Islamic injunction, and then proceed to declare that since this reason is not found in a certain case, that case is thus not covered by that injunction. They also totally ignore an important characteristic of the *Sharī'ah*: that it does not draw vague and obscure boundaries between the lawful and the unlawful. For if it did so, this would make it difficult for people to decide up to which

huge, built-in-cauldrons:[21] "Work, O house of David, in thankfulness[22] (to your Lord). Few of My servants are truly thankful."	وَقُدُورٍ رَّاسِيَٰتٍۚ ٱعۡمَلُوٓاْ ءَالَ دَاوُۥدَ شُكۡرٗاۚ وَقَلِيلٞ مِّنۡ عِبَادِيَ ٱلشَّكُورُ ١٣

point they remain within the limits of the lawful and whereafter they exceed those limits. On the contrary, the *Sharī'ah* draws clear lines of distinction between the lawful and the unlawful that are as clearly visible as a sunny day.

As regards images, it is absolutely clear that images of animate objects are prohibited, whereas the images of inanimate objects are permissible. There is no ambiguity about the matter. Anyone who is desirous of following God's commands will have no difficulty in knowing what is lawful from what is not. Had some animate images been declared permissible and others forbidden, not even the most comprehensive catalogue would have enabled one to distinguish between the permissible and the prohibited. Despite an exhaustive list confusion would nevertheless have remained in distinguishing between one and the other. There is a parallel between the prohibition of pictures and the prohibition of intoxicating drinks. Islam has ordained absolute abstinence from whatever causes intoxication. Had it been ordained that one may consume intoxicants to an amount that falls short of causing intoxication, the lines of demarcation would have been obscure. This would have made it difficult for people to determine what the permissible limit of drinking was. (For further elaboration see this writer's *Rasā'il wa Masā'il*, Vol. 1, pp. 152–155.)

21. This indicates that the scale of Solomon's hospitality was massive, which explains his "basins like water-troughs" and "huge, built-in-cauldrons" respectively to serve and entertain his guests.

22. The Qur'ānic directive is that man should act with a sense of gratitude to God. The verbal acknowledgement of God's bounties by a person who uses them in a manner discordant with His pleasure is an act of futility. The truly grateful servant of God is he who not only verbally acknowledges God's bounties but also makes use of those bounties in accordance with the Benefactor's pleasure.

(14) When We executed Our decree of death on Solomon, nothing indicated to the *jinn* that he was dead except a worm eating away his staff. So when Solomon fell down, the *jinn* realised[23] that had they known what lies in the realm beyond perception, they would not have continued to be in this humiliating chastisement.[24]

فَلَمَّا قَضَيْنَا عَلَيْهِ ٱلْمَوْتَ مَا دَلَّهُمْ عَلَىٰ مَوْتِهِۦٓ
إِلَّا دَآبَّةُ ٱلْأَرْضِ تَأْكُلُ مِنسَأَتَهُۥ ۖ فَلَمَّا
خَرَّ تَبَيَّنَتِ ٱلْجِنُّ أَن لَّوْ كَانُوا۟ يَعْلَمُونَ
ٱلْغَيْبَ مَا لَبِثُوا۟ فِى ٱلْعَذَابِ ٱلْمُهِينِ ﴿١٤﴾

---

23. The words of the verse are *tabayyanat al-jinn*. It can be translated as we have done above. Alternatively, it can also be translated as … "when Solomon fell down the truth about the true state of the *jinn* became evident". In the case of the first translation, the meaning is that when Solomon fell down, the *jinn* realised that all their notions about themselves having knowledge of the realm beyond perception were proved wrong. On the other hand, in the case of the second translation, it would mean that it became evident to the common people that the *jinn* had no access to the realm beyond perception.

24. Some present-day Qur'ān-commentators have put forward the following bizarre interpretation of the verse: The Prophet Solomon's son, Rehoboam, was a good-for-nothing. Being given to a life of ease and luxury, and being surrounded by a host of sycophantish courtiers, he did not prove to be a worthy successor to his distinguished father. A little after his father's death, his vast empire collapsed. Furthermore, the frontier tribesmen, (which in the opinion of some people is meant by the word *jinn*), whom the Prophet Solomon (peace be on him) had harnessed to his service by his overpowering might, got out of control and rebelled. (cf. Sir Sayyid Aḥmad Khān's views in regard to the *jinn* in his *Tafsīr al-Qur'ān wa Huwa al-Hudā wa al-Furqān*, Patna: Khuda Bakhsh Oriental Public Library, 1995, Vol. 3, pp. 57–72, see esp. p. 67 – Ed.)

This contrived interpretation, however, is not at all in concordance with the Qur'ānic text. For the Qur'ān's narrative is as follows: death overtook the Prophet Solomon (peace be on him) at a time when he was either standing or sitting, or reclining against his staff. Supported by the staff, his dead body remained standing where it was and the *jinn* continued to serve him under the impression that he was alive. It was only when worms ate away his staff, making it hollow from within, that his dead body fell down. It was then that the *jinn* realised that Solomon had died.

This simple and straightforward narration is hardly amenable to the far-fetched interpretation to which it has been subjected by these commentators. There is little justification for their laboured interpretation that the staff's being eaten away by worms means that Solomon's son was worthless, that the staff signifies Solomon's power and glory, and that Solomon's death means the utter fragmentation of his vast kingdom. Should God have wanted to say all this, there was no dearth of explicit words in the clear Arabic of the Qur'ān to express these ideas. What need was there to have recourse to such a convoluted and obscure diction to narrate such ordinary facts? The Qur'ān never resorts to a style full of riddles. In any case, how could the ordinary Arabs of the Prophet's time, who were the primary recipients of this Message, have solved these riddles?

The most bizarre aspect of this interpretation is that it equates the *jinn* with the frontier tribesmen of the Prophet Solomon's kingdom. Now, the question arises: have there ever been any tribesmen who have either claimed or who were considered by polytheists to have knowledge of the realm beyond perception? The wording of the verse under discussion underscores reference to a particular species who claimed to have access to the realm beyond perception; or to put it differently, who were perceived to have such knowledge.

The Qur'ānic account thus lays bare the gross ignorance of those who had kept attending the Prophet Solomon (peace be on him) for such a long time after his death, thinking that he was still alive. This account should suffice to make a well-meaning person revise the opinion that those who are being referred to here are frontier tribesmen. However, some people are so overwhelmed by the rampant materialism of the present world that the very idea of believing in the existence of an invisible species called *jinn* makes them blush with shame. As a result, they cling to their fanciful interpretations and this despite the fact that the Qur'ānic account is quite unambiguous.

It is pertinent to note that at several places the Qur'ān plainly states that the polytheists of Arabia regarded the *jinn* as God's partners, even His issue, and sought protection from them:

(15) For Sheba[25] there was also a Sign in their ▶	لَقَدْ كَانَ لِسَبَإٍ فِي مَسْكَنِهِمْ ءَايَةٌ

And yet, some people have come to associate the *jinn* with Allah in His Divinity, even though it is He Who has created them (*al-An'ām* 6:100.)

They have established a kinship between Allah and the *jinn* (*al-Ṣāffāt* 37:158.)

Some from among the humans used to seek protection of some among the *jinn* (*al-Jinn* 72:6.)

Associated with such beliefs was their notion that the *jinn* had access to the realm beyond perception. Accordingly, they used to approach the *jinn* to find out about matters belonging to that realm. God recounts this incident so as to drive home to the Arabian unbelievers that their insistence on holding on to the notions of *Jāhilīyah* was altogether unreasonable; such notions were absolutely baseless. (For further details see n. 63 below.)

25. For a better appreciation of its contents, this verse should be read together with the opening verses of the *sūrah* (see vv. 1–9). In these verses, we are informed that the Arabian unbelievers found the very idea of the Hereafter to be totally contrary to reason. They also emphatically dismissed the Prophet (peace be on him) for teaching them the doctrine of the Hereafter, contending that he either lacked sanity or was a downright fabricator. As a rejoinder to this, God drew attention to some rational evidence as we have elaborated in nn. 7, 8 and 12 above. This account is followed in vv. 10 ff. with the stories of the people of Saba' which supplement the discourse with historical evidence.

The point brought home is that the history of mankind unmistakably points to the fact that the law of requital has been operating through the ages. Were one to cast a reflective glance at mankind's past, it would become evident that the world is not a mad world where things are happening arbitrarily. Far from that, the world is being governed by the All-Seeing, All-Hearing God, Who distinguishes between those that are thankful to Him and those that are thankless.

Anyone who pays attention to the annals of history can derive a lesson from this. Since we find that a distinction is made even in this world between the good and the iniquitous, the ultimate end of the dwelling-place:[26] the two gardens to the right and to the left.[27] "Eat of your Lord's provision, and render thanks to Him. Most pleasant is your land and Most Forgiving is your Lord." (16) But they turned away[28] and so We let loose upon them a devastating flood that swept away the dams[29] ▶

جَنَّتَانِ عَن يَمِينٍ وَشِمَالٍ كُلُوا۟ مِن رِّزْقِ رَبِّكُمْ وَٱشْكُرُوا۟ لَهُۥ ۚ بَلْدَةٌ طَيِّبَةٌ وَرَبٌّ غَفُورٌ ﴿١٥﴾ فَأَعْرَضُوا۟ فَأَرْسَلْنَا عَلَيْهِمْ سَيْلَ ٱلْعَرِمِ

two cannot be the same. God's justice certainly requires that a time should come when both good and evil are fully recompensed.

26. In other words, there was enough indication of the fact that whatever they have was not their own creation but was bestowed upon them by God and by none other than Him. This also points to the fact that God alone deserves to be worshipped, thanked and served. For it is He alone, rather than anyone else, Who bestowed on them the bounties that they are enjoying. It is equally important to note that their possessions are not permanent; possibly, what they have today they will cease to have at a later date.

27. This statement does not mean that there were only two gardens in the whole kingdom. Rather, the statement is simply made to indicate the abundance of greenery in the kingdom. Indeed, one could see gardens throughout the length and breadth of the land of Saba'.

28. In other words, rather than obey God and be thankful to Him, they chose the course of disobedience and ingratitude.

29. The words are "*sayl al-'arim*". The word *'arim* is derived from the South Arabian word *'arman* which means 'dam'. We find this word to have been used frequently in the ancient inscriptions recently excavated from the ruins in Yemen. For example, a tablet dating 592 C.E., or 543 C.E., which the Abyssinian Governor of Yemen, Abrahah, had installed after having the Ma'ārib Dam repaired, uses this word

and replaced their gardens by two others bearing bitter fruits, tamarisks, and a few lote trees.[30] (17) Thus did We retribute them for their ingratitude. And none do We retribute in this manner except the utterly ungrateful.

(18) We placed other prominent towns between them, the towns that We had blessed and had set well-measured stages between them.[31] ▶

وَبَدَّلْنَٰهُم بِجَنَّتَيْهِمْ جَنَّتَيْنِ ذَوَاتَىْ أُكُلٍ
خَمْطٍ وَأَثْلٍ وَشَىْءٍ مِّن سِدْرٍ قَلِيلٍ ﴿١٦﴾
ذَٰلِكَ جَزَيْنَٰهُم بِمَا كَفَرُوا۟ ۖ وَهَلْ نُجَٰزِىٓ
إِلَّا ٱلْكَفُورَ ﴿١٧﴾ وَجَعَلْنَا بَيْنَهُمْ وَبَيْنَ
ٱلْقُرَى ٱلَّتِى بَٰرَكْنَا فِيهَا قُرًى ظَٰهِرَةً
وَقَدَّرْنَا فِيهَا ٱلسَّيْرَ ۖ

over and over again to mean dam. The expression *sayl al-'arim*, therefore, means the flood caused by the dam's breach.

30. As a result of this flood the whole territory suffered destruction, including the canals and the irrigation system. The region once known for its natural beauty was thus reduced to desolation, becoming a jungle of wild trees. Nothing edible was left other than the berries of lote bushes.

31. The expression, "the towns that We had blessed" refers to the region of Palestine and Syria. The Qur'ān generally applies this expression in the context of this region. (See, for example, *al-A'rāf* 7:137; *Banī Isrā'īl* 17:1 and *al-Anbiyā'* 21:71 and 81.)

The expression "prominent towns" refers to the centres of habitation located on the highway, in full view of all, rather than those situated in obscure locations. It may also mean contiguous towns, in so far as one town followed another. No sooner had the signs of a town disappeared than those of another town appeared.

There were milestones on the highway from Yemen to Syria indicating the length of the journey. This seems to be indicated by

Move back and forth between them, night and day, in perfect security. (19) But they said: "Lord, make the stages of our journeys longer."[32] They wronged their own selves so We reduced them to bygone tales, and utterly tore them to pieces.[33] ▶

سِيرُوا۟ فِيهَا لَيَالِىَ وَأَيَّامًا ءَامِنِينَ ﴿١٨﴾ فَقَالُوا۟ رَبَّنَا بَـٰعِدْ بَيْنَ أَسْفَارِنَا وَظَلَمُوٓا۟ أَنفُسَهُمْ فَجَعَلْنَـٰهُمْ أَحَادِيثَ وَمَزَّقْنَـٰهُمْ كُلَّ مُمَزَّقٍ

the saying: "We ... set well-measured stages between them". In other words, the whole journey between Yemen and Syria virtually passed through inhabited territory. While journeying through the desert one halts for rest wherever one feels tired. In contrast, when travelling through inhabited areas, one plans one's journey ahead of time and knows where one will break the journey for rest; in other words, one knows where one will spend the afternoon, and where one will spend the night.

32. This does not necessarily mean that the prayer was made in words. Anyone who fails to give thanks to God's bounties veritably cries out: "I do not deserve these bounties". The same also applies to those nations that misuse God's bounties. Likewise, those who misuse God's bounties virtually call upon God: "O Lord, take away these bounties from us for we are not worthy of them".

They prayed: "Lord, make the stages of our journey longer". This indicates that the people of Saba' had begun to consider their large population to be an encumbrance. Like other senseless nations, they too regarded the rise in population as a dangerous phenomenon and had begun to adopt measures directed at preventing that trend.

33. The people of Saba' were devastated on such a massive scale that their fragmentation became proverbial for the Arabs. Even now if the Arabs speak of a nation's disintegration, they use the expression تفرقوا أيدى سبا (they disintegrated like the people of Saba'.)

When Saba's well-being began to dwindle, several tribes left their home towns and settled in other parts of Arabia. For example, the

Verily there are Signs in this for everyone who is steadfast and thankful.[34] (20) *Iblīs* found his estimate of them to be true, and they followed him, except a party of the believers.[35] ▶

إِنَّ فِي ذَٰلِكَ لَءَايَٰتٍ لِّكُلِّ صَبَّارٍ شَكُورٍ ﴿١٩﴾ وَلَقَدْ صَدَّقَ عَلَيْهِمْ إِبْلِيسُ ظَنَّهُۥ فَٱتَّبَعُوهُ إِلَّا فَرِيقًا مِّنَ ٱلْمُؤْمِنِينَ ﴿٢٠﴾

Ghassānids moved into Jordan and Syria while the Aws and Khazraj tribes found their way to Yathrib, which later came to be known as Madīnah. The Khuzā'ah tribe settled in the region of Tihāmah, near Jeddah, whereas the Azd migrated to 'Umān. The Lakhm, Judhām and Kindah tribes were also forced to move away. In sum, the people of Saba' were so widely scattered that they lost their identity for ever.

34. The "steadfast and thankful" in the present context refer to those who do not lose their equipoise because of the bounties bestowed upon them by God. Their heads are not swayed with arrogance when they come upon an abundance of wealth. They also do not forget God, Who had granted them all that they have. Such people can learn a great many lessons from the past nations that met their doom as a result of disobeying God after they had reached heights of progress and glory.

35. One learns from the history of Saba' that from ancient times there had always been amongst them a group of people who believed in the One True God rather than a multiplicity of deities. The existence of such a group has been corroborated by recent archaeological researches including the inscriptions recovered from the ruins of Yemen. Some inscriptions dating from around 650 B.C. indicate that there were various places of worship in the kingdom of Saba' where the "Lord of the heavens" was exclusively worshipped; He was referred to as *Dhū Samawī* ذو سموى or *Dhū Samāwī* ذوسماوى (that is, Lord of the heavens), or even at places as *Malikun Dhu Samawī* مالكن ذو سموى . This small group flourished for centuries in Yemen. One notes the existence of a similar place of worship in 378 C.E. dedicated to *Ilāh Dhu Samawī* إله ذوسموى. Another inscription of 465 C.E. reads as follows: بنصر وردا إلهن بعل سمين وأرضين. (With the help of God Who is the Lord of the

(21) *Iblīs* had no authority over them and whatever happened was in order that We might know him who believes in the Hereafter as distinct from him who is in doubt about it.[36] Your Lord is watchful over everything.[37]

وَمَا كَانَ لَهُۥ عَلَيْهِم مِّن سُلْطَٰنٍ إِلَّا لِنَعْلَمَ مَن يُؤْمِنُ بِٱلْءَاخِرَةِ مِمَّنْ هُوَ مِنْهَا فِى شَكٍّ ۗ وَرَبُّكَ عَلَىٰ كُلِّ شَىْءٍ حَفِيظٌ ﴿٢١﴾

---

heavens and the earth). Another inscription of 458 C.E. employs the expression *Birada Raḥmanān*, بردارحمنن (with the help of al-Raḥmān) for the same God.

36. Iblīs does not have the power to compel God's devout servants to commit disobedience if they really intend to obey Him. The utmost power that he has is to try to mislead mankind and to prompt those who intend to join his ranks. This power was granted to *Iblīs* so as to distinguish between those who truly believe in the Hereafter and those who are in doubt about it.

The verse declares that only belief in the Hereafter ensures that man will consistently follow the Straight Way. In the absence of this belief, one is bound to go astray, for in that case one would be devoid of all sense of accountability. *Iblīs*'s most effective strategy, therefore, is to make man oblivious of the Hereafter. However, those who see through his mischief can never bring themselves to sacrifice their everlasting success in the Hereafter in exchange for some paltry, material gain in this transient world. By contrast, those who are overwhelmed by Satan's allurements have no concern with the Hereafter and pay no heed to the voice of their conscience. Such people are bound to suffer owing to their rejection of the Hereafter. By the same token, those who follow the Straight Way do so by dint of their belief in the Hereafter.

37. For a better understanding of the Qur'ānic allusions to the history of the people of Saba', it is necessary to bear in mind the information available to us regarding their history from other sources. According to such historical sources, Saba' was the name for a very large nation in South Arabia that comprised several large tribes. On the Prophet's authority, Aḥmad ibn Ḥanbal, Ibn Jarīr al-Ṭabarī, Ibn

Abī Ḥātim, Ibn 'Abd al-Barr and Tirmidhī report that Saba' was the name of the ancestor of the nation that consisted of the following tribes: Kindah, Ḥimyar, Azd, Asha'arīyīn, Madhḥij, Anmār (comprised of two branches – Khath'am and Bajīlah), 'Āmilah, Judhām, Lakhm and Ghassān. (Aḥmad ibn Ḥanbal, *Musnad,* narrated by 'Abd Allāh ibn Abbās; Ṭirmidhī, *Kitāb Tafsīr al-Qur'ān 'an Rasūl Allāh*; Ṭabarī, *Tafsīr,* comments on verse 15; Ibn Kathīr, *Tafsīr*, comments on verse 15.)

Saba' were a celebrated people of Arabia from ancient times. An inscription of 2500 B.C. mentions them as Sābūm. Their account features quite often in Babylonian and Assyrian inscriptions as also in the Bible. (For their reference in the Bible, see *Psalms* 72:15; *Jeremiah* 6:20; *Ezekiel* 27:22 and 38:13, and *Job* 6:19.) The Greek geographer and historian, Theophrastus (d. 287 B.C.) also recorded information about them. The people of Saba' were settled in the south-western corner of the Arabian Peninsula, presently known as Yemen. Saba's rise to prominence commenced from 1100 B.C. By the time of the Prophets David and Solomon (peace be on them) the fame of these people had spread far and wide on account of their fabulous affluence. In the beginning they were sun-worshippers. However, when the Queen of Saba' embraced the true faith under the influence of the Prophet Solomon (965 B.C.-926 B.C.), presumably most Sabaeans became Muslims (that is, submitters to God's Revealed Guidance). However, at some later stage idolatry and polytheism made inroads into their lives. They took to worshipping Almaqah (the moon god), 'Ashtar (Venus), Dhāt Ḥamīm and Dhāt Ba'dān (the sun god), Ḥarmatam or Ḥarīmat and idols representing many other gods and goddesses. Almaqah, however, was their chief deity. Their kings claimed to derive authority from it and presented themselves as its representatives. Numerous inscriptions that have been excavated point to an abundance of temples earmarked for worshipping this deity. People offered thanks to these deities, essentially Almaqah, on every important occasion.

Recent archaeological researches have unearthed around three thousand inscriptions which bring into sharp relief the history of the people of Saba'. With the help of Arabic, Greek and Roman sources, one can compile a fairly good amount of their history. According to the information thus made available the following emerge as the important phases of their history.

i. *Pre-650 B.C. period*. During this period the kings of Saba' were known as Mukarrib Saba'. This was probably a synonym of *muqarrib,* which meant that these kings claimed to be intermediaries between human beings and their deities. In other words, they enjoyed the status of priest-kings. At that time, Ṣirwāḥ was the seat of these kings. To this day its ruins are found to the west of Ma'ārib. This place, which lies at a distance of a day's journey from Ma'ārib, is now known as al-Kharībah. It was during this period that the foundations of the famous Ma'ārib Dam were laid. From time to time, extensions to the dam were later made by a number of kings.

ii. *From 650 B.C. to 115 B.C.* During this period the kings gave up their title of Mukarrib and were simply known as kings and took Ma'ārib as their capital. In other words, the state assumed a markedly political and secular as distinguished from a religious orientation. This was a period of extraordinary growth and development. Ma'ārib, which was 3,900 feet above sea level, was located 60 miles to the east of Ṣan'ā'. To this day its ruins bear witness that there was a time when it was the centre of a highly civilised nation.

iii. *From 115 B.C. to 300 C.E.* During this period the Ḥimyar tribe gained ascendancy in the kingdom of Saba'. This was a constituent tribe of the people of Saba' which outnumbered other tribes. Raydān, which was the Ḥimyar's centre, was made the kingdom's capital. This later came to be known as Ẓafār. Today, its ruins are found at a circular hill near the present town of Yarīm. Near Yarīm there lives a small tribe known as Ḥimyar. When one observes them today it seems hard to imagine that they are the same people who had once scaled great heights of power and glory. During this period the words Yamnat and Yamnāt began to be used for the first time to describe a part of the kingdom. Gradually, the whole region, extending from the south-western coast of Arabia to Aden and from Ḥadramawt to Bāb al-Mandab came to be known as Yaman (Yemen). This was the period during which Saba's decline set in.

iv. *300 C.E. till the rise of Islam.* This was the period of the Sabaeans' ruin. The period was marked by constant civil wars, the destruction of the Sabaeans' trade and commerce, and the collapse of their agriculture. This process culminated in the loss of Saba's independent identity. First, the Abyssinians ruled over Yemen from 340 C.E. to 378 C.E. by taking advantage of the feuds between the Ḥimyar and other tribes. At a later date, the people of Saba' regained their independence. However, their prized Ma'ārib Dam developed cracks and by 450 C.E. it had collapsed, resulting in a wide-ranging deluge, which is referred to in the Qur'ānic verse above (see verse 16). Until the time of Abrahah, the dam was periodically repaired. However, by then the people of Saba' who had become scattered far and wide could not reassemble in their homeland. Nor could

> their remarkable agricultural and irrigation systems ever be restored. In 523 C.E. the Jewish king of Yemen, Dhū Nuwās, ruthlessly persecuted the Christians of Najrān. This event is mentioned in the Qur'ān, as the incident of Aṣḥāb al-Akhdūd. (See *al-Burūj* 85:5–8.) For avenging this wrong, the Christian state of Abyssinia invaded Yemen and conquered the entire country. At a later date, Abrahah, the Abyssinian viceroy in Yemen, mounted his infamous invasion of the Ka'bah aimed at demolishing its prestige and central position in Arabia. In so doing his intention was to bring the whole of western Arabia under Abyssinian control. Abrahah's invasion took place in 571 C.E. shortly before the Prophet Muḥammad's birth. The Qur'ān graphically recounts in *Sūrah al-Fīl* (*Sūrah* 105) the rout Abrahah and his army had to face. Finally, in 575 C.E. the Persians established control over Yemen which ended in 628 C.E. when the Persian governor, Bādhān, embraced Islam.

The rise of the people of Saba' rested on two pillars: their accomplishments in agriculture and trade. Agriculture had developed owing to their excellent irrigation network. Except for Babylon this was unrivalled in ancient times. Surprisingly enough, there were no natural rivers. However, torrents of water during the rainy season would flow from the mountains forming lakes. The people ingeniously converted these torrents of rainwater into a network of canals. As a result, the whole country had become, to borrow the Qur'ānic description, as though it were a garden, (see verse 15, n. 27 above). Their main water resource was a huge reservoir near Ma'ārib in the midst of a valley in the hills called Balaq, a reservoir created by the construction of a dam. However, when God decided to deny them His favours, the Ma'ārib Dam collapsed in the middle of the fifth century and the water overflowing from it deluged everything, particularly the irrigation network, which could never be restored.

God had granted the people of Saba' the best geographical location for trade and commerce and they derived maximum benefit from it. For more than a thousand years they remained intermediaries in the trade between the east and the west. Merchandise such as silk from China, spices from Indonesia and Malabar, fabrics and swords from India, slaves, monkeys, ostrich feathers and ivory from East Africa regularly reached their ports. The Sabaeans used to supply these items to markets in Egypt and Syria, wherefrom these items were exported to Rome and Greece. Furthermore, they themselves produced in huge quantities frankincense, myrrh, amber, and other aromatic objects which were in much demand in Egypt, Syria, Rome and Greece.

So skilled were the merchants of Saba' that they enjoyed control over both sea and land routes. As for the sea route, the people of Saba' maintained a monopoly over maritime trade for a thousand years. This because they alone knew the secrets of the Red Sea's seasonal winds, underwater reefs, and appropriate locations for anchorage. No other nation had the know-how to risk navigating in these dangerous waters. The people of Saba' used to carry their merchandise to the ports of Jordan and Egypt through the sea route. From there were routes which, passing through Aden and Ḥadramawt, converged at Ma'ānib. At this time juncture, a highway leading from al-'Ulā', Tabūk, and Aylah went as far as Petra. Thereafter, the highway forked in two directions – one going to Egypt and the other to Syria. A number of Sabaean colonies dotted the highway from Yemen to the borders of Syria and caravans passed through both by day and night as mentioned in the Qur'ān, (see verse 18). The traces of these colonies are still found along this route, and many Sabaean and Ḥimyarite inscriptions have been unearthed from them.

Around 100 C.E., however, the Sabaeans' trade began to decline. With the growing ascendancy of the Greeks and Romans in the region, much hue and cry was raised against the Sabaeans' control over the region's trade. While the Greeks did not succeed in the undertaking to dislodge the Sabaeans, the Romans were able to vanquish them. In his efforts to displace the Sabaeans, the Egyptian Pharaoh, Ptolemy II (282 B.C.-246 B.C.), who was of Greek stock, reopened the Nile-Red Sea Canal that had originally been dug by Pharaoh Sesostris some seventeen hundred years earlier. The Egyptian naval fleet used this canal to gain control over the Red Sea, but could not achieve a decisive victory over the Sabaeans.

At a later date, however, when Rome established its ascendancy over Egypt, the more resourceful Roman naval and merchant fleet controlled the Red Sea. By then, the people of Saba' had become too weak to resist their onslaught. Subsequently, the Romans set up their trade colonies throughout the region, especially at seaports. Later on when the Romans had established their domination over Egypt, they brought an even more powerful trade fleet to the sea. This was followed by the induction of a naval force to provide protection to Roman maritime trade. In these colonies arrangements had been made to meet the requirements of Roman ships. Moreover, wherever possible, they also served as military bases. Eventually, the Romans established their total control over Aden. The Romans and Abyssinians joined hands against the Sabaeans. As a result, the latter lost even their independence. Having lost control over the sea route, they were left with only the land route to carry out their trade. Many factors,

(22) (O Prophet),[38] say to those who associate others ▶	قُلِ ٱدْعُوا۟ ٱلَّذِينَ زَعَمْتُم

however, affected them adversely even in this regard: the Nabateans expelled the Sabaeans from their colonies covering the entire area from Petra and al-'Ulā to upper Ḥijāz and Jordan. In 106 C.E. the Romans destroyed the Nabatean kingdom and established their own ascendancy up to the borders of Ḥijāz, including Syria and Jordan. Both the Abyssinians and Romans tried to displace the Sabaeans. The former invaded Yemen several times and eventually managed to conquer the whole country. Thus, God's wrath seized the once prosperous Sabaeans and they have never been able to clamber out of the pit of curse in which they were cast.

There was a time when the Sabaeans enjoyed fabulous wealth and both the Greeks and Romans were envious of them. According to Strabo (d. 23 C.E.), they used vessels of gold and silver and their roofs, walls and doors were also overlaid with ivory, gold, silver and precious stones. According to Pliny (d. 79 C.E.), the wealth of Rome and Persia flowed to them and they happened to be the most affluent people in the world. Their kingdom was known for its green and fertile land full of agricultural fields, orchards and cattle. Another chronicler, Artemidorus (fl. 100 B.C.) mentions that they immersed themselves in worldly pleasures. Instead of using ordinary wood for fuel, they used cinnamon, sandalwood and other fragrant objects. Likewise, other Greek historians have noted their unusual fondness for fragrance, relating that when merchant vessels passed by their seacoasts, currents of fragrant wind reached them.

The Sabaeans were the first people in history to construct a skyscraper on the top of a hill in Ṣan'ā', which was known for centuries in the region as Ghumdān Palace. According to Arab historians, this structure had 20 floors and each floor was 36 feet high. However, the Sabaeans enjoyed this splendour and glory only as long as God blessed them with His favours. When they transgressed all limits and became ungrateful to God, He deprived them of His favours. As a result, they are today no more than an obscure relic of history.

38. In the preceding passages (see vv. 1–21), the false notions of the polytheists about the Hereafter were subjected to discussion. The discourse now turns to a refutation of polytheism.

with Allah in His Divinity:[39] "Call upon those whom you fancied to be deities beside Allah. They own not even the smallest particle, neither in the heavens nor on the earth; nor do they have any share in the ownership of either of them. Nor is any of them even a helper of Allah. (23) No intercession can avail with Allah except for him whom Allah permits[40] (to intercede). ▶

مِّن دُونِ ٱللَّهِ ۖ لَا يَمْلِكُونَ مِثْقَالَ ذَرَّةٍ
فِى ٱلسَّمَـٰوَٰتِ وَلَا فِى ٱلْأَرْضِ وَمَا لَهُمْ
فِيهِمَا مِن شِرْكٍ وَمَا لَهُۥ مِنْهُم مِّن ظَهِيرٍ ﴿٢٢﴾
وَلَا تَنفَعُ ٱلشَّفَـٰعَةُ عِندَهُۥٓ إِلَّا لِمَنْ أَذِنَ لَهُۥ ۚ

39. It is God Who makes or mars the destiny of individuals, nations and empires. This is well illustrated by the accounts of the Prophets David and Solomon (peace be on them) and of the people of Saba'. The unbelievers are then asked to invoke their false gods and seek their help for their success and prosperity, and to see if those deities have the power to change anyone's adversity into prosperity or prosperity into adversity.

40. There is no question of anyone owning the universe, or being God's associate in its ownership, or His helper in the creation of and control over the universe. Not only that, there is absolutely no one who can even intercede with God on anyone's behalf as a matter of right. The polytheists are lost in the misunderstanding that there are some beloved or powerful men of God whose intercession He will have to accept. A person will only be able to intercede for those in regard to whom God permits him to present such a plea. (For the distinction between Islamic and polytheistic perspectives on intercession see *Towards Understanding the Qur'ān, Yūnus* 10: nn. 24–26, Vol. IV, pp. 24–25; *Hūd* 11: nn. 84–106, Vol. IV, pp. 120–134; *al-Naḥl* 16: n. 64, Vol. IV, pp. 346–347; *Ṭā Hā* 20: n. 85, Vol. V, pp. 227–228; *al-Anbiyā'* 21: n. 27, Vol. V, p. 262, and *al-Ḥajj* 22: n. 125, Vol. VI, p. 68.)

حَتَّىٰٓ إِذَا فُزِّعَ عَن قُلُوبِهِمۡ قَالُواْ مَاذَا قَالَ
رَبُّكُمۡۖ قَالُواْ ٱلۡحَقَّۖ وَهُوَ ٱلۡعَلِيُّ ٱلۡكَبِيرُ ٢٣
۞ قُلۡ مَن يَرۡزُقُكُم مِّنَ ٱلسَّمَٰوَٰتِ
وَٱلۡأَرۡضِۖ قُلِ ٱللَّهُۖ

When their hearts are relieved of fright they will ask the intercessors: "What did your Lord say?" They will reply: "(He said) what is right, and He is the High, the Great."[41]

(24) Ask them, (O Prophet): "Who provides you sustenance from the heavens and the earth?" Say: "Allah.[42] ▶

41. The Qur'ān here depicts a scene of the Hereafter. A person who intends to intercede on someone's behalf, will seek God's leave to do so. It is clear from the Qur'ānic account that both the interceder and the one on whose behalf he wants to intercede will be in a state of fear and anxiety as they wait for God's response. Later, the interceder receives permission from on high and the one who looks forward to intercession surmises from the interceder's countenance that things are satisfactory. It is then that he heaves a sigh of relief. Thereafter, it is confirmed that the permission to intercede has indeed been granted. All this is being said to give an idea of God's Majesty. It should be clear that there can be no basis for anyone to entertain the notion that someone has the power to prevail upon God and obtain a person's acquittal by obstinately insisting, like a spoiled child, that his protégé will have to be acquitted.

42. There is a subtle gap between the question and its answer by God. Let us recall the fact that the discourse was directed to the polytheists. They not only did not deny God's existence, but also admitted that He alone holds the keys to everyone's sustenance. Notwithstanding this, they associated others with God in His Divinity. When faced with the question: who provides them with sustenance from the heavens and the earth, they were puzzled and did not know what to say. If they named someone other than God as the Provider, this would be contrary to the belief of their own people who might

Now, inevitably only one of us is rightly guided, either we or you; and the other is in manifest error."[43] ▶	وَإِنَّآ أَوْ إِيَّاكُمْ لَعَلَىٰ هُدًى أَوْ فِي ضَلَٰلٍ مُّبِينٍ ۝٢٤

be prompted to contradict their contention. On the other hand, if they were to explicitly acknowledge God as the sole Provider and Sustainer, this too would naturally give rise to the question: if that is so, for what purpose are those whom they have taken as gods? The dilemma facing them made them speechless. They would neither deny God as the Provider nor affirm it. Noting their inability to respond, God, Who had put the question volunteers a response, saying that God alone is the Provider.

43. This enshrines a valuable point pertaining to communicating one's standpoint with wisdom and sensitivity. The logical answer to the question posed above is to affirm that whoever serves and worships God alone is rightly guided whereas those who serve anyone other than God are wallowing in error. In view of this, it should have been explicitly said: "You are in error while we are rightly guided". Such a straightforward statement, howsoever correct it might be, was bound to arouse adamance among the audience. In consequence, their hearts would have become averse to accepting the truth. Now, God's Prophets are not raised merely to proclaim the truth; rather, they are charged with the task to reform, with utmost wisdom, the people to whom they have been sent, people who have fallen prey to erroneous ways. Hence, God did not ask the Prophet (peace be on him) to tell them in plain words: "All of you are in manifest error while we alone are rightly guided". Instead, he is asked to explain to the unbelievers that the deities they worshipped, as they were well aware, did not provide them with anything. Thus there was a major difference between the Muslims and the unbelievers: the Muslims worshipped only the One True God Who provides sustenance to all, whereas the unbelievers worshipped deities that do not provide any sustenance. With this difference readily apparent, it is now impossible for the positions of both parties to be true. Now, since the position of only one of the two parties is correct, inevitably the other party is in error. It was then left to them to reflect and decide which of the two positions was supported by persuasive evidence.

(25) Tell them: "You will not be called to account about the guilt we committed, nor will we be called to account for what you did."[44] (26) Say: "Our Lord will bring us together and then He will rightly judge between us. He is the Great Judge, the All-Knowing."[45] ▶

قُل لَّا تُسْـَٔلُونَ عَمَّآ أَجْرَمْنَا وَلَا نُسْـَٔلُ
عَمَّا تَعْمَلُونَ ﴿٢٥﴾ قُلْ يَجْمَعُ بَيْنَنَا رَبُّنَا ثُمَّ
يَفْتَحُ بَيْنَنَا بِٱلْحَقِّ وَهُوَ ٱلْفَتَّاحُ ٱلْعَلِيمُ ﴿٢٦﴾

---

44. What was said just above – that the position of only one of the two parties can be correct (v. 24) – should have prompted the audience to think seriously. What is being said here reinforces the need to give very serious thought to the question under consideration. People are asked to realise that it is in every man's own interest to ensure that they arrive at the right decision as to which of the two positions is correct. For if one takes the wrong path, one is bound to face its dire consequences. Man should, therefore, think carefully before exercising his choice. The unbelievers should especially examine their position lest they invest all that they have on a false proposition. This because any erroneous judgement on their part will hurt themselves rather than anyone else.

45. The audience are being asked to consider another dimension of the matter. It is obvious that the believers and unbelievers are different from each other in this world as regards the truth and falsity of their doctrinal position. Things, however, do not end in this world. A Day will come when all will have to stand before their Lord, Who fully knows the Truth and is also fully aware of believers as well as of unbelievers. On that Day God will judge as to who was in the right and who was not. On that Day, God will also make it clear what efforts the believers made to explain the Truth to the unbelievers. In like manner, He will also make plain the way the unbelievers reacted to that, and the myriad measures they resorted to in a fit of bigoted adamance to oppose the believers.

(27) Say: "Show me those whom you have attached to Him as His associates[46] (in Divinity)." Nay, Allah alone is Most Mighty, Most Wise.

(28) (O Prophet), We have not sent you forth but as a herald of good news and a warner for all mankind. But most people do not know.[47]

قُلْ أَرُونِيَ ٱلَّذِينَ أَلْحَقْتُم بِهِۦ شُرَكَآءَ ۖ كَلَّا ۚ بَلْ هُوَ ٱللَّهُ ٱلْعَزِيزُ ٱلْحَكِيمُ ﴿٢٧﴾ وَمَآ أَرْسَلْنَٰكَ إِلَّا كَآفَّةً لِّلنَّاسِ بَشِيرًا وَنَذِيرًا وَلَٰكِنَّ أَكْثَرَ ٱلنَّاسِ لَا يَعْلَمُونَ ﴿٢٨﴾

46. The unbelievers are warned that before taking such a huge chance, based on their trust in these deities, they should be sure as to which of these deities is powerful enough to stand up as their defender and supporter before God and save them from His punishment.

47. It is emphasised here that the Prophet Muḥammad (peace be on him) was not raised as God's Prophet only for the city of Makkah, or for Arabia, or for the people of his own time; instead, he was raised as God's Prophet for all mankind till the Day of Judgement. The Makkans of the time, however, did not appreciate the Prophet's true greatness. They were not aware how immense was the favour that God had bestowed on them by raising such a person among them.

That the Prophet Muḥammad (peace be on him) was meant to be God's Prophet to all mankind till the Day of Resurrection is clearly stated at several places in the Qur'ān:

> And this Qur'ān was revealed to me that I should warn you thereby and also whomsoever it may reach, (*al-An'ām* 6:19.)
>
> Say, (O Muḥammad): "O people! I am Allah's Messenger to you all ..." (*al-A'rāf* 7:158.)
>
> We have sent you forth as nothing but mercy to the people of the whole world. (*al-Anbiyā'* 21:107.)
>
> Most blessed is He Who sent down this Criterion on His servant, to be a warner to all mankind, (*al-Furqān* 25:1.)

(29) They ask you: "When will this promise (of Resurrection) be fulfilled, if what you say is true?"[48] ▶	وَيَقُولُونَ مَتَىٰ هَٰذَا ٱلْوَعْدُ إِن كُنتُمْ صَٰدِقِينَ ﴿٢٩﴾

The same truth features in several *aḥādīth* in a variety of ways. According to Abū Mūsa al-Ash'ārī, the Prophet (peace be on him) said: "I have been sent down to the whites and the blacks alike". (Aḥmad ibn Ḥanbal, *Musnad*, narrated by Abū Mūsa al-Ash'ārī.)

> "As for me, I have been sent to all human beings as such. Each of those who preceded me was sent to his own people". (Aḥmad ibn Ḥanbal, *Musnad*, narrated by 'Abd Allāh ibn 'Amr ibn al-'Āṣ.)
>
> "[In the past] a Prophet used to be raised specifically for his people while I have been raised for all human beings as such". (Bukhārī, *Kitāb al-Tayammum, Bāb Qawl Allāh Ta'ālā "fa lam Tajidū mā'an..."*; Muslim, *Kitāb al-Masājid*, on the authority of Jābir ibn 'Abd Allah.)
>
> "My coming [as a Prophet] and the Last Day are like these" – that is, close together like one's two fingers. (Bukhārī, *Kitab al-Riqāq, Bāb Qawl al-Nabī "Bu'ithtu Anā wa al-Sā'ah ka Hātayn ..."*; Muslim, *Kitīb al-Jumu'ah, Bāb Takhfīf al-Ṣalāh wa al-Khuṭbah.*)

The last *ḥadīth* stresses that in the same manner that no third finger separated the Prophet's two fingers from one another, there will be no Prophet between the time of the Prophet Muḥammad (peace be on him) and the Last Day.

48. The Qur'ān had said: "Say: Our Lord will bring us together and then He will rightly judge between them", (see verse 26 above). Alluding to this, the unbelievers asked the Prophet: when will that Promised Day come? They claimed that they had been remonstrating with the Prophet (peace be on him) for a long time. In the course of this remonstration they had often charged him with falsehood and had publicly opposed him in very vehement terms. What, they would arrogantly ask, then keeps that judgement from visiting them?

(30) Say: "Your day is appointed, you can neither hold back its coming by an hour, nor hasten it by an hour."[49]

(31) The unbelievers say: "We shall never believe in this Qur'ān, nor in any Scripture before it."[50] If you could only see the wrong-doers arrayed before their Lord, each bandying charges against the other. Those who were suppressed will say to those who waxed arrogant: "Had it not been for you, we would have been believers."[51] ▸

قُل لَّكُم مِّيعَادُ يَوْمٍ لَّا تَسْتَـْٔخِرُونَ
عَنْهُ سَاعَةً وَلَا تَسْتَقْدِمُونَ ٣٠ وَقَالَ ٱلَّذِينَ
كَفَرُوا۟ لَن نُّؤْمِنَ بِهَـٰذَا ٱلْقُرْءَانِ
وَلَا بِٱلَّذِى بَيْنَ يَدَيْهِ ۗ وَلَوْ تَرَىٰٓ إِذِ
ٱلظَّـٰلِمُونَ مَوْقُوفُونَ عِندَ رَبِّهِمْ يَرْجِعُ
بَعْضُهُمْ إِلَىٰ بَعْضٍ ٱلْقَوْلَ يَقُولُ ٱلَّذِينَ
ٱسْتُضْعِفُوا۟ لِلَّذِينَ ٱسْتَكْبَرُوا۟ لَوْلَآ
أَنتُمْ لَكُنَّا مُؤْمِنِينَ ٣١

49. God's answer to the query stresses that His decree is not subject to the wishes of His creatures. He is not obliged to do something according to the schedule laid down by others. He does everything in accordance with His Will. His scheme of things is well beyond man's grasp. Man does not know the term God has determined for mankind's performance in this world. He also does not know how individuals and nations will be tested in the world. Nor does he know when God will fold up the present order of existence and summon all – be they of earlier or recent times – to stand before Him for judgement. This Hour can neither be held back nor hastened by as much as a second at the behest of others.

50. The reference here is to the unbelieving Arabs who did not recognise any Scripture.

51. That is, the common people who blindly follow their leaders, chiefs, spiritual guides and rulers and are altogether unwilling to

(32) The arrogant ones will retort to those who were suppressed: "What! Did we bar you from the guidance after it came to you? Not at all; rather you yourselves were evil-doers."[52] (33) Those who were suppressed will say to those who waxed arrogant: "By no means; it was your scheming, ▶

قَالَ ٱلَّذِينَ ٱسْتَكْبَرُوا۟ لِلَّذِينَ ٱسْتُضْعِفُوٓا۟
أَنَحْنُ صَدَدْنَٰكُمْ عَنِ ٱلْهُدَىٰ بَعْدَ إِذْ
جَآءَكُم ۖ بَلْ كُنتُم مُّجْرِمِينَ ۝٣٢ وَقَالَ ٱلَّذِينَ
ٱسْتُضْعِفُوا۟ لِلَّذِينَ ٱسْتَكْبَرُوا۟ بَلْ مَكْرُ

give heed to any well-wisher's advice if it is discordant with the orientation of those they follow. On the Day of Judgement, they will know fully what the Truth is and what they had been led to believe. A time will come when these common people will realise how they had been misled by their own leaders to the doom that would then stare them in their faces. They will turn to their leaders in utter disgust and reproachfully scream at them, blaming them for leading them astray and landing them in a mire of woes. Had it not been for their leaders' misguidance, they will contend, they would have accepted the teachings of God's Messengers and prospered.

52. In turn their leaders will point out that they [to wit, their leaders] were few in number and hence did not have the power to force these teeming millions to follow them. If their followers had wanted to believe, they could have overwhelmed their tribal chiefs, religious guides and rulers. On the contrary, it is the mass of followers who provided the necessary manpower to their guides to error and became the source of their strength and material resources. If not for their offerings and tributes, these leaders would have been bereft of the resources necessary to make their enterprise operational. Had they not taken an oath of fealty at the hands of their so-called religious guides, their religious adventure would have been in the doldrums. Had they not raised vociferous slogans to exalt them, they would have had no *locus standi*. These followers were virtually the army of their false leaders whose support strengthened their hold.

As for their failure to follow the way shown by the Messengers, the leaders will claim that the followers themselves are to be blamed for night and day, when you would enjoin us to disbelieve in Allah and set up others as equals to Him."[53] When they are confronted with the chastisement, they will be remorseful in their hearts. ▶

ٱلَّيۡلِ وَٱلنَّهَارِ إِذۡ تَأۡمُرُونَنَآ أَن نَّكۡفُرَ
بِٱللَّهِ وَنَجۡعَلَ لَهُۥٓ أَندَادٗاۚ وَأَسَرُّواْ ٱلنَّدَامَةَ
لَمَّا رَأَوُاْ ٱلۡعَذَابَ

it rather than anyone else. The main reason for their not believing in the Messengers was their own disinclination: they were the slaves of their desires and material interests. It is that which made them averse to the course of piety and uprightness taught by the Messengers. It was because of this weakness that they felt more attracted to the erroneous doctrines and corrupt ways of their false leaders rather than to the teachings of God's Messengers. The common pursuit of material interests and desires served as a mutual bond between them and their leaders. They followed only those degenerate religious leaders who would let them freely indulge in all kinds of sin and still assure them of deliverance on the Day of Judgement, providing they received an offering from them in return. They trusted only those fake religious leaders who could offer them a garbled version of faith and make religion a slave of their whims and fancies. They were interested only in worldly affluence in disregard of the Hereafter. In like manner, corrupt and morally depraved rulers suited them, for they helped them lead the kind of life they wished. In this respect, there was a mutual understanding between these depraved leaders and their followers. Hence, the follower's claim that they were innocent victims who had been compelled into professing false beliefs was simply farcical.

53. "The arrogant ones" will contend that their followers were equally responsible for straying. The followers will contest this and say to their leaders that they had totally enchanted them by their machinations, deceptive moves, and false propaganda. They will also emphatically point out the myriad tactics they constantly employed to entrap God's creatures. They will also argue that in addition to exposing their followers to the charms of worldly life, these leaders had befooled them and employed ever new tricks to entrap them. (For further details see *al-A'rāf* 7:38–39; *Ibrāhīm* 14:21; *al-Qaṣaṣ* 28:63; *al-Aḥzāb* 33:66–68; *al-Mu'min* 40:47–48 and *Ḥā' Mīm al-Sajdah* 41:29.)

We shall put fetters around the necks of the unbelievers. Can people be requited except for their deeds?

(34) We never sent a warner to any town but its wealthy ones said: "We disbelieve in the Message you have brought."[54] (35) They always said: "We have more wealth and children than you have, and we shall not be chastised."[55] ▶

وَجَعَلْنَا ٱلْأَغْلَٰلَ فِىٓ أَعْنَاقِ ٱلَّذِينَ كَفَرُوا۟ ۚ
هَلْ يُجْزَوْنَ إِلَّا مَا كَانُوا۟ يَعْمَلُونَ ﴿٣٣﴾
وَمَآ أَرْسَلْنَا فِى قَرْيَةٍ مِّن نَّذِيرٍ إِلَّا قَالَ
مُتْرَفُوهَآ إِنَّا بِمَآ أُرْسِلْتُم بِهِۦ كَٰفِرُونَ ﴿٣٤﴾
وَقَالُوا۟ نَحْنُ أَكْثَرُ أَمْوَٰلًا وَأَوْلَٰدًا وَمَا نَحْنُ
بِمُعَذَّبِينَ ﴿٣٥﴾

---

54. It is frequently stated in the Qur'ān that the affluent have always been at the forefront of those who oppose the call of the Prophets. (See *al-An'ām* 6:123; *al-A'rāf* 7:60–66, 75, 87 and 90; *Hūd* 11:27; *Banī Isrā'īl* 17:16; *al-Mu'minūn* 23:24, 33–38 and 46–47; and *al-Zukhruf* 43:23.)

55. The affluent unbelievers used to contend that they were nearer to and greater favourites of God than the believers. This was the reason why, they would argue, God had lavished His bounties upon them in great abundance whereas He had deprived the believers of those bounties or had endowed upon them less abundantly. Had He been unfavourably disposed towards the unbelievers, it is inconceivable that He would have lavished upon them such conspicuous prosperity, riches and glory. They further argued that since it could be seen by anyone that the unbelievers enjoyed God's favours in this life, what justified the belief that He would chastise them in the Life-to-Come? It stands to reason, they would say, that if there is to be any chastisement in the Hereafter its victims will not be they but those who are devoid of God's favours in the present life.

At several places the Qur'ān refutes the misconception of those who are excessively enamoured with the glamour of worldly life. See, for example, *al-Baqarah* 2:126–212; *al-Tawbah* 9:55–69; *Hūd* 11:3–27; *al-Ra'd* 13:26; *al-Kahf* 18:37–43; *Maryam* 19:73–77; *Ṭā Hā* 20:131; *al-Mu'minūn*

(36) (O Prophet), say to them: "My Lord grants provision abundantly to whomsoever He pleases and straitens it for whomsoever He pleases. But most people do not know this.[56] (37) It is not your riches nor your children that make you near-stationed to Us, except for him who has faith and acts righteously;[57] ▸

قُلْ إِنَّ رَبِّى يَبْسُطُ ٱلرِّزْقَ لِمَن يَشَآءُ وَيَقْدِرُ
وَلَٰكِنَّ أَكْثَرَ ٱلنَّاسِ لَا يَعْلَمُونَ ۝٣٦
وَمَآ أَمْوَٰلُكُمْ وَلَآ أَوْلَٰدُكُم بِٱلَّتِى
تُقَرِّبُكُمْ عِندَنَا زُلْفَىٰٓ إِلَّا مَنْ ءَامَنَ
وَعَمِلَ صَٰلِحًا

23:55–61; *al-Shu'arā'* 26:111; *al-Qaṣaṣ* 28:76–83; *al-Rūm* 30:9; *al-Muddaththir* 74:11–26, and *al-Fajr* 89:15–20.

56. The unbelievers simply do not understand the purpose and wisdom underlying the distribution of sustenance in the world. They fall prey to the misconception that those who are rolling in wealth are necessarily God's favourites and that those who have been granted provisions on a limited scale are subject to His wrath. Were one to observe things carefully one would see that quite often conspicuous prosperity is the lot of those who are most notoriously wicked and corrupt. On the other hand, those who are upright and whose excellence of character is acclaimed by everyone, live in straitened circumstances. That being the case, how can any reasonable person say that God dislikes people of sterling moral character and likes those that are wicked and mischievous?

57. This verse is open to two meanings and it appears that both are correct. First, that it is not wealth and children that bring one close to God; rather, it is one's faith and one's good deeds that enable one to achieve proximity with Him. Secondly, it is possible that wealth and children might bring one close to God. However, this is possible only in the case of those righteous believers who spend their wealth in God's cause and who undertake their children's education and upbringing in such a manner that they grow up being God-conscious and upright.

it is they who will receive double the recompense for their deeds. They shall live in lofty mansions in perfect peace.[58] (38) As for those who work against Our Signs so as to frustrate them, they shall be arraigned into the chastisement.

(39) Say, (O Prophet): "Verily, my Lord grants provision abundantly to whomsoever He pleases[59] ▶

فَأُوْلَـٰٓئِكَ لَهُمْ جَزَآءُ ٱلضِّعْفِ بِمَا عَمِلُوا۟
وَهُمْ فِى ٱلْغُرُفَـٰتِ ءَامِنُونَ ﴿٣٧﴾ وَٱلَّذِينَ
يَسْعَوْنَ فِىٓ ءَايَـٰتِنَا مُعَـٰجِزِينَ أُوْلَـٰٓئِكَ فِى
ٱلْعَذَابِ مُحْضَرُونَ ﴿٣٨﴾ قُلْ إِنَّ رَبِّى يَبْسُطُ
ٱلرِّزْقَ لِمَن يَشَآءُ مِنْ عِبَادِهِۦ

---

58. Here, one notes a subtle allusion to the fact that the bounties bestowed upon these people will be everlasting, that their reward will never come to an end. This because a person will be constantly apprehensive and unable to enjoy God's bounties if he is filled with the fear that some day he will be deprived of what he presently has.

59. The purpose behind reiterating this point here is to drive home the fact that the extent of livelihood that a person receives depends entirely upon God's will. However, this does not necessarily indicate that those with whom He is pleased receive a greater portion of it whereas those with whom He is displeased receive less. As part of God's dispensation, those who believe in God as well as those who do not believe in Him receive their livelihood. A person's affluence, therefore, does not indicate his proximity with God. By the same token, a person's stringent circumstances do not necessarily indicate God's displeasure with him. It is common knowledge that wrong-doers and dishonest people often amass heaps of wealth even though God disapproves of their wrong-doing and dishonesty. Under God's dispensation, a wicked and dishonest person might flourish although wickedness and dishonesty incur His displeasure. Likewise, under God's dispensation in this world, we find that truthful and honest people sustain financial losses and suffer hardships, and this despite the fact that these qualities enjoy God's pleasure. Hence, those who consider attainment of material possession and benefit to be the

and straitens it for whomsoever He pleases. Whatever you spend, He will replace it. He is the Best of all Providers."[60]

(40) And on the Day when He will muster them all and will ask the angels: "Are they the ones who worshipped you?"[61] ▶

وَيَقْدِرُ لَهُۥ ۚ وَمَآ أَنفَقْتُم مِّن شَىْءٍ فَهُوَ يُخْلِفُهُۥ ۖ
وَهُوَ خَيْرُ ٱلرَّٰزِقِينَ ﴿٣٩﴾ وَيَوْمَ يَحْشُرُهُمْ
جَمِيعًا ثُمَّ يَقُولُ لِلْمَلَـٰٓئِكَةِ أَهَـٰٓؤُلَآءِ إِيَّاكُمْ
كَانُوا۟ يَعْبُدُونَ ﴿٤٠﴾

---

criterion of a person's goodness have completely missed the point. What really matters is the attainment of God's pleasure and the way to attain it is to cultivate those good moral qualities that please Him. If one has these qualities and, in addition to this, enjoys an abundance of worldly bounties, this certainly signifies God's favour upon him. Anyone who is so blessed should thank Him. However, if an evil person rebels against God and is still provided abundant livelihood, this only means that he should get ready to face a rigorous accounting and suffer a woeful chastisement.

60. God is the Provider, the Maker, the Originator and the Bestower. These and other such attributes are essentially God's. Metaphorically, however, some of these might be applied to His creatures. For instance, we say that someone has arranged the means of livelihood for another person, or that he has bestowed something upon another person, or that he has made or invented something. It is in this sense that God has called Himself "the Best of providers". What this means is that as compared with those who are regarded as providers of sustenance, God is by far the Best Provider.

61. From ancient times up to our own polytheists have proclaimed angels to be gods and goddesses, have carved idols in their name and worshipped them. Of these, one might be the god of rain; the other, the god of lightning, and still others of wind, of wealth, of knowledge, and of death and destruction. Now, on the Day of Judgement, God will ask the angels [concerning the unbelievers]: "Are you the ones whom they worshipped?" In other words, did they tell their people that they

(41) They will reply: "Glory to You! You are our Protector, not they.[62] Nay, they rather used to worship the *jinn*. Most of them believe in them."[63] ▶

قَالُواْ سُبْحَـٰنَكَ أَنتَ وَلِيُّنَا مِن دُونِهِمۖ بَلْ كَانُواْ يَعْبُدُونَ ٱلْجِنَّۖ أَكْثَرُهُم بِهِم مُّؤْمِنُونَ ﴿٤١﴾

were the deities whom they should worship? Or did they (that is, the angels) at least desire the people to worship them even if they did not express that desire in so many words? The true purpose of this question is not to ascertain the truth of the matter. What is implicit is whether the angels were happy with the fact that they were made objects of worship? It is also noteworthy that this question will not only be put to angels, but to all those who were ever worshipped in this world. This point is forcefully stressed in a verse of the Qur'ān in these words:

> On the Day when He will muster together all the unbelievers as well as the deities that they worship besides Allah, and He will ask them: "Was it you who caused these servants of Mine to stray away or did they themselves stray away from the Right Path?" (*Al-Furqān* 25:17.)

62. The angels will respond by proclaiming God's glory and holiness. They will declare that none had any share in His Divinity, nor could anyone have a share in His right to be worshipped. They will also plead that they are quit of the polytheists and their misdeeds. They will further claim to be servants of none except the One True God.

63. The reference here is to the devils among the *jinn*. The angels' reply makes it plain that although the polytheists invoked the angels and made statues and idols of them in keeping with their imagination, nonetheless they actually worshipped devils. It was the devils who had misdirected them to the erroneous path they had taken. It was they who misled them into believing that others rather than God should be invoked and it is to them that offerings should be made.

The verse also lays bare the fallacy of those who consider the *jinn* to mean inhabitants of mountainous regions or dwellers of the desert or countryside. For it is simply inconceivable that any rational

(42) Today none of you has the power to benefit or harm another; and We shall say to the evil-doers: "Taste now the chastisement of the Fire which you used to deny, calling it a lie."

(43) When Our Clear Signs are rehearsed to them they say: "This is a person who wants to turn you away from the deities whom your ancestors worshipped." They say: "This is nothing but an invented falsehood." And when the Truth came to the unbelievers they declared: "This is nothing but plain sorcery," (44) whereas We gave them no Books ▶

فَٱلْيَوْمَ لَا يَمْلِكُ بَعْضُكُمْ لِبَعْضٍ نَّفْعًا
وَلَا ضَرًّا وَنَقُولُ لِلَّذِينَ ظَلَمُوا۟ ذُوقُوا۟ عَذَابَ
ٱلنَّارِ ٱلَّتِى كُنتُم بِهَا تُكَذِّبُونَ ﴿٤٢﴾ وَإِذَا تُتْلَىٰ
عَلَيْهِمْ ءَايَـٰتُنَا بَيِّنَـٰتٍ قَالُوا۟ مَا هَـٰذَآ
إِلَّا رَجُلٌ يُرِيدُ أَن يَصُدَّكُمْ عَمَّا كَانَ
يَعْبُدُ ءَابَآؤُكُمْ وَقَالُوا۟ مَا هَـٰذَآ إِلَّآ إِفْكٌ
مُّفْتَرًى ۚ وَقَالَ ٱلَّذِينَ كَفَرُوا۟ لِلْحَقِّ
لَمَّا جَآءَهُمْ إِنْ هَـٰذَآ إِلَّا سِحْرٌ مُّبِينٌ ﴿٤٣﴾
وَمَآ ءَاتَيْنَـٰهُم مِّن كُتُبٍ

---

being will take this verse to mean that people used to worship those who lived in the mountains, or that they worshipped villagers and desert-dwellers.

The verse also throws light on another meaning of *'ibādah*. It indicates that *'ibādah* does not merely consist of acts of worship. Unreservedly following someone's command or rendering someone total obedience also amounts to *'ibādah*. It is even possible that in this sense one might be engaged in the *'ibādah* of someone at whom one hurls curses, provided that one blindly follows the way he prescribes. (One might, in fact, be guilty of performing the *'ibādah* of Satan despite cursing him if one follows his commands.) (For other examples, see *Towards Understanding the Qur'ān, al-Nisā'* 4: n. 145, Vol. II, p. 86; *al-Mā'idah* 5: n. 91, Vol. II, p. 175; *al-Tawbah* 9: nn. 29 and 31, Vol. III, pp. 203 and 204; *Maryam* 19: n. 27, Vol. V, pp. 160–1, and *al-Qaṣaṣ* 28: n. 86, Vol. VII, pp. 239–240.)

that they could study nor sent to them any warner before you.[64] (45) Those who went before them also denounced (Allah's Messengers) as liars. They have not attained even a tenth of what We had given them. But when they rejected My Messengers, calling them liars, how terrible was My chastisement![65]

(46) Say to them, (O Prophet): "I give you but one counsel: stand up (for heaven's sake), singly and in pairs, and then think: what is it in your companion (to wit, Muḥammad) that could be deemed as madness?"[66] ▶

يَدْرُسُونَهَا ۖ وَمَآ أَرْسَلْنَآ إِلَيْهِمْ قَبْلَكَ مِن
نَّذِيرٍ ﴿٤٤﴾ وَكَذَّبَ ٱلَّذِينَ مِن قَبْلِهِمْ وَمَا بَلَغُوا۟
مِعْشَارَ مَآ ءَاتَيْنَـٰهُمْ فَكَذَّبُوا۟ رُسُلِى ۖ فَكَيْفَ
كَانَ نَكِيرِ ﴿٤٥﴾ ۞ قُلْ إِنَّمَآ أَعِظُكُم
بِوَٰحِدَةٍ ۖ أَن تَقُومُوا۟ لِلَّهِ مَثْنَىٰ وَفُرَٰدَىٰ ثُمَّ
تَتَفَكَّرُوا۟ ۚ مَا بِصَاحِبِكُم مِّن جِنَّةٍ

64. Never did God reveal a Book or raise a Messenger to direct mankind to worship anyone other than the One True God. The unbelievers' rejection of the Qur'ān and the Prophet's call is, therefore, based on sheer ignorance rather than knowledge. They have no authoritative basis whatsoever for the attitude they have adopted.

65. It is stressed here that the Makkan unbelievers had not achieved even a fraction of the power, glory and prosperity of some of the nations of the past. But when those nations rejected the truths expounded to them by God's Prophets and persisted in fashioning their lives on false principles, they courted their doom. Their wealth and power simply proved of no avail.

66. Here an appeal is being made to the unbelievers to rise above their interests, desires and biases and for them to give thought, with open minds and purely for God's sake, as individuals and in

He is nothing but a warner, warning you before the coming of a grevious chastisement.[67] (47) Say to them: "Whatever recompense I might ask of you, it shall be yours.[68] My recompense is with Allah, ▶	إِنْ هُوَ إِلَّا نَذِيرٌ لَّكُم بَيْنَ يَدَىْ عَذَابٍ شَدِيدٍ ﴿٤٦﴾ قُلْ مَا سَأَلْتُكُم مِّنْ أَجْرٍ فَهُوَ لَكُمْ إِنْ أَجْرِىَ إِلَّا عَلَى ٱللَّهِ

groups, regarding the Prophet (peace be on him). They should think and earnestly discuss why they brand him as insane, one whom they recognised only a short while earlier as a paragon of wisdom and integrity. After all, it was not long before Muḥammad (peace be on him) had proclaimed himself to be a Prophet that the Makkans unanimously appointed him to arbitrate between the disputing parties on the question of installing the Black Stone in the Ka'bah. The Makkans felt immensely satisfied when, thanks to Muḥammad's wisdom, he was able to amicably resolve that dispute. Thus, they had witnessed at first hand the Prophet's wisdom and sagacity. What change took place in him after that which then warranted that he be called a madman? It is a different matter to deny something out of obstinacy, but do you truly believe with your hearts that which you say with your tongues?

67. The unbelievers are asked: are they labelling the Prophet (peace be on him) with insanity simply because he warned them that a grievous chastisement would come upon them? Do they think that the sign of a person's sanity is that when he sees his people rushing towards their doom, he applauds and encourages them to persist in so following this path of destruction they have chosen for themselves? Do they really think that he who warns people before things get really bad and who directs them to goodness in place of evil is insane?

68. We have translated this part of the verse as follows: "Whatever recompense I ask of you shall be yours". In our opinion, this is one possible meaning of this part of the verse. However, it could also mean that the Prophet (peace be on him) wanted no other recompense except that his people reform themselves. If they did so, that was the recompense he sought. The same truth is propounded elsewhere in the Qur'ān: "Say to them: 'I ask of you no reward for my work. My

and He is a witness over everything."[69] (48) Say to them: "My Lord hurls down the Truth[70] (upon me). He knows fully all that lies beyond the range of perception." (49) Say: "The Truth has come and falsehood can neither originate nor recreate anything." (50) Say: "If I go astray then the hurt of straying will come only upon me. But if I am rightly-guided, that is only because of the revelation that my Lord makes to me. He is All-Hearing, Ever Nigh."[71]

وَهُوَ عَلَىٰ كُلِّ شَيْءٍ شَهِيدٌ ﴿٤٧﴾ قُلْ إِنَّ رَبِّي
يَقْذِفُ بِالْحَقِّ عَلَّامُ الْغُيُوبِ ﴿٤٨﴾ قُلْ جَاءَ
الْحَقُّ وَمَا يُبْدِئُ الْبَاطِلُ وَمَا يُعِيدُ ﴿٤٩﴾
قُلْ إِن ضَلَلْتُ فَإِنَّمَا أَضِلُّ عَلَىٰ نَفْسِي ۖ
وَإِنِ اهْتَدَيْتُ فَبِمَا يُوحِي إِلَيَّ رَبِّي ۚ إِنَّهُ
سَمِيعٌ قَرِيبٌ ﴿٥٠﴾

---

only reward is that whoever so wills may follow the way leading to His Lord'", (*al-Furqan* 25:57).

69. Notwithstanding the baseless charges lavelled at the Prophet (peace be on him) by his opponents, God knows everything. He is a witness that the Prophet (peace be on him) had pursued his mission selflessly and that he had had no axe whatever to grind.

70. The actual words are "*yaqdhifu bi al-ḥaqq*". One meaning of this is that God conveys true knowledge to the Prophet (peace be on him) through revelation. A second meaning is that God makes the truth predominate by having it strike a crushing blow at falsehood.

71. Some people in our time misinterpret this verse, claiming that it affirms that the Prophet (peace be on him) could go astray. In fact, they claim that he used to go astray. They further claim that since that was the case, God made the Prophet (peace be on him) say that he himself was responsible for his straying whenever that happened. They claim, moreover, that he was rightly-guided only when his

(51) If you could only see when the unbelievers will go about in a state of terror. They will have no escape and will be seized from a place near at hand.[72] (52) They will then say: "We believe in it";[73] but whence can they attain it from so far-off a place?[74] ▶

وَلَوۡ تَرَىٰٓ إِذۡ فَزِعُواْ فَلَا فَوۡتَ وَأُخِذُواْ
مِن مَّكَانٖ قَرِيبٖ ٥١ وَقَالُوٓاْ ءَامَنَّا بِهِۦ وَأَنَّىٰ
لَهُمُ ٱلتَّنَاوُشُ مِن مَّكَانِۭ بَعِيدٖ ٥٢

Lord sent revelation [to wit, Qur'ānic verses] to him. Such people are thus trying, by means of this flawed interpretation, to show that the Prophet's life was a mixture of true guidance and error. The Qur'ān, in their view, proclaimed this lest anyone decided to completely follow the Prophet (peace be on him) under the mistaken notion that he was always on the Right Path.

Anyone with even an iota of common sense and who takes into account the context in which the words "if I go astray" occur is bound to conclude that the statement should not be taken in its literal sense. What was being said, in effect, is: "If the Prophet has gone astray, as they allege, and that if his claim to be a Prophet and his call to *tawḥīd* have ensued from his straying, it is the Prophet rather than they who will face the dire consequences of straying. On the contrary, if he is rightly-guided – which he indeed is – this is thanks to the revelation that comes to him from his Lord whereby he receives true knowledge of the Right Way. His Lord is quite close to him. He hears everything. He fully knows whether the Prophet has gone astray or is rightly-guided".

72. On the Last Day, the culprits will be instantly captured as though someone was waiting in ambush for them; no one will be able to escape.

73. That is, they will then profess belief in the teachings expounded by the Prophet (peace be on him) in the world.

74. The unbelievers should have believed while they were in the world, the world they have now left far behind. Once a person has

(53) They disbelieved in it before and indulged in conjectures from far away.[75] (54) A barrier will be placed between them and what they desire, as was done with the likes of them before. Surely they were in a disquieting doubt.[76]

وَقَدْ كَفَرُوا۟ بِهِۦ مِن قَبْلُ ۖ وَيَقْذِفُونَ بِٱلْغَيْبِ
مِن مَّكَانٍۭ بَعِيدٍ ﴿٥٣﴾ وَحِيلَ بَيْنَهُمْ وَبَيْنَ
مَا يَشْتَهُونَ كَمَا فُعِلَ بِأَشْيَاعِهِم مِّن قَبْلُ ۚ
إِنَّهُمْ كَانُوا۟ فِى شَكٍّ مُّرِيبٍۭ ﴿٥٤﴾

set his foot in the Hereafter, the opportunity to believe and repent is gone.

75. The unbelievers levelled all kinds of accusations at the Prophet (peace be on him), hurling a variety of mocking and taunting remarks his way. They variously called him a magician and a madman. On occasion they even made fun of monotheism. On others, they made the Hereafter the butt of their ridicule. They also fabricated fanciful stories about the Prophet (peace be on him), one of them being that a particular person had taught him all that he expounded. They also scoffed at the believers, saying that they followed the Prophet (peace be on him) out of ignorance and naiveté.

76. It goes without saying that no one can embrace polytheism, atheism and denial of the Hereafter on grounds of absolute certainty. This because certainty comes from knowledge and no one knows for sure that God does not exist or that there are many gods or that others have a share in God's Divinity or that it is impossible for the Afterlife to occur. Those who entertain such notions have erected a whole structure merely on the basis of conjecture and speculation, which rests on nothing else but stark scepticism. This scepticism altogether misled them. Thanks to it, they became sceptical about God's existence, about the truth of monotheism, and about the imminence of the Hereafter. They proceeded along this course until scepticism about the objects of belief changed into categorical negation. This took hold of their hearts so completely that they simply refused to accept the teachings of the Prophets and wasted their lives in following a truly flawed way.

Sūrah 35

Fāṭir

(Creator)

(Makkan Period)

Title

The word *Fāṭir,* meaning Creator, occurs in the *sūrah*'s opening verse and marks its title. The only significance of the title is that this is the *sūrah* in which the word *Fāṭir* has been used. Another title for the *sūrah* is *al-Malā'ikah* (the angels). This word too occurs in the *sūrah*'s first verse.

Period of Revelation

The *sūrah*'s stylistic features provide the internal evidence indicating that it was revealed during the middle phase of the Prophet's Makkan life. By then the Makkan unbelievers' opposition to Islam had become severe, whereby they employed all kinds of vile machinations to defeat the Prophet's mission.

Themes and Subject Matter

The *sūrah* aims to warn the Makkan unbelievers, especially their chiefs, about their negative stance towards the Prophet's call to monotheism. It reproaches them in the manner of a sincere well-wisher and explains and admonishes in the manner of a teacher.

The pith of the discourse is that it is in the unbelievers' own interests to respond positively to the Prophet's call. In other words, the unbelievers' anger against that call, their resort to deception, knavery, and vile machinations to frustrate the Prophet (peace be on him) will, in fact, be hurtful only to them. If they do not accept the Prophet's call, the damage so accruing will be all theirs, not the Prophet's. They are urged, therefore, to think dispassionately and to consider whether there was really any flaw in the Prophet's message. True, the Prophet (peace be on him) repudiated polytheism, but does there really exist any reasonable basis for polytheism? He also called on them to affirm God's unity. Now, is there any being other than the Creator of the heavens and of earth, who is possessed of Divine powers and attributes? He emphatically tells them that humans are not irresponsible beings; that they will have to render an account of their deeds to God, and that the present world will be followed by the After-world wherein everyone will have to face the consequences of their actions.

Only a little reflection reveals that it is not at all surprising for a New Life to follow the present one. For, do they not witness day in and day out the unceasing spectacle of life, of death, and of rebirth? What, then, justifies their rejecting as impossible the idea that God, Who once created man from a drop of sperm, will recreate him after he dies? Does your own intellect not testify to the fact that good and evil are dissimilar? Thus, you yourselves decide what makes more sense: that good and evil share the same fate and that both disintegrate and are obliterated, or should good be rewarded with good and evil with evil? Additionally, the *sūrah* re-emphasises the fact that the unbelievers' rejection of these sound doctrines will not harm the Prophet (peace be on him) in any way. Rather, it is they who will be punished for spurning his message. The Prophet's responsibility does not go beyond delivering the message and he has acquitted himself of that task.

The unbelievers are, thus, asked to reflect on the Prophet's message as there is absolutely nothing wrong with it. The Prophet's rejection of polytheism is perfectly valid, for there is not as much as a shred of evidence to support polytheism. The other component of the Prophet's message was monotheism. Now, do the heavens and earth not bear out the existence of the One True God and that no one else has the slightest share in God's power and attributes? The Prophet (peace be on him) also insisted that man is not free to act as he pleases; instead, man will be held accountable in the Afterlife and will be answerable for all his deeds. The unbelievers are asked: is it unreasonable for the good and the wicked to be treated differently? Does it stand to reason that the destiny of those that were upright and those that were evil should be the same, that both should end up in the dust? Is it fair that neither good-doers be rewarded nor evil-doers punished? Evidently, reason and justice require that they be fairly recompensed. However, if, even in the face of these self-evident truths, the unbelievers still choose to lead unbridled lives, this will not harm the Prophet (peace be on him) in any way. He has discharged his duty by preaching the truth to people and warning them against the dire consequences of unbelief, and that is all he was required to do.

In the course of the discourse, the Prophet (peace be on him) is comforted and consoled over and over again and is clearly told that he is not answerable for the unbelievers' persistence in error. The Prophet (peace be on him) is also asked not to grieve over the attitude of those who are averse to his message. He is also asked not to consume himself with concern for those who do not want to be directed to the Right Way. Instead, the Prophet (peace be on him) should focus his attention on bringing about improvements in the believers' lives.

In this regard, the believers are given glad tidings so that their hearts are strengthened and they pursue the Straight Way, fully trusting God's promises.

In the name of Allah, the Most Merciful, the Most Compassionate.

بِسْمِ ٱللَّهِ ٱلرَّحْمَٰنِ ٱلرَّحِيمِ

(1) All praise be to Allah, the Fashioner of the heavens and earth, Who appointed angels as His message-bearers,[1] having two, three, four wings.[2] He adds to His creation whatever He pleases.[3] ▶

ٱلْحَمْدُ لِلَّهِ فَاطِرِ ٱلسَّمَٰوَٰتِ وَٱلْأَرْضِ
جَاعِلِ ٱلْمَلَٰٓئِكَةِ رُسُلًا أُو۟لِىٓ أَجْنِحَةٍ مَّثْنَىٰ
وَثُلَٰثَ وَرُبَٰعَ ۚ يَزِيدُ فِى ٱلْخَلْقِ مَا يَشَآءُ ۚ

---

1. This presumably means that these angels act as the message-bearing intermediaries between God and His Prophets (peace be on them). Alternatively, it might mean that the angels' assignment consists in communicating and putting into effect God's commands. The angels mentioned here are those whom the polytheists recognised as their gods and goddesses. In point of fact, however, they are no more than God's obedient servants. In the manner of a king's servants, they swiftly move from one place to another, carrying out His commands. Being God's servants, however, they are devoid of all authority. All power and authority rests with God, the only True Lord.

2. It is beyond our ability to know the true nature of the angels' wings. However, God has used this word – that is, wings – to describe the angels, a word used in human language to describe the organ that helps birds fly. Hence we can imagine that this word approximately depicts the reality that it seeks to describe.

The verse also mentions these angels as having two, three, or four wings. This indicates that God has endowed them with various levels of ability commensurate with the nature of their tasks.

3. The wording of the verse suggests that four is not necessarily the maximum number of an angel's wings. Some angels in fact have been granted a higher number of wings. According to 'Abd Allāh ibn Mas'ūd, the Prophet (peace be on him) once saw Gabriel with six hundred wings, (Bukhārī, *Kitāb Bad' al-Khalq, Bāb Idhā Qāla Aḥadukum Amīn…*; Muslim,

Verily Allah has power over everything. (2) Whatever Mercy Allah accords to people, none can withhold; and whatever He withholds, no other will be able to release after Him.[4] He is Most Mighty, Most Wise.[5]

(3) O people, remember[6] Allah's favour upon you. ▶

إِنَّ ٱللَّهَ عَلَىٰ كُلِّ شَيْءٍ قَدِيرٌ ۝ مَّا يَفْتَحِ ٱللَّهُ لِلنَّاسِ مِن رَّحْمَةٍ فَلَا مُمْسِكَ لَهَا ۖ وَمَا يُمْسِكْ فَلَا مُرْسِلَ لَهُۥ مِنۢ بَعْدِهِۦ ۚ وَهُوَ ٱلْعَزِيزُ ٱلْحَكِيمُ ۝ يَٰٓأَيُّهَا ٱلنَّاسُ ٱذْكُرُوا۟ نِعْمَتَ ٱللَّهِ عَلَيْكُمْ ۚ

Kitab al-Īmān, Bāb fī Dhikr Sidrat al-Muntahā; Tirmidhī, *Kitāb Tafsīr al-Qur'ān 'an Rasūl Allāh, Bāb Sūrah al-Najm*.) Likewise, 'Ā'ishah reports that the Prophet (peace be on him) saw Gabriel in his true form on two occasions. On both occasions he had six hundred wings and he enveloped the entire horizon, (Tirmidhī, *Kitāb Tafsīr al-Qur'ān 'an Rasūl Allāh, Bāb Sūrah al-Najm*.)

4. This is aimed at removing the polytheists' misconception that some human beings have the power to provide them jobs, grant them children, or cure their ailments. All such polytheistic notions lack substance. Rather, it is God's Mercy that provides the help man seeks. Furthermore, none apart from God has the power to bestow any favour on mankind nor has anyone else the ability to prevent a favour that God wants to bestow. This truth is frequently articulated in the Qur'ān as well as in *aḥādīth* in a variety of ways. The purpose in so doing is to dissuade people from stumbling around, knocking at myriad doors, stretching forth their hands to all possible altars. Only God, and none other than God, has the power to make or mar man's fate.

5. God is Most Mighty; that is, He prevails over all and has absolute sovereignty. None has the power to prevent His will from being carried out. However, along with being Most Mighty, God is also Most Wise. Whenever He decrees something, He does so by dint of absolute wisdom. Whenever He grants anything to someone or withholds it from someone, He does so out of His wisdom.

6. Man is asked not to be ungrateful to God, nor to ignore that it is He Who has bestowed upon him all his possessions. In other words, this

Is there any creator, apart from Allah, who provides you your sustenance out of the heavens and earth? There is no god but He. Whither are you, then, being misdirected?[7] (4) (O Prophet), (there is nothing novel in it) if they cry lies to you;[8] Messengers before you were also cried lies to. To Allah shall all matters be sent back.[9]

هَلْ مِنْ خَـٰلِقٍ غَيْرُ ٱللَّهِ يَرْزُقُكُم مِّنَ ٱلسَّمَآءِ
وَٱلْأَرْضِ ۚ لَآ إِلَـٰهَ إِلَّا هُوَ ۖ فَأَنَّىٰ تُؤْفَكُونَ ﴿٣﴾
وَإِن يُكَذِّبُوكَ فَقَدْ كُذِّبَتْ رُسُلٌ مِّن
قَبْلِكَ ۚ وَإِلَى ٱللَّهِ تُرْجَعُ ٱلْأُمُورُ ﴿٤﴾

---

statement serves as a warning: those who serve or worship any others besides God, or those who ascribe any of God's bounties to others besides Him, or who thank any others rather than God for those bounties, or who seek bounties from others rather than God are all guilty of ingratitude towards Him.

7. There is a subtle gap between the two statements made here, one that is filled by the context of the discourse. In order to appreciate this one should try to bring to mind that the discourse's audience were polytheists. The speaker asks the audience: is there any other than God who has created them and who provides sustenance for them from the heavens and the earth? After posing the question the speaker pauses for a while. Now, instead of responding, the whole audience remains silent, none claiming that someone other than God is their Creator or Provider. This naturally leads to the conclusion that all agree that none other than God is their Creator and Provider. At this point, the speaker breaks the silence and says: "In that case, none other than God can be their deity. All this is crystal clear. Who, then, is misdirecting them?"

8. That is, the Makkan unbelievers denied the Prophet's contention that none other than God is worthy of worship and service. Likewise, they rejected his claim to be God's Prophet, branding that contention as an obvious falsehood.

9. In other words, people do not become liars simply because the unbelievers pronounced them to be so. The judgement on such matters

(5) O people, assuredly Allah's promise is true.[10] So let the life of the world not delude you,[11] and let not the Deluder delude you concerning Allah.[12] ▶

يَـٰٓأَيُّهَا ٱلنَّاسُ إِنَّ وَعْدَ ٱللَّهِ حَقٌّ ۖ فَلَا تَغُرَّنَّكُمُ ٱلْحَيَوٰةُ ٱلدُّنْيَا ۖ وَلَا يَغُرَّنَّكُم بِٱللَّهِ ٱلْغَرُورُ ﴿٥﴾

rests with God. One day He will make it absolutely clear as to who engaged in falsehood. Moreover, He will also make the liars face the dire consequences of their lying.

10. God's promise in the verse refers to His promise in the Hereafter. This was alluded to in the preceding verse by saying: "To Allah shall all matters be sent back".

11. The unbelievers should not delude themselves into supposing that there is nothing beyond the life of this world, that this life will not be followed by the Afterlife wherein people will be called to account. They should also not fall prey to the delusion that when the Afterlife does come about those who flourish here will also flourish there.

12. The word Deluder here refers to Satan, which is evident from the following verse (verse 6). To delude as regards God means that Satan persuades some people to believe that God does not exist at all. He leads others to the misgiving that God originally created the universe and made it operational, but thereafter, for all intents and purposes, He has withdrawn Himself from it. Thus, He is no longer concerned with the affairs of the universe that He Himself created. Satan misleads others into believing that while God is still governing the universe, He has provided no guidance to mankind. All talk of Revelation and Prophethood, therefore, is simply fraud and deception. Satan also convinces others that they may behave as they please for the simple fact that God is Most Forgiving and Most Compassionate! Human beings can, therefore, sin to their hearts' fill and still be sure that He will forgive them out of His Compassion. Satan may also mislead people into cherishing the notion that all they have to do is firmly attach themselves to God's favourites, for they will see to it that they inevitably receive salvation.

(6) Surely Satan is an enemy to you. Therefore, do take him as an enemy. He calls his followers to his way so that they may be among the inmates of the Fire. (7) A severe chastisement lies in store for those that disbelieve,[13] but there is pardon and a great reward for those that believe and work righteous deeds.[14]

(8) (How awful is the straying of the person)[15] for whom his evil deed has been embellished so that it looks fair to him?[16] ▶

إِنَّ ٱلشَّيۡطَٰنَ لَكُمۡ عَدُوّٞ فَٱتَّخِذُوهُ
عَدُوًّاۚ إِنَّمَا يَدۡعُواْ حِزۡبَهُۥ لِيَكُونُواْ
مِنۡ أَصۡحَٰبِ ٱلسَّعِيرِ ٦ ٱلَّذِينَ
كَفَرُواْ لَهُمۡ عَذَابٞ شَدِيدٞۖ وَٱلَّذِينَ
ءَامَنُواْ وَعَمِلُواْ ٱلصَّٰلِحَٰتِ لَهُم مَّغۡفِرَةٞ
وَأَجۡرٞ كَبِيرٌ ٧ أَفَمَن زُيِّنَ لَهُۥ سُوٓءُ
عَمَلِهِۦ فَرَءَاهُ حَسَنٗاۖ

13. By the words "those that disbelieve" are meant those who reject God's Book and His Messenger's call.

14. God will not only overlook their lapses but will also reward them more abundantly than what their good deeds amount to.

15. The preceding verses are addressed to the common people. From here on, the discourse turns to those exponents of erroneous doctrines who spared no effort to frustrate the Prophet's mission and reduce it to humiliation and ignominy.

16. There are some evil-doers who, notwithstanding their lapses, realise that they are indeed guilty of committing evil deeds. Good counsel and admonition are likely to help such people to mend themselves. The reproach of their conscience also occasionally directs them to righteous conduct. This because even though their conduct might not be all that good, their outlook nonetheless remains sound.

There are, however, also others whose outlook is vitiated, who fail to have any sense of distinction between good and evil. As a result, a life

The fact is that Allah causes whomsoever He will to fall into error and shows the Right Way to whomsoever He will. So, (O Prophet), let not your life go to waste sorrowing over them.[17] ▶

فَإِنَّ ٱللَّهَ يُضِلُّ مَن يَشَآءُ وَيَهۡدِي مَن يَشَآءُۖ فَلَا تَذۡهَبۡ نَفۡسُكَ عَلَيۡهِمۡ حَسَرَٰتٍۚ

immersed in sin beckons to them as the very zenith of high living. Such people are repelled by uprightness whereas evil conduct instinctively appeals to them as the very essence of culture and refinement. Such people look down upon uprightness and piety as incorrigible reactionaryism and perceive evil-doing and sinfulness as progressivism. Thus their judgements are reversed: they mistake guidance for error and error for guidance. Understandably, no one's counsel avails them. They are neither conscious of their follies nor heed the words of their well-wishers. It is futile to run after such people and consume oneself out of concern to guide them to the Right Way. One should, instead, pay attention to those whose conscience is still pulsating with life, those who have not bolted their hearts against the Truth.

17. In between the two parts of the statement it has been said that "Allah causes whomsoever He will to fall into error and shows the Right Way to whomsoever He will". The earlier part refers to those diehard unbelievers who allow their minds to utterly wallow in error. When such people are fully immersed in error, God deprives them of His succour that would direct them to the Right Way. He lets them stumble around in the erroneous ways that they insist upon. After clarifying this point, God apprises the Prophet (peace be on him) that it is simply beyond his power to direct those who are so deeply mired in error to the Right Way. He is, therefore, asked to be patient and not to torment himself on account of those for whom God does not care or who have no value near God.

Two points in this context merit attention:

i. The above statement was not made in regard to all Makkan unbelievers as such. It was made, instead, in regard to their chiefs who had no compunction even in resorting to lies, deception and fraud to frustrate the Prophet's call to Islam. Their situation was quite different from those who had fallen prey to some misconception about the Prophet (peace be on him).

Allah is well aware of all that they do.[18] ▶	إِنَّ ٱللَّهَ عَلِيمٌۢ بِمَا يَصۡنَعُونَ ۝٨

As distinct from ordinary unbelievers, these people knew well enough what the Prophet (peace be on him) was calling them to. They were also well aware of the false beliefs and moral corruptions that they wanted to hold on to. They knew all these things and understood them perfectly well. Despite this, they nonetheless had resolved in quite a cool, calculated manner to oppose the Prophet (peace be on him). In opposing him, they felt no qualms of conscience in resorting to all possible means, howsoever lowly or ignoble. They wilfully invented ever new lies against the Prophet (peace be on him) and actively went about spreading them. Such people might deceive the whole world but as far as they themselves were concerned, they fully knew themselves to be liars. They were also quite aware that the Prophet (peace be on him) was free of the charges they levelled against him. Furthermore, they knew that the Prophet (peace be on him) was an utterly truthful, upright and straightforward person. This because even in face of their vile opposition he never deviated from truthfulness and honesty. These people, however, felt no remorse at their misdeeds and persisted in lying and this in sharp contrast to the Prophet's truthfulness. Their unrepentant adamance was sufficiently indicative that they had been overtaken by God's curse and had lost all sense of distinction between good and evil.

ii. The other point to be borne in mind is that God did not simply want to intimate the truth of the matter to the Prophet (peace be on him). Had that alone been the purpose this could have been done without making the matter public. God, however, disclosed it to everyone by a revelation to that effect. The purpose of bringing all this into public knowledge was to alert the common people and make them cognisant of their leaders' mettle – religious as well as otherwise. The crookedness of their mental orientation and the utter corruption of their conduct loudly proclaimed that they were under God's curse.

18. Implicit in this is the unmistakable note of warning that God will ultimately punish them for their misdeeds. A sovereign's declaration that he is well aware of his criminal subjects' deeds is not simply a statement

(9) It is Allah Who sends forth winds which then set the clouds in motion, which We drive to some dead land giving a fresh life to earth after it had become dead. Such will be the resurrection of the dead.[19]

(10) He who seeks glory, let him know that all glory belongs to Allah alone.[20] ▶

وَٱللَّهُ ٱلَّذِىٓ أَرْسَلَ ٱلرِّيَٰحَ فَتُثِيرُ سَحَابًا
فَسُقْنَٰهُ إِلَىٰ بَلَدٍ مَّيِّتٍ فَأَحْيَيْنَا بِهِ ٱلْأَرْضَ
بَعْدَ مَوْتِهَا ۚ كَذَٰلِكَ ٱلنُّشُورُ ﴿٩﴾ مَن كَانَ
يُرِيدُ ٱلْعِزَّةَ فَلِلَّهِ ٱلْعِزَّةُ جَمِيعًا ۚ

---

of fact. Such a statement also necessarily carries the message that he will take them to task.

19. The unbelievers foolishly dismiss the Hereafter simply as something that can never take place. They are under the illusion that regardless of whatever they do in the world, the moment will never come when they will be made to stand before God to render an account of their deeds. Such thinking by the unbelievers, however, is sheer fantasy. For, on the Day of Judgement, at a simple command from God, all the dead will be raised to life. This will happen in the same manner as when a shower of rain revives a seemingly sterile patch of land, causing the long dormant roots that had remained buried in the recesses of earth to blossom forth.

20. It may be noted that whatever the Quraysh chiefs did to oppose the Prophet (peace be on him) was motivated by their privilege and their desire to retain their prestige in society. They thought that should the Prophet's teachings gain currency they would lose their power and pelf over the length and breadth of Arabia. Accordingly, they are told that the prestige they enjoyed was a sham, it lacked firm foundation to sustain it, and was thus bound some day or other to come crashing down. Conversely, true honour and prestige never change into disgrace. Such honour and prestige is only derived by servitude to God. If you turn to Him, you will be honoured. If you turn away from Him, disgrace is your fate.

To Him do good words go up, and righteous action uplifts them.[21] But those who contrive evil deeds,[22] a severe punishment lies in store for them, and their contriving will come to naught.

(11) Allah[23] created you from dust, ▶

إِلَيْهِ يَصْعَدُ ٱلْكَلِمُ ٱلطَّيِّبُ وَٱلْعَمَلُ
ٱلصَّٰلِحُ يَرْفَعُهُۥ ۚ وَٱلَّذِينَ يَمْكُرُونَ ٱلسَّيِّـَٔاتِ
لَهُمْ عَذَابٌ شَدِيدٌ ۖ وَمَكْرُ أُو۟لَٰٓئِكَ
هُوَ يَبُورُ ﴿١٠﴾ وَٱللَّهُ خَلَقَكُم مِّن تُرَابٍ

21. This is the right way to attain glory. False, impure and evil words can never rise in God's sight. He exalts only the word that is true and pure and is grounded in reality, the word that faithfully represents a sound worldview and a wholesome outlook on life. Moreover, what leads to the exaltation of such a word is human support and reinforcement of it by acting according to it. Whenever one's practice goes contrary to the good word, its purity begins to shrink. For, mere verbal exuberance does not exalt a word. It is rather the power of righteous deeds that exalts it and makes it flourish.

It is pertinent to note that the Qur'ān considers a good word and a good deed to be mutually dependent. No deed can be considered righteous unless it rests on the bedrock of right belief. Right belief, on the other hand, is unauthentic if it is not corroborated by righteous action. If a person claims to consider the One True God as the sole object of his worship but in practice worships others than God, this amounts to giving the lie to his claim. To take another instance, a person claims that he considers intoxicating drinks to be forbidden, but at the same time drinks them. In such a scenario, the claim is neither acceptable to God's creatures, nor will it be accepted by God.

22. This refers to people who proclaim false words. They attempt to publicise these through various tricks and fraudulent claims. Their aim is to belittle the true word, even by recourse to the most evil means available.

23. From here on the discourse again turns to the common people.

then from a drop of sperm,[24] then He made you into pairs. No female conceives, nor delivers (a child) except with His knowledge. None is given a long life nor is any diminished in his life but it is written in a Book.[25] Surely that is quite easy for Allah.[26] (12) The two masses of water are not alike.[27] ▶

ثُمَّ مِن نُّطْفَةٍ ثُمَّ جَعَلَكُمْ أَزْوَٰجًا ۚ
وَمَا تَحْمِلُ مِنْ أُنثَىٰ وَلَا تَضَعُ إِلَّا بِعِلْمِهِۦ ۚ
وَمَا يُعَمَّرُ مِن مُّعَمَّرٍ وَلَا يُنقَصُ مِنْ عُمُرِهِۦٓ
إِلَّا فِى كِتَٰبٍ ۚ إِنَّ ذَٰلِكَ عَلَى ٱللَّهِ يَسِيرٌ ﴿١١﴾
وَمَا يَسْتَوِى ٱلْبَحْرَانِ

24. In the first instance, man was brought into being directly from mud. Thereafter, the continuity of his race was ensured by means of sperm drops.

25. God pre-ordains every person's life-span. Those who have a long life have it by dint of God's command. God's command also ensures that some people's life-spans are short. Some ignorant people, however, call attention to the fact that infant mortality rates have fallen dramatically owing to advancements in medicine. Furthermore, they claim that thanks to better resources and better medical care, the average life-span has increased. [The upshot of the claim being that the terms of men's lives are determined by factors other than simply God's will – Ed.] However, this argument can only hold water if it is established that someone's life-span was extended beyond what was pre-ordained by God. Since this cannot be ascertained it is pointless to contest the Qur'ānic statement. The decrease in infant mortality rates or the spurt in longevity does not indicate that man is now able to overrule God's command. One may ask: what is the difficulty, from a rational point of view, in accepting the proposition that God has apportioned different life-spans for people in different times? Also, that it was part of God's decree that man would be able to effectively treat certain diseases at certain periods of time or that he would be able to acquire the resources needed to ensure longevity.

26. It is not difficult at all for God to lay down detailed decisions in respect of His multifarious creatures.

27. One of these two masses of water lies in seas and oceans. The other is held in rivers, springs and lakes.

The one is sweet, sates thirst, and is pleasant to drink from, while the other is salt, bitter on the tongue. Yet from both you eat fresh meat,[28] and extract from it ornaments that you wear;[29] and you see ships cruising through it that you may seek of His Bounty and be thankful to Him. (13) He causes the night to phase into the day and the day into the night,[30] and He has subjected the sun and the moon,[31] each running its course to an appointed term. That is Allah, your Lord; to Him belongs the Kingdom; but those whom you call upon, apart from Allah, possess not so much as the skin of a date-stone.[32] ▶

هَٰذَا عَذْبٌ فُرَاتٌ سَآئِغٌ شَرَابُهُۥ وَهَٰذَا
مِلْحٌ أُجَاجٌ ۖ وَمِن كُلٍّ تَأْكُلُونَ لَحْمًا
طَرِيًّا وَتَسْتَخْرِجُونَ حِلْيَةً تَلْبَسُونَهَا ۖ وَتَرَى
ٱلْفُلْكَ فِيهِ مَوَاخِرَ لِتَبْتَغُوا۟ مِن فَضْلِهِۦ
وَلَعَلَّكُمْ تَشْكُرُونَ ﴿١٢﴾ يُولِجُ ٱلَّيْلَ فِى
ٱلنَّهَارِ وَيُولِجُ ٱلنَّهَارَ فِى ٱلَّيْلِ وَسَخَّرَ ٱلشَّمْسَ
وَٱلْقَمَرَ كُلٌّ يَجْرِى لِأَجَلٍ مُّسَمًّى ۚ ذَٰلِكُمُ
ٱللَّهُ رَبُّكُمْ لَهُ ٱلْمُلْكُ ۚ وَٱلَّذِينَ تَدْعُونَ مِن
دُونِهِۦ مَا يَمْلِكُونَ مِن قِطْمِيرٍ ﴿١٣﴾

28. "Fresh meat" here refers to the flesh of water creatures.

29. That is, pearls, corals, precious stones, and gold.

30. At dusk, daylight begins to slowly recede and the darkness of the night eventually envelopes everything. Likewise, at dawn the initial streak of light gradually develops into bright daylight.

31. That is, God has strictly bound the sun and the moon to a set of laws.

32. *Qiṭmīr* refers to the thin film covering a date-stone. The point of emphasis is that the idols worshipped by polytheists simply own nothing.

(14) If you call upon them, they cannot hear your prayer. And if they hear it, they cannot answer it.[33] On the Day of Resurrection they will disown[34] you for associating others with Allah in His Divinity. No one can inform you of the truth save the All-Aware.[35]

إِن تَدْعُوهُمْ لَا يَسْمَعُوا۟ دُعَآءَكُمْ وَلَوْ سَمِعُوا۟
مَا ٱسْتَجَابُوا۟ لَكُمْ ۖ وَيَوْمَ ٱلْقِيَـٰمَةِ
يَكْفُرُونَ بِشِرْكِكُمْ ۚ وَلَا يُنَبِّئُكَ مِثْلُ
خَبِيرٍ ﴿١٤﴾

33. This does not necessarily mean that the deities they worshipped would cry out and tell them in so many words that their supplication had been accepted or not. Rather, it means that they do not have the power to respond to their supplications. If one pleads to someone who is not authorised to do anything in that matter, then that pleading goes to waste. On the contrary, if a supplication is addressed to one who has the power to act on it, the matter is bound to receive due attention. Thereafter, it will either be accepted or rejected.

34. The deities they worship will plainly state that they never told their devotees that they had a share in God's Divinity. Nor did they ever ask their devotees to worship them. They will further claim that they were not even aware that they were being taken as associates with the Lord of the universe in His Divinity or that prayers were being addressed to them. They will also contend that none of the polytheists' prayers or any of their gifts and offerings ever reached them.

35. The "All-Aware" here is none other than God Himself. The point being made is as follows: The utmost that anyone other than God can do is to proffer rational arguments to refute polytheism and establish the absolute ineffectuality of the polytheists' deities. As distinct from all others, God alone is "All-Aware". It is on the basis of His direct knowledge that He can categorically say that those to whom people had assigned some power and authority in God's Godhead are all utterly powerless. They have no power to make or mar someone's life. God knows by dint of His knowledge that on the Day of Resurrection these deities will themselves refute the polytheistic notions of their devotees.

(15) O people, it is you who stand in need of Allah;[36] as for Allah, He is Self-Sufficient, Immensely Praiseworthy.[37] (16) If He wishes, He can remove you and put in your place a new creation. (17) That surely is not difficult for Allah.[38] ▶

۞ يَـٰٓأَيُّهَا ٱلنَّاسُ أَنتُمُ ٱلْفُقَرَآءُ إِلَى ٱللَّهِ ۖ وَٱللَّهُ
هُوَ ٱلْغَنِىُّ ٱلْحَمِيدُ ﴿١٥﴾ إِن يَشَأْ يُذْهِبْكُمْ
وَيَأْتِ بِخَلْقٍ جَدِيدٍ ﴿١٦﴾ وَمَا ذَٰلِكَ عَلَى
ٱللَّهِ بِعَزِيزٍ ﴿١٧﴾

36. It is clearly emphasised here that it is man who stands in need of God, rather than God standing in need of man. God's dominion is not contingent upon human beings' acceptance of Him as their Lord. Even if they were to disbelieve in Him, it would not cause Him the least harm. On the contrary, man does need God. For he cannot survive for even a moment unless God so wills. Furthermore, it is God Who provides man with the wherewithal to keep him alive and active. Hence, when human beings are told to serve and worship God the reason for it is not that God is sorely in need of their service and worship. Rather, the reason for this urging is that human beings' own success in this world and the Next hinges on it. Were they to pay no heed to this, they will hurt themselves rather than God.

37. God is "Self-Sufficient" because everything that exists is His. He, therefore, does not stand in need of anyone. For Him, no one is indispensable. Moreover, God is "Immensely Praiseworthy" meaning that He is intrinsically worthy of praise. Regardless of whether someone praises him or not, He is worthy of praise and thanks. These two attributes of Self-Sufficiency and being Immensely Praiseworthy have deliberately been juxtaposed. The reason for this is that it is possible for someone to be self-sufficient, but the mere fact that he is self-sufficient does not make him worthy of praise. For it is quite conceivable for someone to have an abundance of resources, but which he does not use to provide benefit to others. Such a person will become praiseworthy when, rather than deriving benefit from others, he diverts his resources to provide them with benefit. God is not simply Self-Sufficient but also Praiseworthy because of His benevolence in providing for the needs of all.

38. People should not forget that if they are strutting about on earth it is not because of any intrinsic power of their own. It would take no more

(18) No one can bear another's burden.[39] If a heavily laden one should call another to carry his load, none of it shall be carried by the other, even though he be a near of kin.[40] ▶

وَلَا تَزِرُ وَازِرَةٌ وِزْرَ أُخْرَىٰ ۚ وَإِن تَدْعُ مُثْقَلَةٌ
إِلَىٰ حِمْلِهَا لَا يُحْمَلْ مِنْهُ شَيْءٌ وَلَوْ كَانَ
ذَا قُرْبَىٰٓ ۗ

---

than a word from God to have them removed from the scene, replacing them by an altogether different people. Hence, they better bear in mind their true position, entertain no illusions, and beware of that evil course which led to the doom of many nations in the past. For, once God decides to destroy a people, no power in the whole universe can prevent that decision from taking effect.

39. The word "burden" here means the burden of responsibility to God. In other words, everyone will be responsible for his deeds, and God will never transfer a person's responsibility to another. Thus, it is not possible for someone to assume another's burden nor is it possible for someone to have themselves seized on another's behalf. This was occasioned by the fact that the relatives and clansmen of those who were converting to Islam said to them: "Abjure this new faith and return to the faith of your ancestors. We bear responsibility for the consequences that will follow".

40. Just prior to this, God's law of justice was enunciated: "No one can bear another's burden". This is an assurance that no one will be seized on account of another person's misdeeds; that God will hold every person responsible for his own sins. Here, reference is made to those who encouraged people to unbelief and sin by assuring them that they would own these acts on the Day of Judgement and volunteer to suffer retribution on their behalf. It was made clear that those people were extending false assurance. When the Day of Judgement comes, everyone will realise how horrible the impending punishment is. Each one will then become absorbed with their own fate. So horrendous will the circumstances facing all be that a brother will distance himself from his brother and a father from his son. No one will show the least inclination to voluntarily bear an atom's weight of any other person's sins.

(O Prophet), you can warn only those who fear their Lord without seeing Him and establish Prayer.[41] Whoever purifies himself does so to his own good. To Allah is the final return. (19) The blind and the seeing are not alike, (20) nor darkness and light; (21) nor cool shade and torrid heat; (22) nor are the living and the dead alike.[42] ▶	إِنَّمَا تُنذِرُ ٱلَّذِينَ يَخْشَوْنَ رَبَّهُم بِٱلْغَيْبِ وَأَقَامُوا۟ ٱلصَّلَوٰةَ ۚ وَمَن تَزَكَّىٰ فَإِنَّمَا يَتَزَكَّىٰ لِنَفْسِهِۦ ۚ وَإِلَى ٱللَّهِ ٱلْمَصِيرُ ﴿١٨﴾ وَمَا يَسْتَوِى ٱلْأَعْمَىٰ وَٱلْبَصِيرُ ﴿١٩﴾ وَلَا ٱلظُّلُمَـٰتُ وَلَا ٱلنُّورُ ﴿٢٠﴾ وَلَا ٱلظِّلُّ وَلَا ٱلْحَرُورُ ﴿٢١﴾ وَمَا يَسْتَوِى ٱلْأَحْيَآءُ وَلَا ٱلْأَمْوَٰتُ ۚ

41. That is, the Prophet's warnings will have no effect on those that are obstinate and haughty. Admonition can avail only those who fear God and are ready to surrender themselves to God, their true Master.

42. These similitudes bring out the distinction between the present and the future of the believers as well as unbelievers. The unbelievers turn a blind eye to the truths that are manifest in their own beings and in the universe at large. By contrast, the believers consider all things with an open and reflective mind and perceive everything to testify to monotheism and to man's ultimate accountability to God.

At one end are those who stray in the dark alleys of assumption, conjecture and superstition and who are averse to going even close to the effulgent lamp kindled by the Prophet (peace be on him). At the other end are those who keep their eyes wide open. Hence, no sooner are they exposed to the light kindled by the Prophet (peace be on him) than it becomes clear to them that the ways followed by the polytheists, unbelievers and atheists lead to doom and destruction. It also becomes clear to them that the way shown by the Prophet (peace be on him) alone leads to true success and felicity.

It follows from this that the people of the two categories pursue different paths in the life of this world. How, then, can their destinations in the Hereafter be the same? In other words, how can those who follow two different paths end up alike, both becoming extinct? How is it possible that the errant will not be punished, and those who follow the Right Way, will

Allah makes to hear whomsoever He wishes, but you, (O Prophet), cannot cause to hear those who are in their graves.[43] (23) You are no more than a warner.[44] (24) We have sent you with the Truth to proclaim good news and to warn. ▶

إِنَّ ٱللَّهَ يُسْمِعُ مَن يَشَآءُ ۖ وَمَآ أَنتَ بِمُسْمِعٍ مَّن فِى ٱلْقُبُورِ ﴿٢٢﴾ إِنْ أَنتَ إِلَّا نَذِيرٌ ﴿٢٣﴾ إِنَّآ أَرْسَلْنَٰكَ بِٱلْحَقِّ بَشِيرًا وَنَذِيرًا

---

be denied their reward? As the following verse eloquently puts it: "The blind and the seeing are not alike, nor darkness and light; nor cool shade and torrid heat nor are the living and the dead alike." (vv. 19–22).

The allusion in these verses is to the fact that while the people of one category will enjoy the "cool shade" of God's mercy, those belonging to the other category will suffer the "torrid heat" of Hell. There is no basis for the illusion that the end of all of them will be the same. It is also significant that the believers have been likened to "the living", and the obstinate unbelievers to "the dead". In other words, the believer is possessed of sensitivity, consciousness and understanding, his living, throbbing conscience constantly reminding him of the distinction between good and evil. As for those who are steeped in obdurateness and the bigotry of unbelief, they are worse than the blind who stagger in darkness. Such people are like the dead who are devoid of every sense and feeling.

43. As for God's Will, it is *sui generis* and no limits can be placed on it. Hence, if God so wills, He can grant the faculty of hearing even to stones. However, there are limits to what the Prophet (peace be on him) can do. For instance, he cannot make his message enter the hearts of those whose conscience is dead. Likewise, he cannot penetrate deaf ears. He can have an impact only on those who are ready to pay heed to that which is fair and reasonable.

44. The Prophet's assigned task is no more than to warn mankind. If the Prophet (peace be on him) fulfils that task and despite this, someone does not come to his senses but keeps stumbling in darkness, then the Prophet (peace be on him) is required to do no more. He is not expected to do the impossible – to make the blind see and the deaf hear.

Never has there been a nation but a warner came to it.[45] (25) If they give the lie to you now, those that went before them also gave the lie to their Messengers when they came to them with Clear Proofs,[46] with Scriptures, and with the Illuminating Book.[47] (26) Then I seized those who denied the Truth, and how terrible was My punishment!

وَإِن مِّنْ أُمَّةٍ إِلَّا خَلَا فِيهَا نَذِيرٌ ﴿٢٤﴾
وَإِن يُكَذِّبُوكَ فَقَدْ كَذَّبَ ٱلَّذِينَ مِن
قَبْلِهِمْ جَآءَتْهُمْ رُسُلُهُم بِٱلْبَيِّنَٰتِ وَبِٱلزُّبُرِ
وَبِٱلْكِتَٰبِ ٱلْمُنِيرِ ﴿٢٥﴾ ثُمَّ أَخَذْتُ ٱلَّذِينَ
كَفَرُوا۟ ۖ فَكَيْفَ كَانَ نَكِيرِ ﴿٢٦﴾

---

45. It is stated quite frequently in the Qur'ān that there has not been a people in the world among whom no Prophet was raised.

> You are only a warner and every people has its guide. (*Al-Ra'd* 13:7.)
>
> (O Muḥammad), certainly We did send Messengers before you among the nations that have gone by. (*Al-Ḥijr* 15:10.)
>
> We raised a Messenger in every community. (*Al-Naḥl* 16:36.)
>
> We never destroyed any habitation but that it had warners. (*Al-Shu'arā'* 26:208.)

However, one should also comprehend the following two points to avoid any misconception. First, that a Prophet suffices for the entire territory whereto his message reaches. It is not at all necessary for separate Prophets to be raised in every town and every nation. Secondly, that the need for a new Prophet does not arise as long as the teachings of an earlier Prophet remain extant and his example is available. It is, therefore, not at all necessary for a separate Prophet to be designated to every generation of people.

46. That is, the Messengers came with "Clear Proofs", thereby corroborating that they were God's Messengers.

47. Presumably the distinction made here between the "Scriptures" and "the Illuminating Book" is that while the former were mainly

(27) Do you not see that Allah sent down water from the sky with which We brought forth fruits of diverse hues? In the mountains there are white and red, of diverse hues, and pitchy black; (28) and human beings too, and beasts, and cattle – diverse are their hues.[48] ▶

أَلَمْ تَرَ أَنَّ ٱللَّهَ أَنزَلَ مِنَ ٱلسَّمَآءِ مَآءً فَأَخْرَجْنَا
بِهِۦ ثَمَرَٰتٍ مُّخْتَلِفًا أَلْوَٰنُهَا ۚ وَمِنَ ٱلْجِبَالِ
جُدَدٌۢ بِيضٌ وَحُمْرٌ مُّخْتَلِفٌ أَلْوَٰنُهَا
وَغَرَابِيبُ سُودٌ ﴿٢٧﴾ وَمِنَ ٱلنَّاسِ وَٱلدَّوَآبِّ
وَٱلْأَنْعَٰمِ مُخْتَلِفٌ أَلْوَٰنُهُۥ كَذَٰلِكَ ۗ

comprised of counsels and moral directives, the latter represents a pervasive, all-embracing *Sharī'ah*.

48. This is to stress that the universe is characterised by its multivariate nature rather than uniformity. This multivariate nature is manifest everywhere. For example, we find that on the same piece of land and watered by the same rainfall, a variety of trees growing on it. Furthermore, two fruits of the same tree vary in colour, size and taste. Even if we were to look at a mountain, we would find in it a variety of colours; in fact, every part of the mountain has a different material composition. Even two issues from the same parentage are not exactly alike. There are people who expect to find uniformity in the temperaments, dispositions and mindsets of people. When they find, instead, the kind of diversity mentioned in verses 19–22 above, they are bewildered. This, however, reflects their own flawed perception.

The fact of the matter is that diversity and variation point to the fact that this Universe was created by the One Who created it with immense wisdom, diversity and variation. They also indicate that the Maker of the Universe is a unique Creator and Matchless Designer, Whose creativity is in no way confined. On the contrary, He is capable of producing any number of patterns and designs. It is not at all accidental that men differ so widely as regards their temperaments and mental faculties. Once again, this fact is a masterpiece of God's creative wisdom. Had all human beings been identical as regards their temperaments, desires, emotions, inclinations and ways of thinking with no room left for any diversity, the very idea of creating man would have been futile. However, since God

From among His servants, it is only those who know that fear Allah.[49] ▶	إِنَّمَا يَخْشَى ٱللَّهَ مِنْ عِبَادِهِ ٱلْعُلَمَـٰٓؤُاْ

decided that humans be created as responsible beings and be granted free will, it necessarily follows that there should be considerable scope for diversity among them. This clearly indicates that far from being an accident, man's creation represents a grand plan based on immense wisdom. Now, if there is a grand plan based on wisdom, it is evident that there must be a Wise Being behind it. Only an imbecile can think of wisdom without there being a Wise Being.

49. The more a person is ignorant of God's attributes, the more fearless he will be of Him. By contrast, the more a person understands attributes such as those of God's power, knowledge, wisdom, and dominance over all, the more one will fear to disobey Him. The expression "those who know" is not used to denote savants in conventional fields of knowledge such as science, philosophy, history and mathematics. A person might be literate or illiterate, but what really matters is whether or not he holds God in awe. A person who is fearless of God is devoid of the knowledge that is meant here and will be deemed to be ignorant, however vast his knowledge of the world may be. By contrast, a person who has a good knowledge of God's attributes and who is God-fearing, will be considered knowledgeable even if he is illiterate. In this regard it should also be borne in mind that the above expression "those who know" does not necessarily refer to those whom we call *'ulamā' al-dīn* (religious scholars), because they have knowledge of the Qur'ān, *Ḥadīth*, *Fiqh* and *Kalām*. This expression only applies to them if they are characterised by God-consciousness. Accordingly, 'Abd Allāh ibn Mas'ūd observed: ليس العلم عن كثرة الحديث ولكن العلم عن كثرة الخشيّة "Knowledge does not come from an abundance of *ḥadīth* but from an abundance of God-fearing".[It could perhaps also mean: "Knowledge does not consist of an abundance of verbal expression, but of an abundance of God-fearing" – Ed.] The same observation was made by Ḥasan al-Baṣrī in the following words:

العالم من خشي الرحمن بالغيب و رغب فيما رغب الله فيه وزهد فيما سخط الله فيه

"A scholar is he who fears God, who is inclined to what pleases God, and who keeps away from whatever leads to God's wrath." (Ibn Kathīr, *Tafsīr*, comments on verse 28).

Verily Allah is Most Mighty, Most Forgiving.[50]

(29) Surely those who recite the Book of Allah and establish Prayer and spend, privately and publicly, out of what We have provided them, look forward to a trade that shall suffer no loss; (30) (a trade in which they have invested their all) so that Allah may pay them their wages in full and may add to them out of His Bounty.[51] ▶

إِنَّ ٱللَّهَ عَزِيزٌ غَفُورٌ ﴿٢٨﴾ إِنَّ ٱلَّذِينَ يَتْلُونَ
كِتَـٰبَ ٱللَّهِ وَأَقَامُوا۟ ٱلصَّلَوٰةَ وَأَنفَقُوا۟
مِمَّا رَزَقْنَـٰهُمْ سِرًّا وَعَلَانِيَةً يَرْجُونَ تِجَـٰرَةً
لَّن تَبُورَ ﴿٢٩﴾ لِيُوَفِّيَهُمْ أُجُورَهُمْ وَيَزِيدَهُم
مِّن فَضْلِهِۦٓ ۚ

50. Such is God's might that He can seize culprits whenever He wills. No one can escape His grip. However, He is also Most Pardoning and Most Forbearing and therefore He continually grants respite to evil-doers.

51. The believers' act of spending in good causes is likened to a trade wherein one invests one's capital, energies and abilities in the hope that one will recover the capital and also be compensated for one's time and effort. Not only that, one also expects to reap rich dividends. By the same token, a believer devotes his time, resources and abilities in obeying, serving and worshipping God and in promoting the cause of the true faith. Like a trader, a believer's devotion is in the expectation that God will not only pay him his wages in full, but will also abundantly compensate him out of His Bounty.

Though there is some similarity between worldly trade and the other type of trade mentioned here, there is also a major difference between them. As far as worldly trade is concerned, it is liable to both profit as well as loss. Quite contrary is the case of the trade which a believer has with God, for in it he runs no risk of loss.

He is Most Forgiving, Most Appreciative.[52] (31) (O Prophet), the Book We have revealed to you is the Truth, confirming the Books that came before it.[53] Verily Allah is well aware of His servants and sees everything.[54] (32) Then We bequeathed the Book to those of Our servants that We chose.[55] ▶

إِنَّهُۥ غَفُورٌ شَكُورٌ ﴿٣٠﴾ وَٱلَّذِىٓ أَوْحَيْنَآ إِلَيْكَ
مِنَ ٱلْكِتَـٰبِ هُوَ ٱلْحَقُّ مُصَدِّقًا
لِّمَا بَيْنَ يَدَيْهِ ۗ إِنَّ ٱللَّهَ بِعِبَادِهِۦ لَخَبِيرٌۢ
بَصِيرٌ ﴿٣١﴾ ثُمَّ أَوْرَثْنَا ٱلْكِتَـٰبَ ٱلَّذِينَ
ٱصْطَفَيْنَا مِنْ عِبَادِنَا ۖ

52. In dealing with His sincere believers God's attitude is unlike that of stingy masters one encounters in this world. These masters strictly take their servants to task for everything, large or small. Even a minor lapse on a servant's part makes them sweep aside his entire record of devoted service and loyalty. Distinguished from such worldly masters, God is noble and magnanimous. He overlooks the lapses of His loyal servants and appreciates even the slightest service that they render.

53. The Qur'ān is not expounding any novel message, one discordant with the teachings of earlier Prophets. Rather, the Qur'ān expounds the eternal truth that was always communicated to people by the Prophets throughout the ages.

54. These attributes of God are mentioned here so as to explain to humans wherein their good lies, which principles are suitable for their guidance and which rules are in conformity with their best interests. This because none but God is truly aware of these matters. He, the Creator, alone has full knowledge of the nature of human beings and their requirements. Furthermore, God alone can take into account their true interests. Human beings do not know themselves as well as God does. Hence what God communicated through revelation only is, and can be true.

55. The reference here is to Muslims. They have been sorted out from all mankind to form the chosen group to whom God's Book was bequeathed and who were required to become its standard-bearers after

Now, some of them wrong themselves and some follow the medium course; and some, by Allah's leave, vie with each other in acts of goodness. That is the great bounty.[56] ▶	فَمِنْهُمْ ظَالِمٌ لِّنَفْسِهِۦ وَمِنْهُم مُّقْتَصِدٌ وَمِنْهُمْ سَابِقٌۢ بِٱلْخَيْرَٰتِ بِإِذْنِ ٱللَّهِ ۚ ذَٰلِكَ هُوَ ٱلْفَضْلُ ٱلْكَبِيرُ ﴿٣٢﴾

the Prophet (peace be on him). Although the Book was presented before all mankind, only those who stepped forward and accepted it were chosen for this honour. That is, to be the inheritors of a book as great as the Qur'ān and the trustees of the teachings of a Prophet as great as Muḥammad (peace be on him).

56. These Muslims, however, are not all alike; rather, they belong to the following three categories:

i. "Those who wrong themselves". These Muslims sincerely believe in the Qur'ān as God's Book and in Muḥammad (peace be on him) as God's Messenger. However, in their practical lives they fail to follow the Book of God and the *Sunnah* of His Prophet (peace be on him) to the extent they should. Despite being believers they still commit sin. While such people might be iniquitous, they are not rebels. Their belief might be a bit feeble, yet they are neither hypocrites nor wilful unbelievers. In recognition of this, the Qur'ān brands them as God's chosen servants to whom His Book has been bequeathed. Such an honour, for sure, could not have been conferred on rebels, hypocrites or unbelievers. Among the believers of all the three categories, they are the first to be mentioned for they constitute the majority of Muslims.

ii. Then come those "who follow the medium course". That is, they are the ones who fulfil, though partially, the requirements ensuing from the bequest of God's Book to them. They represent a mixture of obedience and disobedience. Such people, however, do not give an altogether free rein to their desires; rather, they try to control them. Nevertheless, at times they let their desires loose a bit which leads to sinful behaviour. Thus their conduct is a mixture of both kinds of acts – good and bad. Such people

(33) They shall enter the everlasting Gardens,[57] shall be adorned with bracelets of gold and with pearls, ▶	جَنَّٰتُ عَدْنٍ يَدْخُلُونَهَا يُحَلَّوْنَ فِيهَا مِنْ أَسَاوِرَ مِن ذَهَبٍ وَلُؤْلُؤًا

are less in number than the people of the first category but outnumber those of the third category mentioned below.

iii. Then come those "who vie with one another in acts of goodness". Among the believers, they occupy the forefront. They stand out as the true trustees of the Book of God. They outstrip others as they are exceedingly active in following the Book of God and the *Sunnah* of the Prophet (peace be on him), in communicating God's Message to His servants, in offering sacrifices for the cause of faith, and in doing acts of goodness. They are not the ones who would deliberately commit a sin; but if they happen to fall into sin, they repent as soon as they realise this. In number, these are less than the two groups mentioned above. Although they are mentioned after those groups, they are in fact well ahead of them in acquitting themselves of the trusteeship of the Qur'ān.

The verse concludes with the words: "That is the great bounty". Should these words be considered as referring to the nearest statement – "those who vie with each other in acts of goodness" – the expression would mean that "vying with each other in acts of goodness itself constitutes the great bounty". Hence, those who comprise this group hold the pride of place among Muslims. Another opinion, however, is that these words relate to the following words in the earlier part of the verse: "Then We bequeathed the Book to those of Our servants that We chose". If this view is accepted, then it would mean that the bequeathing of the Book and inclusion in the fold of God's chosen servants constitutes "the great bounty". As a result, those Muslims to whom the Qur'ān was bequeathed and whom God chose to be among His servants have an edge over the rest of God's servants as they attained the distinction of believing in the Qur'ān and in the Prophet Muḥammad (peace be on him).

57. A group of Qur'ān-commentators is of the opinion that the words "they shall enter the everlasting Gardens" ... refer to the people mentioned above – that is, to those who "vie with each other in acts of goodness".

It is in respect of them that the statement about the great bounty was made, and it is they who were assured entry to the everlasting Gardens. However, two other groups – those who "wrong themselves" and those who "follow the medium course" – are also mentioned. According to these commentators, however, the Qur'ān is silent about them. The reason for this silence is to arouse among them serious concern about their ultimate end and to provide them with the impetus to change their present state into a better one. Al-Zamakhsharī forcefully argued for this view and Fakhr al-Dīn al-Rāzī also endorsed it. (See, Zamakhsharī, *al-Kashshāf*, and Rāzī, *al-Tafsīr al-Kabīr,* comments on verses 32–33).

The majority of Qur'ān-commentators, however, are of the opinion that this statement [to wit, "they shall enter the everlasting Gardens"] is connected with the whole preceding statement. In other words, what it means is that all people belonging to the above three groups will eventually enter Paradise. Some will enter without being subjected to reckoning and others after it; some without facing the consequences of that reckoning and some after facing them.

The context of the verse supports this interpretation. This because just a little later on we read of "those who disbelieved, the Fire of Hell awaits them" (verse 36), in contrast to those who have been bequeathed the Book. This shows that all those who believe will be admitted to Paradise and that Hell awaits those who refuse to believe. This interpretation is further corroborated by a tradition from the Prophet (peace be on him) narrated by Abū al-Dardā'. The Prophet (peace be on him) is on record as saying: "Those who vie with each other in acts of goodness shall enter Paradise without reckoning. As for those of the medium course, they will be interrogated, though lightly. However, those 'who wronged themselves', will be detained during the Assembly [of the Last Day], and then God will admit them to His Mercy. They will say: 'All praise be to Allah, Who has taken away all sorrow from us' ". (For this tradition see Aḥmad ibn Ḥanbal, *Musnad*, narrated by Abū al-Dardā'; Ibn Kathīr, *Tafsīr,* comments on verse 32; Ṭabarī, *Tafsīr,* comments on verse 32.)

This *ḥadīth* fully endorses the thrust of the verse under discussion. It points to the different kinds of treatment that will be meted out to each of the three categories of believers. Those believers who follow the medium course will be subjected to light reckoning. This implies that the unbelievers will receive punishment for each of their evil deeds in addition to their punishment for refusing to believe. As distinguished from them, the believers who have a mixed record of good and bad deeds will be treated differently. Their record as a whole, rather than each single item of it, will be subjected to reckoning. It has been stated in the *ḥadīth* cited above that those believers who "wrong themselves" will be detained during the course of the Assembly of the Last Day.

and their apparel therein shall be silk. (34) They will say: "All praise be to Allah Who has taken away all sorrow from us.[58] ▶	وَلِبَاسُهُمْ فِيهَا حَرِيرٌ ﴿٣٣﴾ وَقَالُوا۟ ٱلْحَمْدُ لِلَّهِ ٱلَّذِىٓ أَذْهَبَ عَنَّا ٱلْحَزَنَ ۖ

(One does not know how many centuries long this will be and what will be its attendant severities!) The statement that they shall be detained throughout the course of the Assembly seems to resemble the verdict of our present-day courts that sentence a culprit to remain in "detention till the rising of the court". After being exposed to these severities of the Assembly of the Last Day, God's mercy will envelope them and they will finally be admitted to Paradise. Statements of this import have been narrated on the authority of several Companions such as 'Umar ibn al-Khaṭṭāb, 'Uthmān ibn 'Affān, 'Abd Allāh ibn Mas'ūd, 'Abd Allāh ibn 'Abbās, 'Ā'ishah, Abū Sa'īd al-Khudrī and Barā' ibn 'Āzib. It is obvious that these Companions could not have made such statements unless they had heard something to that effect from the Prophet (peace be on him).

The statement regarding detention for the entire period of the Assembly of the Last Day should, however, not be misunderstood. It does not mean that the punishment of those who wronged themselves will be strictly confined to this detention and that they will not suffer the chastisement of Hell. This is clearly not tenable. This because the Qur'ān and *Ḥadīth* mention several sins in regard to which it has been said that even faith would not be able to prevent those who commit them from being cast into Hell. One such sin, for instance, is the deliberate murder of a believer. God Himself declares that such people will be cast into Hell. (See *al-Nisā'* 4: 93.) Likewise, those who violate the limits laid down by God as regards the laws of inheritance have also been warned of the punishment of Hell. (See *al-Nisā'* 4:6–14.) Again, with regard to those who continue to indulge in usury after its prohibition, it is said in the Qur'ān, that they are the "people of the fire", (*al-Baqarah* 2:275). *Aḥādīth* also identify those who will be consigned to Hell in retribution for certain major sins.

58. Reference here is to their sorrow in a broad sense. They will finally be relieved of any kind of sorrow that might have afflicted them in the course of their lives. Moreover, they will attain deliverance in the Hereafter, which was to them a matter of much concern and anxiety. All such concerns will then have become a matter of the past. As for the future, it will be all milk and honey; a future free of every grief and sorrow.

Surely our Lord is Most Forgiving, Most Appreciative;[59] (35) (the Lord) Who, out of His Bounty, has made us dwell in an abode[60] wherein no toil, nor fatigue affects us.[61]

(36) As for those who disbelieved,[62] the Fire of Hell awaits them. There they shall not be finished off and die; nor will the torment (of Hell) be lightened for them. Thus do We requite every thankless being. (37) They will cry out in Hell and say: "Our Lord, let us out so that we may act righteously, ▶

إِنَّ رَبَّنَا لَغَفُورٌ شَكُورٌ ﴿٣٤﴾ ٱلَّذِىٓ أَحَلَّنَا دَارَ
ٱلْمُقَامَةِ مِن فَضْلِهِۦ لَا يَمَسُّنَا فِيهَا نَصَبٌ
وَلَا يَمَسُّنَا فِيهَا لُغُوبٌ ﴿٣٥﴾ وَٱلَّذِينَ كَفَرُوا۟
لَهُمْ نَارُ جَهَنَّمَ لَا يُقْضَىٰ عَلَيْهِمْ فَيَمُوتُوا۟
وَلَا يُخَفَّفُ عَنْهُم مِّنْ عَذَابِهَا ۚ كَذَٰلِكَ
نَجْزِى كُلَّ كَفُورٍ ﴿٣٦﴾ وَهُمْ يَصْطَرِخُونَ
فِيهَا رَبَّنَآ أَخْرِجْنَا نَعْمَلْ صَٰلِحًا

59. They will recognise God's bounty and be thankful to Him. This because God forgave them their sins. He also showed appreciation for whatever little good they did and rewarded them by admitting them to Paradise.

60. Believers will realise that the worldly existence they went through was just a stage of life as was the Assembly of the Last Day. After having successfully passed through these stages, they will find themselves in Paradise where they are destined to abide forever.

61. Their admittance to Paradise will bring to an end all their toil and suffering. In Paradise, there will be no tasks entailing hardship and exhaustion.

62. Here reference is made to those who do not believe in the Qur'ān, the Book God revealed to the Prophet Muḥammad (peace be on him).

different from what we did before." (They will be told): "Did we not grant you an age long enough for anyone to take heed if he had wanted to take heed?[63] Besides, there came a warner to you. So have a taste of the torment now. None may come to the help of the wrong-doers."

(38) Surely Allah knows the Unseen in the heavens and the earth. He even knows the secrets hidden in people's breasts. (39) It is He Who made you vicegerents in the earth.[64] ▶

غَيْرَ ٱلَّذِي كُنَّا نَعْمَلُ ۚ أَوَلَمْ نُعَمِّرْكُم
مَّا يَتَذَكَّرُ فِيهِ مَن تَذَكَّرَ وَجَآءَكُمُ
ٱلنَّذِيرُ ۖ فَذُوقُوا۟ فَمَا لِلظَّٰلِمِينَ مِن نَّصِيرٍ ﴿٣٧﴾
إِنَّ ٱللَّهَ عَٰلِمُ غَيْبِ ٱلسَّمَٰوَٰتِ
وَٱلْأَرْضِ ۚ إِنَّهُۥ عَلِيمٌۢ بِذَاتِ ٱلصُّدُورِ ﴿٣٨﴾
هُوَ ٱلَّذِي جَعَلَكُمْ خَلَٰٓئِفَ فِى
ٱلْأَرْضِ ۚ

63. This signifies the age during which one acquires the ability to distinguish between good and evil and truth and falsehood and becomes mature enough to turn to guidance in place of error should one so want to. The present verse makes it clear that if one were to die before attaining that age, one will not face accountability. However, those who have attained such age will definitely be held responsible for their deeds. The greater the number of opportunities for a person to mend his ways, the more strictly will he be called to account. Anyone who fails to mend his ways despite reaching old age will have no reason to be extenuated. This point features in the following *ḥadīth* narrated by Abū Hurayrah and Sahl ibn Sa'd al-Sā'idī: "There is an excuse for him who dies at a young age. However, there is no excuse for those who live for sixty years or more". (Bukhārī, *Kitāb al-Riqāq, Bāb man Balagha Sittīn Sanah*; Aḥmad ibn Ḥanbal, *Musnad*, narrated by Abū Hurayrah; Nasā'ī, *Kitāb al-Riqāq*; Ibn Kathīr, *Tafsīr*, comments on verse 37; Ṭabarī, *Tafsīr*, comments on verse 37.)

64. This has two possible meanings: (i) That God settled them in the land after the passing away of the earlier generations and nations.

So whoever disbelieves will bear the burden of his unbelief.[65] The unbelievers' unbelief adds nothing but Allah's wrath against them. The unbelievers' unbelief adds nothing but their own loss.

(40) Say to them (O Prophet): "Have you ever seen those of your associates[66] upon whom you call apart from Allah? Show me what have they created in the earth? Or do they have any partnership (with Allah) in the heavens? ▶

فَمَن كَفَرَ فَعَلَيْهِ كُفْرُهُۥ ۖ وَلَا يَزِيدُ
ٱلْكَٰفِرِينَ كُفْرُهُمْ عِندَ رَبِّهِمْ إِلَّا مَقْتًا ۖ
وَلَا يَزِيدُ ٱلْكَٰفِرِينَ كُفْرُهُمْ
إِلَّا خَسَارًا ﴿٣٩﴾ قُلْ أَرَءَيْتُمْ شُرَكَآءَكُمُ
ٱلَّذِينَ تَدْعُونَ مِن دُونِ ٱللَّهِ أَرُونِى مَاذَا
خَلَقُوا۟ مِنَ ٱلْأَرْضِ أَمْ لَهُمْ شِرْكٌ فِى
ٱلسَّمَٰوَٰتِ

(ii) They enjoyed authority not as owners and masters, but as vicegerents of the True Lord on earth.

65. If the earlier statement is understood to mean that the Muslims were made successors of earlier nations, then this statement means the following: those who do not draw any lesson from the tragic end of past nations and persist in the same unbelief that brought those nations to their catastrophic ends, they will eventually witness the same tragic end that overtook these iniquitous nations of the past.

This statement can also mean that those who disregard their position as God's vicegerents, who arrogate sovereign authority to themselves, and who worship others besides the One True Lord will face terrible consequences for their defiance.

66. The expression used here is "your associates". The significance of this seems to be that in point of fact these deities are not God's associates; rather, it is the polytheists who falsely set them up as God's associates.

Or have We given them a Book so that they have a clear proof (for associating others with Allah in His Divinity)?"[67] Nay, what these wrong-doers promise each other is nothing but delusion.[68] (41) Surely Allah holds the heavens and the earth, lest they should be displaced there, for if they were displaced ▶

أَمْ ءَاتَيْنَٰهُمْ كِتَٰبًا فَهُمْ عَلَىٰ بَيِّنَتٍ مِّنْهُ
بَلْ إِن يَعِدُ ٱلظَّٰلِمُونَ بَعْضُهُم بَعْضًا
إِلَّا غُرُورًا ۝ إِنَّ ٱللَّهَ يُمْسِكُ
ٱلسَّمَٰوَٰتِ وَٱلْأَرْضَ أَن تَزُولَا
وَلَئِن زَالَتَآ

67. The polytheists and unbelievers are pointedly asked whether they have any written sanction from God indicating that He had, for instance, granted certain people the power to cure the sick, or to provide jobs to the unemployed, or to meet the needs of those in distress? No, God has not conferred any such authority upon them. They can neither make nor mar anyone's fate. God has not directed mankind to invoke them or to make offerings to them. They are, therefore, asked to produce evidence in support of their beliefs, if they have any. Now, since they cannot produce such, they had better reconsider their polytheistic beliefs and practices. They are asked to come forward with specific proofs indicating that their idols are indeed God's associates. They, however, have nothing to put forward for there is nothing in any Scripture that lends support to such a notion. Nor do these idols possess any authority from God on the basis of which they have been ascribed special powers. If they have nothing to support their position, they might as well ask themselves: did they own Godhead that made it possible for them to go about lavishing God's powers on whomsoever they wished?

68. These misguided religious leaders, so-called saints and clergymen, preachers, soothsayers and their accomplices exploit the common people. They invent false stories in order to convince them that their devotion to such an idol will carry them to success in this world and to salvation in the Hereafter.

none would be able to hold them after Him.[69] Surely He is Most Forbearing, Most Forgiving.[70]

(42) Swearing by Allah their strongest oaths they claimed that if a warner came to them they would be better-guided than any other people.[71] But when a warner did come to them, his coming only increased their aversion (to the Truth). (43) They began to wax even more proud on earth and contrived evil designs although the contriving of evil designs only overtakes their authors. ▶

إِنۡ أَمۡسَكَهُمَا مِنۡ أَحَدٖ مِّنۢ بَعۡدِهِۦٓۚ إِنَّهُۥ كَانَ
حَلِيمًا غَفُورٗا ﴿٤١﴾ وَأَقۡسَمُواْ بِٱللَّهِ جَهۡدَ
أَيۡمَٰنِهِمۡ لَئِن جَآءَهُمۡ نَذِيرٞ لَّيَكُونُنَّ أَهۡدَىٰ
مِنۡ إِحۡدَى ٱلۡأُمَمِۖ فَلَمَّا جَآءَهُمۡ نَذِيرٞ
مَّا زَادَهُمۡ إِلَّا نُفُورًا ﴿٤٢﴾ ٱسۡتِكۡبَارٗا فِي
ٱلۡأَرۡضِ وَمَكۡرَ ٱلسَّيِّيِٕۚ وَلَا يَحِيقُ ٱلۡمَكۡرُ
ٱلسَّيِّئُ إِلَّا بِأَهۡلِهِۦۚ

69. It is God Who keeps the universe intact. No angel, or *jinn*, no Messenger or saint oversees the workings of the universe. Far from sustaining the universe, those mentioned above cannot maintain even themselves. For, everyone is totally dependent upon God for everything, even as regards his birth and survival. It is thus sheer folly and deception to consider anyone to be God's partner either in His attributes or authority.

70. This underscores God's great forbearance whereby He does not instantly punish the guilty even if they adopt a blasphemous posture towards Him.

71. This was the Arabs' usual comment, especially the Quraysh's, relating to the moral degeneration of the Jews and Christians in pre-Islamic days. Such statements by them are also recorded in *Sūrah al-An'ām* 6:156–157 and *Sūrah al-Ṣāffāt* 37:167–169.

Are they waiting, then, for anything except what happened to the nations before them?[72] You shall not find any change in the Way of Allah; and you shall not find anything that can ever alter the Way of Allah. (44) Have they not journeyed in the earth to behold the end of those who went before them though they were stronger than them in might? Nothing in the heavens nor on earth can frustrate Him in the least. He is All-Knowing, All-Powerful. (45) If Allah were to take people to task for their deeds, He would not leave any living creature on earth, but He grants them respite to an appointed time. When their appointed time comes to an end, surely Allah fully observes His servants.

فَهَلْ يَنظُرُونَ إِلَّا سُنَّتَ ٱلْأَوَّلِينَ ۚ فَلَن
تَجِدَ لِسُنَّتِ ٱللَّهِ تَبْدِيلًا ۖ وَلَن تَجِدَ لِسُنَّتِ
ٱللَّهِ تَحْوِيلًا ﴿٤٣﴾ أَوَلَمْ يَسِيرُوا۟ فِى ٱلْأَرْضِ
فَيَنظُرُوا۟ كَيْفَ كَانَ عَـٰقِبَةُ ٱلَّذِينَ مِن
قَبْلِهِمْ وَكَانُوٓا۟ أَشَدَّ مِنْهُمْ قُوَّةً ۚ وَمَا كَانَ ٱللَّهُ
لِيُعْجِزَهُۥ مِن شَىْءٍ فِى ٱلسَّمَـٰوَٰتِ وَلَا فِى
ٱلْأَرْضِ ۚ إِنَّهُۥ كَانَ عَلِيمًا قَدِيرًا ﴿٤٤﴾
وَلَوْ يُؤَاخِذُ ٱللَّهُ ٱلنَّاسَ بِمَا كَسَبُوا۟ مَا تَرَكَ
عَلَىٰ ظَهْرِهَا مِن دَآبَّةٍ وَلَـٰكِن يُؤَخِّرُهُمْ
إِلَىٰٓ أَجَلٍ مُّسَمًّى ۖ فَإِذَا جَآءَ أَجَلُهُمْ فَإِنَّ ٱللَّهَ
كَانَ بِعِبَادِهِۦ بَصِيرًۢا ﴿٤٥﴾

72. This law is applicable to them in so far as every nation that rejects its Prophet is destroyed.

Sūrah 36

Yā' Sīn

(Makkan Period)

Title

The two opening letters constitute the *sūrah*'s title.

Period of Revelation

The tenor of the *sūrah* indicates that it must have been revealed towards the end of the Makkan period's middle phase. Alternatively, it would have been revealed during the last phase of the Makkan period of the Prophet's mission.

Subject Matter and Themes

The purport of the *sūrah* is to warn the unbelieving Quraysh of the grave consequences for their refusal to believe in the Prophet (peace be on him) and their recourse to oppressive measures, mockery and lampooning in opposing the Prophet's mission. The dominant mood that characterises the *sūrah* is that of warning. However, alongside these warnings the Message is also explicated with the help of argumentation. (i) Arguments in support of monotheism are drawn from natural phenomena and common sense. (ii) Arguments in support of the Hereafter are also drawn from natural phenomena, common sense and man's very own being. (iii) Arguments are also proffered for the veracity of Muḥammad's Messengership. They consist of highlighting (a) the selflessness with which the Prophet (peace be on him) endured hardships in the cause of his Message; (b) the perfectly sound and reasonable character of his teachings, and (c) the fact that acceptance of these teachings was conducive to mankind's good.

Alongside this argumentation, the discourse is punctuated by forceful notes of reproach and warning with a view to jolting the unbelievers from their stupor. This also serves to influence the hearts and minds of those who have even an iota of ability to accept the Truth. Aḥmad ibn Ḥanbal, Abū Dā'ūd, Nasā'ī, Ibn Mājah and Ṭabarānī cite the Prophet's statement on the authority of Ma'qal ibn Yasār that *Sūrah Yā' Sīn* represents the heart of the Qur'ān. (Aḥmad ibn Ḥanbal, *Musnad*, narrated by Ma'qal ibn Yassār; Tirmidhī, *Bāb Faḍā'il al-Qur'ān, Bāb ma jā'a fī Faḍā'il Yā' Sīn* ... (Ed.) *Sūrah al-Fātiḥah* is called *Umm al-Qur'ān* because it encapsulates all the essential teachings of the Qur'ān. *Sūrah Yā' Sīn* has been likened to the Qur'ān's throbbing heart because it forcefully expounds its message. A study of this *sūrah* shatters spiritual stolidity, arousing and activating man's soul. It is again on the authority of the same Ma'qal ibn Yasār (as cited by Aḥmad ibn Ḥanbal, *Musnad*, narrated by Ma'qal ibn Yassār; Abū Dā'ūd, *Kitāb al-Janā'iz, Bāb Qirā'ah 'ind al-Mayyit*; Ibn Mājah, *Kitāb al-Janā'iz, Bāb Mā jā'a fī mā Yuqāl 'ind al-Marīḍ idhā Ḥuḍira*) that the Prophet (peace be on him) said: "Recite *Sūrah Yā' Sīn* when one of you dies". This because the *sūrah* refreshes all the articles of Islamic belief and prompts one to think of what will happen in the Hereafter. This will enable the dying person to realise what stages he will pass through when his term of worldly life ends. In order to achieve this purpose it seems appropriate that this *sūrah* should be recited on this occasion along with its translation for the benefit of those who are not conversant with Arabic.

In the name of Allah, the Most Merciful, the Most Compassionate.

(1) *Yā'. Sīn.*[1] (2) By the Wise Qur'ān, (3) you are truly among the Messengers,[2] (4) on a Straight Way, ▶

بِسْمِ ٱللَّهِ ٱلرَّحْمَٰنِ ٱلرَّحِيمِ

يسٓ ﴿١﴾ وَٱلْقُرْءَانِ ٱلْحَكِيمِ ﴿٢﴾ إِنَّكَ لَمِنَ
ٱلْمُرْسَلِينَ ﴿٣﴾ عَلَىٰ صِرَٰطٍ مُّسْتَقِيمٍ ﴿٤﴾

---

1. *Yā' Sīn,* according to 'Abd Allāh ibn 'Abbās, 'Ikrimah, Ḍaḥḥāk, Ḥasan al-Baṣrī and Sufyān ibn 'Uyaynah means "O man". (Ibn Kathīr, *Tafsīr,* comments on verse 1.) Some Qur'ān-commentators consider *Yā' Sīn* to be the abbreviation of *Yā Sayyid.* Taken in this sense, this constitutes an address to the Prophet (peace be on him).

2. This vigorous affirmation of Muḥammad's Messengership does not in any way imply that the Prophet (peace be on him) had any doubt about his Prophethood and that was thus reassured by God through this verse of the veracity of his claim to be His Messenger. At the time when this *sūrah* was revealed the Makkan unbelievers were engaged in fierce opposition to Muḥammad's claim. Hence, the *sūrah* opens by directly declaring, without any preliminary remarks, that Muḥammad (peace be on him) is "truly among the Messengers". The implication of this declaration is that those who deny his Prophethood are in serious error. This point is made by an oath in the name of the Qur'ān itself, the Book characterised by wisdom. In other words, a clear proof of Muḥammad's Prophethood is the Qur'ān, which overflows with wisdom. That Muḥammad (peace be on him) was presenting a discourse as steeped in wisdom as the Qur'ān, is itself a proof of his being God's Messenger, for no human being could produce anything like it. Those familiar with the Prophet Muḥammad (peace be on him) could never fall prey to the misgiving that he would have made up this discourse himself, or would have acquired it from some other person and then ascribed it to God. (For a detailed explanation of this point see *Towards Understanding the Qur'ān, Yūnus* 10: nn. 21, 45 and 46, Vol. IV, pp. 19–21 and 36–37; *Banī Isrā'īl* 17: nn. 106–108, Vol. V, pp. 73–75; *al-Shu'arā'* 26: n. 1, Vol. VII, p. 52; *al-Naml* 27: n. 93, Vol. VII, pp. 183–184; *al-Qaṣaṣ* 28: nn. 62–64 and 109, Vol. VII, pp. 224–226, 250, and *al-'Ankabūt* 29: nn. 88–91, Vol. VIII, pp. 50–54.)

(5) (and this Qur'ān) is a revelation from the Most Mighty, the Most Compassionate[3] (6) so that you may warn a people whose ancestors were not warned before wherefore they are heedless.[4]	تَنزِيلَ ٱلْعَزِيزِ ٱلرَّحِيمِ ۝٥ لِتُنذِرَ قَوْمًا مَّآ أُنذِرَ ءَابَآؤُهُمْ فَهُمْ غَٰفِلُونَ ۝٦

3. Here we are apprised of the following two attributes of Him Who sent down the Qur'ān. First, that He is the Most Mighty and Supreme, and secondly, that He is the Most Compassionate. The first attribute underscores the point that the Qur'ān is not the counsel of a powerless well-wisher which people may disregard feeling that He is devoid of the necessary power to punish them. It is, instead, the command of the Sovereign of the Universe Whose Will is supreme, One Whose command's enforcement none can prevent, One from Whose powerful grip no one can escape. The second attribute – that He is Most Compassionate – stresses a different point. It is out of His overflowing Compassion that God raised His Messenger to provide guidance to people. Likewise, He revealed this great Book, the Qur'ān, that they might eschew error and tread along the Straight Way which will bring to them success, both in this world and in the Next.

4. In addition to the translation given above, this verse can also be translated thus: "… so that you may warn a people against what their ancestors had been warned for they are heedless".

If one accepts the translation as rendered in the text above, the ancestors would refer to the Arabs' immediate forefathers. This because in the distant past the people of the Arabian Peninsula had witnessed several Prophets who had warned them. However, if one adopts the latter translation suggested in this note, it would mean that the Prophet (peace be on him) should revive the message that had been communicated to their ancestors in the past. Such a revival of that original message was necessary because the people had relegated that message to oblivion. In this respect, there is no basic conflict between the two translations; rather, each of the two is substantially sound.

What is said in this verse might possibly give rise to doubt in some people's minds. The ancestors of these people, according to this verse, had passed through a period in their history when no Messenger came

(7) Surely most of them merit the decree of chastisement; so they do not believe.[5] ▶	لَقَدْ حَقَّ ٱلْقَوْلُ عَلَىٰٓ أَكْثَرِهِمْ فَهُمْ لَا يُؤْمِنُونَ ۝٧

to warn them. The question that arises is the following: why should those who had not been warned be held accountable for the errors they might have succumbed to? The answer to the question is that when God sends a Prophet, his instruction and guidance have a far-reaching impact, one that endures for generations. As long as the traces of the Prophet's teachings remain and there continue to be followers who keep radiating the light of the message, such periods cannot be considered to be eras devoid of True Guidance. However, when a Prophet's teachings are totally lost in oblivion or are distorted beyond recognition, the advent of a new Prophet becomes inevitable. Before the advent of the Prophet Muḥammad (peace be on him), the impact of the message preached earlier by Prophets such as Abraham, Ishmael, Shu'ayb and Moses (peace be on them) was clearly observable throughout Arabia. We also find that from time to time noble souls would rise from within the Arabs' own ranks or would come to them from elsewhere and would renew the impact of the Prophetic message. When, however, this impact almost dissipated and the true teachings of the Prophets were radically distorted, God raised the Prophet Muḥammad (peace be on him) and made iron-cast arrangements so that the Guidance handed down through him would suffer neither obliteration nor distortion, (see *Towards Understanding the Qur'ān, al-Sajdah* 32: n. 5, Vol. VIII, pp. 159–160).

5. The reference here is to those who rejected the Prophet's call out of adamance and obstinacy and had firmly made up their minds not to pay any heed to his teachings. Regarding such people it was remarked: "Surely most of them merit the decree of chastisement, they do not believe". This refers to those who refuse to listen to sound counsel, clinging to their rejection of and fierce opposition to the Truth, even after the Prophets had clearly explained it to them, and thus completed God's argument before them. Such people who continue their hostility to the Truth are left to face the ill consequences of their deeds whereafter they lose the ability to believe. This idea has found explicit expression in verses 10–11 that occur a little after the present verse: "It is all the same for them whether you warn them or do not warn them for they shall not believe. You can warn only him who follows the Admonition and fears the Merciful Lord without seeing Him".

(8) We have put fetters around their necks which reach up to their chins so that they are standing with their heads upright,[6] (9) and We have put a barrier before them and a barrier behind them, and have covered them up, so they are unable to see.[7] (10) It is all the same for them whether you warn them or do not warn them for they shall not believe. (11) You can warn only him who follows the Admonition and fears the Merciful Lord without seeing Him.[8] ▶

إِنَّا جَعَلْنَا فِىٓ أَعْنَـٰقِهِمْ أَغْلَـٰلًا فَهِىَ إِلَى
ٱلْأَذْقَانِ فَهُم مُّقْمَحُونَ ﴿٨﴾ وَجَعَلْنَا مِنۢ بَيْنِ
أَيْدِيهِمْ سَدًّا وَمِنْ خَلْفِهِمْ سَدًّا فَأَغْشَيْنَـٰهُمْ
فَهُمْ لَا يُبْصِرُونَ ﴿٩﴾ وَسَوَآءٌ عَلَيْهِمْ ءَأَنذَرْتَهُمْ
أَمْ لَمْ تُنذِرْهُمْ لَا يُؤْمِنُونَ ﴿١٠﴾ إِنَّمَا تُنذِرُ مَنِ
ٱتَّبَعَ ٱلذِّكْرَ وَخَشِىَ ٱلرَّحْمَـٰنَ بِٱلْغَيْبِ ۖ

6. The word "fetters" in the verse alludes to the unbelievers' obduracy that prevented them from accepting the Truth. Likewise, there is a mention of fetters around the unbelievers' necks "which reach up to their chins" so that "they are standing with their heads upright". This is a reference to the stiffness of the neck that is caused by pride and arrogance. As a result, they have reached a stage where not even the most luminous signs would prompt them to pay any heed.

7. The purpose behind saying that "We have put a barrier before them and a barrier behind them" is to emphasise the unbelievers' obduracy and arrogance. It is thanks to this that they neither derive any lesson from the past nor give any serious thought to the future implications of their attitude. They are encompassed by thick blinkers of misunderstanding. As a result, they have been rendered unable to see those self-evident truths that are observed by everyone who is sensible and unprejudiced.

8. "It is all the same for them whether you warn them or do not warn them for they shall not believe." This does not mean that when that stage is reached there is no point in communicating Islam's message. What is meant is that the message reaches all kinds of people. Among them

Give such a one good tidings of forgiveness and a generous reward.

(12) We shall surely raise the dead to life and We record what they did and the traces of their deeds that they have left behind.[9] We have encompassed that in a Clear Book.

فَبَشِّرْهُ بِمَغْفِرَةٍ وَأَجْرٍ كَرِيمٍ ﴿١١﴾ إِنَّا نَحْنُ نُحْيِ
ٱلْمَوْتَىٰ وَنَكْتُبُ مَا قَدَّمُوا۟ وَءَاثَـٰرَهُمْ ۚ وَكُلَّ
شَىْءٍ أَحْصَيْنَـٰهُ فِىٓ إِمَامٍ مُّبِينٍ ﴿١٢﴾

are some whose characteristics are mentioned above and some who are mentioned in verse 11 below. When one encounters the people of the first group, and realises that they are deeply entrenched in bigoted opposition and hostility, one should leave them alone. At the same time, however, one should not lose heart and abandon one's efforts to spread the word of God out of a feeling of despair. This especially, for one has no means of knowing who among the teeming mass of people are disposed to follow "the Admonition" and to choose the Right Way as a result of their being God-fearing. The Prophet (peace be on him) is told that the real object of his preaching should be this second group of people; it is they whom he should winnow out from the rest. He should leave aside those who are immersed in obdurate hostility to the Truth and focus his efforts instead on accumulating a valuable treasure of decent human beings around him.

9. One learns from this that the record of one's deeds consists of the following three types of entries: (i) All that man does, good or bad, is recorded. (ii) All the impressions that a man leaves on the objects around him or on the organs of his own body are recorded. All these will, at a given time, stand out with utter conspicuousness. As a result, it will be possible to hear the words he spoke in the past in his own voice. It will also be possible to observe a person's ideas, intentions and motives in their fullness for all this will appear as though inscribed on his mind's tablet. Thus it will be possible to have a full picture of all a person's good and bad deeds, and of all his movements. (iii) The full impact of a person on others, both good and evil: the impact on his own future generations, on his society and on mankind at large, will also be entered in this record.

(13) Recite to them, as a case in point, the story of the people of the town when the Messengers came to them.[10] ▶	وَٱضْرِبْ لَهُم مَّثَلًا أَصْحَٰبَ ٱلْقَرْيَةِ إِذْ جَآءَهَا ٱلْمُرْسَلُونَ ﴿١٣﴾

As long as a person's impact lasts, it will be credited to his account. A complete record of his impact after his demise on subsequent generations, on his own society and on humanity at large, with all its ramifications, will be entered into his record. The good or bad upbringing of his children, the contributions he made to spreading good or evil in his society and among mankind will also be maintained and will be kept extant as long as his deeds continue to affect human behaviour in the world.

10. Earlier Qur'ān-commentators are generally disposed to identify this town as Antioch (Anṭākiyah) in Syria. As for the "Messengers" mentioned in the verse, they were the emissaries of the Prophet Jesus (peace be on him) whom he had directed to preach the Truth in that town. The details mentioned in regard to this story include that at that time Antiochus was the king. Qatādah, 'Ikrimah, Ka'b al-Aḥbār and Wahb ibn Munabbih, however, have narrated the whole story on the basis of unauthentic Christian traditions. Historically speaking, these traditions are devoid of any basis whatsoever. Antioch was then under the suzerainty of the Seleucid dynasty. Thirteen kings of this dynasty bore the name Antiochus. The political power of the last king with that name, and in fact the dynasty itself, came to an end in 65 B.C. In the days of the Prophet Jesus (peace be on him), the whole region of Syria and Palestine, including Antioch, was under Roman control. There are no authentic Christian reports to indicate that the Prophet Jesus (peace be on him) sent any of his apostles to Antioch to preach his mission there. On the contrary, it appears from *Acts* that Christian missionaries reached Antioch a few years after the Crucifixion. Those who decided to preach faith at their own behest, without having been sent either by God or His Prophet, cannot be considered God's Messengers. Moreover, according to the Bible, a large number of non-Israelites living in Antioch had embraced Christianity, the Christian mission there being a great success. By contrast, the Qur'ānic allusion is to a town that had rejected the Messengers' calls, and as a result, incurred God's punishment. Furthermore, no piece of historical evidence suggests that Antioch itself was ever struck by the kind of calamity that takes place when people reject a Messenger's mission.

(14) We sent to them two Messengers and they rejected both of them as liars. Then We strengthened them with a third (Messenger). They said: "We have been sent to you as Messengers." (15) The people of the town said: "You are only human beings like ourselves,[11] ▶

إِذۡ أَرۡسَلۡنَآ إِلَيۡهِمُ ٱثۡنَيۡنِ فَكَذَّبُوهُمَا فَعَزَّزۡنَا
بِثَالِثٖ فَقَالُوٓاْ إِنَّآ إِلَيۡكُم مُّرۡسَلُونَ ۝١٤ قَالُواْ
مَآ أَنتُمۡ إِلَّا بَشَرٞ مِّثۡلُنَا

The above report, therefore, is altogether unacceptable. The Qur'ān does not specify the identity of the town. Moreover, the names of these Messengers are also not mentioned in any authentic *ḥadīth*. The purpose for which this story has been narrated here, however, does not require that the true name of this town or the real names of these Messengers be known. This because the purpose of narrating this story was to convey a specific message to the Quraysh. The message was as follows: "You are treading a path that was trodden in the past by the people of this town – the path of obduracy, bigoted prejudice and rejection of the Truth. If you tread that very path, you should be ready to face the same calamitous end that befell the people of that town". (Ibn Kathīr, *Tafsīr,* comments on verses 13 and 29.)

11. In other words, the Makkan unbelievers virtually said that since the Prophet (peace be on him) was a human being, he could not be God's Messenger. It is pertinent to mention that the unbelievers of earlier times held exactly the same view regarding Messengers:

> They say: "What sort of a Messenger is this: he eats food and walks about in the markets?" (*Al-Furqān* 25:7.)
>
> The wrong-doers whisper to one another: "This person is no more than a mortal like yourselves. Will you then be enchanted by sorcery while you see?". (*Al-Anbiyā'* 21:3.)

The Qur'ān refutes this fallacious notion held by the Makkan unbelievers, pointing out that the grounds for their rejection are not new. Ignorant people have all along entertained the erroneous notion that a mortal human being such as themselves cannot be God's Messenger. The same point, for example, was made by the Prophet Noah's community.

> This is none other than a mortal like yourselves who desires to attain superiority over you. Had Allah wanted to send any Messengers, He would have sent down angels. We have heard nothing like this in the time of our forbears of old (that humans were sent as Messengers). (*Al-Mu'minūn* 23:24.)

The people of 'Ād made an almost identical observation about the Prophet Hūd (peace be on him):

> This is no other than a mortal like yourselves who eats what you eat and drinks what you drink. If you were to obey a human being like yourselves, you will certainly be losers. (*Al-Mu'minūn* 23:33–34.)

The same was the basis for the rejection of the Prophet Ṣāliḥ (peace be on him) by the Thamūd:

> Are we to follow a single mortal, one from among ourselves? (*Al-Qamar* 54:24.)

Unbelievers of all times and places treated God's Messengers in the same manner, rejecting them on the basis of their humanity. The Messengers themselves, however, never ceased to emphasise that they were no more than mortals:

> Indeed we are only human beings like yourselves, but Allah bestows His favour on those of His servants whom He wills. (*Ibrāhīm* 14:11.)

According to the Qur'ān, this flawed attitude has always prevented people from embracing the True Guidance. Ultimately too, it led to their destruction:

> Has the news of the unbelievers of the past not reached you? (They disbelieved) and then tasted its evil consequence. A grievous chastisement awaits them. This was because their Messengers would come to them with clear signs, but they would say: "Shall mortals (like ourselves) guide us to the right way?" They rejected the truth and turned away. Thereupon Allah became unconcerned with them. (*Al-Taghābun* 64:5–6.)

and the Merciful Lord has revealed nothing.[12] You are simply lying."

(16) The Messengers said: "Our Lord knows that we have indeed been sent to you ▶

وَمَآ أَنزَلَ ٱلرَّحْمَـٰنُ مِن شَىْءٍ إِنْ أَنتُمْ
إِلَّا تَكْذِبُونَ ﴿١٥﴾ قَالُوا۟ رَبُّنَا يَعْلَمُ إِنَّآ إِلَيْكُمْ
لَمُرْسَلُونَ ﴿١٦﴾

> Whenever guidance came to people, nothing prevented them from believing except that they said: "Has Allah sent a human being as a Messenger?"(*Banī Isrā'īl* 17:94.)

The Qur'ān asserts that it is only human beings that were raised as Messengers. For only they, rather than angels, are possessed of the ability to guide their fellow human beings to truth:

> (O Muḥammad), even before you We never sent any other than human beings as Messengers, and to them We sent revelation. Ask the people of the Book if you do not know. We did not endow the Messengers with bodies that would need no food; nor were they immortals. (*Al-Anbiyā'* 21:7–8.)
>
> (O Muḥammad), We never sent any Messengers before you but they ate food and walked about in the markets. (*Al-Furqān* 25:20.)
>
> Say: "Had angels been walking about in peace on earth, We would surely have sent to them an angel from the heavens as Messenger". (*Banī Isrā'īl* 17:95.)

12. This is another folly to which the Makkan unbelievers had fallen prey. Interestingly, this is a folly which many rationalists of our own time share with them. From the earliest times the deniers of Revelation and Prophethood have been victims of this misconception. Such people have always fancied that God does not provide any Revelation to guide humankind. For, according to their belief, God is solely concerned with matters pertaining to the higher realm, leaving human affairs to human beings themselves.

(17) and our duty is no more than to clearly convey the Message."[13] (18) The people of the town said: "We believe you are an evil omen for us.[14] If you do not desist, we will stone you or you will receive a grievous chastisement from us." (19) The Messengers replied: "Your evil omen is with you.[15] ▶

وَمَا عَلَيْنَآ إِلَّا ٱلْبَلَٰغُ ٱلْمُبِينُ ﴿١٧﴾ قَالُوٓا۟ إِنَّا
تَطَيَّرْنَا بِكُمْ ۖ لَئِن لَّمْ تَنتَهُوا۟ لَنَرْجُمَنَّكُمْ
وَلَيَمَسَّنَّكُم مِّنَّا عَذَابٌ أَلِيمٌ ﴿١٨﴾ قَالُوا۟
طَٰٓئِرُكُم مَّعَكُمْ ۚ

13. The task of a Messenger is no more than to faithfully deliver God's message to people. Once the message has been delivered, it is for people to accept it or not. It is not a part of a Messenger's task to force people to accept that message. Were they to reject the message, the responsibility would lie at the door of the people rather than with the messengers.

14. The unbelievers dismissed the Messenger sent to them as an evil omen for them. They thought that his denunciation of their idols had incurred the latter's wrath upon them. Thus the real cause of all their afflictions was their Messenger. Exactly the same charge was levelled by the Arab unbelievers and hypocrites against the Prophet Muḥammad (peace be on him): "When some misfortune befalls them, the unbelievers say: "This is because of you (O Muḥammad)", (*al-Nisā'* 4:78). It was in a similar vein that the unbelieving Thamūd used to say to their Messenger: "We augur ill of you and those who are with you", (*al-Naml* 27:47). The same attitude was held by Pharaoh and his people. But whenever prosperity came their way, they said: "This is our due." And whatever hardship befell them, they attributed it to the misfortune of Moses and those who followed him. (*Al-A'rāf* 7:131.)

15. No one is an evil omen for others. Everyone's destiny lies fastened to his own neck. Whatever good or evil act comes a person's way is, in either case, a part of his fate. As the Qur'ān says: "We have fastened every man's omen to his neck". (*Banī Isrā'il* 17:13.)

(Are you saying this) because you were asked to take heed? The truth is that you are a people who have exceeded all bounds."[16]

(20) In the meantime a man came running from the far end of the town, saying: "My people, follow the Messengers; (21) follow those who do not ask any recompense from you and are rightly-guided.[17] ▶

أَئِن ذُكِّرْتُمۚ بَلْ أَنتُمْ قَوْمٌ مُّسْرِفُونَ ﴿١٩﴾
وَجَآءَ مِنْ أَقْصَا ٱلْمَدِينَةِ رَجُلٌ يَسْعَىٰ قَالَ
يَـٰقَوْمِ ٱتَّبِعُوا۟ ٱلْمُرْسَلِينَ ﴿٢٠﴾ ٱتَّبِعُوا۟ مَن
لَّا يَسْـَٔلُكُمْ أَجْرًا وَهُم مُّهْتَدُونَ ﴿٢١﴾

16. The Prophets (peace be on them) pointed out to them that in truth they wanted to flee from goodness, preferring error to Guidance. Hence rather than distinguish between truth and falsehood on the basis of any rational evidence they resorted to superstition and hankered after one pretext or another to legitimise their evil ways.

17. In this one little statement, this true believer encapsulates all the arguments that confirm the truthfulness of Prophethood. One may judge the claim of a person to be a Prophet for the following two reasons: (i) his words and deeds, and (ii) his selflessness. The purpose of that person's argument was to stress that the Prophets (peace be on them) were expounding the truth and that their character was absolutely unblemished. Further, no one can identify any selfish motive in the Prophets' calling people to the religious faith they espoused. For all these reasons taken together, there is no reason why a person should not believe in them. The Qur'ān, by reproducing this argument, provided people with a criterion to judge any person's claim to be a Prophet. Muḥammad's own words and deeds clearly indicate that he is on the Right Way. Moreover, there is no trace of any selfish motive in the work he is engaged in. There is, thus, no valid basis for a sane person to reject his message.

(22) Why should I not serve the One Who created me and to Whom all of you shall be sent back?[18] (23) What! Shall I take any deities apart from Him whose intercession will not avail me the least were the Merciful One to bring any adversity upon me, nor will they be able to rescue me?[19] (24) Surely in that case[20] I should indeed be in evident error. ▶

وَمَا لِيَ لَآ أَعۡبُدُ ٱلَّذِي فَطَرَنِي وَإِلَيۡهِ
تُرۡجَعُونَ ﴿٢٢﴾ ءَأَتَّخِذُ مِن دُونِهِۦٓ ءَالِهَةً إِن
يُرِدۡنِ ٱلرَّحۡمَٰنُ بِضُرّٖ لَّا تُغۡنِ عَنِّي
شَفَٰعَتُهُمۡ شَيۡـٔٗا وَلَا يُنقِذُونِ ﴿٢٣﴾ إِنِّيٓ إِذٗا
لَّفِي ضَلَٰلٖ مُّبِينٍ ﴿٢٤﴾

18. This statement is comprised of two parts. The first part is a masterpiece of persuasive argumentation. As for the second part, it represents the very zenith of consummate wisdom in the preaching of the true faith. In the first part it has been shown that to serve the Creator is, in every respect, a requirement of reason and human nature. If anything could be considered unreasonable, it would be that a person should serve those who have not created him rather than serve his Creator. In the second part, the person who came running from the far end of the town draws his people's attention to the fact that they are destined to die and return to the same God serving Whom they find objectionable. They are asked to consider what good can they expect as a result of turning away from Him?

19. Why should man take deities other than God? No one is so favoured by God that his intercession on someone's behalf will necessarily secure God's forgiveness for him. Nor is anyone so influential with God that by his persistent pleading he will secure a person's release even though God wants to punish him.

20. That is, even if I take others apart from God as my deities, despite knowing that they are powerless.

(25) I believe in your Lord;[21] so listen to me."

(26) (Eventually they killed him and he was told): "Enter Paradise."[22] The man exclaimed: "Would that my people knew (27) for what reason Allah has forgiven me and placed me among the honoured ones."[23]

إِنِّيٓ ءَامَنتُ بِرَبِّكُمۡ فَٱسۡمَعُونِ ٢٥
قِيلَ ٱدۡخُلِ ٱلۡجَنَّةَۖ قَالَ يَٰلَيۡتَ قَوۡمِي
يَعۡلَمُونَ ٢٦ بِمَا غَفَرَ لِي رَبِّي وَجَعَلَنِي مِنَ
ٱلۡمُكۡرَمِينَ ٢٧

---

21. Implicit in this is a subtle suggestion as to how one should preach the truth. By so saying the person concerned reminds those people that it is God in Whom he believes, and He is not only *his* but also *their* Lord. The statement further suggests that he made no mistake by deciding to believe in Him. Rather, they had made a mistake by not believing in Him.

22. No sooner had that person attained martyrdom, than he was given the glad tidings of Paradise. When he reached the Next Life, after passing through the portal of death, angels were in waiting to welcome him and inform him that Paradise looked forward to his arrival.

There is some disagreement among Qur'ān-commentators regarding the interpretation of this sentence. Qatādah, for example, is of the view that God instantly admitted him to Paradise where he is alive and receives his sustenance. However, Mujāhid points out that this was uttered by the angels by way of giving glad tidings to him. Therefore, he will enter Paradise along with other believers on the Day of Judgement. (Ibn Kathīr, *Tafsīr*, comments on verse 26.)

23. This brings to the fore the moral excellence of that paragon of faith. He did not have any grudge or rancour against those who had assassinated him that would prompt him to imprecate against them. On the contrary, he still seeks their well-being. After his death at the hands of his own people, all that he wishes is that his people may come to know of the happy state in which he now is. He thought that his people would perhaps learn a useful lesson from him after his death even if they failed to learn anything from him while he was alive. It is such people who have

(28) After him, We did not send down any hosts from the heaven; We stood in no need to send down any host. (29) There was but a single Blast and suddenly they became silent and still.[24] (30) Alas for My servants! Never does a Messenger come to them but they mock him. ▶

وَمَآ أَنزَلۡنَا عَلَىٰ قَوۡمِهِۦ مِنۢ بَعۡدِهِۦ مِن جُندٖ
مِّنَ ٱلسَّمَآءِ وَمَا كُنَّا مُنزِلِينَ ﴿٢٨﴾ إِن كَانَتۡ
إِلَّا صَيۡحَةٗ وَٰحِدَةٗ فَإِذَا هُمۡ خَٰمِدُونَ ﴿٢٩﴾
يَٰحَسۡرَةً عَلَى ٱلۡعِبَادِۚ مَا يَأۡتِيهِم مِّن رَّسُولٍ
إِلَّا كَانُواْ بِهِۦ يَسۡتَهۡزِءُونَ ﴿٣٠﴾

---

been applauded in a tradition in these words: نصح قومه حيا و ميتاً ("He served as a well-wisher of his people, both in his life and death".)

By narrating this episode, God explains an important fact to the Makkan unbelievers: Muḥammad (peace be on him) and his fellow believers are their well-wishers just as this believer had been for his own nation. Despite the travails the unbelievers inflict upon them, the Muslims do not hold any personal enmity or desire for revenge against them. Their enmity is not with the unbelievers but rather with their misguided state. Their only purpose in opposing them is that they come to the Right Path.

Incidentally, this is one of the verses that conclusively establishes life in *barzakh*. One also learns that the period commencing from one's death until the Day of Resurrection will not be a state of nothingness, a state of absolute non-existence as some ignorant people fancy. After death, one's soul continues to exist though without its body. The soul retains its faculties of speech and hearing and is characterised by feeling and emotion. It experiences joys and sorrows and maintains an interest in those living in the world. Had it not been so, this believing man would not have been given the glad tidings of Paradise after his death and he would not have expressed the wish that his people be informed of the happy end at which he had arrived.

24. There is a subtle irony in this statement. Those people, who were quite proud of their physical prowess, were burning with bigoted hostility towards the true faith. They were under the illusion that they would be able to totally blot out all three Prophets as well as their followers. Their fury was like a fierce blaze. But the very first touch of God's scourge extinguished that flame!

(31) Have they not seen how many nations before them did We destroy? Thereafter they never came back to them.[25] (32) All of them shall (one day) be gathered before Us.

(33) Let[26] the dead earth be a Sign for them.[27] We gave it life and produced from it grain whereof they eat. (34) We made in it gardens of date-palms and vines, and We caused springs to gush forth ▶

أَلَمْ يَرَوْا۟ كَمْ أَهْلَكْنَا قَبْلَهُم مِّنَ ٱلْقُرُونِ
أَنَّهُمْ إِلَيْهِمْ لَا يَرْجِعُونَ ٣١ وَإِن كُلٌّ
لَّمَّا جَمِيعٌ لَّدَيْنَا مُحْضَرُونَ ٣٢ وَءَايَةٌ لَّهُمُ
ٱلْأَرْضُ ٱلْمَيْتَةُ أَحْيَيْنَٰهَا وَأَخْرَجْنَا مِنْهَا
حَبًّا فَمِنْهُ يَأْكُلُونَ ٣٣ وَجَعَلْنَا فِيهَا
جَنَّٰتٍ مِّن نَّخِيلٍ وَأَعْنَٰبٍ وَفَجَّرْنَا
فِيهَا مِنَ ٱلْعُيُونِ ٣٤

25. They were totally obliterated so much so that today no one is left even to remember them. Not only their culture and civilisation, but their entire race stands utterly destroyed.

26. In the preceding verses (see vv. 1–32), the Makkan unbelievers were reproached for their rejecting, opposing, and giving the lie to the Prophet (peace be on him). The discourse now turns to the main point of contention, indeed what became conflict, between the unbelievers and the Prophet (peace be on him). The contention between the two parties mainly related to the doctrines of monotheism and the Afterlife expounded by the Prophet (peace be on him). In this regard a set of arguments are over and again marshalled in support of these doctrines. Thereby people are asked to continue to reflect over these doctrines. Their attention is drawn to natural phenomena. Do they [to wit, the natural phenomena themselves] not clearly confirm the truth expounded by the Prophet (peace be on him)?

27. The sign indicating that monotheism represents the truth whereas polytheism is utterly baseless.

(35) that they might eat of its fruits. It was not their hands that made them.[28] Will they not, then, give thanks?[29] ▶	لِيَأْكُلُوا۟ مِن ثَمَرِهِۦ وَمَا عَمِلَتْهُ أَيْدِيهِمْ ۖ أَفَلَا يَشْكُرُونَ ﴿٣٥﴾

28. We have translated this above as: "… that they might eat of its fruits. It was not their hands that made them". It can, however, be alternatively translated as: "… so that they may eat of its fruits and whatever their hands make". This latter rendering signifies secondary food products manufactured by people from natural produce. Bread, cooked dishes, jams, pickles, chutney and innumerable other edibles are its good illustrations.

29. Here, the soil's fertility is presented as an argument in support of the doctrine of the Hereafter. It runs like this: man is sustained day and night by what is produced by land. He is, however, inclined to consider the produce he reaps from the land a matter of ordinary routine. If he reflects, however, he will realise that the sprouting of blooming fields and verdant gardens, and the flow of streams, springs and rivers on earth do not take place automatically. All this is the outcome of immense wisdom, power and providence. Soil is made of certain lifeless constituents which, in themselves, are devoid of the potential for growth. All its constituents are both separately and after all possible combinations intrinsically devoid of organic life. This obviously raises the question: what has made it possible for this lifeless soil to bring forth vegetation? When one studies this issue, one comes to know that some major factors account for it. Had they not already been in existence, vegetation would not have come to be.

These factors are as follows: first, certain parts of the land have layers endowed with materials that provide nutrition to plants. These layers are soft, enabling the roots of the plants to draw nourishment from them. Secondly, water was provided to the land in a variety of ways enabling the assimilation of the nourishing materials by the plants' roots. Thirdly, the air present in the outer atmosphere protects the earth against natural calamities, and causes rainfall. Moreover, it also contains the gases that are essential for plant life and its growth. Fourthly, a special nexus has been established between the sun and the earth ensuring that plants enjoy both a suitable temperature and climate.

These four major factors (each of which represents a combination of several sub-factors) were provided in order that plant life might become possible. After providing these suitable factors, plants were created and

(36) Holy is He Who[30] created all things in pairs, ▶	سُبْحَـٰنَ ٱلَّذِى خَلَقَ ٱلْأَزْوَٰجَ كُلَّهَا

endowed with the ability to reproduce themselves providing suitable conditions relating to soil, water, air and climate were available. Each plant species was granted a seed possessed of the remarkable quality of perpetuating itself along with its distinguishing characteristics. Above all, numberless species of plants were brought into existence and were invested with the ability to fulfil the myriad needs of animals as well as humans for food, medicine, clothing and countless other items. Anyone who studies this consummate arrangement with an open mind will be impelled to testify that such a marvellous system could not have come into being on its own. No one other than the Lord of the universe could have taken into account these multifarious considerations relating to soil, air, water and climate and could have established this astounding correspondence between plants, animals and human beings. This can, in no way, be the result of an accident. Also, it evidently signifies that it cannot be the accomplishment of a multiplicity of gods. On the contrary, it represents the achievement of the One True God, Who is the sole Creator and Lord of earth, wind, water, the sun, plants, animals and humans. Had they been the creatures of several gods, they would not have displayed such immaculate harmony and coordination. Nor could this system continue to function flawlessly without any interruption for millions of years.

After adducing this argument in support of God's unity, the Qur'ān poses the question: "Will they not give thanks?" (See v. 35.) This question suggests, by implication, that these unbelievers are a bunch of thankless and perfidious folk. God provided them with the wherewithal for their existence, yet they give thanks to others rather than to their Bounteous Provider. They stoop to prostrating before false gods who created nothing, but they fail to prostrate themselves before God, their Creator.

30. "Holy is He ..." suggests that God is free from every conceivable imperfection, flaw or weakness. He is also free from having any partner or associate. Generally speaking, the Qur'ān employs such expressions while refuting polytheistic notions. This because every polytheistic notion essentially amounts to ascribing some kind of flaw or imperfection to God. Those who take others as God's associates assume that He is unable, on His own, to govern the universe that He Himself created. Or that He is too weak to dispense with the support of others or that others are intrinsically

whether it be of what the earth produces, and of themselves, and of what they do not know.[31]

(37) And the night is another Sign for them. We strip the day from it and they become plunged in darkness.[32] ▶

مِمَّا تُنۢبِتُ ٱلۡأَرۡضُ وَمِنۡ أَنفُسِهِمۡ
وَمِمَّا لَا يَعۡلَمُونَ ﴿٣٦﴾ وَءَايَةٞ لَّهُمُ ٱلَّيۡلُ
نَسۡلَخُ مِنۡهُ ٱلنَّهَارَ فَإِذَا هُم مُّظۡلِمُونَ ﴿٣٧﴾

---

so powerful that they interfere in matters relating to God's overlordship and yet God puts up with their interference. Alternatively, they conceive Him to be like a worldly sovereign with a retinue of favourite courtiers, sycophantish companions, and pet princes and princesses who have some share in several of His powers. In the first place, people could not have subscribed to polytheism had such ignorant notions not been in currency. Accordingly, the Qur'ān repeatedly affirms that God is free from all such flaws, defects and imperfections that the polytheists ascribe to Him.

31. This is yet another argument in support of monotheism. Here too attention is drawn to some commonplace facts. People observe these facts day in and day out and go about their business without pondering over them. This despite the fact that these objects are signs that could direct them to the Truth. One of these observable things is the division of human beings into males and females, which is a cause of their procreation. A similar division in the animal species also accounts for the continuation of their species. The same kind of gender coupling is operating in plant life. In a sense, the same also holds true for inanimate objects, as they too are comprised of pairs. We know that matter consists of positive and negative electrical charges and that they produce energy. Only an imbecile can attribute these elaborate arrangements to mere accident and coincidence. It is also hard to conceive that several gods would have created numerous pairs and bound them together so perfectly. The fact of this binary division and the resultant birth of new objects unmistakably points to the Oneness of the Creator.

32. The alternation of day and night is also one of those commonplace phenomena that man constantly observes. He, however, scarcely regards

it as worthy of any special attention. Should he, however, consider how day and night follow each other, and ponder the wisdom underlying this alternation, it would become evident that this ordinary phenomenon provides luminous proof of the existence and unity of the All-Mighty and All-Wise Creator. A day cannot phase into night nor can night phase into day unless their positions *vis-à-vis* each other remain changing rather than constantly the same. We also know that the regularity found in this alternation of day and night would not have been possible if the sun and the earth were not part of an inexorable system that strictly governs the alternation of day and night. Moreover, the alternation of day and night has an enormous bearing on earth's creatures. This, once again, underscores that it is a Wise Being who has put this arrangement in place. The distance between the sun and the earth accounts for the existence of animals, plants, humans, and minerals. Moreover, different regions of the earth regularly face the sun and then move away. Without this, life could not have existed on planet earth. Had the sun been too far from the earth or too close to it, or had one region of the earth always been engulfed by night and the other by day life as we know it could not have existed. The same would be the case if the alternation between day and night had been too fast or too slow, or had it been erratic so that suddenly there would be sunshine or suddenly night enveloped the earth. Even the shape and structure of non-living entities would have been much different from what it is.

If one is not blinded by bias, one can easily perceive the Hand of the All-Wise God in this natural arrangement. It is evident that it is the One True God Who willed the creation of certain kinds of beings on earth and accordingly established a perfect correspondence between the sun and the earth that was needed for life and survival. Someone might not be convinced that God's existence and unity is a rationally convincing proposition. Such a person would do well to think of the other alternative explanations of the phenomenon such as there being a host of gods behind the order of the universe. Or consider if its underlying cause was a set of blind laws of nature that automatically came into being without the involvement of a conscious Will. Can such assumptions be regarded as patently more reasonable than the acceptance of the One True God's will and wisdom as being responsible for the order that characterises the universe?

The assertions to the contrary mentioned above are obviously preposterous. This makes one wonder about the wisdom of those for whom the order, wisdom and purposiveness found in the universe are not enough proof for God's existence. On the other hand, the very same people accept absolutely irrational explanations of universal phenomenon merely on the basis of sheer guess and conjecture, unsupported by any kind of rational proof whatsoever.

(38) The sun is running its course to its appointed place.[33] That is the ordaining of the All-Mighty, the All-Knowing. (39) We have appointed stages for the moon till it returns in the shape of a dry old branch of palm-tree.[34] (40) Neither does it lie in the sun's power to overtake the moon[35] ▶

وَٱلشَّمۡسُ تَجۡرِي لِمُسۡتَقَرّٖ لَّهَاۚ ذَٰلِكَ تَقۡدِيرُ
ٱلۡعَزِيزِ ٱلۡعَلِيمِ ۝٣٨ وَٱلۡقَمَرَ قَدَّرۡنَٰهُ مَنَازِلَ
حَتَّىٰ عَادَ كَٱلۡعُرۡجُونِ ٱلۡقَدِيمِ ۝٣٩ لَا ٱلشَّمۡسُ
يَنۢبَغِي لَهَآ أَن تُدۡرِكَ ٱلۡقَمَرَ

33. This might refer to the place where the sun will ultimately come to a halt. Or it might refer to the time when it will come to a halt. One can only grasp the true meaning of the verse if one acquires a sound knowledge of the facts relating to the universe. Human knowledge, however, is constantly in a state of flux. The knowledge that mankind has been able to accumulate till today is also liable to change. In olden days, the common belief derived from visual observation was that the sun revolved around the earth. Further observation and research subsequently led to the notion that the sun was stationary whereas the planets of the solar system were revolving around the sun. However, this theory too did not endure. Subsequent observations gave rise to the belief that all stars that were considered stationary are moving in a set direction with speeds varying from 10 to 100 miles per second. As for the sun, it revolves along with the entire solar system at a speed of just over 20 kilometres (approximately 12 miles) per second. (Q.v. "star" and "sun" in *The Encyclopaedia Britannica,* xiv edition – Ed.)

34. During one month, the course of the moon changes every day. First, it rises as a crescent. Thereafter it continues to grow day after day until it becomes a full moon by the fourteenth day. This is followed by recession until it eventually returns to its original shape of a crescent. This has been taking place for millions of years; never has any change been noted in the phases of the moon. As a result, it is easy to work out its phase on any given day.

35. This is open to two equally valid meanings: (i) That it is not possible for the sun to pull the moon towards itself or to collide with it

nor can the night outstrip the day.[36] All glide along, each in its own orbit.[37]	وَلَا ٱلَّيۡلُ سَابِقُ ٱلنَّهَارِۚ وَكُلٌّ فِي فَلَكٖ يَسۡبَحُونَ ۝٤٠

by entering into the latter's orbit. (ii) That the sun cannot appear at the hours designated for the rise of the moon. It is simply impossible that the sun should suddenly appear on the horizon, when the moon is shining at night.

36. It never happens that night sets in before the time appointed for the day comes to an end, or that it finds its way with its attendant darkness at a time earmarked for daylight.

37. *Falak* in Arabic denotes a planetary orbit. It is altogether different from *samā'* (sky). The Qur'ān says that "all glide along, each in its orbit". This lays bare the following truths: (i) That not only the sun and the moon, but all stars, planets and heavenly bodies are in a state of motion. (ii) That each has its own orbit. (iii) That orbits do not move along with heavenly bodies. Rather, the heavenly bodies move along with their orbits. (iv) That the movement of stars is akin to the floating of an object in a liquid.

These verses are not meant to furnish detailed astronomical information; rather, they seek to press home the point that if man were to look around himself carefully he will perceive proofs indicating God's existence and unity. On the other hand, there is no indication whatsoever of atheism or polytheism in the universe. The solar system, of which our earth is a part, has a massive size. The sun is 300,000 times larger than the earth and the farthest planet of our solar system, Neptune, is at least 2,793 million miles away from the sun. However, were one to regard Pluto as the most distant planet, it lies at a massive distance of some 4,600 million miles away from the sun. Notwithstanding its gigantic proportions, our solar system is only an infinitesimal part of the galaxy that includes it, for this galaxy alone contains as many as 3,000 million suns. It takes four years for the light of our nearest sun to reach earth. It is also worth mentioning that this galaxy does not comprise the whole universe: it is just one of around two million spiral nebulae. The light of the nebulae which is closest to earth takes one million years to reach us. As for the celestial bodies farthest from us that are visible to the eyes of our instruments, billions of years are needed for their light to reach us. Even this does not bring to light the whole universe. For so far we have managed to observe only a tiny part of God's creation. It is hard to say

(41) Another Sign for them is that We carried all their offspring in the laden vessel[38] (42) and then created for them other vessels like those on which they ride.[39] ▶

وَءَايَةٌ لَّهُمْ أَنَّا حَمَلْنَا ذُرِّيَّتَهُمْ فِى ٱلْفُلْكِ
ٱلْمَشْحُونِ ﴿٤١﴾ وَخَلَقْنَا لَهُم مِّن مِّثْلِهِۦ
مَا يَرْكَبُونَ ﴿٤٢﴾

---

what will be the size of the universe that will dawn upon us in the future when better means of observation become available.

The facts regarding the universe that have come to our knowledge till now show that it is composed of the same material of which the earth is constituted. Also, the same laws of nature are at work in the entire universe. Had this not been so, we would not have been able to fathom the workings of the universe. All this conclusively proves that the whole universe is the creation of the One True Lord Who reigns supreme. The order, wisdom and interconnectedness characterising the numerous galaxies with countless planets revolving in them indicate beyond any shadow of doubt that this universe did not come into being of its own or as a result of some accident. Is it conceivable that there be order in the universe without there being the One Who gave shape to that order, that there be wisdom without their being the Wise One? That there can be design and immaculate work without there being the Designer, and that there be planning without there being the Planner?

38. The "laden vessel" here denotes the Prophet Noah's Ark. That men were directed to board it may mean that the Prophet Noah (peace be on him) was instructed to take his companions along with him. Those who did embark in Noah's Ark are the ancestors of all future generations of human beings, for on that occasion all the children of Adam, except these believers, were drowned in the Flood. The human beings of the period that followed were all issues of those who had boarded the Ark.

39. This seems to imply that this was the first boat in the history of mankind. Before that man had no idea how he could traverse rivers and oceans. It was God Who taught Noah for the first time to make this vessel. However, when it became possible for a few souls to survive the Flood, they began to build and use boats for maritime voyages.

(43) Should We so wish, We can drown them, and there will be none to heed their cries of distress, nor will they be rescued. (44) It is only Our Mercy (that rescues them) and enables enjoyment of life for a while.[40]

(45) When it is said to such people: "Guard yourselves against what is ahead of you and what has preceded you[41] ▶

وَإِن نَّشَأْ نُغْرِقْهُمْ فَلَا صَرِيخَ لَهُمْ وَلَا هُمْ يُنقَذُونَ ﴿٤٣﴾ إِلَّا رَحْمَةً مِّنَّا وَمَتَاعًا إِلَىٰ حِينٍ ﴿٤٤﴾ وَإِذَا قِيلَ لَهُمُ ٱتَّقُوا۟ مَا بَيْنَ أَيْدِيكُمْ وَمَا خَلْفَكُمْ

40. Some signs were mentioned in the preceding passage by way of evidence in support of monotheism. Attention is now drawn to this particular sign to make people realise that whatever control they exercise over things is thanks to the powers granted to them by God. In other words, man has not acquired these powers himself. Furthermore, it is God Who instructed him in how to exercise his powers; he would not have been able to find out on his own how to utilise his faculties and powers. Man enjoys this authority only as long as God wills so. When God wills differently, man is deprived of the power to control the forces of nature; rather, the same forces of nature make life difficult for him and he finds himself totally helpless. God mentions sea voyages as an example to illustrate this. Had God not instructed the Prophet Noah (peace be on him) how to build the Ark, the entire human race would have perished in the Flood. Again, it was God Who guided the believers to board the Ark as a result of which they survived and were later able to settle in various parts of the earth. The principles of boat-building and thereby undertaking sea voyages enabled mankind to move around. Notwithstanding all the advancements accomplished by man in the various modes of transport, he cannot claim total mastery over the sea. To this day, God reigns supreme and, as and when He wills, ships along with their passengers are wrecked.

41. This was experienced by earlier nations.

that mercy be shown to you" (they pay scant heed to it). (46) Never does any Sign of their Lord come to them, but they turn away from it.[42] (47) And when it is said to them: "Spend (in the Way of Allah) out of the sustenance that Allah has provided you," the unbelievers say to the believers: "Shall we feed him whom, Allah would have fed, had He so wished?" Say: "You are in evident error."[43]

(48) They[44] say: "When will this threat (of Resurrection) ▶

لَعَلَّكُمْ تُرْحَمُونَ ﴿٤٥﴾ وَمَا تَأْتِيهِم مِّنْ
ءَايَةٍ مِّنْ ءَايَٰتِ رَبِّهِمْ إِلَّا كَانُوا۟
عَنْهَا مُعْرِضِينَ ﴿٤٦﴾ وَإِذَا قِيلَ لَهُمْ أَنفِقُوا۟
مِمَّا رَزَقَكُمُ ٱللَّهُ قَالَ ٱلَّذِينَ كَفَرُوا۟ لِلَّذِينَ
ءَامَنُوٓا۟ أَنُطْعِمُ مَن لَّوْ يَشَآءُ ٱللَّهُ أَطْعَمَهُۥٓ إِنْ
أَنتُمْ إِلَّا فِى ضَلَٰلٍ مُّبِينٍ ﴿٤٧﴾ وَيَقُولُونَ
مَتَىٰ هَٰذَا ٱلْوَعْدُ

42. "Signs" also denote the verses of the Qur'ān through which human beings are provided right counsel. Signs, however, also mean the signs that are found in the cosmic phenomena and in man's own being and in history which can make man derive a lesson providing he is ready for it.

43. Unbelief not only causes mental blindness but also numbs man's moral sense. As a result, such people become incapable of using sound reason in regard to God. Nor do they adopt an appropriate attitude towards God's creatures. Furthermore, when such people receive good advice, they simply spurn it, and have a ready explanation to justify their rejection of it. They also have no dearth of legitimising philosophies for every doctrinal error and moral corruption of theirs. They are ever prone to flee from every act of goodness and always have some pretext to justify their attitude.

44. The other contentious issue after monotheism between the Prophet (peace be on him) and the unbelievers was that of the Hereafter.

come to pass? Tell us if indeed you are truthful."[45] (49) The Truth is that they are waiting for nothing but a mighty Blast to seize them the while they are disputing (in their worldly affairs), (50) and they will not even be able to make a testament, nor to return to their households.[46] ▶

إِن كُنتُمْ صَٰدِقِينَ ﴿٤٨﴾ مَا يَنظُرُونَ إِلَّا
صَيْحَةً وَٰحِدَةً تَأْخُذُهُمْ وَهُمْ يَخِصِّمُونَ ﴿٤٩﴾
فَلَا يَسْتَطِيعُونَ تَوْصِيَةً وَلَآ إِلَىٰٓ أَهْلِهِمْ
يَرْجِعُونَ ﴿٥٠﴾

The present verses depict a terrible scene of the Life-to-Come. This is in order to impress on the unbelievers that the Last Day is imminent regardless of their rejection of it. A day is bound to come when all will inexorably experience what has been destined.

45. What is meant here is not that the unbelievers were genuinely interested in knowing the exact date when the Day of Resurrection would arrive. Hence, if they were informed of that date their doubts would be removed and they would feel satisfied. Far from it, for they had taken recourse to posing this kind of question in order to emphasise that the very idea of the Next Life was simply fanciful and that by being told that it would come, they were being subjected to a totally empty threat. Hence, in response to the unbelievers' query: "When will the threat (of the Hereafter) pass by?" they are not informed of the date of its occurrence. Instead, they are jolted by the declaration that the Day of Resurrection is imminent and when it does come "a mighty Blast will seize them the while they are disputing".

46. The Last Day will not approach with slow, measured steps enabling mankind to observe it in a leisurely fashion. Rather, it will suddenly overtake people while they are engaged in their worldly pursuits. At the time of its coming it will not occur to the people concerned that the end of the world has arrived. There will be a sudden and huge Blast and everything will come to an end. 'Abd Allāh ibn al-'Āṣ and Abū Hurayrah narrate from the Prophet (peace be on him): "While people are walking about the market shopping, and talking in their assemblies, suddenly

(51) Then the Trumpet shall be blown and lo! they will come out of their graves[47] and be on the move towards their Lord, (52) (nervously) exclaiming. "Alas for us! Who roused us out of our sleeping-place?"[48] ▶

وَنُفِخَ فِى ٱلصُّورِ فَإِذَا هُم مِّنَ ٱلْأَجْدَاثِ
إِلَىٰ رَبِّهِمْ يَنسِلُونَ ﴿٥١﴾ قَالُوا۟ يَٰوَيْلَنَا مَنۢ
بَعَثَنَا مِن مَّرْقَدِنَا ۜ

---

the Trumpet will be blown. He who is engaged in buying a piece of cloth will die instantly before even laying down that piece of cloth. Likewise, someone will fill a tank to provide water for his cattle but before the cattle drink that water, the Last Day will come to pass. There will be someone who will sit down to eat but will die even before he is able to put a bite of food into his mouth".

47. For a detailed note on the Trumpet, see *Towards Understanding the Qur'ān,Ṭā Hā* 20: n. 78, Vol. V, pp. 223–224. It is narrated by Abū Hurayrah that the Prophet (peace be on him) said: "Isrāfīl has his lips on the Trumpet and his gaze is fixed on the Throne, and he is waiting for God's command to blow it. It will be blown three times. By the first blow of the Trumpet (called *nafkhat al-faza'*) (the trumpet of terror) all the creatures of the heavens and the earth will be struck with terror. The second blow (called *nafkhat al-ṣa'q*) (the trumpet of lightning) will cause everyone to fall down dead. Therefore, when no one remains alive, except the One True God, the earth will be transformed. It will be spread flat and smooth without there being any crease or wrinkle in it. Then, God will issue a command whereupon everyone will rise at the spot where he had fallen dead. This blowing of the Trumpet will be called *nafkhat al-qiyām li Rabb al-'ālamīn* (the trumpet to make all rise and stand before the Lord of the Universe). This is supported by several allusions in the Qur'ān. (See, for example, *Towards Understanding the Qur'ān, Ibrāhīm* 14: nn. 56–57, Vol. IV, pp. 276–277; *Ṭā Hā* 20: nn. 82–83, Vol. V, pp. 225–226.)

48. People will not realise that they had died and been resurrected after a very long time. Rather, they will be under the impression that they had been asleep and that thereafter they had been woken by some terrible incident and were hastily rushing along. (For further explanation,

"This is what the Merciful One had promised, and what (His) Messengers had said was true."[49] (53) Then there will simply be one single Blast, and all will have gathered before Us.

(54) Today[50] no one shall suffer the least injustice, and you shall not be recompensed except according to your deeds. (55) Indeed, the people of Paradise will be busy enjoying themselves:[51] ▶

هَـٰذَا مَا وَعَـدَ ٱلرَّحۡمَـٰنُ وَصَدَقَ
ٱلۡمُرۡسَلُونَ ۝٥٢ إِن كَانَتۡ إِلَّا صَيۡحَةٗ
وَٰحِدَةٗ فَإِذَا هُمۡ جَمِيعٞ لَّدَيۡنَا مُحۡضَرُونَ ۝٥٣
فَٱلۡيَوۡمَ لَا تُظۡلَمُ نَفۡسٞ شَيۡـٔٗا وَلَا تُجۡزَوۡنَ
إِلَّا مَا كُنتُمۡ تَعۡمَلُونَ ۝٥٤ إِنَّ أَصۡحَٰبَ
ٱلۡجَنَّةِ ٱلۡيَوۡمَ فِي شُغُلٖ فَٰكِهُونَ ۝٥٥

---

see *Towards Understanding the Qur'ān, Ibrāhīm* 14: n. 18, Vol. IV, p. 259; *Ṭā Hā* 20: n. 78, Vol. V, pp.223–224.)

49. Here it has not been explicitly stated who will articulate this response. It is likely that this truth will dawn on the unbelievers whereafter they will engage in a soliloquy, reproaching themselves: "This is what the Merciful One had promised and what [His] Messengers had said was true". It is also possible that the believers will remove the unbelievers' misunderstanding and inform them that they have not risen from sleep but have been raised to life after having been dead. Yet another possibility is that this response will be conveyed by the overall conditions obtaining on the Last Day, or that God's angels will explain the truth of the matter to the people concerned.

50. This is how God will address the unbelievers, polytheists, and the evil ones when they appear before Him on the Day of Judgement.

51. Note that true believers will not be detained in the Grand Assembly of the Last Day, but will rather be admitted to Paradise after a light interrogation. Alternatively, they might be spared interrogation altogether, for their record will be clean. Regardless, they will not have to wait for long. In the Assembly itself, God will point all this out to the

(56) they and their spouses shall be reclining on their couches in shady groves; (57) therein there will be all kinds of fruits to eat, and they shall have all that they desire. (58) "Peace" shall be the word conveyed to them from their Merciful Lord. (59) Criminals, separate yourselves from others today![52] (60) Children of Adam, did I not command you not to serve Satan – he is to you an open enemy (61) and serve Me alone: this is the Straight Way?[53] ▶

هُمْ وَأَزْوَٰجُهُمْ فِى ظِلَـٰلٍ عَلَى ٱلْأَرَآئِكِ
مُتَّكِـُٔونَ ﴿٥٦﴾ لَهُمْ فِيهَا فَـٰكِهَةٌ وَلَهُم
مَّا يَدَّعُونَ ﴿٥٧﴾ سَلَـٰمٌ قَوْلًا مِّن
رَّبٍّ رَّحِيمٍ ﴿٥٨﴾ وَٱمْتَـٰزُوا۟ ٱلْيَوْمَ أَيُّهَا
ٱلْمُجْرِمُونَ ﴿٥٩﴾ ۞ أَلَمْ أَعْهَدْ إِلَيْكُمْ يَـٰبَنِىٓ
ءَادَمَ أَن لَّا تَعْبُدُوا۟ ٱلشَّيْطَـٰنَ ۖ إِنَّهُۥ لَكُمْ
عَدُوٌّ مُّبِينٌ ﴿٦٠﴾ وَأَنِ ٱعْبُدُونِى ۚ هَـٰذَا
صِرَٰطٌ مُّسْتَقِيمٌ ﴿٦١﴾

---

unbelievers who used to make fun of the believers, for the latter will enjoy the delights of Paradise while the former will be subjected to rigorous interrogation.

52. This can be understood in two different ways. (i) That this will be a command to the criminals on the Day of Resurrection asking them to separate themselves from upright believers. During the course of worldly life, these evil-doers might have lived together with the believers. It is even possible that they belonged to the same family, social fraternity or political entity. All this will, however, come to an end in the Hereafter where all affinity between the two groups will be sundered. (ii) The criminals will be ordered to separate themselves from one another. In the Hereafter their integral solidarity as a cohesive party of unbelievers is sundered; the ties that had kept them bound together will be dissolved. As a result, each person will be made to account for himself purely in his individual capacity.

53. Here again the word *'ibādah* has been employed to mean obedience. We have elucidated this point at several places in our work. (See *Towards*

Understanding the Qur'ān, al-Nisā' 4: n. 145, Vol. II, p. 86; *al-An'ām* 6: nn. 87 and 107, Vol. II, pp. 270 and 278–279; *al-Tawbah* 9: n. 31, Vol. III, p. 204; *Ibrāhīm* 14: n. 32, Vol. IV, pp. 266–267; *al-Kahf* 18: n. 50, Vol. V, p. 113 and *Saba'* 34: n. 63, see p. 197 above.) While explaining this verse in his *al-Tafsīr al-Kabīr,* Rāzī points out that "do not serve Satan" means "do not obey Satan". It is not only forbidden to prostrate before him; it is equally forbidden to obey him. Hence, obedience to someone amounts to serving him. After making this point, Rāzī asks: "If *'ibādah* means obedience, then what is meant by the command 'to obey Allah, and His Messenger and those in authority among you'"? Does it mean that we are required to serve and worship the Messenger and those in authority among us? Rāzī responds to this by saying that obedience to the Messenger and to those in authority among the Muslims amounts to serving and obeying God if the order to obey is in accord with God's command. Obedience to them, however, will be reckoned as serving and worshipping them [rather than God] when people obey them in matters where obeying them has no sanction. He adds: "The angels prostrated before Adam at God's command, [and since it was in compliance with God's command], this was an act of worshipping none other than God. Obedience of rulers will become service and worship of those rulers if one obeys them in a matter which does not enjoy God's sanction". Rāzī continues: "If someone were to come to you and ask you to carry out a command, consider whether this command conforms to God's command or not. If it does not conform to God's command, then his companion is Satan. In such a case, if one obeys him one is guilty of worshipping that person and his Satan. Likewise, if a person's self prompts him to do something he should consider whether God's Law permits that act or not. If that act is not permitted, then his self itself is Satan or Satan's companion. In case he follows the prompting of his own self, one is guilty of worshipping one's self". Rāzī further points out that there are various degrees of worshipping Satan. At times one does something in which all of one's limbs including one's tongue as well as one's heart work in union. In other cases while one's limbs take part in the task, one's heart and tongue do not participate in it. Likewise, sometimes one commits a sin while one's heart is not happy with it and the tongue seeks God's forgiveness for that act, the person concerned confessing that the act is an evil. In such a case, the person concerned is guilty of worshipping Satan only with his limbs. There are, however, other people who commit a misdeed and whereby their heart is quite satisfied and their tongue too expresses happiness. Such people are Satan's worshippers, internally as well as externally. (Rāzī, *al-Tafsīr al-Kabīr,* comments on verses 60–61.)

(62) Still, he misguided a whole throng of you. Did you have no sense?[54] (63) Now this is the Hell of which you were warned. (64) Burn in it on account of your disbelieving.

(65) Today We shall put a seal on their mouths, and their hands will speak to Us and their feet shall bear witness to what they had been doing.[55]

وَلَقَدْ أَضَلَّ مِنكُمْ جِبِلًّا كَثِيرًا ۖ أَفَلَمْ تَكُونُوا۟
تَعْقِلُونَ ﴿٦٢﴾ هَٰذِهِۦ جَهَنَّمُ ٱلَّتِى كُنتُمْ
تُوعَدُونَ ﴿٦٣﴾ ٱصْلَوْهَا ٱلْيَوْمَ بِمَا كُنتُمْ
تَكْفُرُونَ ﴿٦٤﴾ ٱلْيَوْمَ نَخْتِمُ عَلَىٰٓ أَفْوَٰهِهِمْ
وَتُكَلِّمُنَآ أَيْدِيهِمْ وَتَشْهَدُ أَرْجُلُهُم بِمَا كَانُوا۟
يَكْسِبُونَ ﴿٦٥﴾

54. The unbelievers are told that had they been devoid of reason and understanding, they could have put this forward as an extenuating reason for their choosing Satan, their enemy, rather than God as the object of their worship. The fact, however, is that God has endowed human beings with reason of which they make good use in all their worldly affairs. Not only that, God warned them through his Messengers, with regard to Satan. If they fall victim to the deceptions of their enemy, Satan, then they cannot acquit themselves of their responsibility in committing this folly.

55. This command will be issued as regards those supercilious culprits who simply refuse to own their guilt, deny the testimony of the witnesses, and contest the veracity of their scroll of deeds. It is at this point that God will call a halt to their protestations, and will ask them to witness the tale of their misdeeds as narrated by their own limbs. Mention is made here only of the testimony given by the hands and feet of these culprits. At other places, however, it is stated that their eyes, ears, tongues and skins will bear testimony to their misdeeds. The following verses are illustrative: "They should not disregard the Day when their own tongues, their hands and their feet will testify against their misdeeds" (*al-Nūr* 24:24), and "When they reach there, their ears, their eyes and their skin will testify to what they did" (*Ḥa' Mīm al-Sajdah* 41:20).

One is, however, faced with a difficulty in this regard. For, on the one hand, God declares that He will seal their mouths while at another

(66) If We so willed, We would have put out their eyes, then they would rush to see the Way, but how would they be able to see? (67) If We so willed, We would have transformed them where they were so that they would not go forward or backward.[56] (68) Whomsoever We grant a long life, We reverse him in his constitution.[57] Do they still not understand?

وَلَوۡ نَشَآءُ لَطَمَسۡنَا عَلَىٰٓ أَعۡيُنِهِمۡ فَٱسۡتَبَقُواْ
ٱلصِّرَٰطَ فَأَنَّىٰ يُبۡصِرُونَ ﴿٦٦﴾ وَلَوۡ نَشَآءُ
لَمَسَخۡنَٰهُمۡ عَلَىٰ مَكَانَتِهِمۡ فَمَا ٱسۡتَطَٰعُواْ
مُضِيّٗا وَلَا يَرۡجِعُونَ ﴿٦٧﴾ وَمَن نُّعَمِّرۡهُ
نُنَكِّسۡهُ فِي ٱلۡخَلۡقِۚ أَفَلَا يَعۡقِلُونَ ﴿٦٨﴾

place it is asserted that their tongues will testify against them. So, how does one reconcile these two statements? In our opinion, the sealing of their mouths means depriving them of the faculty of speech. In other words, it will no longer be possible for them to speak as they like. As for the testimony by the tongues, it means that they themselves will relate their misdeeds. Their tongues will elaborate upon how they were put to misuse by these wrong-doers in uttering blasphemy and lies and in fomenting mischief.

56. After depicting a scene of the Hereafter, the unbelievers are reminded of how they dismissed the Afterlife as something quite remote from reality. Yet they should observe with open eyes that in fact in this life too they are quite helpless beings under the control of the All-Mighty God. True, they are able to see everything around them with their eyes, but a simple command from God can make them instantly blind. Likewise, their legs which enable them to move about freely can be paralysed by God's command, thus rendering them incapable of even walking a step. As long as people enjoy the physical faculties granted to them by God, they remain deluded by an overly inflated egotism. As soon as they lose any of these faculties, they realise the true extent of their helplessness.

57. What is emphasised here is that in old age one is reverted to the state of one's infancy. The elderly suffer from the same weaknesses,

(69) We did not teach him (to wit, the Messenger) poetry and it does not behove him.[58] This is none but an Admonition, and a Clear Book (70) that he may warn him who is alive[59] and establish an argument against those that deny the Truth.

(71) Do they not see Our handiwork:[60] ▶

وَمَا عَلَّمْنَـٰهُ ٱلشِّعْرَ وَمَا يَنۢبَغِى لَهُۥٓ ۚ إِنْ هُوَ
إِلَّا ذِكْرٌ وَقُرْءَانٌ مُّبِينٌ ﴿٦٩﴾ لِّيُنذِرَ مَن كَانَ
حَيًّا وَيَحِقَّ ٱلْقَوْلُ عَلَى ٱلْكَـٰفِرِينَ ﴿٧٠﴾
أَوَلَمْ يَرَوْا۟ أَنَّا

infirmities and dependencies that marked their infant lives. Others help them to rise and put them to bed and feed them. They even lose control over themselves in such ordinary matters as answering the call of nature. Furthermore, they engage in foolish prattle causing people to burst into laughter. In short, in old age they revert to the same stage of weakness through which they had passed in their infancy.

58. This constitutes the Qur'ānic rejoinder to the unbelievers' dismissal of the Prophet's statements about monotheism, the Hereafter, Life-after-Death, Paradise and Hell, as sheer poetry. For them, these statements were as worthless as flights of fancy which one notes in poetry. (For further details see *Towards Understanding the Qur'ān*, *Sūrah al-Shu'arā'* 26: nn. 142–145, Vol. VII, pp. 126–129.)

59. He "who is alive" refers to him who thinks and understands, unlike a piece of stone. Such people who are devoid of understanding and feeling, are truly pieces of stone. No matter how reasonably a distinction is made between truth and falsehood before them, and no matter how sincerely a person tenders sincere advice to them, they are unmoved. For they neither hear, nor understand. Nor do they budge an inch from their position.

60. The word handiwork has been used here with regard to God in a figurative sense. This usage does not necessarily mean that God has a body and that, like human beings, He works with His hands. Recourse

We created for them cattle which they own? (72) We have subjected the cattle to them so that some of them they ride and eat the flesh of others. (73) They derive a variety of benefits and drinks from them. Will they, then, not give thanks?[61] (74) They set up deities apart from Allah, hoping that they will receive help from them. (75) Those deities can render them no help. Yet these devotees act as though they were an army in waiting for them.[62] ▶

خَلَقْنَا لَهُم مِّمَّا عَمِلَتْ أَيْدِينَآ أَنْعَـٰمًا فَهُمْ
لَهَا مَـٰلِكُونَ ﴿٧١﴾ وَذَلَّلْنَـٰهَا لَهُمْ فَمِنْهَا
رَكُوبُهُمْ وَمِنْهَا يَأْكُلُونَ ﴿٧٢﴾ وَلَهُمْ فِيهَا
مَنَـٰفِعُ وَمَشَارِبُ ۖ أَفَلَا يَشْكُرُونَ ﴿٧٣﴾
وَٱتَّخَذُوا۟ مِن دُونِ ٱللَّهِ ءَالِهَةً لَّعَلَّهُمْ
يُنصَرُونَ ﴿٧٤﴾ لَا يَسْتَطِيعُونَ نَصْرَهُمْ وَهُمْ
لَهُمْ جُندٌ مُّحْضَرُونَ ﴿٧٥﴾

---

has been made to this word to emphasise that God Himself created all these things; that no one had any part in God's act of creation.

61. Ingratitude consists in crediting someone other than the True Benefactor as the source of the bounty that one has received, or giving thanks for it to anyone other than Him, or expecting or seeking it from anyone other than Him. In like manner, using God's bounty in ways that do not please Him also amounts to ingratitude. Therefore, a polytheist, unbeliever, hypocrite or transgressor cannot be regarded as God's grateful servant merely because he verbally thanks God. The Makkan unbelievers did not deny that God had created their cattle. They also did not contend that any of their idols had a role in creating them. Yet they thanked their gods for the bounties conferred upon them by God, offering them sacrifices and invoking them for the bestowal of further bounties. This, therefore, made their verbal expression of gratitude to God meaningless. They were, therefore, branded as thankless.

62. That is, those idols were dependent on their devotees for their existence, security and other needs. If not for the hordes of these devotees

(76) Let not their words grieve you. Surely We know all things about them, what they conceal and what they reveal.[63]

(77) Does man[64] not see that We created him of a sperm-drop, ▶

فَلَا يَحْزُنكَ قَوْلُهُمْ إِنَّا نَعْلَمُ مَا يُسِرُّونَ
وَمَا يُعْلِنُونَ ﴿٧٦﴾ أَوَلَمْ يَرَ الْإِنسَانُ أَنَّا خَلَقْنَاهُ
مِن نُّطْفَةٍ

they could not have survived for a day. These devotees served them as though they were an army in waiting for them who set up and decorated their shrines. They carried out propaganda campaigns to exalt them and to turn people into their zealous supporters. They went about quarrelling and fighting on their behalf. It is thanks to a combination of these factors that the Godhead of these deities flourished. Had these factors not been there none would even care to utter their names. They are altogether unlike the One True God Whose sovereign control over the universe is not contingent on people's acknowledgement of Him as their Lord.

63. This is addressed to the Prophet (peace be on him). It has been said that "We know all things about them, what they conceal and what they reveal". This alludes to the storm of false propaganda and the campaign of slander and calumny against the Prophet (peace be on him) mounted by the Quraysh chiefs. They admitted in their private councils that their charges against the Prophet (peace be on him) were baseless. Yet they dubbed him as a madman, a poet, a soothsayer and a magician in order to prejudice people's minds against him. All the while, however, they knew in their heart of hearts that they had fabricated false charges in order to discredit him. God, therefore, asks the Prophet (peace be on him) not to lose heart on account of their slanderous campaign. Those who oppose the truth and cling to falsehood will be disgraced both in this life and in the Next.

64. This represents the Qur'ānic response to the query posed by the unbelievers mentioned in verse 48 above. The unbelievers often asked: when will the Last Day come? Their true purpose in asking this question was not to find out the actual date of the Last Day's arrival. Rather, their intent was to depict the occurrence of Resurrection as not

and lo! he is flagrantly contentious?[65] (78) He strikes for Us a similitude[66] and forgot his own creation.[67] He says: "Who will quicken the bones when they have decayed?" ▶

فَإِذَا هُوَ خَصِيمٌ مُّبِينٌ ۝٧٧ وَضَرَبَ لَنَا مَثَلًا وَنَسِيَ خَلْقَهُۥ ۖ قَالَ مَن يُحْيِ ٱلْعِظَـٰمَ وَهِيَ رَمِيمٌ ۝٧٨

---

only impossible but also evidently irrational. Hence, arguments are put forward in response to the unbelievers' query to confirm that the Hereafter is certainly possible.

The traditions narrated by 'Abd Allāh ibn 'Abbās, Qatādah and Sa'īd ibn Jubayr inform us that a Makkan chief once brought the bone of a dead man from a graveyard. He broke that bone into pieces and then scattered them into the air before the Prophet (peace be on him) and asked: "O Muḥammad, you say that the dead will be raised to life after death. Now, who will bring this disintegrated bone back to life?" The verse in question was instantly revealed in response to this query. (Ibn Kathīr, *Tafsīr,* comments on verse 77).

65. A drop of semen, which simply contained the basic germ of life, was of little significance as such. It is, however, God Who made it grow and then endowed it with life. Thanks to God's will it began to move about and derive nourishment, and was also granted myriad faculties – of consciousness and reason, of understanding and argumentation, of speech and effective articulation – faculties which had not been conferred on any other living species. All this carried man to such heights of vanity as to make him bold enough to argue even with God.

66. The unbelievers mistakenly consider God to be helpless, somewhat like the creatures which He created. As man himself cannot resurrect the dead, he suffers from the illusion that God too does not have the power to do so.

67. The unbelievers forget that God caused their birth out of a lifeless drop of semen and then let them grow into a speaking, thinking creature. Disregarding all this, man indulges in specious argumentation before God.

(79) Say: "He Who first brought them into being will quicken them; He knows well about every kind of creation; (80) He Who created from a green tree a fire for you, a fire to light your stoves with."[68] (81) Has He Who created the heavens and the earth no power to create the likes of them? Yes, indeed, He is the Superb Creator. (82) Whenever He wills a thing, He just commands it "Be" and it is. (83) Holy is He Who has full control over everything, and to Him you shall all be recalled.

قُلۡ يُحۡيِيهَا ٱلَّذِىٓ أَنشَأَهَآ أَوَّلَ مَرَّةٖۖ وَهُوَ
بِكُلِّ خَلۡقٍ عَلِيمٌ ٧٩ ٱلَّذِى جَعَلَ لَكُم
مِّنَ ٱلشَّجَرِ ٱلۡأَخۡضَرِ نَارٗا فَإِذَآ أَنتُم مِّنۡهُ
تُوقِدُونَ ٨٠ أَوَلَيۡسَ ٱلَّذِى خَلَقَ ٱلسَّمَٰوَٰتِ
وَٱلۡأَرۡضَ بِقَٰدِرٍ عَلَىٰٓ أَن يَخۡلُقَ مِثۡلَهُمۚ بَلَىٰ
وَهُوَ ٱلۡخَلَّٰقُ ٱلۡعَلِيمُ ٨١ إِنَّمَآ أَمۡرُهُۥٓ إِذَآ
أَرَادَ شَيۡـًٔا أَن يَقُولَ لَهُۥ كُن فَيَكُونُ ٨٢
فَسُبۡحَٰنَ ٱلَّذِى بِيَدِهِۦ مَلَكُوتُ كُلِّ
شَيۡءٖ وَإِلَيۡهِ تُرۡجَعُونَ ٨٣

---

68. This either means that God has granted such characteristics to green trees that man is able to use them as fuel. Or else it is an allusion to the two well-known trees called *markh* and *'ufār* (trees whose wood easily ignites). Arabs used to strike the green branches of these trees against one another and this produced sparks. In olden times, Arab bedouins employed this means to kindle fire, and maybe they continue to do so even today.

Sūrah 37

Al-Ṣāffāt

(The Rangers)

(Makkan Period)

Title

The word *al-ṣāffāt*, meaning the rangers, used in the opening verse constitutes the *sūrah*'s title.

Period of Revelation

It appears from the content and style of the *sūrah* that it was presumably revealed in the middle phase, and possibly even during the last stage of the middle phase, of the Prophet's Makkan life. The tenor of the discourse clearly reveals that fierce hostility to Islam was dominant, and that the Prophet (peace be on him) and his Companions were confronted with the most daunting of circumstances.

Subject Matter and Themes

The Makkan unbelievers are sternly warned in the *sūrah* against their rejection of the Prophet's call to monotheism and the Hereafter. The unbelievers had greeted this call with a volley of jest, derision and ridicule. They had also vehemently dismissed his claim to be God's Messenger. These unbelievers are now being unequivocally told that soon enough the Prophet (peace be on him), whom they had mockingly dismissed, will prevail over them, and they will find God's hosts occupying their very courtyards (see vv. 171–179). Significantly enough, the unbelievers were served with this warning at a time when apparently there existed no tokens of the Prophet's success. Rather, these early Muslims, who have been designated as God's hosts (verse 173), were the victims of savage persecution. About three fourths of these Makkan Muslims had already migrated from their home town. No more than 40 to 50 Muslims were left with the Prophet (peace be on him) in Makkah and they had to put up with all manner of hardships. It was inconceivable in the face of these harsh realities that the Prophet (peace be on him) and his handful of resourceless followers would eventually triumph. On the contrary, it appeared that the Prophet's call would be buried in the sands of Makkah's valleys. But hardly 15 or 16 years had passed before Makkah was conquered by the Muslims and what was foretold in this *sūrah* (see vv. 171–173) came true.

The *sūrah* combines its warning to the unbelievers with an address providing words of counsel and a persuasive exposition of Islam's teachings. Convincing arguments are also succinctly advanced in the course of the *sūrah* to corroborate the Islamic doctrines of monotheism and the Hereafter. Furthermore, the fallacious notions entertained by the polytheists are also effectively critiqued to lay bare the absurdity of their beliefs. They are apprised of the dire consequences of the errors in which they were mired and also informed, by way of contrast, of the splendid results of adhering to sound belief and righteous conduct. In this context, examples are provided by referring to the annals of human history. These examples clearly show how God dealt in the past with earlier Prophets and their nations; the myriad ways in which He lavished His favours on His loyal servants and punished those who gave the lie to His Prophets.

Of the historical stories narrated in this *sūrah*, the most instructive one relates to the life of the Prophet Abraham (peace be on him).

The most important event of Abraham's life is that no sooner had he realised that God wanted him to sacrifice his only son, than he made up his mind to do so. There was a lesson for all in the example set by Abraham (peace be on him) and not just for the Quraysh who boasted of their Abrahamic ancestry. There was also a lesson in it for the Muslims who believed in God and His Messenger (peace be on him). By recounting this story the Muslims were intimated of the essence and spirit of Islam: that after accepting Islam as one's faith, a true believer should be ready to sacrifice his all to please God. The *sūrah*'s concluding verses provide not only a warning for the Makkan unbelievers, but also glad tidings for the true believers who endured untold hardships in the course of supporting the Prophet (peace be on him). Through these verses the believers were given the message that the hardships confronting them in this early stage of their mission should not dishearten them. For, eventually, the Muslims are bound to gain the upper hand over the forces of unbelief and falsehood. Within just a few years' time these tidings came true. These verses were thus not merely a source of consolation for Muslims but also enshrined a prophecy that soon enough became a reality.

In the name of Allah, the Most Merciful, the Most Compassionate.

بِسْمِ ٱللَّهِ ٱلرَّحْمَٰنِ ٱلرَّحِيمِ

(1) By those who range themselves in rows; (2) by those who reprove severely, (3) and those who recite the Exhortation;[1] ▶

وَٱلصَّٰٓفَّٰتِ صَفًّا ﴿١﴾ فَٱلزَّٰجِرَٰتِ زَجْرًا ﴿٢﴾
فَٱلتَّٰلِيَٰتِ ذِكْرًا ﴿٣﴾

---

1. The majority of Qur'ān-commentators are agreed that all the three groups mentioned here belong to the angels. This is the interpretation of the verses made by 'Abd Allāh ibn Mas'ūd, 'Abd Allāh ibn 'Abbās, Qatādah, Masrūq, Sa'īd ibn Jubayr, 'Ikrimah, Mujāhid, al-Suddī, Ibn Zayd and Rabī' ibn Anas (Ibn Kathīr, *Tafsīr,* comments on verses 1–3). Some commentators, however, do interpret the verses differently. However, the context in which the verses occur lends support to the view that those referred to here are angels.

The significance of the statement that they "range themselves in rows" is that the angels who manage the whole order of the universe are no more than God's servants and bondsmen. As such, they are always in a state of readiness to obey God and carry out His commands. This truth is reiterated in verse 165 below, where the angels introduce themselves as follows: "We range ourselves in rows (as humble servants)".

As for the words "those who reprove severely" (v. 2), according to some commentators, they mean that some angels direct the clouds and bring about rainfall. Even though this meaning of the verse is not incorrect, what seems more plausible in view of the contents of the verses that follow, is the meaning that there is a group of angels who severely reprove the disobedient and afflict the guilty. This reproof, however, is not simply verbal but may also afflict the disobedient and the guilty in the form of natural disasters and historic calamities.

The statement that they "recite the Exhortation" (v. 3) means that among these angels are also those that constantly remind people of the truth so that they take heed. This exhortation may also take the form of the devastations that occurred in the past teaching human beings a lesson. It may also be in the form of the teachings that these angels convey to the Prophets, and also in the form of the inspirations that reach virtuous people through them.

(4) surely your God is One,[2] (5) the Lord[3] of the heavens and the earth and of whatever lies between the two, the Lord of the Easts.[4]

إِنَّ إِلَٰهَكُمْ لَوَاحِدٌ ۝٤ رَّبُّ ٱلسَّمَٰوَٰتِ وَٱلْأَرْضِ وَمَا بَيْنَهُمَا وَرَبُّ ٱلْمَشَٰرِقِ ۝٥

2. The proclamation of this truth is accompanied by taking an oath in the name of the angels. In other words, it is affirmed that the workings of the whole universe reflect its servitude to God. Also, natural phenomena expose before man the evil consequences of deviating from God's servitude. Moreover, it has been a part of the universe's scheme of things that people are reminded of one and the same truth in varying ways. All these bear out that man's lord is none but the One True God.

The word *ilāh* that occurs here has two connotations. In one sense, it means the deity that is an object of actual service and worship. In the other, it means the deity that truly deserves to be worshipped. The word *ilāh* is employed in this verse in its latter sense. For evidently it could not have been used to denote the false gods that human beings invented and which they worshipped.

3. The truth, brought home by these verses, is that only the Lord and Sovereign of the universe is mankind's True God. It would be absolutely irrational that in the presence of the True *Rabb* (that is, Lord, Sovereign, Guardian and Sustainer) anyone else should be deemed deserving of worship. What underlies man's worship of God is his recognition of the Being Who is the source of all benefits and losses and of the fulfilment of all of his needs and requirements. It is a recognition of He Who can mar his fate, and in fact upon Whom his very existence and survival depend. It is, therefore, an innate requirement of human nature to recognise God's supremacy and to surrender to Him. Once man realises this truth, he can readily grasp that it is pointless and absurd to worship false gods for they have absolutely no power. Worship is exclusively the right of the One Who has absolute power. Powerless entities, by contrast, are not entitled to any worship. Man can gain nothing by turning to them. False gods are incapable of doing anything. Turning to them, and praying to them rather than to the All-Powerful God is as foolish an act as approaching subjects of the Sovereign who themselves invoke God's mercy.

4. The sun does not always rise at the same point. Furthermore, it appears in different parts of the earth at varying times. This explains the

(6) We have adorned the lower heaven[5] with the adornment of the stars (7) and have protected it from every rebellious satan.[6] (8) These satans cannot listen to what transpires in the High Council for they are pelted away from every side (9) and are repelled. Theirs is an unceasing chastisement. ▶

إِنَّا زَيَّنَّا ٱلسَّمَآءَ ٱلدُّنْيَا بِزِينَةٍ ٱلْكَوَاكِبِ ۝٦
وَحِفْظًا مِّن كُلِّ شَيْطَٰنٍ مَّارِدٍ ۝٧
لَّا يَسَّمَّعُونَ إِلَى ٱلْمَلَإِ ٱلْأَعْلَىٰ وَيُقْذَفُونَ
مِن كُلِّ جَانِبٍ ۝٨ دُحُورًا ۖ وَلَهُمْ عَذَابٌ
وَاصِبٌ ۝٩

Qur'ānic use of the word *mashāriq* (Easts) in its plural form. It is significant that the Qur'ān does not use the corresponding word *maghārib* (Wests) here (the word *maghrib* singular of *maghārib* signifies the direction in which the sun sets). The reason is that the word Easts also implies the word "Wests". However, in *Sūrah al-Ma'ārij* 70:40, God is described as the Lord of "the easts and the wests".

5. By "the lower heaven" is meant the heaven nearer to us, one which we see with our naked eyes, without the aid of any external equipment such as a telescope. The worlds that can be observed with the help of telescopes, and the worlds that we have not yet been able to observe even with the help of the equipments of observation available to us are the "farther heavens". In this regard, it ought to be clarified that *samā'* is not a fixed, static object. This word and its equivalents have been used from earliest times to denote the heavens, or simply, the sphere above us.

6. The upper sphere is not an empty space that may be trespassed by anyone. On the contrary, it is strictly guarded and barriers have been erected in its various regions so that it is impossible for any rebellious devils to trespass it. Every planet has its own orbit and sphere and it is impossible for another to enter it, or for the planet itself, to move out of it. While looking around one feels that there is nothing else but space. In truth, however, this space contains numerous check posts, each of which forms a formidable barrier. One can have some idea of this by acquainting oneself with the myriad difficulties being experienced by man in his effort to reach the moon, the earth's closest neighbour. In like manner, the *jinn* face insurmountable difficulties in ascending to the heavens.

(10) And if any is able to snatch a fragment, he is pursued by a piercing flame.[7]

إِلَّا مَنْ خَطِفَ ٱلْخَطْفَةَ فَأَتْبَعَهُۥ شِهَابٌ ثَاقِبٌ ﴿١٠﴾ فَٱسْتَفْتِهِمْ أَهُمْ أَشَدُّ خَلْقًا أَم مَّنْ خَلَقْنَآ

(11) So ask them (that is, human beings): "Were they harder to create than the objects We created?"[8] ▶

---

7. To better appreciate this, one should recall that soothsaying was quite rampant in Arabia at that time. Such soothsayers claimed to have control over the *jinn* and devils, which brought to them all kinds of information. It was against this backdrop that when Muḥammad (peace be on him) was designated a Prophet, he was dubbed a soothsayer for he began to recite the verses of the Qur'ān which contained information about man's past and his future. The Prophet (peace be on him) also informed people that he received this revelation from an angel. Upon hearing this, the unbelievers immediately began to accuse him of being a practitioner of this craft and said that like other soothsayers, he too had links with the devils who informed him of tidings from on high.

The present verse refutes this charge, asserting that devils have no access to the heavens. Moreover, the devils are incapable of deriving any information from the angels. If, however, anything the angels say accidentally reaches their ears, then even before they descend to earth, they are hotly pursued by meteors. In other words, devils cannot interfere in the workings of the universe; they do not even have any access to the basic information regarding it. (For further details see *Towards Understanding the Qur'ān, Sūrah al-Ḥijr* 15: nn. 8 and 10–12, Vol. IV, pp. 284–286.)

8. This is in response to the Makkan unbelievers' doubts about the Hereafter. Indeed they ruled out the Hereafter as something impossible. It was inconceivable for them that the dead would be brought back to life. The Qur'ān advances a series of arguments in order to corroborate the doctrine of the Hereafter. First, it raises the question: if the unbelievers think that God does not have the power to resurrect mankind, then what is their position regarding the fact that God created the heavens and the earth? This, not to mention the innumerable other objects that exist in the heavens and the earth! There is, therefore, no reason for them to think that God lacks the power to bring the dead back to life.

We created them from sticky clay.[9] (12) You marvel (at the wondrous creations of Allah) and they scoff at it, (13) and when they are admonished, they pay no heed; (14) and if they see any Sign, they laugh it away (15) and say: "This is nothing but plain sorcery.[10] ▶

إِنَّا خَلَقْنَٰهُم مِّن طِينٍ لَّازِبٍۭ ﴿١١﴾ بَلْ
عَجِبْتَ وَيَسْخَرُونَ ﴿١٢﴾ وَإِذَا ذُكِّرُوا۟
لَا يَذْكُرُونَ ﴿١٣﴾ وَإِذَا رَأَوْا۟ ءَايَةً
يَسْتَسْخِرُونَ ﴿١٤﴾ وَقَالُوٓا۟ إِنْ هَٰذَآ
إِلَّا سِحْرٌ مُّبِينٌ ﴿١٥﴾

9. There is nothing all that unusual about man. After all, what he was made from was sticky clay and he can be created from the same material again.

The present verse means that the first man was created from sticky clay and, thereafter, the human race multiplied from the semen of that first man. It also means that every human being is made from sticky clay in so far as the whole substance of man's existence is derived from earth. The semen of which man is created is a product of food. From the time of man's conception till the moment of his death, man's whole body is made of constituents drawn from food. Whether food is derived from animal or vegetable origins, its ultimate source is clay. When clay is combined with water it becomes possible to grow grain and vegetables and fruit, and also to nourish animals which supply milk and meat for man's consumption. The basis of the argument is as follows: had the clay not been invested with the ability to receive the essence of life, how could people be alive today? On the other hand, if clay already has the ability to receive the essence of life – something that is clearly proved by the existence of human beings – then why is it not plausible that through the same clay it will be possible to recreate them at some future date?

10. The unbelievers reject every notion about the Hereafter as belonging to the realm of magic and sorcery. For them, the Next Life the Prophet (peace be on him) talks about, one which involves the revival of the dead, the holding of God's Court of Reckoning, the award of Paradise and Hell, was just fantasy. Alternatively, this can be taken to mean that they regarded the Prophet (peace be on him) as enchanted, as someone who, under the spell of enchantment, talked of such bizarre things.

(16) Is it ever possible that after we die and are reduced to dust and (a skeleton of) bones, we will be raised to life? (17) And so also shall our forefathers of yore be raised to life?" (18) Tell them: "Yes; and you are utterly helpless[11] (against Allah)."

(19) There will be a single stern rebuff and lo, they will be observing with their own eyes (all that they had been warned against).[12] (20) They will then say: "Woe for us. This is the Day of Judgement." (21) "Yes, this is the Day of Final Decision ▶

أَءِذَا مِتْنَا وَكُنَّا تُرَابًا وَعِظَٰمًا أَءِنَّا
لَمَبْعُوثُونَ ﴿١٦﴾ أَوَءَابَآؤُنَا ٱلْأَوَّلُونَ ﴿١٧﴾ قُلْ
نَعَمْ وَأَنتُمْ دَٰخِرُونَ ﴿١٨﴾ فَإِنَّمَا هِىَ زَجْرَةٌ
وَٰحِدَةٌ فَإِذَا هُمْ يَنظُرُونَ ﴿١٩﴾ وَقَالُوا۟
يَٰوَيْلَنَا هَٰذَا يَوْمُ ٱلدِّينِ ﴿٢٠﴾ هَٰذَا
يَوْمُ ٱلْفَصْلِ

11. The unbelievers are told that God has the absolute power to make them as He wants. When God so willed He brought human beings into existence by simply hinting at what He wills. Likewise, whenever God so wills all human beings will instantly perish. By the same token, they will be resurrected whenever He so wills.

12. When the time for it comes, recreating the world will not be a difficult task for God to accomplish. A mere "rebuff" from God will suffice to awaken the dead. The Qur'ānic expression employed in this context seems to suggest that all human beings, from the very the beginning of time up till the Last Day, have been in a state of sleep. Then there will be a sudden, reproachful command: "Wake up!" All will then be instantly up and awake.

that you used to deny as a lie."[13] (22) (Then will the command be given): "Muster all the wrong-doers[14] and their spouses and the deities[15] whom they used to serve (23) apart from Allah,[16] and direct them to the path of Hell, ▶

ٱلَّذِى كُنتُم بِهِۦ تُكَذِّبُونَ ﴿٢١﴾ ۞ ٱحْشُرُوا۟
ٱلَّذِينَ ظَلَمُوا۟ وَأَزْوَٰجَهُمْ وَمَا كَانُوا۟
يَعْبُدُونَ ﴿٢٢﴾ مِن دُونِ ٱللَّهِ فَٱهْدُوهُمْ إِلَىٰ
صِرَٰطِ ٱلْجَحِيمِ ﴿٢٣﴾

13. This might be the remark made by the believers to the unbelievers, or by the angels. It is also possible that the prevailing state of affairs in the Hereafter will convey this message to them. Alternatively, this might be the reaction of concerned people as a part of their soliloquy. In other words, addressing themselves, they will say: "You thought all along that there would be no Day of Judgement. Now, that Day is come and woe has betaken you".

14. The word "wrong-doers" used here consists not only of those who had wronged others. The Qur'ānic usage of the term applies to all those who are rebellious, headstrong, and disobedient of God.

15. The word *azwāj* used here might denote their wives who were accomplices in their rebellion against God, or it might denote all those who, like them, were rebellious, defiant and disobedient of God. The verse may also mean that the culprits of each category will be classified separately.

16. The reference here is to two kinds of deities: (i) Those human beings and devils who desired and strove in order that human beings abandon God and worship them instead of Him. (ii) The idols, trees and stones and so on that have been the objects of worship in the world. The deities of the former category will be reckoned as culprits and hurled into Hell. As for the deities of the second category, they will be cast into Hell along with their devotees so that the latter may perpetually witness them and remain immersed in shame and remorse. In addition to them there is a third category of deities. This category consists of those that were objects of people's worship but this was never at their behest or

(24) and detain them there; they will be called to account. (25) How is it that you are not helping one another? (26) Indeed, today they are surrendering themselves completely."[17] (27) They will then turn towards each other (and start wrangling). (28) (The followers will say to their leaders): "You used to come to us from the right hand."[18] ▶

وَقِفُوهُمْۖ إِنَّهُم مَّسْـُٔولُونَ ٢٤ مَا لَكُمْ
لَا تَنَاصَرُونَ ٢٥ بَلْ هُمُ ٱلْيَوْمَ مُسْتَسْلِمُونَ ٢٦
وَأَقْبَلَ بَعْضُهُمْ عَلَىٰ بَعْضٍ يَتَسَآءَلُونَ ٢٧
قَالُوٓاْ إِنَّكُمْ كُنتُمْ تَأْتُونَنَا عَنِ ٱلْيَمِينِ ٢٨

with their approval. These consist of angels, Prophets, and saints who always asked people not to worship anyone besides the One True God. Quite obviously there is no question of these deities being cast into Hell along with their devotees.

17. The first part of the statement will be addressed to the culprits and the second to the general public as they watch those culprits being dispatched to Hell. This passage depicts the true state of those culprits. They will not be able to muster any resistance. The so-called honourable and respectable figures of this world will be publicly disgraced. The clergy with pretensions to Divinity will also be thrown into Hell. Devotees will no longer care for their lords. Rather, they will turn away from them. Even passionate lovers will desert one another. In portraying this scene the Qur'ān stresses the point that the mutual ties of men, rooted in rebellion of God, will be severed in the Hereafter. Those who strut about arrogantly in the world will be made to eat dust.

18. The word *al-yamīn* carries many connotations. If it is taken in the sense of power and strength, it would mean that the weak were dragged by the strong to the path of error. Alternatively, if it is taken to mean goodness, it would mean that they betrayed them although they pretended to be their sincere well-wishers, for they assured the weak that the path they showed them would lead to their success. This is what

(29) They will say: "Nay, you yourselves were not the ones who would believe. (30) We had no power over you. You were a rebellious people, (31) and so we became deserving of the Word of our Lord that we shall be made to suffer chastisement. (32) So we led you astray; we ourselves were strayed."[19]

(33) On that Day, they will all share the chastisement.[20] (34) Thus do We treat the culprits. (35) Whenever it was said to them: "There is no true deity apart from Allah," they waxed proud (36) and said: "Shall we forsake our deities for the sake of a distracted poet?" ▶

قَالُواْ بَل لَّمۡ تَكُونُواْ مُؤۡمِنِينَ ٢٩ وَمَا كَانَ
لَنَا عَلَيۡكُم مِّن سُلۡطَٰنِۭۖ بَلۡ كُنتُمۡ
قَوۡمًا طَٰغِينَ ٣٠ فَحَقَّ عَلَيۡنَا قَوۡلُ رَبِّنَآۖ إِنَّا
لَذَآئِقُونَ ٣١ فَأَغۡوَيۡنَٰكُمۡ إِنَّا كُنَّا
غَٰوِينَ ٣٢ فَإِنَّهُمۡ يَوۡمَئِذٖ فِي ٱلۡعَذَابِ
مُشۡتَرِكُونَ ٣٣ إِنَّا كَذَٰلِكَ نَفۡعَلُ
بِٱلۡمُجۡرِمِينَ ٣٤ إِنَّهُمۡ كَانُوٓاْ إِذَا قِيلَ لَهُمۡ
لَآ إِلَٰهَ إِلَّا ٱللَّهُ يَسۡتَكۡبِرُونَ ٣٥ وَيَقُولُونَ
أَئِنَّا لَتَارِكُوٓاْ ءَالِهَتِنَا لِشَاعِرٖ مَّجۡنُونِۭ ٣٦

---

deceived them. If, however, this word is regarded as a synonym of an oath, it would mean that they swore that what they were expounding was nothing but the truth.

19. For further details see *Towards Understanding the Qur'ān, Sūrah Saba'* 34: nn. 51–53, pp. 190–192 above.

20. Both false gods and their devotees, the leaders as well as the led, will share a terrible punishment in the Hereafter. The devotees' plea that they were misled by others will not be entertained. Nor will those who mislead them be exonerated on the grounds that the latter were not seekers of the Truth.

(37) (They say so although) he brought the Truth and confirmed the veracity of the Messengers.[21] (38) (They will be told): "You shall taste the grievous chastisement. (39) You will only be recompensed according to your deeds."

(40) But Allah's chosen servants (shall be spared this woeful end). (41) For them awaits a known provision,[22] (42) a variety of delicious fruits;[23] and they shall be honoured (43) in the Gardens of Bliss. ▶

بَلْ جَآءَ بِٱلْحَقِّ وَصَدَّقَ ٱلْمُرْسَلِينَ ﴿٣٧﴾
إِنَّكُمْ لَذَآئِقُواْ ٱلْعَذَابِ ٱلْأَلِيمِ ﴿٣٨﴾
وَمَا تُجْزَوْنَ إِلَّا مَا كُنتُمْ تَعْمَلُونَ ﴿٣٩﴾
إِلَّا عِبَادَ ٱللَّهِ ٱلْمُخْلَصِينَ ﴿٤٠﴾ أُوْلَٰٓئِكَ لَهُمْ
رِزْقٌ مَّعْلُومٌ ﴿٤١﴾ فَوَٰكِهُ ۖ وَهُم مُّكْرَمُونَ ﴿٤٢﴾
فِى جَنَّٰتِ ٱلنَّعِيمِ ﴿٤٣﴾

21. Bearing out the veracity of the Messengers carries the following three meanings and it appears that all three are intended here: (i) That he did not oppose any earlier Messenger; rather, he affirmed belief in all of God's earlier Messengers. Hence there was no reasonable basis for the followers of a messenger to be prejudiced against him. (ii) That he did not expound any novel message; rather, his message consisted of what the earlier Messengers had expounded from the very beginning. (iii) That the tidings given by the earlier Messengers about him were fully applicable to him.

22. "For them awaits a known provision", one whose qualities have already been described. This provision they feel fully assured of receiving, and receiving continually.

23. Implicit in this is the subtle hint that food in Paradise will be for enjoyment rather than for nutrition. Food there will not be the fuel for the body because man will not experience hunger. Nor will man be in need of food for survival. This explains why the word *fawākih* (fruits) is mentioned in connection with the food of Paradise, which carries the dominant nuance of enjoyment rather than simply of nutrition.

(44) They will be seated upon couches set face to face; (45) a cup filled with wine[24] from its springs,[25] will be passed around to them;[26] ▶	عَلَىٰ سُرُرٍ مُّتَقَـٰبِلِينَ ﴿٤٤﴾ يُطَافُ عَلَيْهِم بِكَأْسٍ مِّن مَّعِينٍ ﴿٤٥﴾

24. The verse does not make a specific mention of wine. It is, however, implied by the use of the word *ka's*. This word is used only for the cup that contains an intoxicating drink. This word is never used if the cup contains milk or water, or even if it is empty.

25. It will be unlike the wine that is produced in the world from fruit and grain by means of fermentation. Rather, it will flow naturally in the form of springs and lakes. This point is elaborated in the following words in the Qur'ān elsewhere: "In Paradise there shall be rivers of wine, of delight to those that drink", (*Muḥammad* 47:15).

26. It is not specified as to who will circulate the goblets of wine among the inmates of Paradise. This point is elaborated in the following verses:

> Youths as fair as hidden pearls will be set apart to wait upon them; they will be running to and fro to serve them, (*al-Ṭūr* 52:24).
>
> There boys of everlasting youth shall go about attending them: when you see them, you would think that they are scattered pearls, (*al-Dahr* 76:19).

The preceding point has been amplified in the *aḥādīth* narrated by Anas ibn Mālik and Samurah ibn Jundub. According to these traditions, the children of polytheists will serve as page boys for the inmates of Paradise (Abū Dā'ūd, al-Ṭayālisī, Ṭabarānī and Bazzār). These reports are weak in terms of their chains of narrators. It is, nonetheless, evident from other *aḥādīth* that young children will be admitted to Paradise. We also learn from *aḥādīth* that righteous parents will enjoy the company of their children in Paradise. This leaves out only those parents who will not enter Paradise. It is, therefore, logical that their children will serve as page boys in Paradise. (For a detailed discussion see Ibn Ḥajar al-'Asqalānī, *Fatḥ al-Bārī, Kitāb al-Janā'iz, Bāb mā Qīla fī Awlād al-Mushrikīn*; Badr al-Dīn al-'Aynī, *'Umdat al-Qārī, Kitāb al-Janā'īz, Bāb mā Qīla fī Awlād*

(46) white, sparkling (wine), a delight to the drinkers. (47) There will neither be any harm in it for their body nor will it intoxicate their mind.[27] (48) Theirs shall be wide-eyed maidens[28] with bashful, restrained glances,[29] (49) so delicate as the hidden peel under an egg's shell.[30]

بَيۡضَآءَ لَذَّةٖ لِّلشَّٰرِبِينَ ٤٦ لَا فِيهَا غَوۡلٞ
وَلَا هُمۡ عَنۡهَا يُنزَفُونَ ٤٧ وَعِندَهُمۡ
قَٰصِرَٰتُ ٱلطَّرۡفِ عِينٞ ٤٨ كَأَنَّهُنَّ بَيۡضٞ
مَّكۡنُونٞ ٤٩

al-Mushrikīn. See also the author's work in Urdu, *Rasā'īl wa Masā' īl*, Vol. 3, pp. 177–187.)

27. This wine will be free from both the defects that usually mar wine in the world. These defects are: its stench which is unbearable; its bad taste also offends, and the fact that it hurts both the stomach and the brain. Then it soars upwards to the brain and causes severe headaches. It also adversely affects the liver and ruins one's health as such. Another big disadvantage of drinking is that it causes intoxication followed by a hangover. One loses self control and acts in a foolish manner. One drinks wine only for the sake of transient pleasure, exposing oneself to all these harms. God makes it clear that while wine in Paradise "will be a delight to the drinkers", it will be altogether free of the kind of defects mentioned above.

28. That is, their glances will be restricted to their spouses.

29. It is likely that these may be the girls who died before reaching the age of discretion and whose parents do not deserve to enter Paradise. This is analogous to the case of the young boys whose parents are not admitted to Paradise, and who will serve as page boys there, (see n. 26 above). Likewise, such girls will serve as houries. Their state of youth will endure. And God knows best.

30. Literally, this stands for hidden or preserved eggs. Scholars of *tafsīr*, however, have interpreted it variously. The true interpretation of it is evidently that narrated by Umm Salamah from the Prophet (peace be on him). When she requested him to define it, he replied: "They will

(50) Then some of them will turn to others, and will ask each other. (51) One of them will say: "I had a companion in the world (52) who used to say: 'Are you also one of those who confirm the Truth[31] (of life after death)? (53) After we are dead and have become all dust and bones shall we still be requited?' (54) He will say: 'Do you wish to know where he is now?' (55) Then he will look downwards, and will see him in the depths of Hell. (56) He will say to him: 'By Allah, you almost ruined me. (57) But for Allah's favour, I should be one of those who have been mustered here.[32] ▶

فَأَقْبَلَ بَعْضُهُمْ عَلَىٰ بَعْضٍ يَتَسَآءَلُونَ ﴿٥٠﴾
قَالَ قَآئِلٌ مِّنْهُمْ إِنِّى كَانَ لِى قَرِينٌ ﴿٥١﴾ يَقُولُ
أَءِنَّكَ لَمِنَ ٱلْمُصَدِّقِينَ ﴿٥٢﴾ أَءِذَا مِتْنَا وَكُنَّا
تُرَابًا وَعِظَـٰمًا أَءِنَّا لَمَدِينُونَ ﴿٥٣﴾ قَالَ هَلْ
أَنتُم مُّطَّلِعُونَ ﴿٥٤﴾ فَٱطَّلَعَ فَرَءَاهُ فِى سَوَآءِ
ٱلْجَحِيمِ ﴿٥٥﴾ قَالَ تَٱللَّهِ إِن كِدتَّ
لَتُرْدِينِ ﴿٥٦﴾ وَلَوْلَا نِعْمَةُ رَبِّى لَكُنتُ مِنَ
ٱلْمُحْضَرِينَ ﴿٥٧﴾

---

be as soft and tender as the fine covering inside the eggshell", (Ṭabarī, *Tafsīr,* comments on verse 49).

31. The unbelievers used to tease the believers, asserting that their affirmation of the After-life simply betrayed their superstitiousness.

32. This points to the faculties of sight, hearing and speech granted to man in the Hereafter. A person sitting in Paradise will easily be able to know the condition of someone who is undergoing severe punishment in Hell. He will be able to do so just by casting his glance downwards to see him without using any equipment such as a television. He will also be able to remain directly in touch and even converse with others even though there might be a great distance separating them.

(58) So, are we not going to die, (59) except for our first death? And shall we suffer no chastisement?'"[33]

(60) Surely this is the supreme triumph. (61) For the like of it should the workers work. (62) Is this a better hospitality or the tree of al-Zaqqūm?[34] (63) We have made this tree a trial for the wrong-doers.[35] (64) It is a tree that grows in the nethermost part of Hell. ▶

أَفَمَا نَحْنُ بِمَيِّتِينَ ﴿٥٨﴾ إِلَّا مَوْتَتَنَا ٱلْأُولَىٰ
وَمَا نَحْنُ بِمُعَذَّبِينَ ﴿٥٩﴾ إِنَّ هَٰذَا لَهُوَ
ٱلْفَوْزُ ٱلْعَظِيمُ ﴿٦٠﴾ لِمِثْلِ هَٰذَا فَلْيَعْمَلِ
ٱلْعَٰمِلُونَ ﴿٦١﴾ أَذَٰلِكَ خَيْرٌ نُّزُلًا أَمْ شَجَرَةُ
ٱلزَّقُّومِ ﴿٦٢﴾ إِنَّا جَعَلْنَٰهَا فِتْنَةً لِّلظَّٰلِمِينَ ﴿٦٣﴾
إِنَّهَا شَجَرَةٌ تَخْرُجُ فِىٓ أَصْلِ ٱلْجَحِيمِ ﴿٦٤﴾

---

33. It is evident from the tenor of the discourse that while speaking to an inmate of Hell the dwellers of Paradise will turn to soliloquy. What he says in this regard fully expresses his sense of ecstatic wonder at the idyllic state in which he finds himself. Clearly, this is not directed at anyone in particular, for he is found talking to himself and is expressing his innermost feelings. He marvels at his good fortune in so far as he is immune from death and punishment. His admission to Paradise has brought to an end every hardship and suffering. He is also blessed with everlasting life. Overpowered by these feelings, he is unable to contain himself and exclaims, asking whether all this is true?

34. Zaqqūm is the name of a tree that grows in Tihāmah. It has an intensely bitter taste as well as a bad odour. The juice released by its leaves causes swelling in the body. (This is perhaps the very same tree that is called *thūhar* in the Subcontinent.)

35. On hearing this, those who denied the Hereafter found another pretext to taunt the Qur'ān and ridicule the Prophet (peace be on him). They would giggle uncontrollably at the idea that trees should grow in a Hell that is filled with blazing fire.

(65) Its spathes are like the
heads of satans.[36] (66) (The
people of Hell) will surely
eat of it, filling their bellies
with it. (67) Then on top of
it they will have a brew of
boiling water. (68) Then their
return will be to the same
blazing Hell.[37] (69) These
are the ones who found
their fathers steeped in error,
(70) and they are running in
their footsteps.[38] (71) Before
them a multitude of people
of olden times had erred,
(72) and We had sent among
them Messengers to warn
them. ▶

طَلۡعُهَا كَأَنَّهُۥ رُءُوسُ ٱلشَّيَٰطِينِ ﴿٦٥﴾ فَإِنَّهُمۡ
لَأٓكِلُونَ مِنۡهَا فَمَالِـُٔونَ مِنۡهَا ٱلۡبُطُونَ ﴿٦٦﴾
ثُمَّ إِنَّ لَهُمۡ عَلَيۡهَا لَشَوۡبٗا مِّنۡ حَمِيمٖ ﴿٦٧﴾ ثُمَّ
إِنَّ مَرۡجِعَهُمۡ لَإِلَى ٱلۡجَحِيمِ ﴿٦٨﴾ إِنَّهُمۡ أَلۡفَوۡاْ
ءَابَآءَهُمۡ ضَآلِّينَ ﴿٦٩﴾ فَهُمۡ عَلَىٰٓ ءَاثَٰرِهِمۡ
يُهۡرَعُونَ ﴿٧٠﴾ وَلَقَدۡ ضَلَّ قَبۡلَهُمۡ أَكۡثَرُ
ٱلۡأَوَّلِينَ ﴿٧١﴾ وَلَقَدۡ أَرۡسَلۡنَا فِيهِم مُّنذِرِينَ ﴿٧٢﴾

---

36. This should not give rise to the misunderstanding that since no one has seen the head of Satan, it cannot be likened to the spathes of the Zaqqūm tree. For this is an imaginative simile. Such similes are an integral part of the literature of every language. For example, "fairy" is a common metaphor to indicate the zenith of feminine beauty. By the same token, "witch" is used as a metaphor for describing utmost ugliness. A pious person with a halo of spirituality around him is likened to an "angel". In contrast, an evil person is likened to Satan.

37. This shows that when the inmates of Hell are overpowered by hunger and thirst, they will be dragged to a spot full of Zaqqūm trees and springs of boiling water. Then, after they have had their fill of both, they will be returned to Hell.

38. They never made use of their reason to examine their inherited ways. Blindly, they turned to the ways they had found their predecessors treading.

(73) Observe, then, what was the end of those that had been warned, (74) except for the chosen servants of Allah?

(75) Noah[39] had called upon Us[40] (earlier). See, how excellent We were in answering him! (76) We delivered him and his household from the great calamity;[41] (77) and made his offspring the only ones to survive,[42] ▶

فَانظُرْ كَيْفَ كَانَ عَاقِبَةُ الْمُنذَرِينَ ﴿٧٣﴾
إِلَّا عِبَادَ اللَّهِ الْمُخْلَصِينَ ﴿٧٤﴾ وَلَقَدْ نَادَانَا
نُوحٌ فَلَنِعْمَ الْمُجِيبُونَ ﴿٧٥﴾ وَنَجَّيْنَاهُ وَأَهْلَهُ
مِنَ الْكَرْبِ الْعَظِيمِ ﴿٧٦﴾ وَجَعَلْنَا ذُرِّيَّتَهُ
هُمُ الْبَاقِينَ ﴿٧٧﴾

---

39. This relates to verses 72–74. If we bear in mind the content of those verses, it is evident why these stories are being narrated here.

40. Reference here is to the supplication of the Prophet Noah (peace be on him) in a state of utter despair after he had preached the truth to his people for centuries. This supplication is mentioned in the Qur'ān in these words: "Then he called upon his Lord: 'Verily I am vanquished. So come to my aid'", (*al-Qamar* 54:10).

41. The subtle point suggested here is that in the same manner that God had delivered the Prophet Noah (peace be on him) and his companions from the "great calamity", He will also deliver the Prophet Muḥammad (peace be on him) and his Companions from a similar calamity, the one they were facing at the hands of the Makkans.

42. This is open to the following two meanings: (i) The detractors of the Prophet Noah (peace be on him) were obliterated while only Noah's progeny has survived. (ii) Almost all the human race was removed from the scene. Only the descendants of the Prophet Noah (peace be on him) survived and later populated the world. Generally, Qur'ān-commentators prefer the latter interpretation, although the text of the Qur'ān is not explicit in this regard. God alone knows the truth. (Ibn Kathīr, *Tafsīr*, comments on verse 77).

(78) and We established for him a good name among posterity. (79) Peace be upon Noah among all the nations.[43] (80) Thus do We reward all those who do good. (81) Surely he was one of Our truly believing servants. (82) Thereafter We caused the others to be drowned.

(83) Abraham was on the self-same way (as Noah). (84) When he came to his Lord with a pure heart,[44] (85) and said to his father and his people:[45] "Whom do you worship? ▶

وَتَرَكْنَا عَلَيْهِ فِى ٱلْـَٔاخِرِينَ ﴿٧٨﴾ سَلَـٰمٌ عَلَىٰ
نُوحٍ فِى ٱلْعَـٰلَمِينَ ﴿٧٩﴾ إِنَّا كَذَٰلِكَ نَجْزِى
ٱلْمُحْسِنِينَ ﴿٨٠﴾ إِنَّهُۥ مِنْ عِبَادِنَا ٱلْمُؤْمِنِينَ ﴿٨١﴾
ثُمَّ أَغْرَقْنَا ٱلْـَٔاخَرِينَ ﴿٨٢﴾ ۞ وَإِنَّ مِن شِيعَتِهِۦ
لَإِبْرَٰهِيمَ ﴿٨٣﴾ إِذْ جَآءَ رَبَّهُۥ بِقَلْبٍ سَلِيمٍ ﴿٨٤﴾
إِذْ قَالَ لِأَبِيهِ وَقَوْمِهِۦ مَاذَا تَعْبُدُونَ ﴿٨٥﴾

43. No one who would speak ill of the Prophet Noah (peace be on him) has survived. In contrast, for thousands of years since the Flood, praise has been constantly showered on him.

44. This means that a heart free of evil motives and intentions, exclusively turns to God. Moreover, this was done with a "pure heart", that is a heart free from all errors relating to both belief and practice. This is a heart that has been purged of unbelief, polytheism, scepticism, rebellion, egotism and evil intentions; a heart free from crookedness and complexity, free from evil inclinations and vile desires, free from rancour, envy and ill-will.

45. For a detailed account of the Prophet Abraham's story see also *al-An'ām* 6:74–84; *Maryam* 19:41–50; *al-Anbiyā'* 21:51–73; *al-Shu'arā'* 26:69–89, and *al-'Ankabūt* 29:16–27.

(86) Is it false deities that you want to serve rather than Allah? (87) What do you think of the Lord of the whole Universe?"[46]

(88) Then[47] he looked carefully at the stars[48] (89) and said: "I am sick."[49] ▶

أَئِفْكًا ءَالِهَةً دُونَ ٱللَّهِ تُرِيدُونَ ﴿٨٦﴾
فَمَا ظَنُّكُم بِرَبِّ ٱلْعَـٰلَمِينَ ﴿٨٧﴾ فَنَظَرَ نَظْرَةً
فِى ٱلنُّجُومِ ﴿٨٨﴾ فَقَالَ إِنِّى سَقِيمٌ ﴿٨٩﴾

---

46. Abraham pointedly asked the unbelievers what their view of God was. Do they believe that their statues of wood and stone are His equivalents? Do they ascribe partnership to them in God's Divinity? Abraham asked them: can they really be God's associates in His attributes and authority? Do they think they can indulge in this kind of blasphemy and still escape God's Punishment?

47. This particular event is described in *al-Anbiyā'* 21:51–73 and *al-'Ankabūt* 29:16–27.

48. Ibn Abī Ḥātim quotes Qatādah, the leading Qur'ān-commentator of the generation of the Successors, that the Arabs used the expression نظر في النجوم (he looked upon the stars) in an idiomatic sense; the word *naẓar* meaning "to consider", "to ponder". Ibn Kathīr has given preference to this opinion. (Ibn Kathīr, *Tafsīr,* comments on verse 88.) Moreover, it is common knowledge that when one is seized with a question that deserves serious reflection, one tends to look up above for a while, before responding.

49. This is considered to be one of the three things about which the Prophet Abraham (peace be on him) is said to have lied during his life. Before saying so, however, it should be ascertained whether at that time Abraham was really suffering from some indisposition (as he said) or whether he merely uttered this by way of pretext. If the former is the case, he cannot be considered a liar. We have discussed this point at length in *Towards Understanding the Qur'ān, Sūrah al-Anbiyā'* 21: n. 60, Vol. V, pp. 275–277. (See also the writer's work in Urdu, *Rasā'īl wa Masā'īl*, Vol. 2, pp. 35–39.)

(90) So turning their backs, they went away from him.[50] (91) Then he went quietly to the (temple of the deities) and said: "What is the matter with you, why do you not eat?[51] (92) What is the matter with you, why do you not speak?" (93) Then he turned upon them, striking them with his right hand, (94) whereupon people came to him running.[52] (95) Abraham said to them: "Do you worship what you yourselves have carved with your own hands (96) while it is Allah Who has created you and all that you make?" ▶

فَتَوَلَّوْا۟ عَنْهُ مُدْبِرِينَ ﴿٩٠﴾ فَرَاغَ إِلَىٰٓ ءَالِهَتِهِمْ
فَقَالَ أَلَا تَأْكُلُونَ ﴿٩١﴾ مَا لَكُمْ
لَا تَنطِقُونَ ﴿٩٢﴾ فَرَاغَ عَلَيْهِمْ ضَرْبًۢا بِٱلْيَمِينِ ﴿٩٣﴾
فَأَقْبَلُوٓا۟ إِلَيْهِ يَزِفُّونَ ﴿٩٤﴾ قَالَ أَتَعْبُدُونَ
مَا تَنْحِتُونَ ﴿٩٥﴾ وَٱللَّهُ خَلَقَكُمْ وَمَا تَعْمَلُونَ ﴿٩٦﴾

---

50. This clarifies the actual situation. Apparently the members of Abraham's community were on their way to attend a fair and they presumably asked him to accompany them. Abraham, however, excused himself on the grounds of his indisposition. Since his family members accepted his excuse and left him behind it is evident that he was suffering from some kind of indisposition, maybe a cold or cough or any other ailment with such visible signs. It is this which prompted his family members to go ahead without him (see vv. 89–90).

51. This indicates that a variety of food items were placed before idols as offerings.

52. This event is described here in a summarised form. Its details feature in *Sūrah al-Anbiyā'* (*Sūrah* 21). When Abraham's people returned home they found that their idols had been demolished. They began to inquire and were told that the young Abraham used to speak ill of these idols. These people asked that Abraham be brought before them. A group of them then hastened to Abraham and brought him to the public assembly.

(97) They spoke among themselves: "Build him a pyre and then throw him into the furnace." (98) They had contrived an evil plan against him, but We abased them all.[53]

(99) Abraham said:[54] "I am going to my Lord;[55] He will guide me. ▶

قَالُواْ ٱبْنُواْ لَهُۥ بُنْيَـٰنًا فَأَلْقُوهُ فِى ٱلْجَحِيمِ ﴿٩٧﴾
فَأَرَادُواْ بِهِۦ كَيْدًا فَجَعَلْنَـٰهُمُ ٱلْأَسْفَلِينَ ﴿٩٨﴾
وَقَالَ إِنِّى ذَاهِبٌ إِلَىٰ رَبِّى سَيَهْدِينِ ﴿٩٩﴾

---

53. It is stated elsewhere in the Qur'ān that God made the fire "coolness and safety" for Abraham, (*al-Anbiyā'* 21:69 and *al-'Ankabūt* 29:24). One learns, therefore, that while the unbelievers hurled the Prophet Abraham (peace be on him) into the fire, God saw to it that he remained safe. The wording of the verse that "the unbelievers had contrived an evil plan against him, but Allah abased them all" (verse 98), cannot be considered to mean that although they had wanted to throw the Prophet Abraham (peace be on him) into the fire, they could not do so. Instead, if one reads this verse in conjunction with the verses referred to above, it clearly emerges that what they were unsuccessful in doing was burning him to death, even though they did hurl him into the fire. Abraham's miraculous survival established his inordinately exalted position and the unbelieving members of his community were publicly humiliated.

The purpose of narrating this incident is to warn the Quraysh who boasted of being Abraham's descendants. They are being told that it is not they but Muḥammad (peace be on him) who followed Abraham's way. Now, if they resort to evil designs against the Prophet Muḥammad (peace be on him) in the manner the unbelieving members of the Prophet Abraham's people once did, they too will bite the dust. They may do whatever they wish to, but in no way will they be able to thwart the mission of the Prophet Muḥammad (peace be on him).

54. After being delivered from the fire, Abraham decided to bid adieu to his homeland. He uttered the words, "I am going to my Lord" at the time of his departure.

55. Abraham's words, "I am going to my Lord", mean that he was leaving his hearth and home in God's cause. His people had turned

(100) Lord, grant me a righteous son."[56] (101) (In response to this prayer) We gave him the good news of a prudent boy;[57] (102) and when he was old enough to go about and work with him, (one day) Abraham said to him: "My son, I see in my dream that I am slaughtering you.[58] ▶

رَبِّ هَبْ لِى مِنَ ٱلصَّٰلِحِينَ ﴿١٠٠﴾ فَبَشَّرْنَٰهُ بِغُلَٰمٍ حَلِيمٍ ﴿١٠١﴾ فَلَمَّا بَلَغَ مَعَهُ ٱلسَّعْىَ قَالَ يَٰبُنَىَّ إِنِّىٓ أَرَىٰ فِى ٱلْمَنَامِ أَنِّىٓ أَذْبَحُكَ

against him on account of his exclusive devotion and allegiance to God. Also, there was no particular place to which Abraham could go. Hence, he was setting out for God's sake, and in so doing, his trust was entirely in Him. He was ready to go wherever God wanted to take him.

56. It is evident from this supplication that at that time Abraham (peace be on him) had no children of his own. It also appears from other Qur'ānic passages that he had left the country along with his wife and his nephew, Lot. In this situation the desire naturally arose within him that God grant him a righteous child whose presence would be a solace to him in this grievous state of exile.

57. This should not give rise to the misconception that this happy tiding of the birth of a son came instantly on the heels of Abraham's supplication. It appears from *Sūrah Ibrāhīm* 14:39 that it took many years before Abraham's prayer was granted. According to the Bible, the Prophet Abraham (peace be on him) was 86 years old at the time of Ishmael's birth (*Genesis* 16:16) and was 100 years old when Isaac was born (*Genesis* 21:5).

58. It is noteworthy that the Prophet Abraham (peace be on him) did not dream that he had slaughtered his son; rather, he dreamt that he was slaughtering him. He, nonetheless, interpreted this dream to mean that he was directed to slaughter his son. It was for this reason that he prepared himself to carry out that task. The subtle point that whatever happened was a part of God's plan is uncovered below in verse 105.

So consider (and tell me) what you think."[59] He said: "Do as you are bidden.[60] You will find me, if Allah so wills, among the steadfast." (103) When both surrendered (to Allah's command) and Abraham flung the son down on his forehead,[61] (104) We cried out:[62] ▶

فَٱنظُرْ مَاذَا تَرَىٰ ۚ قَالَ يَـٰٓأَبَتِ ٱفْعَلْ مَا تُؤْمَرُ ۖ
سَتَجِدُنِىٓ إِن شَآءَ ٱللَّهُ مِنَ ٱلصَّـٰبِرِينَ ﴿١٠٢﴾
فَلَمَّآ أَسْلَمَا وَتَلَّهُۥ لِلْجَبِينِ ﴿١٠٣﴾ وَنَـٰدَيْنَـٰهُ

59. Abraham did not mention his dream to his son in order to seek the latter's consent to carry out God's command. Instead, he wanted to ascertain how righteous his son was. It is significant that Abraham's prayer to God was to grant him "a righteous child". The latter's willingness to be slaughtered indicated that his prayer had been granted in full. Ishmael was thus not only his son in a biological sense, but was also a true descendant of Abraham in moral and spiritual terms.

60. It is clear from Ishmael's words that he took his father's dream to be an indication of God's command. Had this indeed not been God's command, the Qur'ān would have indicated, whether explicitly or implicitly, that this was a misunderstanding. But there is nothing to show that this was a misunderstanding. This explains the Islamic doctrine that a Prophet's dream is one mode of revelation. Had the Prophet Abraham (peace be on him) erred in grasping the import of his dream, God would have corrected him. It is impossible for anyone who believes the Qur'ān to be the Word of God to accept that God can commit such lapses.

61. Just as the Prophet Abraham (peace be on him) was about to undertake the slaughter, he placed his son with his face downwards. He did so because he did not wish to look at his son's face lest out of overwhelming affection, his hand might falter while he was slaughtering him.

62. Concerning verses 103–104, some grammarians are of the opinion that the letter "*wa*" (in v. 104) means "then" rather than "and". Thus the verses in question: "When both surrendered (to Allah's command) and Abraham flung his son down on the forehead, then We cried out: 'O Abraham ...'"

"O Abraham, (105) you have indeed fulfilled your dream.[63] Thus do We reward the good-doers."[64] (106) This was indeed a plain trial.[65] ▶

أَن يَـٰٓإِبْرَٰهِيمُ ﴿١٠٤﴾ قَدْ صَدَّقْتَ ٱلرُّءْيَآ ۚ إِنَّا
كَذَٰلِكَ نَجْزِى ٱلْمُحْسِنِينَ ﴿١٠٥﴾ إِنَّ هَـٰذَا
لَهُوَ ٱلْبَلَـٰٓؤُا۟ ٱلْمُبِينُ ﴿١٠٦﴾

Other grammarians, however, contest this interpretation. They are of the opinion that the answer to *lammā* (when) in verse 103 is omitted and has been left to the understanding of the reader. (Rāzī, *al-Tafsīr al-Kabīr,* comments on verse 104). The matter was of such tremendous proportions that rather than verbally express it, it was better left to the audience's imagination. In other words, God witnessed how readily the age-stricken father had agreed to slaughter his own son whose birth he had sought so fervently, and the son also expressed his full readiness to be slaughtered for God's pleasure. One can imagine how strongly this would have aroused God's mercy and compassion for both Abraham and his son; how the loyalty of both of them would have endeared them to God. This too is better left to the imagination rather than stated in words, for words can never do full justice to it.

63. In his dream Abraham had seen himself slaughtering his son, but not that he had slaughtered him. So, when he had made all preparations for that act, God treated this as indicating that the actual object of the dream had been fulfilled. God's purpose was not to take Ishmael's life, but to ascertain the readiness of Abraham and Ishmael to do His will.

64. God does not put His righteous servants to test with a view to subjecting them to unnecessary hardship. Rather, these tests are meant to bring out their latent excellence and to help them attain higher ranks. Also, God sees to it that they are safely rescued from the hardships in which they are placed. The Prophet Abraham's readiness to sacrifice his son was sufficient for the bestowal of an exalted rank on him, one which would normally have only been granted to him after the performance of the act itself.

65. God did not want the Prophet Abraham (peace be on him) to slaughter his son. The purpose of the test was to ascertain whether Abraham held God's pleasure dearer than everything else, including his son.

(107) And We ransomed him with a mighty sacrifice,[66] (108) and We preserved for him a good name among posterity. (109) Peace be upon Abraham. (110) Thus do We reward the good-doers. (111) Surely he was one of Our believing servants. (112) And We gave him the good news of Isaac, a Prophet and among the righteous ones. (113) And We blessed him and Isaac.[67] ▶

وَفَدَيْنَـٰهُ بِذِبْحٍ عَظِيمٍ ﴿١٠٧﴾ وَتَرَكْنَا عَلَيْهِ
فِى ٱلْـَٔاخِرِينَ ﴿١٠٨﴾ سَلَـٰمٌ عَلَىٰٓ إِبْرَٰهِيمَ ﴿١٠٩﴾
كَذَٰلِكَ نَجْزِى ٱلْمُحْسِنِينَ ﴿١١٠﴾ إِنَّهُۥ مِنْ
عِبَادِنَا ٱلْمُؤْمِنِينَ ﴿١١١﴾ وَبَشَّرْنَـٰهُ بِإِسْحَـٰقَ
نَبِيًّا مِّنَ ٱلصَّـٰلِحِينَ ﴿١١٢﴾ وَبَـٰرَكْنَا عَلَيْهِ
وَعَلَىٰٓ إِسْحَـٰقَ ۚ

66. The reference here is to the ram, which according to both Islamic and Biblical sources, was made available to Abraham in order that it be sacrificed instead of his son. This is referred to as "the great sacrifice" in so far as it served as the ransom to preserve the son of God's obedient servant, Abraham. God made that ram the means for an unprecedented sacrifice. This incident is also known as "the great sacrifice" because God prescribed that believers should henceforth offer animal sacrifice and commemorate this great example of loyalty and selfless allegiance to Him.

67. One is faced here with the question of determining as to who was that son of the Prophet Abraham, he whom he wanted to sacrifice and who readily accepted to be sacrificed.

> ... God tested Abraham and said to him, "Abraham! Take your son, your only son Isaac, whom you love, and go to the land of Moriah, and offer him there as a burnt offering upon one of the mountains of which I shall tell you", (*Genesis* 22:1–2).

This passage specifies Isaac and declares him to be the only son of the Prophet Abraham (peace be on him). At other places, however, the Bible speaks of a second son of Abraham as well. Let us consider the following Biblical passages as illustrative:

> Now Sarai, Abram's wife, bore him no children. She had an Egyptian maid whose name was Hagar; and Sarai said to Abram, "Behold now, the Lord has prevented me from bearing children, go in to my maid; it may be that I shall obtain children by her." And Abram hearkened to the voice of Sarai. So, after Abram had dwelt ten years in the land of Canaan, Sarai, Abram's wife, took Hagar the Egyptian, her maid, and gave her to Abram her husband as wife. And he went in to Hagar, and she conceived ... (*Genesis* 16:1–4).
>
> And the angel of the Lord said to Hagar, "Behold, you are with child, and shall bear a son; you shall call his name Ishmael". (*Genesis* 16:11).
>
> Abram was eighty-six years old when Hagar bore Ishmael to Abram, (*Genesis* 16:16).
>
> And God said to Abram, "As for Sarai, your wife, ... I will give you a son by her; ... and you shall call his name Isaac ... Sarah shall bear to you Isaac at this season next year" ... Then Abraham took Ishmael his son and every male among the men of Abraham's house and he circumcised the flesh of their foreskins that very day, as God had said to him. Abraham was ninety-nine years old when he was circumcised in the flesh of his foreskin. And Ishmael his son was thirteen years old when he was circumcised in the flesh of his foreskin. (*Genesis* 17:15–25).
>
> Abraham was a hundred years old when his son Isaac was born to him. (*Genesis* 21:5).

These Biblical passages betray inner contradictions. For 14 years, Ishmael was the only son of Abraham (peace be on him). If God had asked him to offer his only son, then this could only refer to Ishmael; for then he was his only son. Had God's intent been that Isaac be the offering, the insistence on the only son would be incongruous.

However, even the traditions in the Islamic sources on this question are characterised by serious contradictions. The traditions narrated by Qur'ān-commentators on the authority of Companions and Successors show considerable disagreement. One group of commentators, for example, affirms, on the basis of reports narrated by Companions and Successors, that it was Isaac who was earmarked for the sacrifice. To this group belong 'Umar, 'Alī, 'Abd Allāh ibn Mas'ūd, 'Abbās ibn 'Abd al-Muṭṭalib, 'Abd Allāh ibn 'Abbās, Abū Hurayrah, Qatādah, 'Ikrimah,

Ḥasan al-Baṣrī, Sa'īd ibn Jubayr, Sha'bī, Masrūq, Makḥūl, Zuhrī, 'Aṭā', Muqātil, Suddī, Ka'b al-Aḥbār and Zayd ibn Aslam.

Another group, however, asserts that it was Ishmael who was marked for the sacrifice. Notable authorities of this group are Abū Bakr, 'Alī, 'Abd Allāh ibn 'Umar, 'Abd Allāh ibn 'Abbās, Abū Hurayrah, Mu'āwiyah, 'Ikrimah, Mujāhid, Yūsuf ibn Mahrān, Ḥasan al-Baṣrī, Muḥammad ibn Ka'b al-Quraẓī, Sha'bī, Sa'īd ibn al-Musayyib, Ḍaḥḥāk, Muḥammad ibn 'Alī ibn al-Ḥusayn (Muḥammad al-Bāqir), Rabī' ibn Anas and Aḥmad ibn Ḥanbal.

When we compare the names in the two lists, we find that some names feature in both of them. In other words, at times two opposite views are ascribed to the same people. According to 'Ikrimah, 'Abd Allāh ibn 'Abbās identified Isaac on this count. 'Aṭā' ibn Abī Rabāḥ, however, credits the same 'Abd Allāh ibn 'Abbās with the following statement: "The Jews contend that it was Isaac; but the Jews lied". Likewise, Ḥasan al-Baṣrī appears in a report supporting the view that Isaac was the one who was to be sacrificed. On the contrary, in another report, 'Amr ibn 'Ubayd declares that Ḥasan al-Baṣrī wholly subscribed to the view that it was Ishmael whom the Prophet Abraham (peace be on him) was asked to sacrifice.

As a result of this disagreement, Muslim scholars stand divided into two camps. Ibn Jābir, Qāḍī 'Iyāḍ and some others are of the firm view that Isaac was the intended offering. Ibn Kathīr, Jalāl al-Dīn al-Suyūṭī and some others appear undecided on the issue. In contrast, some scholars emphatically declare that Ishmael was the intended offering. A scrutiny of the whole issue, however, leads one to the view that beyond any shadow of doubt God's command to the Prophet Abraham (peace be on him) was to sacrifice Ishmael. This view rests on the following pieces of evidence:

i. As already noted, while migrating from his home town the Prophet Abraham (peace be on him) had prayed to God that he be blessed with a righteous son. In response, God gave him the glad tidings of the birth of a forbearing son. It is clear from the context that at the time he prayed he did not have a child. These tidings, therefore, relate to the birth of his first child. It also emerges from the context that Abraham was directed to present the same son as an offering. That Ishmael was his first son is indisputable. The Qur'ān speaks of his sons in the following order: "Abraham said: ... All praise be to Allah Who, despite my old age, has given me Ishmael and Isaac". (*Ibrāhīm* 14:39.)

ii. All the Qur'ānic references to Isaac designate him as a "knowledgeable son". Instances in point are as follows: "They [the angels] announced to him (Abraham) the good news of (the birth of) a boy endowed with knowledge", (*al-Dhāriyāt* 51:28). They (the angels) said: "We give you (O Abraham) the good news of a wise boy", (*al-Ḥijr* 15:53). When the Qur'ān speaks of Ishmael, he is mentioned as a forbearing boy (see *al-Ṣāffāt* 37:101). The two sons thus had qualities distinct from each other. The Qur'ānic command to sacrifice was meant for the "forbearing boy", that is, Ishmael, rather than for the boy "endowed with knowledge", that is, Isaac.

iii. While giving the good news about Isaac's birth, the Qur'ān also gave the good news of the birth of a son to him called Jacob: "We gave her (Abraham's wife) the good news of (the birth of) Isaac, and after Isaac, of Jacob", (*Hūd* 11:71). Thus the situation was the following: Abraham was given the tidings that a son (Isaac) would be born to him and that a worthy son (Jacob) would be born to Isaac. Then Abraham (peace be on him) was shown in a vision that he was sacrificing his son. In the circumstance it would be well nigh impossible for Abraham to conclude that he was being asked to offer Isaac as a sacrifice. Ibn Jarīr al-Ṭabarī explains his viewpoint about the matter by saying that possibly Abraham had that vision after Jacob was born to Isaac. This, however, is a very tenuous contention. For the Qur'ān states that the Prophet Abraham's dream belongs to the period when his son had become "old enough to go about and work with him", (*al-Ṣāffāt* 37:102). Anyone who pays an unbiased attention to this will consider it to refer to a young, say eight or ten year old boy, rather than to a fully grown adult who had already fathered a child.

iv. After narrating this whole account the Qur'ān concludes with the observation: "And We gave him the good news of Isaac, a Prophet and among the righteous ones", (*al-Ṣāffāt* 37:112). This, once again, establishes that Isaac was not to be sacrificed. Rather, the glad tiding about another son had been given earlier, and as he grew old enough to go about and work, God directed Abraham that he be sacrificed. After the Prophet Abraham (peace be on him) had successfully passed the test to which he was put, the good news of the birth of another son was given to him.

This sequence of events makes it clear that Isaac was not the son intended for the sacrifice. Rather, the allusion was to Ishmael who had been born 14 years earlier. Ibn Jarīr al-Ṭabarī dismisses this sequence of events, saying that the glad tidings related to Isaac's birth. Also, as he expressed his readiness to be sacrificed in order to obtain God's pleasure, he was rewarded with the conferment of the Messenger's office. This, however, is an even less convincing and less plausible statement than the one already cited. Had Isaac been the intended offering, the Qur'ān would not have said: "And We gave him the good news of Isaac, a Prophet and among the righteous ones", (v. 112). Rather, it would have been mentioned: "And We gave him the good news that this son of yours will be a Prophet among the righteous ones".

v. Authentic reports indicate that the horns of the ram which was slaughtered as a ransom for Ishmael were preserved inside the Ka'bah up to the days of 'Abd Allāh ibn al-Zubayr. At a later date, when Ḥajjāj ibn Yūsuf laid siege on 'Abd Allāh ibn al-Zubayr inside the Ka'bah and demolished it, these horns were lost. Both 'Abd Allāh ibn 'Abbās and Sha'bī testify that they saw these horns inside the Ka'bah. (Ibn Kathīr, *Tafsīr,* comments on verses 107–113). This also proves that the offering was made in Makkah, not in Syria, and that it was Ishmael who was to be sacrificed. That is why this relic was befittingly preserved within the precincts of the Ka'bah, which had been built by the Prophets Abraham and Ishmael (peace be on them).

vi. The Arabs have held on to the belief down the ages that the event of the offering took place in Minā. This was far from being a mere report. Since the time of the event till the life-time of the Prophet Muḥammad (peace be on him), the Arabs used to sacrifice their animals, as one of their pilgrimage rites. They did this at the spot where the Prophet Abraham (peace be on him) had made the offering. This rite was retained as part of *Ḥajj* by the Prophet Muḥammad (peace be on him). Up to this day, millions of pilgrims sacrifice their animals in Minā. This practice, for more than four and a half thousand years, conclusively establishes that Ishmael was the intended offering. Significantly, no such rite is performed by Isaac's descendants. Furthermore, Ishmael's people have observed this practice for centuries in order to commemorate the offering that involved the Prophets Abraham and Ishmael (peace be on them). (Ibn Kathīr, *Tafsīr,* comments on verses 107–113, *Faṣl fī Dhikr al-Āthār al-Wāridah 'an al-Salaf fī anna al-Dhabīḥ man huwa?;* Ṭabarī, *Tafsīr,* comments on verse 107.)

In the face of these incontrovertible pieces of evidence it is astonishing how even some Muslims entertained the idea that Isaac was the intended offering. The Jewish insistence on conferring this honour

Among the offspring of the two some did good and some plainly wronged themselves.[68]	وَمِن ذُرِّيَّتِهِمَا مُحْسِنٌ وَظَالِمٌ لِّنَفْسِهِۦ مُبِينٌ ﴿١١٣﴾

on their progenitor, Isaac, is understandable. However, it defies one's understanding why so many Muslims endorsed this Jewish claim. Ibn Kathīr offers the following answer to this intriguing question:

> The truth is known to God alone. Nonetheless, it appears that all the reports identifying Isaac as the intended offering have originated from Ka'b al-Aḥbār. When he embraced Islam during Caliph 'Umar's era, he occasionally narrated to the Caliph passages from the Jewish and Christian Scriptures. Others [that is, other Companions] too, received similar reports from him, irrespective of their authenticity. The Muslims did not stand in need of any report from these sources. (Ibn Kathīr, *Tafsīr,* comments on verses 107–113, *Faṣl fī Dhikr al-Āthār al-Wāridah 'an al-Salaf fī anna al-Dhabīḥ man huwa?*)

The issue is further elaborated in a report on the authority of Muḥammad ibn Ka'b al-Quraẓī. He states:

> There was discussion at the court of Caliph 'Umar ibn 'Abd al-'Azīz on the issue as to who was the intended offering: Isaac or Ishmael. Among those present there was a devout Muslim who had converted from Judaism to Islam. He remarked: "O Commander of the Faithful! By God, it was Ishmael. This fact is well known to the Jews. However, swayed by their jealousy towards the Arabs, they confer this honour upon Isaac". (Ṭabarī, *Tafsīr*, comments on verse 107.)

In sum, it was as a result of Jewish propaganda that some Muslims bought the story of Isaac being the intended offering. Since the Muslims were unbiased on these academic issues, they uncritically accepted false reports paraded by the Jews as scriptural statements. They failed to discern the Jewish ploy permeating such reports.

68. This brings out the lesson inherent in the Prophet Abraham's story. Two major communities emerged from the Prophet Abraham's two sons. One of them were the Children of Israel among whom there emerged two major religions – Judaism and Christianity. The other were

(114) Verily We bestowed Our favours on Moses and Aaron (115) and We delivered both of them and their people from the great calamity.[69] (116) We succoured them, and they gained the upper hand (against their enemies). (117) We granted them a Clear Book, (118) and showed them the Straight Way, (119) and preserved for them a good name among posterity. (120) Peace be upon Moses and Aaron. (121) Thus do We reward the good-doers. (122) Surely both of them were among Our believing servants.

وَلَقَدْ مَنَنَّا عَلَىٰ مُوسَىٰ وَهَـٰرُونَ ﴿١١٤﴾
وَنَجَّيْنَـٰهُمَا وَقَوْمَهُمَا مِنَ ٱلْكَرْبِ
ٱلْعَظِيمِ ﴿١١٥﴾ وَنَصَرْنَـٰهُمْ فَكَانُوا۟ هُمُ
ٱلْغَـٰلِبِينَ ﴿١١٦﴾ وَءَاتَيْنَـٰهُمَا ٱلْكِتَـٰبَ
ٱلْمُسْتَبِينَ ﴿١١٧﴾ وَهَدَيْنَـٰهُمَا ٱلصِّرَٰطَ
ٱلْمُسْتَقِيمَ ﴿١١٨﴾ وَتَرَكْنَا عَلَيْهِمَا فِى
ٱلْـَٔاخِرِينَ ﴿١١٩﴾ سَلَـٰمٌ عَلَىٰ مُوسَىٰ
وَهَـٰرُونَ ﴿١٢٠﴾ إِنَّا كَذَٰلِكَ نَجْزِى
ٱلْمُحْسِنِينَ ﴿١٢١﴾ إِنَّهُمَا مِنْ عِبَادِنَا
ٱلْمُؤْمِنِينَ ﴿١٢٢﴾

---

the Children of Ishmael. At the time the Qur'ān was revealed, they were considered the leaders of the whole of Arabia. Among them were the Quraysh of Makkah, who occupied a pre-eminent position in the whole of Arabia. After relating this most important event in the history of this family, God reminds them that they were exalted to great heights. This was in recognition of their godliness, sincerity and submission to God, as exemplified by their ancestors – the Prophets Abraham, Ishmael and Isaac (peace be on them). God endowed His bounties on them according to His plan. This was not a haphazard bestowal of His grace. The descendants of these Prophets cannot lay claim to the endowment of the same favours simply because of their blood ties with their ancestors. Rather, God will test them as to whether they are righteous or wrong-doers and He will treat them accordingly.

69. In other words, their deliverance from the great calamity they suffered at the hands of Pharaoh and his people.

(123) Surely, Elias too was among the Messengers.[70] (124) (Call to mind) when he said to his people: "Will you not fear Allah? ▶

وَإِنَّ إِلۡيَاسَ لَمِنَ ٱلۡمُرۡسَلِينَ ﴿١٢٣﴾ إِذۡ قَالَ
لِقَوۡمِهِۦٓ أَلَا تَتَّقُونَ ﴿١٢٤﴾

---

70. The Prophet Elias/Elijah was raised among the Children of Israel. His name occurs at only two places in the Qur'ān – in the present verse and in *Sūrah al-An'ām* 6:85. Scholars of the present time believe that he flourished between 875–850 B.C. He hailed from Gilead which is now part of the northern districts of Jordan and lies to the south of the Yarmūk River. In the Bible, he is referred to as Elijah the Tishbite. Here is a brief account of the Prophet Elias/Elijah as gleaned from the Bible.

After the Prophet Solomon's death, his son, Rehoboam proved incompetent in handling the affairs of the kingdom with the result that it split into two. One part of the kingdom, which comprised Jerusalem and southern Palestine, fell under the control of the Prophet David's descendants. The other, comprising northern Palestine, emerged as an independent state called Israel, with Samaria as its capital. Although both states were plagued with problems, Israel's orientation from the very beginning was perverted. As a result, it became inundated with polytheism and idolatry, tyranny and oppression, sin and wickedness. When King Ahab married Jezebel, daughter of the king of Sidon (located in present-day Lebanon), this marked the lowest ebb in its history. For, under the evil influence of his polytheistic wife, Jezebel, King Ahab also succumbed to polytheism. He built a temple and an altar devoted to Ba'al in Samaria and spared no effort in promoting the worship of Ba'al instead of the One True God. Offerings dedicated to Ba'al were made publicly throughout the kingdom.

This was the time when the Prophet Elias/Elijah (peace be on him) appeared on the scene. He arrived in Samaria from Gilead and warned Ahab that his kingdom would not receive any rainfall as a punishment for his outrageous misdeeds, so much so that his land would even be deprived of dew-drops. This warning, issued by a Prophet of God, came true. For more than three years there was no rainfall in the kingdom. This brought Ahab back to his senses and he sent for Elias/Elijah. Before praying to God for rainfall, however, Elias/Elijah gathered people together in an assembly with a view to helping them discern the tremendous difference between the Lord of the universe and Ba'al. Accordingly, he asked the devotees of Ba'al to present an offering to their deity in that assembly whereas he would dedicate his offering to the One True Lord. Then, he proposed the following test: whichever of the two offerings was consumed by fire from on high, without any human intervention, would be deemed to be true. Ahab accepted the test. Accordingly, 850 priests, who owed allegiance to Ba'al, assembled at Mount Carmel. This test was held in a public gathering of Israelites, marking the encounter between the worshippers of Ba'al and the Prophet Elias/Elijah (peace be on him). In this test, Ba'al's devotees were thoroughly exposed and disgraced because the Prophet Elias/Elijah (peace be on him) publicly demonstrated that Ba'al was a false god. This event also established the truth of the One True Lord and of Elias'/Elijah's credentials as God's Messenger. In the same assembly he had Ba'al's worshippers put to the sword and then prayed to God for rainfall. His prayer was readily answered. The whole kingdom of Israel was subsequently blessed with rain.

Even after witnessing these miracles, Ahab was still under the sway of his idolatrous wife. She became so hostile towards the Prophet Elias/Elijah (peace be on him) that she vowed to have him killed, just as the devotees of Ba'al had been put to death. The Prophet Elias/Elijah (peace be on him), therefore, had to leave Israel and take refuge in a cave in Mount Sinai for several years. His plight is reflected in his supplication, as recorded in the Bible:

> The people of Israel have forsaken thy covenant, thrown down thy altars, and slain thy Prophets with the sword; and I, even I only, am left; and they seek my life, to take it away. (I *Kings* 19:10.)

During the same period, Jehoram, the ruler of the Jewish state of Jerusalem, married the daughter of Ahab, the King of Israel. This led to the spread of polytheism and idolatry in Jerusalem as well. The Prophet Elias/Elijah (peace be on him) warned against this evil as a part of his Prophetic mission. He wrote, for example, the following letter to Jehoram, admonishing him:

> Thus says the Lord, the God of David your father, 'Because you have not walked in the ways of Jehoshaphat your father, or in the ways of Asa, King of Judah, but have walked in the ways of the kings of Israel, and have led Judah and the inhabitants of Jerusalem into unfaithfulness, just as the house of Ahab led Israel into unfaithfulness, and also you have killed your brothers, of your father's house, who were better than yourself; behold, the Lord will bring a great plague on your people, your children, your wives, and all your possessions, and you yourself will have a severe sickness

(125) Do you call upon Baal[71] and forsake the Best of the Creators? (126) Allah is your Lord and the Lord of your ancestors of yore." ▶

أَتَدْعُونَ بَعْلًا وَتَذَرُونَ أَحْسَنَ ٱلْخَـٰلِقِينَ ﴿١٢٥﴾ ٱللَّهَ رَبَّكُمْ وَرَبَّ ءَابَآئِكُمُ ٱلْأَوَّلِينَ ﴿١٢٦﴾

> with a disease of your bowels, until your bowels come out because of the disease, day by day. (2 *Chronicles* 21:12–15.)

All that this letter forewarned came true. First, Jehoram's kingdom was destroyed as a result of invasions. Even Jehoram's wives were taken captives. At a later date, Jehoram died, suffering from a disease of the bowels.

Later on, the Prophet Elias/Elijah (peace be on him) returned to Israel and tried his level best to direct Ahab and his son, Ahaziab, to the Straight Way. They were, however, too deeply steeped in iniquity to pay any attention to his call. Eventually, Elias'/Elijah's curse also brought an end to the state of Israel. It was at this juncture that God recalled him from the world. (For further details of the events relating to the Prophet Elias/Elijah (peace be on him), see 1 *Kings* 17–19 and 21; 2 *Kings* 1–2, and 2 *Chronicles* 21.)

71. Literally, Ba'al means "master". It is also used for husband. This expression features in the last-mentioned sense in the Qur'ān itself. (Instances in point are: *al-Baqarah* 2:228; *al-Nisā'* 4:127; *Hūd* 11:72, and *al-Nūr* 24:31.) Ancient Semitic nations, however, used this word as a synonym for God. They designated a certain idol as Ba'al. Special mention in this context should be made of the Phoenicians, the inhabitants of Lebanon. Ba'al and his spouse Ash'taroth were taken by them respectively as their chief god and goddess. Scholars differ in identifying Ba'al with either the Sun or Jupiter and Ash'taroth with either the Moon or Venus. What is, nonetheless, on record is that Ba'al worship had been in vogue from Babylonia to Egypt, virtually encompassing the whole of the Middle East. Polytheistic communities living in Lebanon, Syria and Palestine were prominent in their devotion of Ba'al. After migrating from Egypt, the Israelites settled in Palestine and Trans-Jordan. In defiance of the stringent prohibitions contained in the Torah they engaged in inter-marriages with members of the polytheistic communities of the region. As a result, they took to idolatry. According to the Bible, moral and religious

(127) But they denounced him as a liar, so they will surely be arraigned (for punishment), (128) except Allah's chosen servants.[72] (129) We preserved a good name for him among posterity.[73] ▶

فَكَذَّبُوهُ فَإِنَّهُمْ لَمُحْضَرُونَ ﴿١٢٧﴾ إِلَّا عِبَادَ اللَّهِ الْمُخْلَصِينَ ﴿١٢٨﴾ وَتَرَكْنَا عَلَيْهِ فِي الْآخِرِينَ ﴿١٢٩﴾

---

decline afflicted the Israelites soon after the death of Joshua, the Prophet Moses' successor:

> And the people of Israel did what was evil in the sight of the Lord, and served the Ba'als ... They forsook the Lord, and served the Ba'als and the Ash'taroth. (*Judges* 2:11–13.)
>
> So the people of Israel dwelt among the Canaanites, the Hittites, the Amorites, the Per'izzites, the Hivites, and Jeb'usites; and they took their daughters to themselves for wives, and their own daughters they gave to their sons; and they served their gods. (*Judges* 3:3–6.)

Ba'al worship was so rampant at the time that an altar dedicated to Ba'al was erected in one of their towns where animal sacrifices were made. When a pious Israelite saw this he could not contain his anger and demolished the altar in the darkness of night. The next morning a huge crowd assembled there, demanding the beheading of the Israelite who had so destroyed their centre of idolatry, (*Judges* 6:25–32). Eventually Samuel, Saul and the Prophets David and Solomon (peace be on them) managed to put an end to this sad state of affairs. Not only did they reform the recalcitrant Israelites, but also suppressed polytheism and idolatry in their kingdom. After the Prophet Solomon's death, polytheistic practices again resurfaced among the Israelites. Ba'al worship was particularly pronounced in northern Palestine, which formed part of the kingdom of Israel.

72. Only those who did not give the lie to the Prophet Elias/Elijah (peace be on him) and who were chosen by God from among that nation to serve Him were to be spared the punishment.

73. We have already noted to what extent the Children of Israel persecuted the Prophet Elias/Elijah (peace be on him). Subsequently,

(130) Peace be upon Elias.[74] (131) Thus do We reward the good-doers. ▶	سَلَـٰمٌ عَلَىٰٓ إِلْ يَاسِينَ ﴿١٣٠﴾ إِنَّا كَذَٰلِكَ نَجْزِى ٱلْمُحْسِنِينَ ﴿١٣١﴾

however, their attitude towards him changed altogether and they began to hold him in unusual esteem and respect. Other than Moses, they hardly held anyone in such high esteem. They believe that he was raised alive to the heavens by a whirlwind, (2 *Kings* 2). They also maintain that he will return to this world. The following Biblical passage throws further light on Jewish popular beliefs about him:

> Behold, I will send you Elijah the Prophet before the great and terrible day of the Lord comes. (*Malachi* 4:5.)

Essentially, the Jews looked forward to the advent of the following three: (i) Elias/Elijah, (ii) the Christ, and (iii) the Prophet (that is, the Prophet Muḥammad). As John the Baptist (peace be on him) embarked upon his Prophetic mission and baptised people, Jewish rabbis asked him:

> "Who are you? Are you the Christ?" He confessed, "I am not the Christ." And they asked him, "What then? Are you Elijah?" He said, "I am not." "Are you the Prophet?" And he answered, "No." They asked him, "Then why are you baptizing, if you are neither the Christ, nor Elijah, nor the Prophet?" (*John* 1:19–25.)

When the Prophet Jesus (peace be on him) launched his mission, the Jews thought that the Prophet Elias/Elijah (peace be on him) had reappeared (*Mark* 6:14–15). Even some disciples of the Prophet Jesus (peace be on him) had looked forward to Elias'/Elijah's advent. The Prophet Jesus (peace be on him) removed their misunderstanding, telling them that Elias/Elijah had already appeared, though few recognised him. He also informed them about John the Baptist, urging them not to mistake him for Elijah who had appeared 800 years earlier. (*Matthew* 11:14 and 17:10–13.)

74. The actual words are سلام على إل ياسين (Peace be upon Elias). Some Qur'ān-commentators consider Ilyāsīn as another name for the Prophet Elias/Elijah, in the same way that another name for Abraham was Abram. Other scholars, however, point out that it represents only a variant form of the same Hebrew name. They also point out that some Hebrew names

(132) He was one of Our believing servants.

(133) And Lot too was one of the Messengers. (134) (Call to mind) when We delivered him and all his kinsfolk, (135) except for an old woman who was among those that stayed behind.[75] (136) Then We utterly destroyed the rest of them. (137) You pass by their desolate habitations in the morning (138) and at night.[76] Do you still not understand?

(139) And Jonah too was one of the Messengers.[77] ▶

إِنَّهُۥ مِنْ عِبَادِنَا ٱلْمُؤْمِنِينَ ﴿١٣٢﴾ وَإِنَّ لُوطًا لَّمِنَ
ٱلْمُرْسَلِينَ ﴿١٣٣﴾ إِذْ نَجَّيْنَٰهُ وَأَهْلَهُۥٓ أَجْمَعِينَ ﴿١٣٤﴾
إِلَّا عَجُوزًا فِى ٱلْغَٰبِرِينَ ﴿١٣٥﴾ ثُمَّ دَمَّرْنَا
ٱلْءَاخَرِينَ ﴿١٣٦﴾ وَإِنَّكُمْ لَتَمُرُّونَ عَلَيْهِم
مُّصْبِحِينَ ﴿١٣٧﴾ وَبِٱلَّيْلِ ۚ أَفَلَا تَعْقِلُونَ ﴿١٣٨﴾ وَإِنَّ
يُونُسَ لَمِنَ ٱلْمُرْسَلِينَ ﴿١٣٩﴾

---

were variously pronounced by the Arabs. The same angel, for instance, was known by three different names: Mīkāl, Mīkā'īl and Mīkā'īn. The same happened with the Prophet Elias/Elijah. In the Qur'ān itself we find the same mountain mentioned both as Ṭūr Sīnā and Ṭūr Sīnīn. (Ibn Kathīr, *Tafsīr,* comments on verse 120.)

75. This allusion is to the Prophet Lot's wife. She did not accompany her husband and preferred to stay behind with her people. Accordingly, she was seized by God's scourge.

76. The Quraysh traders always passed through this same region in the course of their trade journeys to Syria and Palestine. The ruins of the Prophet Lot's towns were located on the highway.

77. This represents the third instance in which the Prophet Jonah (peace be on him) is mentioned in the Qur'ān. Reference to him also

(140) Call to mind when he fled to the laden ship,[78] (141) cast lots, and was among the losers. (142) Then a fish swallowed him, and he was blameworthy.[79] (143) Had he not been one of those who glorify Allah,[80] ▶

إِذْ أَبَقَ إِلَى ٱلْفُلْكِ ٱلْمَشْحُونِ ﴿١٤٠﴾ فَسَاهَمَ فَكَانَ مِنَ ٱلْمُدْحَضِينَ ﴿١٤١﴾ فَٱلْتَقَمَهُ ٱلْحُوتُ وَهُوَ مُلِيمٌ ﴿١٤٢﴾ فَلَوْلَآ أَنَّهُۥ كَانَ مِنَ ٱلْمُسَبِّحِينَ ﴿١٤٣﴾

---

occurs in *Sūrahs Yūnus* and *al-Anbiyā'*. (See *Towards Understanding the Qur'ān, Yūnus* 10: nn. 98–100, Vol. IV, pp. 66–68, and *al-Anbiyā'* 21: nn. 82–85, Vol. V, p. 292.)

78. The word *abaqa* is used in Arabic to denote a slave who runs away from his master. The word *ibāq*, according to *Lisān al-'Arab*, means: الإباق: هرب العبد من سيده "*ibāq* means a slave's running away from his master" (*Lisān al-'Arab*, q.v. *abq*).

79. Were we to consider verses 139 and 148 together it would be clear that the following is what happened: (i) When the Prophet Jonah (peace be on him) boarded the ship, it was already loaded beyond its capacity. (ii) Most probably when it was realised that this overloading posed a serious threat to the lives of all passengers, lots were drawn to cast someone over-board so as to shed the load. (iii) The Prophet Jonah's name appeared in this lot and consequently he was thrown into the sea and was swallowed by a fish. (iv) Jonah faced this plight because he had left his station without God's leave. Let us bring to mind the use of the term *abaqa* with regard to him, a term whose meaning we have explained in n. 78 above. The use of the expression *mulīm* reinforces that sense as it denotes a guilty person who deserves to be reproached, irrespective of whether he is actually reproached or not. (يقال قد الام الرجل إذا أتى ما يلام عليه من الأمر و إن لم يلم) Ṭabarī, *Tafsīr*, comments on verse 142.)

80. This carries two meanings and both are intended: (i) The Prophet Jonah (peace be on him) even beforehand was one of those who constantly remembered God. (ii) When he entered the belly of the fish, he turned only to God and glorified Him. This comes out sharply from the following

(144) he would certainly have remained in its belly till the Day of Resurrection.[81] (145) But We threw him on a wide bare tract of land while he was ill;[82] (146) and caused a gourd tree[83] to grow over him, ▶

لَلَبِثَ فِي بَطْنِهِۦٓ إِلَىٰ يَوْمِ يُبْعَثُونَ ۝١٤٤ ۞ فَنَبَذْنَٰهُ بِٱلْعَرَآءِ وَهُوَ سَقِيمٌ ۝١٤٥ وَأَنۢبَتْنَا عَلَيْهِ شَجَرَةً مِّن يَقْطِينٍ ۝١٤٦

Qur'ānic passage: "Eventually he cried out in the darkness: 'There is no god but You. Glory be to You. I have done wrong'", (*al-Anbiyā'* 21:87).

81. This does not mean that the fish would have remained alive till the Day of Resurrection and that Jonah would have remained in the belly of that fish. What it really means is that the belly of the fish would have been Jonah's grave till the Day of Resurrection. The famous Qur'ān-commentator Qatādah interpreted the verse to mean so, (Ṭabarī, *Tafsīr*, comments on verse 144).

82. When the Prophet Jonah (peace be on him) admitted his lapse and engaged in God's glorification as a true believer, at God's behest the fish cast him onto the coast. The coast was a level plane, without any vegetation. Some pseudo-rationalists contend that it is impossible for anyone to come out alive from a fish's belly. However, exactly the same kind of incident took place in a coastal town in England, the centre of pseudo-rationalists! A group of fishermen went into the deep seas in August 1891 on the ship "Star of the East" to hunt whales. They managed to injure a huge whale, which was 20 ft. long, 5 ft. wide and weighed 100 tonnes. However, James Bartley, one of the fishermen, was swallowed up by the whale in the presence of his friends during this encounter. The next day they found the dead whale and transported it with much difficulty to the coast. On cutting open its belly, James Bartley was found alive. He had been in the whale's belly for more than 60 hours.

83. The word *yaqṭīn* is used for a tree which does not stand on a stem but rather grows and spreads like a creeper, such as a gourd, pumpkin, cucumber and melon. God miraculously allowed a creeper to grow over there. Its leaves provided shade to the Prophet Jonah (peace be on him) and its fruit served him both as food and drink.

(147) and We sent him forth to a nation of a hundred thousand or more,[84] (148) and they believed. So We let them enjoy life for a while.[85]

وَأَرْسَلْنَٰهُ إِلَىٰ مِائَةِ أَلْفٍ أَوْ يَزِيدُونَ ﴿١٤٧﴾

فَـَٔامَنُوا۟ فَمَتَّعْنَٰهُمْ إِلَىٰ حِينٍ ﴿١٤٨﴾

---

84. The figure "one hundred thousand or more" does not indicate that God does not accurately know their number. What is meant here is that an observer would have surmised that the town had a population of one hundred thousand or more. It was presumably the same town from where the Prophet Jonah (peace be on him) had departed. After his departure, the inhabitants of the town embraced faith as they saw God's scourge approaching them. In view of their acceptance of faith, which amounted to repentance, the scourge was averted. The Prophet Jonah (peace be on him) was sent back to them so that they might embrace faith at his hands and lead their lives as believers. (For a better comprehension of this see *Yūnus* 10:98.)

85. Some people have taken exception to our version of the Prophet Jonah's story, as featured in *Sūrahs Yūnus* (*Sūrah* 10) and *al-Anbiyā'* (*Sūrah* 21); it would be pertinent to reproduce below the version of this story as offered by some Qur'ān-commentators.

While elucidating *Yūnus* 10: 98, the distinguished Qur'ān-commentator, Qatādah says the following:

> There has been no community that committed unbelief and believed after God's punishment had come to them, and yet they were spared punishment. The only exception are the people of Jonah. As the Divine scourge approached they looked for their Messenger and could not locate him in their midst, so God instilled repentance in their hearts. (Ibn Kathīr, *Tafsīr*, comments on *Sūrah Yūnus* 10:98.)

Ālūsī offers the following explanation:

> The Prophet Jonah (peace be on him) was sent to the people of Nineveh in the region of Mosul. They were unbelievers. The Prophet Jonah (peace be on him) urged them to worship the One True God and to give up idolatry. However, they rejected his call

> and denounced him as a liar. The Prophet Jonah (peace be on him) warned them that a Divine scourge would befall them after three days. He left the town in the night before the appointed day of their punishment. The next day, as God's scourge almost encompassed them, they realised that they were on the verge of death and destruction. It was then that they desperately looked for their Messenger but they could not find him. Eventually they assembled in the open along with their children and cattle. At that stage they professed faith and repented their sins ... God took pity on them and accepted the repentance. (*Rūḥ al-Ma'āni*, comments on *Sūrah Yūnus* 10: 98).

In a similar vein Ālūsī explains *Sūrah al-Anbiyā'* 21:87:

> The Prophet Jonah's departure, in a fit of anger directed against his community, no doubt constituted his migration. God, however, had not directed him to do so. (*Rūḥ al-Ma'āni*, comments on *Sūrah al-Anbiyā'* 21:87.)

As for the Prophet Jonah's confession that he had done wrong (*al-Anbiyā'* 21:87), Ālūsī writes:

> His confession of doing wrong underscores the haste with which he migrated. This did not befit a Messenger of God. He confessed his lapse in order to win God's acceptance of his repentance. (*Rūḥ al-Ma'āni*, comments on *Sūrah al-Anbiyā'* 21:87.)

Mawlānā Ashraf 'Alī Thānawī's gloss on *al-Anbiyā'* 21:87 reads as follows:

> He left the town, angry with his community over their unbelief. He did not return to them even after the Divine scourge had been averted from them. His departure from the town did not have God's sanction. (*Bayān al-Qur'ān* comments on *Sūrah al-Anbiyā'* 21:87.)

Mawlānā Shabbīr Aḥmad 'Uthmānī explains the Prophet Jonah's conduct thus:

> Enraged at the misdeeds of his community, he [Jonah] left the town in a fit of anger. In so doing, he did not wait for the Divine directive. He had threatened his community with the Divine scourge which would overtake them after three days. Nonetheless, he later admitted his mistake in having left the town in haste

> without God's command and having abandoned his people. (*Tafsīr 'Uthmānī*, comments on *Sūrah al-Anbiyā'* 21:87.)

Rāzī's explanation of *al-Ṣāffāt* 37:148 is as follows:

> God had promised to annihilate the unbelieving people of the Prophet Jonah's town. While apprehending the imminent Divine scourge, the Prophet Jonah (peace be on him) lost patience and left the town, thus neglecting his mission to guide his community to the truth. He was obliged to continue his mission, for the possibility remained that God would decide not to destroy them. (*Al-Tafsīr al-Kabīr*, comments on *al-Ṣāffāt* 37:148.)

While explaining *al-Ṣāffāt* 37:140, Ālūsī states:

> *Abq* denotes a slave's running away from his master. As the Prophet Jonah (peace be on him) had left his community without his Lord's leave, this expression is befittingly used of him. It was on the third day that he left the town. Unable to trace their Messenger, the community members went out, along with their cattle. As the Divine scourge was approaching them, they turned to God, crying fervently over their misdeeds and sought God's pardon. God accepted their repentance. (*Rūḥ al-Ma'ānī*, comments on *al-Ṣāffāt* 37:140.)

On the import of *al-Ṣāffāt* 37:142, Mawlānā Shabbīr Aḥmad 'Uthmānī writes as follows:

> The Prophet Jonah (peace be on him) stood charged with having committed a mistake in the exercise of his discretion. It was so both in his choice of departing from the town without God's leave and in fixing the day the Divine scourge would strike his people. (*Tafsīr 'Uthmānī*, comments on *al-Ṣāffāt* 37:142.)
>
> The Prophet Muḥammad (peace be on him) was instructed not to behave towards the unbelievers in the manner of the Prophet Jonah (peace be on him) which was characterised by a certain lack of magnanimity and patience towards those who falsified the truth. (*Tafsīr 'Uthmānī*, comments on *al-Qalam* 68:48.)
>
> Maulānā 'Uthmānī, referring to the words in the verse وهو مكظوم ("choking with grief"), says as follows: "This shows that Jonah was filled with anger towards his people which prompted him, in a state of irritation, to hurriedly imprecate against them and even

(149) So ask their opinion:[86] "(Are you convinced) that your Lord should have daughters and you should have sons?[87] (150) Did We create the angels as females the while they witnessed?" (151) Behold, it is one of their fabrications that they say: ▶

فَٱسْتَفْتِهِمْ أَلِرَبِّكَ ٱلْبَنَاتُ وَلَهُمُ ٱلْبَنُونَ ﴿١٤٩﴾
أَمْ خَلَقْنَا ٱلْمَلَـٰٓئِكَةَ إِنَـٰثًا وَهُمْ شَـٰهِدُونَ ﴿١٥٠﴾
أَلَآ إِنَّهُم مِّنْ إِفْكِهِمْ لَيَقُولُونَ ﴿١٥١﴾

---

make a prophecy [regarding the time of God's scourge]." (*Tafsīr 'Uthmānī*, comments on *al-Qalam* 68:48.)

It emerges from all the above that the Prophet Jonah (peace be on him) had incurred God's displeasure because of the following three lapses: (i) He himself fixed a date for God's scourge, though God had not specified it. (ii) He migrated from the town before God's scourge had arrived. A Messenger is not supposed to leave his station without God's permission. (iii) Moreover, he did not return to his home town even after God's scourge was averted.

86. This marks the beginning of a new discourse. The earlier discourse commenced with verse 11. It began with posing to the Makkan unbelievers the question: "Were they harder to create than the objects We created?" At this stage, they are asked another question. The objective of the former question was to jolt the unbelievers, those who had ruled out the possibility of the Afterlife, Resurrection and Divine retribution, and mocked the Prophet (peace be on him) because he expounded these doctrines. The present question, however, seeks to alert them to their ignorance, for they ascribed children to God. They gave free rein to their imagination and confirmed ties of kinship between God and whomsoever they wanted.

87. We learn from traditions in a variety of sources that the Quraysh, Juhaynah, Banū Salimah, Khuzā'ah, Banū Mulayḥ and some other tribes considered angels to be the daughters of God. The Qur'ān refers to this in the following instances: *al-Nisā'* 4:117; *al-Naḥl* 16:57–58; *Banī Isrā'īl* 17:40; *al-Zukhruf* 43:16–19, and *al-Najm* 53:21–27.

(152) "Allah has begotten." They are liars! (153) Did He choose daughters rather than sons? (154) What is the matter with you that you make such strange judgements? (155) Will you then not take heed? (156) Do you have any clear authority for such claims? (157) Bring your Book, if you are truthful.[88]

(158) They have established a kinship between Allah and the angels;[89] and the angels know well that these people will be arraigned (as culprits). (159) (They say): "Exalted be Allah above what they attribute to Him, ▶

وَلَدَ ٱللَّهُ وَإِنَّهُمْ لَكَـٰذِبُونَ ۝١٥٢ أَصْطَفَى
ٱلْبَنَاتِ عَلَى ٱلْبَنِينَ ۝١٥٣ مَا لَكُمْ كَيْفَ
تَحْكُمُونَ ۝١٥٤ أَفَلَا تَذَكَّرُونَ ۝١٥٥ أَمْ
لَكُمْ سُلْطَـٰنٌ مُّبِينٌ ۝١٥٦ فَأْتُوا۟ بِكِتَـٰبِكُمْ
إِن كُنتُمْ صَـٰدِقِينَ ۝١٥٧ وَجَعَلُوا۟ بَيْنَهُۥ
وَبَيْنَ ٱلْجِنَّةِ نَسَبًا ۚ وَلَقَدْ عَلِمَتِ ٱلْجِنَّةُ
إِنَّهُمْ لَمُحْضَرُونَ ۝١٥٨ سُبْحَـٰنَ ٱللَّهِ
عَمَّا يَصِفُونَ ۝١٥٩

88. There could evidently be no more than two grounds for considering the angels to be God's daughters. The first of these could be observation. Alternatively, it could have a scriptural basis. In other words, there should be a statement on God's authority that the angels are His daughters. The unbelievers, however, cannot substantiate their claim on either of these two grounds. It was the height of their ignorance and folly that they entertained a baseless notion as an article of faith. They attributed to God what was patently ridiculous and outrageous.

89. The Qur'ān employs the word *jinn*. Some leading Qur'ānic scholars, however, contend that the word *jinn* has been used here in the literal meaning of 'hidden creatures', thereby signifying angels since the angels are essentially hidden creatures. The text that follows also corroborates that the word has been used here to denote angels.

(160) all of them except the chosen servants of Allah. (161) So you and your deities (162) shall not be able to tempt anyone away from Allah (163) except him who shall roast in the Blazing Fire.[90] (164) As for us, there is none but has an appointed station.[91] (165) Verily we range ourselves in rows (as humble servants) (166) and we are of those who glorify Allah."

(167) They used to say before: (168) "If only we had the Reminder which had been granted to the people of yore (169) we would surely have been Allah's chosen servants."[92] ▶

إِلَّا عِبَادَ ٱللَّهِ ٱلْمُخْلَصِينَ ﴿١٦٠﴾ فَإِنَّكُمْ
وَمَا تَعْبُدُونَ ﴿١٦١﴾ مَآ أَنتُمْ عَلَيْهِ بِفَـٰتِنِينَ ﴿١٦٢﴾
إِلَّا مَنْ هُوَ صَالِ ٱلْجَحِيمِ ﴿١٦٣﴾ وَمَا مِنَّآ
إِلَّا لَهُۥ مَقَامٌ مَّعْلُومٌ ﴿١٦٤﴾ وَإِنَّا لَنَحْنُ
ٱلصَّآفُّونَ ﴿١٦٥﴾ وَإِنَّا لَنَحْنُ ٱلْمُسَبِّحُونَ ﴿١٦٦﴾
وَإِن كَانُوا۟ لَيَقُولُونَ ﴿١٦٧﴾ لَوْ أَنَّ عِندَنَا ذِكْرًا
مِّنَ ٱلْأَوَّلِينَ ﴿١٦٨﴾ لَكُنَّا عِبَادَ ٱللَّهِ
ٱلْمُخْلَصِينَ ﴿١٦٩﴾

90. This may alternatively be translated as follows: "So you and your worship shall not be able to tempt anyone away from God except ..." Taken in this sense, the angels will tell their devotees that they will be unable to tempt them to err by their act of worshipping them. In other words, the devotees could beguile only those who have been caught in the vortex of their doom. As for the angels, they will simply not oblige their devotees by falling into their trap.

91. Far from being God's children, angels cannot dare to deviate even slightly from the roles assigned to each of them.

92. The same truth is enshrined in *Sūrah Fāṭir* 35:42.

(170) But when it came to them, they rejected it. They shall soon come to know (the end of such an attitude). (171) We have already given Our promise to Our Messengers (172) that they shall certainly be succoured, (173) and that Our hosts shall triumph.[93] (174) So, (O Prophet), leave them alone for a while, (175) and see, and soon they too shall see.[94] (176) Do they seek to hasten Our chastisement? ▶

فَكَفَرُواْ بِهِۦۖ فَسَوۡفَ يَعۡلَمُونَ ١٧٠ وَلَقَدۡ
سَبَقَتۡ كَلِمَتُنَا لِعِبَادِنَا ٱلۡمُرۡسَلِينَ ١٧١ إِنَّهُمۡ
لَهُمُ ٱلۡمَنصُورُونَ ١٧٢ وَإِنَّ جُندَنَا لَهُمُ
ٱلۡغَٰلِبُونَ ١٧٣ فَتَوَلَّ عَنۡهُمۡ حَتَّىٰ حِينٖ ١٧٤
وَأَبۡصِرۡهُمۡ فَسَوۡفَ يُبۡصِرُونَ ١٧٥ أَفَبِعَذَابِنَا
يَسۡتَعۡجِلُونَ ١٧٦

---

93. God's "hosts" comprise the believers who follow His Prophet and support His cause, thereby signifying angels since the latter are essentially hidden creatures. The text that follows also corroborates that the word has been used here to denote angels, including the invisible powers that help the votaries of truth by God's leave. God's help and support, however, do not necessarily mean that every Prophet of God and his followers will enjoy political ascendancy in every age. Wherever God's Prophets do not have such ascendancy, they enjoy moral ascendancy. By the same token, the nations that do not follow those Prophets and follow a path contrary to their teachings, ultimately meet their doom. All theories and doctrines that are rooted in ignorance and error prosper only for a short while. Even when these are forcibly put into effect, they fail to strike deep roots. However, the truths expounded by God's Prophets since time immemorial continue to be immutable. None can shake their roots.

94. The Prophet's Companions are assured that the Makkan unbelievers will soon witness their own defeat and the victory of the believers. That indeed came true. Within 15 years of the revelation of these verses, the Makkan unbelievers helplessly watched the Prophet

(177) When that chastisement will descend upon their courtyard, evil shall that Day be for those who had been warned. (178) Leave them alone for a while, (179) and see; and they too shall soon see.

(180) Exalted be your Lord, the Lord of Glory, above what they attribute to Him, (181) and peace be upon the Messengers, (182) and all praise be to Allah, the Lord of the Universe.

فَإِذَا نَزَلَ بِسَاحَتِهِمْ فَسَآءَ صَبَاحُ
ٱلْمُنذَرِينَ ﴿١٧٧﴾ وَتَوَلَّ عَنْهُمْ حَتَّىٰ حِينٍ ﴿١٧٨﴾
وَأَبْصِرْ فَسَوْفَ يُبْصِرُونَ ﴿١٧٩﴾ سُبْحَٰنَ
رَبِّكَ رَبِّ ٱلْعِزَّةِ عَمَّا يَصِفُونَ ﴿١٨٠﴾ وَسَلَٰمٌ
عَلَى ٱلْمُرْسَلِينَ ﴿١٨١﴾ وَٱلْحَمْدُ لِلَّهِ رَبِّ
ٱلْعَٰلَمِينَ ﴿١٨٢﴾

(peace be on him) enter their town, Makkah, as a conqueror. Then, a decade later, the Muslims had established their superiority over both superpowers of the time – the Persians and the Romans.

Glossary of Terms

'Ahd (covenant) refers to God's eternal command to His servants that they render their service, obedience and worship to Him, and Him alone.

Ahl al-Bayt literally means one's family members: one's spouse(s) and children. Used in the context of the Prophet (peace be on him) in *al-Aḥzāb* 33:33, it signifies all his wives and children.

Al-Ākhirah (After-Life, Hereafter, Next World). The term embraces the following ideas:

1. That man is answerable to God.
2. That one day the present order of existence will come to an end.
3. That when that happens, God will bring another order into being in which He will resurrect all human beings, gather them together and examine their conduct, and reward them with justice and mercy.
4. That the persons who believe and do good will be sent to Paradise whereas the evil-doers will be consigned to Hell.
5. That the true measure of a person's success or failure is not the extent of his prosperity in the present life, but his success in the Next.

Amānah (trust) encompasses all types of trust which either God or society or an individual places in someone's charge.

Āyah (pl. *āyāt*), means a sign which directs one to something significant. In the Qur'ān the word has been used in four different senses:

(i) sign or indication; (ii) the phenomena of the universe (called *āyāt*) of God because the reality to which they indicate is hidden behind the veil of appearances; (iii) miracles performed by God's Prophets; and (iv) individual units (i.e. verses) of the Book of God.

Barzakh is an Arabicized form of the Persian word *pardah* (signifying barrier). According to the Qur'ān, there presently exists a barrier between those who are dead and the present world. This barrier prevents the dead from returning to life and so they will stay where they are till the Day of Judgement. In technical Islamic usage, the term signifies the stage following death until one's resurrection for God's final judgement.

Dhibḥ 'Adhẓīm: literally "mighty sacrifice". It alludes to the ram that the angels brought before the Prophet Abraham (peace be on him) so that he might slaughter it instead of his son, Ishmael. It is called "a mighty sacrifice" because it served as a ransom from a very faithful servant of God, Abraham for as patient and obedient a son as Ishmael. Another reason for calling it "a mighty sacrifice" is that Allah made it incumbent on the believers to offer animal sacrifice on the same day the world over so as to keep fresh the memory of that great event which epitomizes fidelity and devotion of the highest order to Allah.

Dhikr means remembrance. In the Islamic context it is used in the sense of "remembrance of God". In *al-Baqārah* 2:199, *dhikr* refers to remembering God on a specific occasion and a specific place namely at Minā during the Pilgrimage.

Ghayb literally means "hidden, covered, or concealed". As a Qur'ānic term, it means all that is unknown and is not accessible to man by the means of acquiring knowledge normally available to him. *Ghayb,* therefore, refers to the realm that lies beyond the ken of sense-perception.

Ḥadīth literally means communication or narration. In the Islamic context it has come to denote the record of what the Prophet (peace be on him) said, did, or tacitly approved. According to some scholars, the word *ḥadīth* also applies to reports about the sayings and deeds, etc., of the Companions of the Prophet in addition to the Prophet himself. The whole corpus of these reports is termed *Ḥadīth* and its science, *'Ilm al-Ḥadīth.*

Ḥamd literally means "praise". Whenever we praise someone, we do so for two reasons. First, because excellence calls for praise. Second, we praise one whom we consider to be our benefactor. God is worthy of praise on both counts: in recognition of His infinite excellence and also because of our gratitude to Him for the blessings He has lavished upon us.

'Ibādah is used in three meanings: (i) worship and adoration; (ii) obedience and submission; and (iii) service and subjection. The fundamental message of Islam is that man, being God's creature, should direct his *'ibādah* to Him and Him alone in all the above-mentioned meanings.

Iblīs literally means "thoroughly disappointed; one in utter despair". In Islamic terminology it denotes that particular *jinn* who, out of arrogance and vanity, refused to obey God's command to prostrate before Adam. He also asked God to allow him a term wherein he might mislead and tempt mankind to error. This term was granted to him by God whereafter he became the chief promoter of evil and prompted Adam and Eve to disobey God's command which led to his exit from Paradise. He is also called *al-Shayṭān* (Satan), who is possessed of a specific personality and is not just an abstract force.

'Iddah denotes the waiting period that a woman is required to observe as a consequence of the nullification of her marriage with her husband or because of the husband's death. The waiting period of a widow is four lunar months and ten days (and nights), and for a divorcee it is three menstrual cycles according to some schools of law, and three clear periods according to others. Neither a widow nor a divorcee may marry until the waiting period comes to an end. However, if a widow or divorcee is pregnant the waiting period comes to an end with the completion of pregnancy.

Ijmā' refers to the consensus of eminent scholars (*mujtahidūn*) of Islam in a given age. *Ijmā'* comes next to the Qur'ān and the *Sunnah* as a source of Islamic doctrines.

Jāhilīyah denotes all those worldviews and ways of life which are based on rejection or disregard of Heavenly Guidance communicated to mankind through God's Prophets and Messengers; the attitude of living one's life – whether wholly or partly – as independent of God's Guidance. Since the above-mentioned attitude to God's Guidance characterized Arabia on the eve of the Prophet's advent, this period of Arabia's history is called *Jāhilīyah*.

Jinn are an independent species of creation about which little is known except that unlike human beings who were created out of clay, the *jinn* were created out of fire. But like human beings, a Divine Message has also been addressed to them and they too have been endowed with the capacity, again like human beings, to choose between good and evil, and between obedience and disobedience to God.

Khalīfah or vicegerent is he who exercises the authority delegated to him by his principal. Man has been called *khalīfah* in the Qur'ān since God appointed him as His vicegerent on earth.

Khātam al-Nabīyīn (the Seal of the Prophets), that is the Prophet Muḥammad (peace be on him) after whom God will raise no Prophet or Messenger.

Kufr: its original meaning is "to conceal". This word has been variously used in the Qur'ān to denote: (i) the state of absolute lack of faith; (ii) the rejection or denial of any of the essentials of Islam; (iii) the attitude of ingratitude and thanklessness towards God; and (iv) the non-fulfilment of the basic requirements of faith. In the accepted technical sense, *kufr* consists in the rejection of the Divine Guidance communicated through God's Prophets and Messengers. More specifically, since the advent of the last of the Prophets and Messengers, Muḥammad (peace be on him), wilful rejection of the teachings revealed to him by God constitutes *kufr*.

Mahr (bridal gift) signifies the amount of payment that is settled between the spouses at the time of marriage which the husband is required to pay to his bride. *Mahr* symbolizes the financial responsibility that a husband assumes towards his wife by virtue of entering into the contract of marriage. In Islamic parlance the word *ṣadāq* is also used as an equivalent of *mahr*.

Maḥram refers to those whom it is prohibited to marry.

Muhājirūn: (Emigrants), (single. *muahājir*), are those who migrated in the Prophet's time from Makkah to Madīnah (or Abyssinia) in the cause of God at a time when it had become extremely difficult for them to live in their home town according to the requirements of their faith. Though originally used to signify the emigrants in the cause of God during the Prophet's time, its application is extended to all those who forsake their hearth and home in God's cause regardless of space and time context.

Nabī, a word for which we have used the word "Prophet" in this work as an equivalent, refers to a person chosen by God to whom He entrusts the task to warn people against that which would lead to their perdition and to direct them to the way that would lead to their felicity. Prophets are enabled to perform this task because of the special knowledge that is providentially made available to them, because of the special power that is bestowed upon them by God (which is evident from the miracles they are enabled to perform), and because of the special ability to live a life of absolute probity. The function of a *nabī* is close to, but not necessarily identical with, that of a *rasūl* (q.v. *rasūl*).

Nikāḥ, as a technical term, denotes the contract of marriage, including copulation which follows it.

Rasūl, plural *rusul,* literally means "message-bearer", has been used in the Qur'ān with reference both to the angels who bear God's Message to the Prophets and to the humans entrusted with the communication of God's Message to other humans. Technically, it is commonly used in Islamic parlance in the latter sense. There is some disagreement among Muslim scholars as to whether the terms *nabī* (Prophet) and *rasūl* (Messenger) are equivalent, and which of the two – *nabī* or *rasūl* has a higher status. The majority of scholars are of the opinion that while every *rasūl* (Messenger) is a *nabī (*Prophet), every *nabī* is not necessarily a *rasūl;* and that the Messengers (*rusul*), therefore, have a higher status and are entrusted with an even greater mission than the Prophets.

Ṣalāh literally means prayer. In Islamic parlance *ṣalāh* signifies the ritual which is so called because it includes praying. *Ṣalāh* is an obligatory act of devotion which all adult Muslims are required to perform five times a day and consists of certain specific acts such as *takbīr* which signals the commencement of *ṣalāh*, and includes such other acts as *qiyām* (standing), *rukū'* (bowing), and *sujūd* (prostration). Apart from obligatory *ṣalāh*, there are other kinds of *ṣalāh* as well. (For one such kind of *ṣalāh*, *q.v. Tahajjud*.)

Shahādah, literally the act of witnessing, is the declaration of belief in the unity of God and the Prophethood of the Prophet Muḥammad (peace be on him). Its pronouncement is considered one of the Five Pillars of Islam. When one proclaims it, one is considered to have officially declared oneself to be a Muslim. It is also used to denote martyrdom for the act of laying down one's life in God's cause, is the highest form of bearing witness to one's faith.

Sharī'ah signifies the entire Islamic way of life, especially the Law of Islam.

Shirk consists in associating anyone or anything with the Creator either in His Person, or Attributes, or in the exclusive rights (such as worship) that He has against His creatures.

Sunnah means a way, course, rule, mode or manner of acting or conduct of life. In Islamic parlance it denotes the way of the Prophet Muḥammad (peace be upon him) as evidenced by his authentic precepts and practices.

Tabarruj: literally, to make manifest, apparent, conspicuous or elevated. In *al-Aḥzāb* 33:33 the word has been used in the context of women in so far as they have been asked not to go about deliberately displaying their allurements in the manner it was customary in the Time of Ignorance (*Jāhilīyah*) and this despite the morally refining teachings of Islam. *Tabarruj* can take place in the following ways: (i) by a woman's intended show of her physical charms; (ii) by her making an alluring display of her dress and jewellery, (iii) and by her making a show of her alluring gait and other enticing gestures. The Qur'ān directs the believing women to abstain from all these.

Tahajjud is the Prayer offered in the last quarter of the night, any time before the commencement of the time of *Fajr* Prayer. It is a recommended rather than an obligatory Prayer, but one which has been emphasized in the Qur'ān and in the *Ḥadīth* as an act that merits great reward from God.

Takhyīr: the husband's granting his wife the right to continue the wedlock or seek separation. This signifies delegating to one's wife the right to obtain divorce. In accordance with the command contained in *al-Aḥzāb* 33:28, the Prophet (peace be on him) had granted this right to his four wives which he had at the time when these verses were revealed – Sawdah, 'Ā'ishah, Ḥafṣah, and Umm Salamah.

Tasbīḥ has two meanings: (i) to proclaim God's glory, and (ii) to exert oneself earnestly and energetically to do God's will.

Tashahhud, literally "testimony", is a declaration of the Muslim faith towards the end of the Prayers, immediately after the recitation of *Taḥīyah, Tashahhud* is performed while one is sitting on one's knees with the forefinger of his right hand extended to witness the unity of God and the Prophethood of Muḥammad (peace be on him).

Tawḥīd means affirmation of the unity of God's Essence, and the uniqueness of His Attributes, and the consecration of worship, devotion and obedience to Him.

Waqf, as a technical term, signifies the appropriation or dedication of a property to charitable uses in service to God. It is an endowment the object of which must be of a perpetual nature so that the property so endowed may not be sold or transferred. Thus, while the substance of the property is retained, its usufruct is devoted to the good purposes laid down by the owner of the *waqf* who, however, forfeits his power of its disposal by willing that his property will be perpetually devoted to the purposes that are pleasing to God.

Zakāh (Purifying Alms) literally means purification, whence it is used to express a portion of property bestowed in alms as a means of purifying the person concerned as well as the property that is left with him after the payment of *zakāh*. It is among the Five Pillars of Islam and refers to the mandatory amount that a Muslim is required to pay out of his property. The rules of *zakāh* are laid down in the major collections of *Ḥadīth* and in the manuals of *Fiqh*.

Ẓālim is the wrong-doer; he who exceeds the limits of right; the unjust.

Zaqqūm is the name of the tree that will grow in the depths of Hell and the inmates of Hell will be obliged to eat of it.

Ẓihār was one of the recognized forms of divorce in pre-Islamic Arabia. It consisted of a person's statement in which he declared his wife to be like his mother, daughter or sister. Islam abolished this form of divorce and if a person makes such a statement, he would commit a sin for which he is required to expiate. Nevertheless, the divorce so pronounced will take legal effect.

Zinā means illegal sexual intercourse and embraces both fornication and adultery.

Biographical Notes

'Abd Allāh ibn 'Abbās, see Biographical Notes, Vol. I.

'Abd Allāh ibn 'Amr ibn al-'Āṣ, see Biographical Notes, Vol. I.

'Abd Allāh ibn Mas'ūd, see Biographical Notes, Vol. I.

'Abd Allāh ibn Ubayy ibn Salūl, see Biographical Notes, Vol. I.

'Abd Allāh ibn 'Umar, see Biographical Notes, *Towards Understanding the Qur'ān*, Abridged Version.

'Abd al-Razzāq, see Biographical Notes, Vol. VII.

'Abd ibn Ḥumayd, d. 249 AH/863 CE, hailed from Jurjān and is acclaimed as a *Ḥadīth* scholar. His original name was said to be 'Abd al-Ḥamīd which was presumably shortened to 'Abd ibn Ḥumayd.

'Abd Allāh ibn Rawāḥah, d. 8 AH/629 CE, of the Khazraj tribe in Madīnah, was a devout Companion and a poet who attained martyrdom in the Battle of Mu'tah.

Abraham (Ibrāhīm), see Biographical Notes, Vol. III.

Abū Bakr, 'Abd Allāh ibn 'Uthmān, see Biographical Notes, Vol. I.

Abū al-Dardā', 'Uwaymir ibn Mālik, see Biographical Notes, Vol. I.

Abū Dā'ūd Sulaymān ibn al-Ash'ath, see Biographical Notes, Vol. I.

Abū Ḥanīfah, al-Nu'mān ibn Thābit, see Biographical Notes, Vol. VIII.

Abū Ḥumayd al-Sā'idī, belonged to the Khazraj tribe and embraced Islam after the Prophet's *Hijrah* to Madīnah. He participated in the Battle of Uḥud and all later battles.

Abū Hurayrah, see Biographical Notes, Vol. I.

Abū Jahl, 'Amr ibn Hishām ibn al-Mughīrah, see Biographical Notes, Vol. I.

Abū Mūsā al-Ash'arī, 'Abd Allāh ibn Qays, see Biographical Notes, Vol. I.

Abū Sufyān, Ṣakhr ibn Ḥarb ibn Umayyah, see Biographical Notes, Vol. I.

Abū Ṭalḥah, Zayd ibn Sahl ibn al-Aswad, see Biographical Notes, *Towards Understanding the Qur'ān*, Abridged Version.

Abū Thawr, Ibrāhīm ibn Khālid ibn abī al-Yamān al-Kalbī, d. *circa* 240 AH/854 CE, was a leading *Ḥadīth* scholar and jurist.

Abū al-Ṭufayl, 'Āmir ibn Wāthilah ibn 'Abd Allāh al-Laythī al-Kinānaī, d. 100 AH/718 CE, was a poet, warrior and one of the chiefs of Kinānah. He was born on the day of the Battle of Badr and narrated nine traditions from the Prophet (peace be on him). He was among the prominent supporters of 'Alī and was presumably the last of the Companions to have died.

'Abū 'Ubaydah, d. 209 AH/824 CE, was an acclaimed grammarian.

Aḥmad ibn Ḥanbal, see Biographical Notes, Vol. I.

'Ā'ishah, see Biographical Notes, Vol. I.

'Alī ibn Abī Ṭālib, see Biographical Notes, Vol. I.

Al-Ḥusayn ibn 'Alī ibn Abī Ṭālib, d. 61 AH/680 CE, was Fāṭimah's son. He enjoyed great respect because of his many qualities, including piety, besides his distinguished lineage as the Prophet's grandson. Soon after Yazīd assumed power, Ḥusayn went to Kūfah at the invitation of his supporters who promised to install him as the caliph. Accompanied by the members of his family and a band of staunch supporters, he was intercepted by the Umayyad soldiers and brutally martyred along with his family members and followers.

Al-Alūsī, Maḥmūd ibn 'Abd Allāh al-Ḥusaynī, see Biographical Notes, Vol. I.

'Amr ibn 'Ubayd, d. 144 AH/761 CE, was a client of the Taym tribe. He was a prominent Mu'tazilī scholar of Baṣrah. 'Amr became known for his learning and ascetic piety.

'Āmir ibn Shuraḥbīl al-Sha'bī, see Biographical Notes, Vol. II. See also al-Sha'bī, 'Āmīr ibn Shuraḥbīl.

Anas ibn Mālik, see Biographical Notes, Vol. I.

'Aṭā' ibn Abī Rabāḥ, see Biographical Notes, Vol. I.

Al-Awzā'ī, 'Abd al-Raḥmān ibn 'Amr, see Biographical Notes, Vol. II.

Al-Baghawī, 'Abd Allāh ibn Muḥammad Abī al-Qāsim, see Biographical Notes, Vol. II.

Al-Bāhillī, Abū Umāmah Ṣudayy ibn 'Ajlān ibn Wahb, d. 81 AH/701 CE, was a Companion who supported 'Alī ibn Abī Ṭālib in the Battle of Ṣiffīn.

Al-Barā' ibn 'Āzib, see Biographical Notes, Vol. I.

Al-Bayḍāwī, 'Abd Allāh ibn 'Umar, d. 685 AH/1286 CE, served as chief *qāḍī* in Shīrāz. His fame rests on his famous *tafsīr* called *Anwār al-Tanzīl wa Asrār al-Ta'wīl*, popularly known as *Tafsīr al-Bayḍāwī.*

Al-Bayhaqī, Abū Bakr Aḥmad ibn al-Ḥusayn ibn 'Alī, see Biographical Notes, Vol. V.

Al-Bazzār, Aḥmad ibn 'Amr ibn 'Abd al-Khāliq, see Biographical Notes, Vol. VI.

Al-Bukhārī, Muḥammad ibn Ismā'īl, see Biographical Notes, Vol. I.

Buraydah ibn al-Ḥusayb ibn 'Abd Allāh ibn al-Ḥārith al-Aslamī, see Biographical Notes, Vol. V.

Ḍaḥḥāk, Abū 'Āṣim al-Nabīl ibn Makhlad ibn Ḍaḥḥāk ibn Muslim al-Shaybānī, see Biographical Notes, Vol. VI.

Al-Dārimī, 'Abd Allāh ibn 'Abd al-Raḥmān, see Biographical Notes, Vol. I.

Fāṭimah bint Muḥammad, see Biographical Notes, *Towards Understanding the Qur'ān*, Abridged Version.

Al-Ghazālī, Abū Hāmid Muḥammad ibn Muḥammad, see Biographical Notes, Vol. V.

Ḥafṣah, see Biographical Notes, Vol. I.

Ḥajjāj ibn Yūsuf, d. 95 AH/714 CE, was a powerful administrator during the Umayyad period who was noted for his ruthlessness in the execution of his policies.

Al-Ḥākim al-Naysābūrī, Muḥammad ibn 'Abd Allāh Ḥamdawayh, see Biographical Notes, Vol. V.

Ḥamzah ibn 'Abd al-Muṭṭalib, see Biographical Notes, Vol. III.

Al-Ḥasan al-Baṣrī, see Biographical Notes, *Towards Understanding the Qur'ān*, Abridged Version.

Ḥasan ibn Ṣāliḥ al-Zaydī, see Biographical Notes, Vol. VI.

Ḥudhayfah ibn al-Yamān, see Biographical Notes, Vol. II.

Ḥudhayfah ibn Asīd al-Ghifārī, see Biographical Notes, Vol. V.

Ibn Abī Ḥātim, 'Abd al-Raḥmān, see Biographical Notes, Vol. VIII.

Ibn Abī Laylā, d.148 AH/765 CE, was a celebrated jurist and judge of Iraq and is known for his contribution to Islamic law.

Ibn al-Mundhir, Muḥammad ibn Ibrāhīm, see Biographical Notes, Vol. VIII.

Ibn Ḥazm, 'Alī ibn Aḥmad, see Biographical Notes, Vol. II.

Ibn Hishām, 'Abd al-Malik, see Biographical Notes, Vol. I.

Ibn Isḥāq, Muḥammad, see Biographical Notes, Vol. IV.

Ibn Kathīr, Ismā'īl ibn 'Umar, see Biographical Notes, Vol. I.

Ibn Mājah, Muḥammad ibn Yazīd, see Biographical Notes, Vol. I.

Ibn Sa'd, Muḥammad, see Biographical Notes, *Towards Understanding the Qur'ān*, Abridged Version.

Ibn Sīrīn, Muḥammad, see Biographical Notes, *Towards Understanding the Qur'ān*, Abridged Version.

Ibn Taymīyah, Taqī al-Dīn Aḥmad ibn 'Abd al-Ḥalīm, see Biographical Notes, Vol. I.

Ibrāhīm al-Nakha'ī, see Biographical Notes, Vol. I.

Ibrāhīm, see Abraham.

'Ikrimah ibn 'Abd Allāh al-Barbarī al-Madanī, see Biographical Notes, Vol. VIII.

'Ikrimah ibn Abī Jahl, see Biographical Notes, Vol. II.

'Imrān ibn Ḥuṣayn ibn 'Ubayd, see Biographical Notes, Vol. VIII.

Isaac (Isḥāq), see Biographical Notes, Vol. VIII.

'Īsā, see Jesus.

Isḥāq, see Isaac.

Isḥāq ibn Rāhawayh ibn Ibrāhīm ibn Makhlad al-Marwazī, see Biographical Notes, Vol. V.

Jābir ibn 'Abd Allāh, see Biographical Notes, Vol. I.

Jābir ibn Zayd, see Biographical Notes, *Towards Understanding the Qur'ān*, Abridged Version.

Al-Jaṣṣāṣ, Aḥmad ibn 'Alī, see Biographical Notes, Vol. I.

Jesus ('Īsā), see Biographical Notes, Vol. VIII.

Juwayrīyah, d. 50 AH/670 CE, one of the wives of the Prophet (peace be on him), was the daughter of Ḥārith, chief of the Muṣṭaliq tribe, whom he married after her husband was killed in a battle.

Khadījah bint Khuwaylid, see Biographical Notes, *Towards Understanding the Qur'ān*, Abridged Version.

Khālid ibn al-Walīd, see Biographical Notes, Vol. I.

Al-Khudrī, Abū Sa'īd ibn Mālik ibn Sinān al-Anṣārī, see Biographical Notes, *Towards Understanding the Qur'ān*, Abridged Version.

Al-Layth ibn Sa'd, see Biographical Notes, Vol. II.

Lot (Lūṭ), see Biographical Notes, Vol. VIII.

Lūṭ, see Lot.

Mālik ibn Anas, see Biographical Notes, Vol. I.

Maymūnah bint al-Ḥārith, see Biographical Notes, Vol. VI.

Moses (Mūsā), see Biographical Notes, Vol. VIII.

Mūsā, see Moses.

Mu'āwiyah ibn Abī Sufyān, see Biographical Notes, Vol. II.

Muḥammad al-Bāqir ibn 'Alī Zayn al-'Ābidīn ibn al-Ḥusayn, see Biographical Notes, *Towards Understanding the Qur'ān*, Abridged Version.

Muḥammad ibn Ka'b al-Quraẓī, see Biographical Notes, Vol. VIII.

Mujāhid ibn Jubayr, see Biographical Notes, *Towards Understanding the Qur'ān*, Abridged Version.

Mujamma' ibn Jāriyah, d. *circa* 50 AH/*circa* 670 CE, was among those few Companions who collected the Qur'ān from the Prophet (peace be on him). The second Caliph, 'Umar ibn al-Khaṭṭāb, reportedly deputed him to Kūfah to teach Kūfans the Qur'ān.

Muqātil ibn Sulaymān, see Biographical Notes, Vol. I.

Muslim ibn al-Ḥajjāj al-Nīsābūrī, see Biographical Notes, Vol. I.

Al-Nasā'ī, Aḥmad ibn 'Alī, see Biographical Notes, Vol. I.

Nīsābūrī, Niẓām al-Dīn al-Ḥasan ibn Muḥammad, d. after 850 AH/ after 1445 CE, gained much fame in his time for his contribution to the fields of *tafsīr*, philosophy and mathematics. He was the author of *Gharā'ib al- Qur'ān wa Raghā'ib al-Furqān*, popularly known as *Tafsīr al-Nīsābūrī*.

Noah (Nūḥ), see Biographical Notes, Vol. VIII.

Nūḥ, see Noah.

Qāḍī 'Iyāḍ ibn Mūsā, see Biographical Notes, Vol. VI.

Al-Qārī al-Mullā 'Alī, see Biographical Notes, Vol. VII.

Qatādah ibn Di'āmah, see Biographical Notes, *Towards Understanding the Qur'ān*, Abridged Version.

Al-Qurṭubī, Muḥammad ibn Aḥmad, see Biographical Notes, Vol. I.

Rabī' ibn Anas, see Biographical Notes, *Towards Understanding the Qur'ān*, Abridged Version.

Rayḥānah bint Zayd ibn 'Amr, d. 10 AH/632 CE, belonged to the Qurayẓah tribe and was one of the wives of the Prophet (peace be on him). Originally a Jew, she later embraced Islam. The Prophet (peace be on him) admired her for her excellence of conduct and eloquence.

Al-Rāzī, Muḥammad ibn 'Umar Fakhr al-Dīn, see Biographical Notes, Vol. III.

Ruqayyah bint Muḥammad d. 2 AH/624 CE, was married before the advent of Islam to 'Utbah ibn Abī Lahab who divorced her at the insistence of his father. She later embraced Islam and was married to 'Uthmān ibn 'Affān, along with whom she migrated to Abyssinia when it became difficult for Muslims to live and practice Islam in Makkah.

Sa'd ibn Abī Waqqāṣ, see Biographical Notes, Vol. III.

Sa'd ibn Mu'ādh, see Biographical Notes, Vol. III.

Sa'd ibn 'Ubādah al-Khazrajī al-Anṣārī, see Biographical Notes, Vol. VI.

Safīnah, d. *circa* 90 AH/709 CE, was a client of the Prophet (peace be on him) and was among the People of Ṣuffaḥ.

Ṣafīyah, see Biographical Notes, Vol. I.

Sahl ibn Sa'd al-Khazrajī al-Anṣārī, see Biographical Notes, Vol. VI.

Sa'īd ibn Jubayr, see Biographical Notes, Vol. II.

Sa'īd ibn al-Musayyib, see Biographical Notes, Vol. I.

Ṣāliḥ, see Biographical Notes, *Towards Understanding the Qur'ān*, Abridged Version.

Sālim, *mawlā* of Abū Ḥudhayfah, see Biographical Notes, Vol. I.

Al-Salmānī, 'Ubaydah ibn 'Amr, d. 72 AH/691 CE, was a Successor from Yemen who embraced Islam on the occasion of the conquest of Makkah. He, however, did not have the privilege of the Prophet's Companionship. He migrated to Madīnah during the Caliphate of 'Umar ibn al-Khaṭṭāb and took part in several military expeditions on behalf of Muslims.

Samurah ibn Jundub, d. 54 AH/673 CE, was a Companion who participated in almost all the battles led by the Prophet (peace be on him).

Sawdah bint Zam'ah ibn Qays, see Biographical Notes, *Towards Understanding the Qur'ān*, Abridged Version.

Al-Sha'bī, 'Āmir ibn Shuraḥbīl, see 'Āmir ibn Shuraḥbīl al-Sh'abī.

Al-Shāfi'ī, Muḥammad ibn Idrīs, see Biographical Notes, Vol. I.

Sufyān ibn Abī 'Uyaynah , d. 198 AH/813 CE, was a Successor who is rated highly for his contribution to the field of *Ḥadīth.*

Al-Suyūṭī, Jalāl al-Dīn, see Biographical Notes, Vol. VII.

Al-Ṭabarānī, Sulaymān ibn Aḥmad ibn Ayyūb, see Biographical Notes, Vol. VII.

Al-Ṭabarī, Muḥammad ibn Jarīr, see Biographical Notes, Vol. I.

Al-Taftāzānī, Sa'd al-Dīn, d. 793 AH/1390 CE, was an illustrious scholar of Arabic language, rhetoric, logic and theology. His commentary on Nasafī's *'Aqā'id* is an influential work in the field of Islamic theology.

Ṭalḥah ibn 'Ubayd Allāh ibn 'Uthmān, see Biographical Notes, Vol. III.

Thānawī, Ashraf 'Alī, d. 1362 AH/1943 CE, was among the most celebrated religious scholars and reformers of Muslim South Asia in the twentieth century. He has left dozens of works in virtually all fields of Islamic scholarship, including *tafsīr* and *taṣawwuf.*

Al-Thawrī, Sufyān ibn Sa'īd, see Biographical Notes, Vol. II.

Al-Tirmidhī, Muḥammad ibn 'Īsā, see Biographical Notes, Vol. I.

Ubayy ibn Ka'b, see Biographical Notes, Vol. I.

'Umar ibn al-Khaṭṭāb, see Biographical Notes, Vol. I.

Umm Ḥabībah Ramlah bint Abī Sufyān, see Biographical Notes, Vol. V.

Umm Kulthūm, d. 9 AH/630 CE, was one of the Prophet's daughters from his first wife, Khadījah bint Khuwaylid. She was married before the advent of Islam to 'Utaybah ibn Abī Lahab who divorced her. Her sister Ruqayyah was married to 'Uthmān ibn 'Affān. After Ruqayyah died, she too was married to 'Uthmān and died while she was in 'Uthmān's wedlock.

Umm Salamah, Hind bint Abī Umayyah, see Biographical Notes, Vol. I.

'Urwah ibn al-Zubayr, see Biographical Notes, Vol. II.

'Uthmān ibn 'Affān, see Biographical Notes, Vol. I.

'Uthmānī, Shabbīr Aḥmad, d. 1369 AH/1949 CE, was among the most prominent scholars of the Deobandī school. His major works include his *tafsīr*, popularly known as *Tafsīr 'Uthmānī*, and his famous commentary on Muslim's *Ṣaḥīḥ*. He gained fame for effectively supporting the Pakistan movement. After the establishment of Pakistan he was regarded as the most esteemed religious authority and was popularly called Shaykh al-Islām.

Al-Wāqidī, Muḥammad ibn 'Umar, see Biographical Notes, Vol. I.

Wāthilah ibn Asqa', d. 83 AH/702 CE, was among the People of Ṣuffah.

Ẓāhirīs, see Biographical Notes, Vol. I.

Al-Zamakhsharī, Maḥmūd ibn Muḥammad ibn Aḥmad, see Biographical Notes, Vol. IV.

Zayd ibn Aslam al-'Adawī al-'Umarī, see Biographical Notes, Vol. VI.

Zayd ibn Ḥārithah ibn Sharāḥīl (or Shuraḥbīl) al-Kalbī, see Biographical Notes, *Towards Understanding the Qur'ān*, Abridged Version.

Zayd ibn Thābit, see Biographical Notes, Vol. I.

Zaynab bint Jaḥsh al-Asadīyah, see Biographical Notes, *Towards Understanding the Qur'ān*, Abridged Version.

Zufar ibn al-Hudhayl, see Biographical Notes, Vol. II.

Al-Zuhrī, Muḥammad ibn Muslim ibn Shihāb, see Biographical Notes, Vol. I.

Bibliography

Abū Dāwūd, Sulaymān ibn al-Ash'ath al-Sijistānī, *al-Sunan*.

Abū al-Ḥanafī al-'Izz, *Sharḥ al-Ṭaḥāwīyah fī al-'Aqīdah al-Salafīyah*, Riyadh, Wakālat al-Ṭibā'ah wa al-Tarjamah, 1413 AH.

Abū Ḥayyān, *al-Baḥr al-Muḥīṭ*.

Akmal al-Dīn Muḥammad ibn Maḥmūd, *al-'Ināyah Sharḥ al-Hidāyah*, 9 vols., Quetta, al-Maktabah al-Rashīdīyah, 1985 on the margin of Kamāl al-Dīn 'Abd al-Wāḥid, Quetta, Fatḥ al-Qadīr, 9 vols., al-Maktabah al-Rashīdīyah, 1985.

Al-Ālūsī, Maḥmūd ibn 'Abd Allāh al-Ḥusaynī, *Rūḥ al-Ma'ānī*, 30 vols., Cairo, Idārat al-Ṭibā'ah al-Munīrīyah, n.d.

Al-'Asqalānī, Ibn Ḥajar, *Fatḥ al-Bārī*, 13 vols., Cairo, al-Maṭba'ah al-Khayrīyah, 1325 AH.

Al-'Aynī, Badr al-Dīn, *'Umdat al-Qārī*, 12 vols., Dār al-Ṭibā'ah al-'Āmirah, n.d.

Āzād, Abū al-Kalām, *Tarjumān al-Qur'ān*, New Delhi, 1970.

Al-Azharī, *Tahdhīb al-Lughah*, Cairo, 1967.

Al-Baghawī, 'Abd Allāh ibn Muḥammad Abī al-Qāsim, *Ma'ālim al-Tanzīl*, eds. Khālid 'Abd al-Raḥmān al-'Ak and Marwān Sawar, 4 vols., second edition, Beirut, Dār al-Ma'rifah, 1987.

———, *Sharḥ al-Sunnah*, ed. Zuhayr al-Shāwīsh and Shu'ayb al-Arnā'ūṭ, 16 vols., second edition, Beirut, al-Maktab al-Islāmī, 1983.

Al-Baghdādī, 'Alā' al-Dīn, *Tafsīr al-Khāzin*, eds. 'Abd al-Salām Muḥammad 'Alī Shāhīn, 4 vols., Beirut, Dār al-Kutub al-'Ilmīyah, 1995.

Al-Bayḍāwī, 'Abd Allāh ibn 'Umar, *Anwār al-Tanzīl*, 5 vols., Beirut, Dār al-Fikr, n.d.

Al-Bayhaqī, Abū Bakr Aḥmad ibn al-Ḥusayn ibn 'Alī, *al-Sunan*.

Al-Bukhārī, Muḥammad ibn Ismā'īl, *al-Jāmi' al-Ṣaḥīḥ*.

Al-Dāraquṭnī, 'Alī ibn 'Umar, *al-Sunan*, 4 vols., Beirut, 'Ālam al-Kutub, n.d.

Al-Dārimī, Abū Muḥammad 'Abd Allāh ibn 'Abd al-Raḥmān, *al-Sunan*, 2 vols., Cairo, Dār al-Fikr, 1975.

Doughty, Charles Montagu, *Travels in Arabia Deserta*, London, 1888.

Encyclopaedia of the Qur'ān, 5 vols., ed. Jane D. McAuliffe, Leiden and Boston, Brill, 2001–2006.

The Encyclopaedia of Religion and Ethics, 12 vols., ed. James Hastings, Edinburgh, 1959.

Al-Firūzābādī, *al-Qāmūs al-Muḥīṭ*, second edition, Cairo, al-Ḥalabī, 1952.

Al-Ghazālī, Abū Hāmid Muḥammad ibn Muḥammad, *al-Iqtiṣād fī al-I'tiqād*, Beirut, Dār al-Kutub al-'Ilmīyah, 1403/1983.

Gibbon, Edward, *Decline and Fall of the Roman Empire*, 5th ed., London, Methuen, 1924.

Goitein, S.D., *Studies in Islamic History and Institutions*, Leiden, E.J. Brill, 1966.

Al-Ḥākim al-Naysābūrī, Muḥammad ibn 'Abd Allāh Ḥamdawayh, *al-Mustadrak 'alā al-Ṣaḥīḥayn fī al-Ḥadīth*, 4 vols., Riyadh, Maktabat al-Ma'ārif, n.d.

Al-Ḥamawī, Yāqūt, *Mu'jam al-Buldān*, 5 vols., Beirut, Dār Ṣādir, 1977.

Hershon, Paul Isaac, *Talmudic Miscellany*, London, 1880.

Al-Hindī, 'Alā' al-Dīn, *Kanz al-'Ummāl fī Sunan al-Aqwāl wa al-Af'āl*, Beirut, Mu'assasat al-Risālah, 1985.

The Holy Bible, Revised Standard Edition, New York, 1952.

Howley, G.C.D., *A Bible Commentary for Today*, London, Pickering & Inglis Ltd., 1979.

Ibn Abī Ḥāṭim, *Tafsīr*.

Ibn Abī Shaybah, *al-Muṣannaf*, 15 vols., Karachi, Idarat al-Qur'ān wa al-'Ulūm al-Islāmīyah, 1986.

Ibn Aḥmad al-Makkī, *Manāqib al-Imām al-A'ẓam Abī Ḥanīfah*, Hyderabad, India, 1321 AH.

Ibn al-'Arabī, Abū Bakr, *Aḥkām al-Qur'ān*.

Ibn Baṭṭūṭah, *Muhadhdhab Riḥlat Ibn Baṭṭūṭah*, ed. Aḥmad al-'Awāmir Muḥammad Jād al-Mawlā, Cairo, al-Amīrīyah, 1934.

Ibn Ḥanbal, Aḥmad, *Musnad*, 6 vols., Cairo, al-Maktabah al-Maymanīyah, 1313 AH.

Ibn Ḥazm, 'Alī ibn Aḥmad, *Jawāmi' al-Sīrah*.

———, *Al-Muḥallā*, ed. Muḥammad Munīr al-Damishqī, 11 vols., Cairo, Idarat al-Ṭibā'ah al-Munīrīyah, 1352 AH.

Ibn Hishām, 'Abd al-Malik, *Sīrah*, eds. Muṣṭafā al-Saqqā et al., second edition, Cairo, 1955.

Ibn Isḥāq, *The Life of Muḥammad*, tr. and notes by A. Guillaume, Karachi, Oxford University Press, 1955.

Ibn al-Jawzī, *Zād al-Masīr*.

Ibn Kathīr, Ismā'īl ibn 'Umar, *al-Bidāyah wa al-Nihāyah*, Cairo, Dār Iḥyā' al-Turāth al-'Arabī, 1988.

———, *Tafsīr al-Qur'ān al-'Aẓīm*.

Ibn Mājah, Muḥammad ibn Yazīd, *al-Sunan*.

Ibn Manẓūr, *Lisān al-'Arab*, Beirut, Dār Ṣādir, n.d.

Ibn Rushd, *Bidāyat al-Mujtahid*, 2 vols., Cairo, n.d.

Ibn Sa'd, Muḥammad, *Al-Ṭabaqāt Al-Kubrā*, 8 vols., Beirut, 1957–60.

Ibn al-Sinnī, Abū Bakr Aḥmad ibn Muḥammad, *'Amal al-Yawm wa al-Laylah*, Hyderabad (Deccan), second edition, Maṭba'at Dā'irat al-Ma'ārif al-'Uthmānīyah, 1359 AH.

Ibn Taymīyah, Taqī al-Dīn, *Majmū' Fatāwā Ibn Taymīyah*, ed. Muḥammad ibn 'Abd al-Raḥmān ibn Qāsim, 37 vols., Riyadh, 1398 AH.

Al-'Imādī, Abū Sa'ūd, *Irshād al-'Aql al-Salīm ilā Mazāyā al-Kitāb al-Karīm*, 9 vols., Beirut, Dār Iḥyā' al-Turāth al-'Arabī, n.d.

Al-'Irāqī, Abū al-Ḥasan, *Tanzīh al-Sharī'ah al-Marfū'ah 'an al-Aḥādīth al-Mawḍū'ah*, 2 vols., first edition, Cairo, Maktabat al-Qāhirah, n.d.

Al-Jaṣṣāṣ, Aḥmad ibn 'Alī, *Aḥkām al-Qur'ān*, 3 vols., Cairo, 1347 AH.

Al-Jazīrī, 'Abd al-Raḥmān, *al-Fiqh 'alā al-Madhāhib al-Arba'ah*, 5 vols., Beirut, Dar Iḥyā' al-Turāth, 1980.

The Jewish Encyclopaedia, 12 vols., ed. Isidore Singer, New York, KTAV Publishing House, n.d.

Kamāl al-Dīn Muḥammad ibn 'Abd al-Wāḥid, *Fatḥ al-Qadīr*, 9 vols., Quetta, al-Maktabah al-Rashīdīyah, 1985.

Al-Kardarī, Muḥammad ibn Muḥammad ibn al-Bazzāz, *Manāqib al-Imām al-A'ẓam Abī Ḥanīfah*, Quetta, Maktabah Islāmīyah, 1407 AH.

Khān, Sir Sayyid Aḥmad, *Tafsīr al-Qur'ān wa Huwa al-Hudā wa al-Furqān*, Patna: Khuda Bakhsh Oriental Public Library, 1995.

Mālik ibn Anas, *al-Muwaṭṭa'*, ed. Muḥammad Fu'ād 'Abd al-Bāqī, 2 vols., Cairo, 1951.

Mawdūdī, Sayyid Abūl A'lā, *Rasā'īl wa Masā'īl* (Urdu), Lahore, 1957.

Muslim ibn al-Ḥajjāj al-Nīsābūrī, *al-Ṣaḥīḥ*.

Al-Nasā'ī, Aḥmad ibn 'Alī, *al-Sunan*.

Al-Nīsābūrī, Niẓām al-Dīn al-Ḥasan ibn Muḥammad, *Gharā'ib al-Qur'ān wa Raghā'ib al-Furqān*, 30 vols., Beirut, Dār al-Kutub al-'Ilmīyah, 1996.

Polano, H., *The Talmud Selections*, London, Frederick Warne & Co.

Al-Qāḍī 'Iyāḍ ibn Mūsā, *Al-Shifā bi Ta'rīf Ḥuqūq Muṣṭafā*, ed. 'Alī Muḥammad al-Bajāwī, 2 vols., Beirut, Dār al-Kutub al-'Arabī, 1984.

Al-Qārī, Mullā 'Alī, *Sharḥ al-Fiqh al-Akbar*, Karachi, Muḥammad Sa'īd and Sons, n.d.

Al-Qurṭubī, *al-Jāmi' li Aḥkām al-Qur'ān*, 8 vols., Cairo, Dār al-Sha'b, n.d.

Al-Rāzī, Muḥammad ibn 'Umar Fakhr al-Dīn, *Mafātīḥ al-Ghayb*, 8 vols., Cairo, al-Maṭba'ah al-Khayrīyah, 1308 AH.

Al-Ṣābūnī, Muḥammad 'Alī, *Ṣafwat al-Tafāsīr*, 3 vols., fourth edition, Beirut, 1402/1981.

Al-Ṣāliḥ, Ṣubḥī, *Mabāḥith fī 'Ulūm al-Qur'ān*, Beirut, 1977.

Al-Sarakhsī, Shams al-Dīn, *al-Mabsūṭ*, 30 vols., Cairo, Maṭba'at al-Sa'ādah, 1324 AH.

Al-Shahrastānī, Tāj al-Dīn Abū al-Fatḥ Muḥammad ibn 'Abd al-Karīm, *al-Milal wa al-Niḥal*.

Al-Suyūṭī, Jalāl al-Dīn, *al-Jalālayn*, Qatar, Mu'asassat al-Risālah, 1995.

———, *al-Durr al-Manthūr fī al-Tafsīr bī al-Ma'thūr*, 6 vols., Tehran, al-Maktabah al-Islāmīyah wa al-Maktabah al-Ja'farīyah, n.d.

———, *Lubāb al-Nuqūl fī Asbāb al-Nuzūl*, 2nd edition, Cairo, Muṣṭafā al-Ḥalabī, n.d.

Sykes, Percy, *A History of Persia*, London, Macmillan, 1958.

Al-Ṭabarānī, Sulaymān ibn Aḥmad ibn Ayyūb, *al-Mu'jam al-Kabīr*, ed. Ḥamdī 'Abd al-Mājid, 23 vols., second edition, Baghdad, Wazārat al-Awqāf, n.d.

———, *al-Mu'jam al-Wasīṭ*, Cairo: Dār al-Ḥaramayn, 1405.

Al-Ṭabarī, Muḥammad ibn Jarīr, *Ta'rīkh*, 8 vols., Beirut, Mu'sassat al-A'lamī, n.d.

———, *Jāmi' al-Bayān 'an Tā'wīl Āyi al-Qur'ān*, ed. Ṣadqī Jamīl, 15 vols., Beirut, Dār al-Fikr, 1995.

Al-Tabrayzī, Muḥammad ibn 'Abd Allah, *Mishkāt al-Maṣābīḥ*, ed. Nāṣir al-Dīn Albānī, third edition, Beirut, al-Maktab al-Islāmī, 1985.

Thānawī, Ashraf 'Alī, *Bayān al-Qur'ān*, 2 vols., Lahore, Shaykh Ghulām 'Alī and Sons, n.d.

———, *Kashshāf Iṣṭilāḥāt al-Funūn*, Calcutta, 1863.

Al-Tirmidhī, Muḥammad ibn 'Īsā, *al-Sunan*.

'Uthmanī, Shabbīr Aḥmad and Maḥmūd al-Ḥasan, *Qur'ān Majīd: Mutarjam wa Muḥashshā* [popularly known as *Tafsīr 'Uthmānī*], Karachi.

Al-Wāqidī, Muḥammad ibn 'Umar, *al-Maghāzī*, ed. M. Jones, 3 vols., Cairo, 1966.

Wensinck, A.J., *Concordance et indices de la tradition musulmane*, 7 vols., Leiden, 1939–69.

Winston, William, *The Life and Works of Flavius Josephus*, Philadelphia, John C. Winston Company, n.d.

Al-Zamakhsharī, Maḥmūd ibn Muḥammad ibn Aḥmad, *al-Kashshāf 'an Ḥaqā'iq Ghawāmiḍ al-Tanzīl*, 4 vols., Beirut, Dār al-Kitāb al-'Arabī, 1366 AH.

Subject Index

Adoption of a child:
- Allah's directive regarding it, 63–64
- The Prophet (pbuh) changed this practice at Allah's command, 65, 66
- The Prophet's initial hesitation, 19, 22, 29, 65
- The Prophet Muḥammad (pbuh) was directed to change this practice, 15, 67, 68
- This practice had created legal complications, 15, 16, 65, 66

Al-Ākhirah (see Hereafter)

Angels:
- Arab polytheists regarded them as Allah's daughters, 32, 322
- No evidence for the above misconception, 321
- Recognise their position, 322
- Supplicate for the believers, 69
- Their assignment, 208, 280, 283
- Worshipped by polytheists in every age, 196, 197

Animal sacrifice: 302, 303

Arabs:
- Did not accept any Scripture, 190
- Looked forward to a Messenger before the Prophet Muḥammad's advent, 237, 238, 323
- Prophets in Arabia before the Prophet Muḥammad (pbuh), 242, 243
- Regarded angels as Allah's daughters, 321, 322
- Their condition in *Jāhilīyah* period, 242, 243
- Their erroneous notions, 198, 321

- They had some idea of monotheism even in the pre-Islamic days, 176, 177
- They recognized that Allah is the Sustainer, 185, 186

Associating others with Allah in His Divinity (*shirk*):
- Allah has not sanctioned it, 235
- Calling on someone besides Allah, 235
- False gods, 286, 287
- It amounts to God's imperfection, 257, 258
- It betrays ingratitudes to Allah, 272
- It harms man, 209
- It is illogical, 281
- It stems from doubt, 203
- Its terrible end in the Hereafter, 109, 196, 286–288, 313
- The Qur'ānic arguments against it, 182, 183, 184, 185, 186, 197, 198, 199, 203, 205, 208, 209, 210, 216–218, 219, 235, 236, 251, 252, 298, 312, 313, 321, 322
- Taking angels as God's daughters, 321, 322

Āyah, pl. *Āyāt* (Sign, signs):
- As signs of Allah's power, 152, 173, 175, 254, 258, 261, 263, 283
- Divine punishment for those who reject these, 194, 195
- End of those who reject these, 153
- Standing for the Book and Divine commandments, 53, 153, 263
- Who benefits from these, 156, 157

Backbiting:
- How it differs from calumny, 100

Barzakh:
- Life in *barzakh*, 253–254

Battle of Aḥzāb (the battle of *Khandaq* or the Trench):
- Allah's invisible hosts helped Muslims in this battle, 12, 31, 32
- Distinction between a *ghazwah* and *sariyah*, 2
- Its causes and its account, 1–13
- Its impact, 10, 32, 38–41
- The Qur'ānic critique on it, 31–41
- Tremendous sacrifices by Anṣār of Madīnah in this battle, 11, 12

Battle of Banū Qurayẓah:
- Banū Qurayẓah themselves had appointed the Aws chief, 14
- Its account, 9, 10–11, 12, 13, 31, 32

- The Qur'ānic critique on it, 42, 43
- Sa'd ibn Mu'adh the arbiter, 14
- Were besieged at Allah's directive, 13, 14

Battle of Uḥud:
- Its impact, 1
- The Prophet's strategy, 2

The Bible: 303, 304, 311, 312, 313, 314

Blessed land:
- The Qur'ān brands Syria and Palestine as blessed lands, 175, 176

Blind Conformity:
- As a cause of error, 107, 294
- Conformity to the Prophet (pbuh) is the only way to success, 251

Call to the Truth: 187–188

Calumny (*buhtān*):
- How it differs from backbiting, 100, 101
- Its meaning, 100–101

Children of Israel (*Banī Isrā'īl*):
- Their brief history, 310–313
- Their decline after the demise of the Prophet Solomon (pbuh), 310–314
- Their degeneration after the demise of the Prophet Moses (pbuh), 311, 312, 313
- Their opposition to the Prophet Solomon (pbuh), 161, 162
- Their release from Pharaoh's bondage, 310
- Their treatment of the Messengers of Allah, 107, 108, 311, 312
- Their treatment of the Prophet Moses (pbuh), 107, 108
- They are descendants of the Prophet Isaac (pbuh), 309
- Why they rejected the Prophet Jesus (pbuh), 145

Christianity:
- Its main error, 135
- When the Prophet Jesus (pbuh) reappears, he will disown it, 135

Companions of the Prophet (pbuh):
- Their sincerity and sacrifices, 2–3, 10–11, 12–13, 37–40

Covenant: 28, 31, 34

Dajjāl: 134–147

Deity (*ilāh*):
- Allah is the One True God, 281
- Its meaning, 281
- No god besides Allah, 209, 288
- Prophet Abraham's argument against false gods, 296, 297
- Why Allah is the Only Deity, 209, 281

Divine decree:
- Allah alone directs one to follow the right way, 228
- Allah may guide whom He pleases, 212, 213
- Distinction between Allah's pleasure and His decree, 195
- How Allah misguides one, 212, 213
- How Allah seals one's heart, eyes and ears, 212, 213
- Its nexus with one's error, 263
- It is preordained, 258
- Man cannot escape his destiny, 249
- Man endowed with authority in order to test him, 108–110
- Man responsible for his choice of good and evil, 233, 234
- No one can alter it, 106, 237
- One's span of life is fixed, 217
- One's sustenance is preordained, 193, 194, 195
- Who is not shown guidance, 242, 243

Divine forgiveness:
- Who will be blessed with it, 56, 60, 108, 153, 212, 245, 252

Divine revelation:
- Messengers' dream as a mode of revelation, 300
- The Qur'ān as revelation, 228

Error:
- How Allah directs one to error, 213
- Is in not recognizing evil as evil, 212, 213
- It consists in disobeying Allah and His Messenger, 61, 62
- Its causes, 107, 154, 176, 177, 190–193, 247–249, 251, 262, 263, 264, 267–270, 294, 321
- Who are in error, 61, 62

Establishing faith:
- An arduous task, 37, 38, 39
- Angels assist those seeking to establish faith, 68, 69
- Those working for it are reinforced, 67, 68

Faith (*Īmān*):
- Allah helps believers in both the worlds, 323
- Allah is kind to believers, 109
- Allah's directive for believers, 108
- Allah's favours to believers, 68, 69
- Allah's promise of help to believers, 37, 38
- Angels pray for believers, 68, 69
- Believers and unbelievers are not alike, 222
- Believers to get unending reward, 73
- Believers' relationship with the Prophet (pbuh), 26, 27, 107, 108
- Consists in obeying the Prophet (pbuh), 47, 53, 60, 61, 108
- Definition of a believer, 57, 58
- Difference between a believer, an unbeliever and a hypocrite, 222, 228
- Excellent end of those who believe in the Prophet (pbuh) and the Qur'ān, 227, 233
- Features of believers, 36–41, 56–60, 66, 67, 108, 220, 221, 222, 226, 227, 243, 322
- Good deed without faith is pointless, 35, 36
- Its criteria, 35, 36, 60, 61
- Its increase or decrease, 37–41
- Its link with good deeds, 152, 194, 212, 214, 215, 216
- Its prerequisites, 60, 61, 67, 68, 69, 91, 99, 108, 279
- Reward for faith and good deeds, 41, 56, 60, 68, 73, 152, 153, 194, 212, 214, 215, 216, 226, 227, 295, 303, 310, 313, 314, 315, 318
- What one's faith in the Prophet (pbuh) demands, 53, 60, 61, 68, 86, 88, 89, 90, 91, 92, 93, 98, 108
- Who is a true believer, 37–41

Fighting in Allah's cause (*Jihād fī sabīl Allāh*):
- For eliminating the enemies within, 104
- How should women carry it out, 51
- Hypocrites' crime, 32, 33
- Those avoiding it are hypocrites, 32, 37–39

Finality of the Prophet Muḥammad's Messengership:
- How Qadyanis misinterpret this doctrine, 29–30
- Its exposition, 67, 68, 111–133
- No need for a new Prophet, 131, 132
- Significance of this doctrine, 130, 131
- War was waged against Musaylimah in view of his false claim to Prophethood, 119–120

Glorifying Allah (*tasbīḥ*):
- Its meaning, 68, 195, 196, 254, 257

God (Allah):
- Accountability to Him, 34
- All-Appreciative, 228, 233
- All are dependent on Him, 219
- All-Aware, 22, 56, 151, 218, 227
- All-Forgiving, 26, 42, 84, 105, 109, 152, 174, 228, 233, 237
- All-Hearing, 201
- All-Knowing, 22, 86, 187, 238, 260, 276
- All-Pardoning, 227
- All praise is for Him, 151, 208, 325
- All-Powerful, 42, 208, 238
- All-Seeing, 228
- All-Subtle, 56
- Alternates day and night, 218
- Always states the truth, 23
- Best of creators, 312
- Created man, 209
- Creates everything, 272
- Creator, 276
- Deserves all praise and thanks, 219, 220
- Does not feel shy of stating the truth, 89
- Does not have a child, 322
- Everyone has to return to Him, 222, 276
- Free from all that the polytheists ascribe to Him, 325
- Fully aware of what man does, 22, 23
- Grants one what He wills, 208, 209
- Grants respite and does not instantly seize the culprits, 151, 235, 236
- Great, 185
- Guardian, 23, 74
- Has bound the sun and the moon to a set of laws, 218
- Has power over everything, 42, 208, 276
- He alone is the best guide, 23, 24
- He alone is the One True God, 280, 281
- He controls the heavens and the earth, 235
- He decides all issues, 186, 210
- His creative wonders, 225, 226, 276
- His excellent names are related to the context of the verses in which they occur, 22, 23, 26, 56, 67, 84, 85, 86, 90, 91, 92, 103, 151, 152, 153, 154, 185, 186, 187, 209, 219, 220, 226, 227, 236

- His favours to man, 217, 218
- His is the dominion, 218
- His knowledge is all-embracing, 67, 151, 216
- His perfect justice, 47, 48, 314, 315, 316, 317
- His reckoning is to be feared, 67
- His way does not change, 106, 237
- Holds all power and authority, 208, 209, 276
- Holds all power to punish or pardon, 41
- How He succours the believers, 31
- How to gain proximity to Him, 194, 214
- Immensely praiseworthy, 154
- Infinitely Mighty, 42, 187, 209, 226, 241, 258
- Is man's only Guardian, 235, 236
- Knows all that is hidden and manifest, 152
- Knows best what is good and what is not, 22, 227, 228
- Knows even the secrets of man's heart, 84, 234
- Knows what man publishes or hides, 90, 273
- Lord of human beings, 312
- Lord of the worlds, 297
- Lord, 265, 325
- Man should fear only Him, 22
- Man should have trust in Him, 22, 73
- Manages the entire universe, 151, 208, 280, 281
- May guide or misguide anyone, 212, 213
- May honour or disgrace anyone, 214, 325
- May increase or decrease one's sustenance, 193, 194, 195
- May replace one community with another, 219, 220
- Most Compassionate to the believers, 35
- Most Compassionate, 26, 41, 83, 103, 109, 151, 241, 267
- Most Exalted, 185
- Most forbearing, 86, 236
- Most Merciful, 244, 249, 252, 263
- Most Wise, 22, 151, 188, 209
- Near everyone who supplicates to Him, 200
- No god besides Him, 210, 288
- No one can escape His grip, 34
- No one can stop His decree, 209
- No power on earth can frustrate Him, 237
- Overlooks man's misdeeds, 237, 238
- Overwhelms everyone, 209
- Owner of all that is in the heavens and on earth, 281
- Perfect, 325
- Possessor of all honour, 325

- Reckoner, 67
- Resurrection of mankind is not hard for Him, 245
- Self-Sufficient, 220
- Signs of His power and wisdom, 217, 218, 225, 226, 276
- Strong, 42
- Suffices for everything, 67
- Took a firm covenant from Messengers, 28, 29
- Watches everything, 87, 176, 200
- Watches man's deeds, 31, 214
- Watchful, 86
- Who benefits from His signs, 156

Gratitude:
- How man is punished for ingratitude, 174, 175
- Its meaning, 175, 176, 273
- Its significance, 175, 176
- What is ingratitude, 209

Guidance:
- Allah may bestow it on who He pleases, 212, 213
- How can man follow it? 176, 177
- Its sources, 226
- Only divine revelation can guide man to the straight way, 227, 228
- Out of Allah's grace and mercy, 292
- Who gains it, 220, 223

Ḥadīth: 24, 25, 26, 27, 52, 53, 54, 55, 57, 60, 72, 73, 78, 94, 98, 99, 108, 109, 114–117, 133–141, 162–165, 188, 208, 229, 230, 231, 265, 290, 291, 292

Heaven:
- Adorned with the adornment of stars, 282
- As a sign of Allah's creative power, monotheism and the Hereafter, 151, 154–157, 185, 209, 235, 236, 258–262, 276, 282
- Distinction between *samā'* and *falak*, 261
- How it is protected against devils, 281, 282
- Meaning of the lower heaven, 282

Hell:
- The dispute between unbelievers and their leaders there, 191, 287
- False gods will be hurled into it along with polytheists, 286
- The food of its inmates, 293
- It is eternal, 106, 107, 233
- Its inmates will not have any helper, 107

– Its punishment, 106, 233, 293, 294
– Unbelievers will curse their leaders there, 107
– Who will enter it, 80, 109, 197, 233, 270, 286, 292, 293, 322

Hereafter (The Life to Come; the Next Life; the Next World, the World to Come):
– All differences will be settled there, 186
– All the unbelievers and their idols will be consigned to Hellfire, 286, 288
– All ties between culprits will be severed there, 267, 268
– Allah will gather everyone there, 187, 253, 265
– An appointed term for the present order, 218
– Arguments for it, 153, 173, 274, 275, 282, 283, 284, 285
– Both the misguiding leaders and their followers will face punishment there, 288
– Concern for it is a great virtue, 37, 42
– Condition of culprits there, 286, 287, 288
– Consequences of its rejection, 176, 177, 178, 283, 284
– Culprits will be recompensed for their misdeeds, 288
– The culprits' limbs will testify against them, 270, 271
– The above testimony will be presented in the case of those culprits who deny their misdeeds, 270
– The culprits will wish that they could return to the world, 233
– The response to their above wish, 233
– Day of Recompense, 284
– Everyone has to return to Allah, 222, 276
– Everyone will be called to account for his/her deeds, 185, 186, 187
– The evil and the pious will not be treated alike there, 222
– False gods will disown there their polytheistic devotees, 195, 196, 218, 219
– How arguments will be clinched against unbelievers there, 233
– How will the believers be welcomed there, 68, 69
– How will children be treated there, 290, 291
– How will the Muslim community be treated there, 227–233
– How will witnesses bear out their testimony there, 71, 72
– The interrogation there, 195, 196, 197
– It is bound to happen, 210, 211
– Its nature, 264, 265, 284
– Its purpose, 152, 153
– Its rejection is a serious error, 154, 155
– Its significance, 152, 153, 154, 157, 176, 177, 205
– Law of retribution there, 193, 194, 288
– Man should strive for success there, 293

– Man will be recompensed for his deeds, 288
– Man will be restored to the same body, 152, 153, 154, 155, 270, 271
– Man will not get any more chances there, 201
– Man will only be recompensed there; he will not be able to do any act or embrace faith there, 201
– Man's faculties of hearing and sight there will be different, 292
– Man's good deeds will not be wasted there, 226, 227
– The mighty will be humbled there, 286
– The misguiding leaders and their followers will blame each other, 190–193, 286, 287
– No one will be wronged there, 267, 286
– No one will carry another's burden there, 219, 220
– No one will come to anyone's rescue there, 196, 219, 220, 286
– No one will help the culprits there, 233
– One will not be burdened there with someone else's record of deeds, 219
– Perfect judgement there, 186, 187, 287
– Reason and justice demand it, 153
– The righteous will be immediately admitted to Paradise, 267, 268
– Terrible end of those who reject it, 201, 202
– Those who reject it, 176, 177, 203
– Unbelievers ask how they will be brought back to life there, 154, 155, 274, 275, 276, 284, 285, 292
– Unbelievers ask that their ancestors be revived, 284, 285
– Unbelievers mistakenly think they will have success there, 193
– Unbelievers mockingly ask when it will happen, 106, 264, 265
– The unbelievers will be full of remorse, 107
– Unbelievers will curse their leaders and demand a double punishment for them, 107
– The unbelievers will curse themselves for their foolishness, 284
– Unbelievers will recognize the truth there which they used to reject in this world, 201
– Unbelievers' arguments against, 152
– Unbelievers' objections against it, 154, 155
– Who will be punished and who will be spared there, 294
– Who will undergo punishment there, 288, 313
– Why unbelievers reject it, 156

Hypocrites:
– Distinction between a believer and a hypocrite, 222, 228
– Their misconduct, 32, 36–40
– Their punishment, 109

- Their role in Madīnah, 2–3, 15, 32–37, 63, 103
- To be dealt with sternly, 103
- What is hypocrisy? 104, 105

Iḥsān (doing good):
- It exalts one's rank 214
- Its meaning, 43–44
- Its reward, 291, 301, 302, 310, 313
- Who are the doers of good, 43–44

Intercession:
- Islamic doctrine, 185
- Its polytheistic version, 252
- No one can intercede without Allah's leave, 183–185

Islam:
- Consists in obedience to Allah and His Messenger, 53
- Its essence and spirit, 35, 279
- Its essential values, 60
- Its real message, 241, 242
- Those obeying Allah and His Messenger attain a great success, 108
- Types of Muslim, 229
- A universal faith, 187, 188
- Who is Muslim, 56, 57, 58

Islamic law:
- About the adoption of a child, 14, 15, 16, 17, 24
- About apostasy, 119, 120
- About constitution, 60, 62, 63, 276
- About exile, 103, 106
- About gender segregation, 18, 19, 21–53, 87–90, 101–105
- About inheritance, 14, 15, 23, 26, 28
- About marriage and divorce, 14, 24, 43–47, 65, 66, 75, 76, 77, 78, 79, 80, 86, 87
- About spreading false rumours, 103, 104, 106
- About war, 12, 13
- All believers are equal before law, 41
- Command belongs only to Allah, 218
- Does not allow mixed gatherings of men and women, 50, 51, 90, 91, 104, 105
- Essence of Islamic social laws, 103, 104
- The lawful and the unlawful clearly demarcated, 169, 170

- Legal distinction between a rebel and an apostate, 20
- Making images is forbidden, 161–170
- No Muslim to disregard what is commanded by Allah and His Messenger, 60–62
- No one is responsible for another's conduct, 219, 220
- No penalty for an unintentional act, 25
- The Prophet's role in it, 11, 12
- *Sharī'ah* as prescribed by the Prophet (pbuh) and practised by Companions, 166

Islamic society:
- Adopted children to be attributed to their father, 24, 25
- Based on universal equality, 15, 16, 17, 61
- Enemies of Islam cannot flourish in it, 103, 106
- Status of women, 49, 50, 51, 52, 53
- One whose father is not known is to be called a brother in faith, 24, 25
- Ties of kinship superior to all else, 26

Islamic state:
- Its principles, 60, 61
- Sovereignty belongs only to Allah, 218
- Those opposing it cannot be allowed to flourish within it, 103, 106

Jāhilīyah (Former Time of Ignorance):
- Its meaning, 52–53

Jews:
- Dajjāl will be from among them, 145, 146
- Looked forward to Messengers, 313, 314
- Their belief about the Promised Messiah, 144, 145
- Why their rabbis regard the Prophet Isaac (pbuh) as the one sacrificed, 308

Jinn:
- Arab polytheists' belief about them, 172–173
- As angels, 322
- Their nature, 158, 172, 173
- Their sphere is limited to this world, 281, 282
- They were made subservient to the Prophet Solomon (pbuh), 159, 170–173
- Those in error, serve them, 196

Knowledge:
- Not to conform blindly, 294
- Those endowed with knowledge fear Allah, 226
- What the Qur'ān means by knowledge, 226

Last Day:
- Culprits will be seized then, 201
- Day of gathering all human beings, 195
- How will it overtake man?, 264, 265, 284
- Is inevitable, 152
- Is preordained, 187, 190
- Its signs as foretold in *Ḥadīth*, 139
- May happen at any time, 156
- Only Allah knows when it will be, 106, 152
- The Qur'ānic rejoinder to the unbelievers' demands, 188, 190
- Who will intercede on that Day? 184, 185
- Why the unbelievers asked as to when it will be, 106, 152, 188, 189, 190, 265
- Why will it be? 152, 153
- Will be sudden, 264

Making images or pictures:
- Photograph, 168, 169
- The ruling in the Torah, 160, 161
- *Sharī'ah* forbids it, 160–170

Man:
- Allah grants him respite, 237, 238
- Allah guides him, 292
- Allah overlooks his misdeeds, 237, 238
- Allah's favours to him, 271, 272
- Differences in his nature are preordained, 225, 226
- Gives little thanks, 170
- Has only One True God, 280, 281
- Has to return to Allah, 253, 276
- Helpless before Allah's powers, 271
- His accountability, 156, 185, 186
- His audacity, 274
- His choice between faith and unbelief, 108–110
- His condition in old age, 271, 272
- His non-serious attitude, 108–110
- His obedience to Satan lands him in Hell, 210, 211, 212
- His record of deeds, 245

- His role in life, 108–110, 234
- His span of life is preordained, 217
- His vicegerency, 108–110, 234
- Is dependent upon Allah's mercy, 262, 263
- Is totally under Allah's grip, 156, 157
- Meaning of his being ignorant and unjust, 110
- Not responsible for someone's conduct, 219, 220
- Owes all his authority to Allah, 262, 263
- The Qur'ānic account of man's creation, 216, 274, 283
- Satan being his eternal enemy, 210, 212, 267, 268
- Satan's tricks in order to deceive him, 176, 210
- Serving Allah is his only right way, 268
- Signs for him to turn to Allah, 156
- Stages of man's life, 233
- Will be resurrected, 245
- Worshipping Allah is innate in his nature, 281

Marriage: 75

Messengers:
- Convey Allah's message to mankind, 72
- Did all that Allah commanded, 66
- Their addressees, 193

Messengership:
- The affluent ones always reject Messengers, 193
- Allah grants it to whom He pleases, 131
- Both Allah and the Messenger are to be obeyed, 53, 54, 60, 61, 107, 108
- Even Messengers cannot escape punishment, if they were to commit a mistake, 316–319
- Every community had a Messenger, 223, 224
- How Allah reinforces them, 294, 295, 310
- How is a Messenger to be tested, 250, 251
- How it stands distinct from Prophethood, 127, 128
- How Messengers warned their communities, 310–312
- Its acceptance as a deciding factor on the Day of Judgement, 233
- Its role, 207, 220, 221, 223, 224, 249, 294
- Its significance in Islam, 130
- Messengers as witnesses on the Day of Judgement, 70–72
- Messengers brought clear arguments, Scriptures and divine guidance, 223, 224
- Messengers cannot guide those who are not keen on it, 220–223

– Messengers do not fear anyone other than Allah, 66, 67
– Messengers faced trials, 223, 224
– Messengers fear Allah most, 65, 66
– Messengers reinforced by wisdom, 53, 56
– Messengers were rejected because they were human, 247–249
– Messengers' covenant with Allah, 28–31
– Messengers' dream as a mode of divine revelation, 300, 301
– Modes of divine revelations, 227, 228
– One's kinship with a Messenger cannot save him, 47, 48
– Only in one instance three Messengers were sent at the same time, 247
– Opposition to Messengers, 210, 223, 246–251
– Sustained by divine revelation, 227, 228
– Terrible end of those who reject it, 199, 223, 224, 252, 294, 313, 323
– Those obedient to Messengers will be spared divine punishment, 313, 314
– When is a Messenger sent down? 242, 243

Miracle(s):
– How the Prophet Abraham (pbuh) was rescued from fire, 299
– In the life of the Prophet Jonah (pbuh), 316, 317

Monotheism (*tawḥīd*):
– Allah is above and beyond having a child, 322
– Arguments for it, 151, 182, 183, 205, 208, 209, 210, 216–218, 224, 235, 236, 251, 252, 254, 262, 272, 280, 281, 312, 313
– It is pointless to invoke anyone other than Allah for help, 218, 219
– Man needs to worship Allah, 219
– Signs of Allah's wisdom and creative wonders, 224

Morals and Moral teachings: 87, 88, 89, 293

Paradise (*Jannah*):
– Allah's blessings on its inmates, 267
– Believers will thank Allah on entering it, 231, 292
– Conversation between the inmates of Paradise and Hell, 292
– Conversation of its inmates, 291
– *Ḥūr* and *ghilmān*, 277, 291
– Its bounties, 194, 229–233, 267, 288–291
– Its drinks, 290, 291
– It is eternal life, 292, 293
– It is eternal, 194, 195, 228, 233
– It is for martyrs, 252

– Its inmates will not suffer any fatigue, 233
– Who will enter it, 194, 228, 288, 289

Patience:
– Its meaning, 57, 58, 175, 176
– Its significance, 57, 58, 175, 176

People of the Book:
– How they fell to idolatry, 162
– Their attitude before the Prophet Muḥammad's advent, 236, 323

Piety (*taqwā*):
– Demands that unbelievers and hypocrites be not followed, 22
– Its end, 108
– Its prerequisites, 47–48, 78, 108, 310, 312

Polygamy: 83

Prayer:
– Benefits of establishing Prayer, 226, 227
– Establishing Prayer as an essential feature of believers, 226
– Its significance in Islam, 222
– To be established, 50, 53

Principles of Jurisprudence (*fiqh*):
– How jurists have deduced commands from the Qur'ān, 43–47, 61, 62, 75–79
– How *Sharī'ah* lifts unnecessary restrictions, 23, 24, 65, 66
– *Sharī'ah* commands based on expediency, 47, 49, 65, 66, 80–83, 87, 88, 167–170

The Prophet Muḥammad's wives:
– As models for Muslim women, 47–49
– As mothers of believers, 26, 27
– The choice granted to them, 17, 42
– Muslims forbidden to marry them, 21, 89, 90, 91
– The Prophet (pbuh) not to divorce such wives who had chosen him, 43, 86
– The Prophet (pbuh) treated them fairly, 84, 85
– Their firm faith, 43
– Their names and number, 79, 80
– Their transmission of the Prophet's teachings, 56

The Prophet Muḥammad's family (*Ahl al-Bayt*):
- Are they infallible, 54
- Their obligations, 55
- Who is included, 53–55

Punishment:
- As a sign of God, 314
- Disgraceful punishment, 91, 92
- No more respite when divine punishment overtakes one, 201
- One's status cannot avert it, 47, 48
- Terrible punishment, 31
- Who will be punished, 31, 91, 109, 153, 154, 191, 192, 193, 194, 195, 196, 212, 218, 233, 242, 243, 288, 324
- Who will incur a double punishment, 47, 48
- Why various communities have been punished, 174, 175, 199, 224, 237, 253, 254, 294, 295, 314

Qadyanism: 147

Qur'ānic commands: 22, 23, 24, 26, 28, 36, 37, 43, 44, 47–50, 50–60, 61, 66, 67, 68, 75, 78–87, 87–91, 92, 101–104, 107, 108, 159, 170, 174, 175, 220, 221, 226, 227, 251, 267, 268, 276

Qur'ānic Oaths:
- Their types and purpose, 241, 242, 280, 281

Qur'ānic Parables: 213, 214, 242, 243, 244, 254, 291, 293, 294

Quraysh:
- Branded the Qur'ān as magic, 198
- Dismissed the fact that a fellow human being could be a Messenger of God, 247–249
- How they misled new Muslims, 221
- Prediction about the defeat of their designs, 323, 324
- The Qur'ānic account of their condition, 243
- Rejected divine revelation and Messengership, 249, 250
- Resented the birth of daughters, 321
- Their arguments for rejecting the Prophet Muḥammad (pbuh), 198
- Their false allegations against the Prophet (pbuh), 199, 200, 282, 283, 288

Record of Deeds: 245

Rememberance of Allah: 59, 60, 67, 68

Repentance: 109

Reward:
- Who will get a double reward, 47, 48
- Who will get a generous reward, 69
- Who will get a great reward, 43, 56, 60
- Who will get it, 43, 212, 226, 227, 245

Reward and punishment:
- Allah rewards good and punishes evil, 193, 194, 267, 288
- How it works in this world, 91, 106, 174, 175, 223, 224, 237, 253, 254, 294, 295, 314
- Its divine law, 47, 48, 315, 316–321

Straight Way: 267, 268

Supplication:
- Invoking anyone other than Allah constitutes polytheism, 235, 236
- Only Allah listens to it, 218, 219

Sustenance:
- Allah enlarges or restricts it, 193, 194, 195
- In Paradise, 288
- Its divine dispensation, 193, 194, 195
- Allah as the Sustainer, 195

Takhyīr (a husband authorising his wife to continue or dissolve their marriage): 43–47

Test:
- How believers are tested, 301, 302, 303
- How Allah tests man, 34, 39, 40, 41, 176

The Torah:
- It forbids making images, 161, 162
- Its teachings, 310
- All Ismaelite Messengers abided by it, 161

Trust, 108, 110

Trust in Allah:
- Its meaning, 23, 27
- Why one should trust in Allah, 22, 73

Unbelief:
- Consists in rejecting the Qur'ān and the Prophet Muḥammad (pbuh), 190, 233, 234
- Difference between a believer and an unbeliever, 222
- Is to dispute the signs of Allah, 31
- Its punishment, 152, 153
- Its signs, 262, 263
- Its tormenting consequences, 31, 106, 107, 193, 201, 202, 203, 212, 224, 225, 233–235, 270
- No one can rescue unbelievers from Allah's grip, 106, 107
- Stems from doubt, 202, 203
- Unbelievers are not to be followed, 22
- Unbelievers will be utter losers, 234, 235
- Unbelievers will stand away from believers on the Day of Judgement, 267
- Will land one in Hell, 270

Universe:
- Created by Almighty, All-Wise Allah, 225, 255–262
- Created for a fixed time, 218
- Each planet moving within its orbit, 261
- The sun and the moon have been made subservient, 259

Vicegerency (*Khilāfah*):
- Its meaning, 109
- Man as vicegerent, 108, 234
- Meaning of man's vicegerency, 108–110

Wine:
- As a drink in Paradise, 290, 291
- Its harms, 291

Wisdom (*ḥikmah*):
- How to follow it in preaching Islam, 185–187, 244, 245, 251, 252
- Synonymous with the Prophet's *Sunnah*, 53, 56

Witness:
- Glad tidings of Paradise, 252
- In what sense is the Prophet (pbuh) a witness, 70–73

– Testimony, 69, 70, 91
– Testimony in the Hereafter, 71, 72, 270, 271

Woman:
– 'Ā'ishah's participation in the battle of Jaml not to be taken as a precedent, 51, 52
– Her *Jihād*, 51
– Her status in Islamic society, 49–53, 90, 91, 104, 105
– Is subject to divine reward and punishment, 109
– Should avoid unnecessary talk with unrelated males, 50, 51
– Will get the same reward for her good act which a male performs, 56, 58, 59, 60

World:
– The All-Wise has brought it into being, 225, 226
– A test for man, 233, 234
– How man is deluded by it, 210, 211
– Its real nature, 194
– Rememberance of Allah, 59, 60, 67, 68
– Worldly glory cannot save man from Allah's punishment, 199
– Worldly bounties do not signify Allah's approval of the person getting these, 193, 194

Worship (*'ibādah*):
– As obedience, 267–270
– As service, 195, 196
– Demanded by reason and nature, 251
– Innate in the human nature, 281
– Man asked to worship only the One True God, 281
– Only Allah is to be worshipped, 268

Wrong-doing:
– Committed by polytheists, 196, 197
– Consists in rejecting truth, 233
– Ingratitude to Allah, 175
– Is to believe in something without any basis, 235, 236
– Its meaning, 284, 285, 286, 308
– Who commits it, 286
– Wrong-doers will not have any helper in the Hereafter, 233

Zakāh: 52

Zaqqum: 293

Name Index

Aaron, 116, 117, 309
'Abbās ibn 'Abd al-Muṭṭalib, 304
'Abd Allāh ibn 'Abbās, 47, 54, 61, 72, 78, 94, 102, 124, 163, 165, 166, 179, 232, 241, 275, 280, 304, 305, 307
'Abd Allāh ibn Aḥmad ibn Maḥmūd al-Nasafī, 125
'Abd Allāh ibn 'Amr ibn al-'Āṣ, 78, 116, 139, 189
'Abd Allāh ibn Jaḥsh, 61
'Abd Allāh ibn Mas'ūd, 45, 47, 51, 72, 78, 97, 108, 163, 164, 208, 226, 232, 280, 304
'Abd Allāh ibn Rawāḥah, 10
'Abd Allāh ibn Ubayy, 4
'Abd Allāh ibn 'Umar, 25, 47, 97, 118, 125, 164, 165, 305
'Abd Allāh ibn al-Zubayr, 307
'Abd al-Raḥmān ibn Jubayr, 116
'Abd al-Razzāq, 94
Abī al-'Izz al-Hanafī, 122
Abrahah, 174, 180, 181
Abraham, 29, 54, 94, 95, 97, 118, 243, 278, 279, 296, 297, 298, 299, 300, 301, 302, 303, 304, 305, 306, 307, 308, 309, 314
Abū Bakr, 43, 63, 83, 120, 121, 141, 305
Abū Bakr al-Bazzār, 51, 290
Abū Bakr al-Jaṣṣāṣ, 47, 78, 79, 85, 102
Abū al-Dardā', 47, 52, 72, 231
Abū al-Faḍl 'Iyāḍ ibn Mūsā ibn 'Iyāḍ ibn 'Amr, 99, 124, 305
Abū al-Hiyāj al-Asadī, 166
Abū al-Ṭufayl, 116
Abū Dā'ūd, 25, 78, 85, 94, 95, 100, 108, 115, 116, 117, 137, 138, 139, 165, 240, 290
Abū Ḥanīfah, 41, 45, 78, 98, 121, 122, 167
Abū Ḥumayd al-Sā'idī, 94, 95
Abū Hurayrah, 95, 115, 118, 135, 136, 137, 162, 234, 265, 266, 304, 305
Abū Ja'far Aḥmad ibn Muḥammad al-Azdī al-Ṭaḥāwī, 121
Abū Ja'far M. ibn al-Ḥabīb, 103
Abū Jahl, 83
Abū Juḥayfah, 162
Abū Mas'ūd al-Anṣārī, 97
Abū Muḥammad al-Hudhalī, 162
Abū Mūsa al-Ash'ārī, 189
Abū Razīn, 85
Abū Sa'īd al-Khudrī, 54, 95, 115, 232
Abū Salamah, 2, 4
Abū Sufyān, 3, 5, 83
Abū Ṭalḥah al-Anṣārī, 165, 166
Abū Thawr, 45
Abū 'Ubaydah, 52
Abū Umāmah al-Bāhillī, 140
Abū Yusūf, 122
Abū Zur'ah, 162
Abyssinia, 162, 180, 181
'Ād, 248
'Aḍal, 2, 10
Adam, 78, 262, 268, 269
Aden, 180, 182
Afīq, 141
Africa, 146, 181
Ahab, 310, 311, 312
Ahaziab, 312
Aḥmad Ibn al-Nujaym, 127
Aḥmad ibn Ḥanbal, 44, 51, 54, 60, 72, 73, 78, 94, 95, 98, 108, 115, 116, 117, 135, 136, 137, 138, 139, 140, 141, 162, 163, 164, 165, 167, 178, 179, 189, 231, 234, 240, 305

Aḥmad, Mirzā Ghulām, 111, 147, 148
Aḥzāb, 3, 7, 13, 15, 16, 19, 31, 38, 43, 44, 47
'Ā'ishah, 18, 27, 43, 51, 54, 55, 79, 83, 85, 119, 141, 162, 164, 165, 166, 209, 232
'Alā' al-Dīn al-Baghdādī, 126
'Alī ibn Abī Ṭālib, 13, 14, 27, 47, 54, 55, 63, 116, 117, 120, 162, 163, 165, 166, 167, 304, 305
Almaqah, 179
Ālūsī, 65, 86, 91, 99, 129, 143, 318, 319, 320
al-Ālūsī, Maḥmūd ibn 'Abd Allāh, 129
'Āmilah, 179
'Āmir al-Sha'bī, 45, 78, 305, 307
Amorites, 313
'Amr ibn 'Ubayd, 305
Anas ibn Mālik, 45, 46, 51, 54, 72, 73, 79, 89, 95, 98, 115, 116, 164, 165, 166, 167, 290
Andalus, 129
al-Andalusī, Abū Muḥammad 'Alī ibn Aḥmad Ibn Ḥazm, 103, 122
Anmār, 179
Anṣār, 10, 11, 28, 29
Antioch, 246
Antiochus, 246
'Aqabat Afīq, 141
Arabia, 2, 5, 7, 10, 17, 40, 83, 172, 176, 178, 179, 180, 181, 188, 215, 243, 283, 309
Arabian Peninsula, 139, 179, 242
Arabic, 53, 54, 75, 96, 101, 112, 113, 114, 130, 172, 179, 240, 261, 316
Artemidorus, 183
Asa, 311
Asad, 7
Asha'arīyīn, 179
Ashja', 7, 11
'Ashtar, 179
Ash'taroth, 312, 313
'Āṣim, 127, 128
'Aṭā, 45, 305
'Aṭā' ibn Abī Rabāḥ, 305
'Atīq ibn 'Ā'idh al-Makhzūmī, 103
Aurangzeb 'Ālamgīr, 128
Aws, 14, 177
Awzā'ī, 45
Aylah, 182
al-'Aynī, Badr al-Dīn, 167, 290
Azd, 177, 179

Ba'al, 310, 311, 312, 313
Bāb al-Mandab, 180
Babylon, 181
Babylonia, 145, 179, 312
Bādhān, 181
Badr, 5
al-Baghawī, Abū Muḥammad Ḥusayn ibn Mas'ūd, 57, 123, 124
Bajīlah, 179
Banū 'Āmir, 2
Banū Asad, 2, 4, 7
Banū Ghaṭafān, 2, 4, 5, 11, 12
Banū Ḥanīfah, 120, 121
Banū Ma'ān, 63
Banū Muḥārib, 2
Banū Mulayḥ, 321
Banū al-Muṣṭaliq, 80
Banū Naḍīr, 2, 4, 7, 9, 14, 18
Banū Qayn ibn Ḥabr, 63
Banū Qaynuqā', 7, 14
Banū Qurayẓah, 1, 4, 9, 10, 12, 13, 14, 15, 16, 31, 33, 38, 39, 42, 43, 80
Banū Salimah, 321
Banū Sulaym, 2, 7
Banū Tha'labah, 2
Barā' ibn 'Āzib, 232
Bartley, James, 317
al-Bayḍāwī, 'Abd Allāh ibn 'Umar, 125
Bayhaqī, 54, 118
Bethlehem, 158
Bi'r Ma'ūnah, 2
Bukhārī, 13, 25, 26, 47, 53, 72, 73, 85, 89, 94, 95, 114, 116, 117, 135, 136, 162, 163, 164, 165, 166, 189, 208, 234
Buraydah al-Khuzā'ī, 95

Caesar, 40
Canaan, 304
Canaanites, 313
China, 181
Chosroes, 40

Ḍaḥḥāk, 241, 305
Dajjāl, 116, 136, 137, 138, 139, 140, 141, 143, 145, 146, 147
Damascus, 138, 146, 147
David, 150, 158, 170, 179, 184, 310, 311, 313

Dhakwān, 2
Dhāt al-Riqā', 5
Dhāt Ba'dān, 179
Dhāt Ḥamīm, 179
Dhū Nuwās, 181
Dūmat al-Jandal, 5, 7

Egypt, 5, 80, 181, 182, 312
Elijah, 310, 311, 312, 313, 314, 315
England, 317

Fāṭimah, 27, 54, 55, 102, 103
Fazārah, 7
Fīq, 141

Gabriel, 13, 165, 208, 209
Ghassān, 179
Ghaṭafān, 7, 12
al-Ghazzālī, Abū Ḥāmid Muḥammad ibn Muḥammad, 122, 123
Ghumdān Palace, 183
Gilead, 310
Gog and Magog, 139
Goliath, 158
Greece, 181
Gulf of Aqaba, 158

Ḥadramawt, 180
Ḥafṣah, 19, 43, 79, 83, 85
Hagar, 304
Ḥajjāj ibn Yūsuf, 307
al-Ḥākim, 54, 116, 140, 141, 146
Ḥakīm ibn Ḥizām, 63
Ḥamrā' al-Asad, 3
Ḥamzah, 3
Ḥanash al-Kinānī, 166
Ḥarīmat, 179
Ḥārithah ibn Sharāḥīl, 63
Ḥarmatam, 179
Ḥasan, 54, 55
Ḥasan al-Baṣrī, 45, 226, 241, 305
Ḥasan ibn Ṣāliḥ, 78
Ḥaqqī, Ismā'īl, 127
Hebron, 158
Ḥijāz, 183
Ḥimyar, 179, 180
Hind, 103
Hind ibn Abī Hālah, 103
Hishām ibn Muḥammad al-Sa'īd al-Kalbī, 103
Hittites, 313
Hivites, 313
Ḥudhayfah ibn Asīd al-Ghifārī, 139
Hudhayl, 2, 7
Ḥusayn, 54, 55
Ḥuyayy ibn al-Akhṭab, 9

Iblīs, 177, 178
Ibn 'Abd al-Barr, 103, 179
Ibn Abī Ḥātim, 54, 85, 94, 102, 297
Ibn Abī Laylā, 78
Ibn Abī Nujayḥ, 52
Ibn Abī Shaybah, 51, 94, 168
Ibn Aḥmad al-Makkī, 121
Ibn al-'Arabī, 43, 47, 167
Ibn al-Mundhir, 51, 101
Ibn Ḥajar al-'Asqalānī, 167, 290
Ibn Ḥazm, 103, 122
Ibn Jarīr al-Ṭabarī, 54, 94, 101, 102, 121, 178, 306
Ibn Kathīr, 51, 52, 54, 65, 79, 120, 126, 179, 226, 231, 234, 241, 247, 253, 275, 280, 295, 297, 305, 307, 308, 315, 318
Ibn Mājah, 72, 73, 78, 85, 94, 95, 98, 116, 136, 138, 140, 164, 165, 240
Ibn Marduwayh, 102
Ibn Sa'd, 51, 61, 103
Ibn Ṣayyād, 137, 138
Ibn Sīrīn, 101, 168
Ibn Zayd, 45, 280
Ibrāhīm al-Nakha'ī, 45, 78
'Ikrimah ibn Khālid, 54, 168, 241, 246, 280, 304, 305
Ilyāsīn, 314
'Imrān ibn Ḥaṣīn, 141
India, 121, 128, 129, 139, 146, 181
Indonesia, 181
Iraq, 5
Isaac, 300, 303, 304, 305, 306, 307, 308, 309
al-Iṣfahānī, Rāghib, 75
Isḥāq ibn Rāhwayah, 97
Ishmael, 243, 300, 301, 302, 304, 305, 306, 307, 308, 309
Israel, 29, 117, 138, 141, 146, 308, 310, 311, 312, 313

Jābir ibn 'Abd Allāh, 43, 44, 45, 97, 99, 115, 137, 138, 164, 189
Jābir ibn Zayd, 45
Jacob, 306
al-Jawf, 5

Jeb'usites, 313
Jeddah, 2, 177
Jehoram, 311, 312
Jehoshaphat, 311
Jerusalem, 147, 158, 310, 311
Jezebel, 310
John the Baptist, 314
Jordan, 141, 177, 182, 183, 310, 312
Joshua, 313
Judah, 158, 311
Judhām, 177, 179
Juhaynah, 321
al-Juwayanī, 167
Juwayrīyah, 80, 83

Ka'b al-Aḥbār, 246, 305, 308
Ka'b ibn 'Ujrah, 94
Kalb, 63
Khadījah, 63, 103
Khālid ibn al-Walīd, 83
al-Khalīl, 158
Khān, Sir Sayyid Aḥmad, 159, 171
Khath'am, 179
Khawwāt ibn Jubayr, 10
Khaybar, 5, 7, 32, 80
Khazraj, 177
Khubayb ibn 'Adī, 2
Khuzā'ah, 177, 321
Kindah, 177, 179

Lake Ṭabarīyā, 141
Lakhm, 177, 179
Layth ibn Sa'd, 78
Lebanon, 310, 312
Lod, 138
Ludd, 138, 139, 140, 147
Ludhiana, 147
Lydda, 138

Ma'ānib, 182
Ma'ārib Dam, 174, 180, 181
Madhḥij, 179
Madīnah, 2, 3, 4, 5, 7, 9, 10, 11, 13, 14, 18, 28, 31, 32, 38, 80, 101, 105, 117, 118, 120, 136, 162, 163, 177
Makḥūl, 305
Makkah, 2, 3, 32, 63, 118, 188, 278, 307, 309, 325
Malabar, 181
Mālik, 45, 46, 51, 72, 73, 78, 79, 89, 95, 98, 115, 116, 164, 165, 166, 167, 290
Ma'qal ibn Yasār, 240
Māriyah the Copt, 80
Marr al-Ẓahrān, 5
Mary, 29, 136, 137, 138, 139, 140, 141, 142, 145, 146, 147, 168
Masrūq, 47, 51, 280, 305
Maymūnah, 81, 118
Messiah, 134, 136, 142, 145, 146, 147, 148
Mīkā'īl, 315
Mīkā'īn, 315
Mīkāl, 315
Minā, 307
Moriah, 303
Morocco, 129
Moses, 29, 108, 116, 161, 250, 314
Mosul, 318
Mount Carmel, 311
Mount Sala', 9
Mount Sinai, 117, 311
Mount Uḥud, 9
Mu'ādh, 10, 11, 14
Mu'ādh ibn Anas al-Juhanī, 60
Mu'āwiyah, 305
Al-Mubarrad, 52
Muhājirūn, 28, 29
Muḥammad Bāqir, 97
Muḥammad ibn 'Alī al-Shawkānī, 128, 129
Muḥammad ibn al-Ḥanafīyah, 120
Muḥammad ibn al-Ḥasan, 78, 122
Muḥammad ibn Isḥāq, 103, 117
Muḥammad ibn Ka'b al-Quraẓī, 97, 305, 308
Mujāhid, 45, 52, 78, 253, 280, 305
Mujammi' ibn Jāriyah al-Anṣārī, 139, 140
Muqātil ibn Ḥayyān, 97
Muqawqis, 80
Murrah, 7
Musaylimah the Liar, 119, 120, 121
Muslim (Imām), 25, 26, 44, 54, 57, 72, 73, 85, 89, 94, 95, 98, 115, 116, 118, 135, 137, 138, 139, 162, 189, 208

Najd, 2, 4, 32
Najrān, 181
Nakha'ī, 45, 78
Al-Nasā'ī, 25, 44, 85, 94, 95, 116, 139, 162, 163, 164, 165, 166, 234, 240
Nawwās ibn Sam'ān al-Kilābī, 138

Nineveh, 318
al-Nīsābūrī, Niẓām al-Dīn, 102
Nu'aym ibn Mas'ūd, 11, 12, 13
al-Nu'mān ibn Thābit, 121

Pakistan, 146
Palestine, 138, 145, 175, 246, 310, 312, 313, 315
Per'izzites, 313
Persia, 183
Petra, 182, 183
Pharaoh, 54, 97, 182, 250, 309
Pharaoh Sesostris, 182
Pliny, 183
Prophet Elias, 310, 311, 312, 313, 314, 315
Prophet Hūd, 248
Prophet Jesus, son of Mary, 29, 72, 124, 125, 126, 127, 128, 134, 135, 136, 138, 139, 140, 141, 142, 143, 144, 145, 161, 168, 246, 314
Prophet Jonah, 315, 316, 317, 318, 319, 320, 321
Prophet Muḥammad, 2, 3, 4, 5, 7, 9, 10, 11, 12, 14, 15, 16, 17, 18, 19, 20, 22, 23, 26, 27, 28, 29, 30, 32, 33, 34, 35, 36, 38, 39, 41, 43, 44, 47, 48, 49, 53, 55, 62, 63, 66, 67, 68, 70, 71, 72, 73, 79, 80, 81, 82, 83, 84, 85, 88, 89, 90, 91, 92, 94, 95, 96, 97, 98, 99, 100, 101, 105, 106, 108, 111, 112, 113, 114, 116, 117, 118, 119, 120, 121, 122, 123, 124, 125, 126, 127, 128, 129, 130, 131, 132, 133, 134, 138, 142, 143, 144, 145, 146, 149, 150, 152, 154, 155, 160, 162, 163, 164, 165, 166, 181, 183, 185, 188, 189, 194, 195, 200, 201, 202, 205, 206, 207, 208, 210, 213, 214, 222, 223, 228, 229, 230, 233, 235, 239, 240, 241, 243, 247, 249, 250, 251, 254, 255, 264, 266, 274, 275, 277, 278, 283, 291, 295, 299, 301, 307, 314, 320
Prophet Noah, 248, 262, 263, 295, 296
Prophet Ṣāliḥ, 248
Prophet Solomon, 56, 118, 145, 150, 158, 159, 160, 161, 170, 171, 172, 179, 184, 310, 313
Ptolemy II, 182

Qāḍī 'Iyād, 99, 124, 167, 305
Qāḍī Shurayḥ, 101
Qādiyān, 111, 147
Qārah, 2, 10
Qāsim, 103
Qatādah, 45, 52, 102, 246, 253, 275, 280, 297, 304, 317, 318
Quraysh, 4, 5, 7, 12, 13, 17, 61, 63, 155, 215, 237, 239, 247, 274, 279, 299, 309, 315, 321

Rabī' ibn Anas, 280, 305
Rābigh, 2
Rajī', 2, 10
al-Rawḥā, 3, 136
Raydān, 180
Rayḥānah, 80, 83
al-Rāzī, Fakhr al-Dīn, 125, 231
Red Sea, 182
Rehoboam, 171, 310
Ri'l, 2
River Euphrates, 145, 158
River Jordan, 141
River Nile, 145, 182
Rome, 181, 182, 183
Ruqayyah, 103

Saba', 149, 173, 176, 177, 178, 179, 180, 181, 182, 184
Sa'd, 7, 14, 15
Sa'd ibn Abī Waqqāṣ, 25, 117
Sa'd ibn Mu'ādh, 10, 11, 14
Sa'd ibn 'Ubādah, 10, 11, 99
Ṣafīyah, 83
Sa'īd ibn Abī al-Ḥasan, 163
Sa'īd ibn al-Musayyib, 78, 305
Sa'īd ibn Jubayr, 168, 275, 280, 305
Sābūm, 179
Safīnah, 141
Sahl ibn Sa'd al-Sā'idī, 234
Sālim ibn 'Abd Allāh, 165, 166, 168
Samaria, 310
Samuel, 158, 313
Samurah ibn Jundub, 141, 290
Ṣan'ā', 180, 183
Sarai, 304
Satan, 51, 96, 178, 198, 211, 212, 268, 269, 270, 282, 294
Saul, 158, 313
Sawdah, 19, 43, 79, 82, 85
Sha'bī, 45, 97, 305, 307
Shāfi'ī, 45, 46, 97

al-Shahrastānī, Tāj al-Dīn Abū al-Fatḥ Muḥammad ibn 'Abd al-Karīm, 125
Sidon, 310
Ṣirwāḥ, 179
Strabo, 183
Su'dā bint Tha'labah, 63
al-Suddī, 102, 280, 305
Sufyān al-Thawrī, 45, 78, 167
Sufyān ibn 'Uyaynah, 241
Sulaymān ibn 'Abd Allāh al-Baḥrānī, 27
al-Suyūṭī, Jalāl al-Dīn, 126, 305
Syria, 5, 141, 147, 175, 176, 177, 181, 182, 183, 246, 307, 312, 315

Ṭabarānī, 118, 140, 240, 290
al-Ṭabrasī, Abū Manṣūr Aḥmad ibn Abī Ṭālib, 27
Al-Tabrayzī, 137, 138
Tabūk, 117, 182
Taftāzānī, Sa'd al-Dīn Mas'ūd ibn 'Umar, 143
Ṭāhir, 103
Ṭā'if, 63
Ṭalḥah, 95, 165, 166
al-Tamīmī, Abū Hālah, 103
al-Ṭayālisī, Abū Dā'ūd, 115, 117, 290
Ṭayy, 63
Ṭayyib, 103
Tel Aviv, 138
Thamūd, 248, 250
Thānawī, Ashraf 'Alī, 319
Thawbān, 117, 139
Theophrastus, 179
Tihāmah, 177, 293
Tirmidhī, 25, 51, 54, 72, 73, 78, 94, 98, 100, 101, 108, 115, 116, 135, 138, 140, 163, 164, 165, 166, 179, 209, 240
Torah, 161, 312
Ṭūr Sīnā, 315
Ṭūr Sīnīn, 315
Turkey, 129

'Ubaydah, 52, 101
Ubayy ibn Ka'b, 115
Uḥud, 1, 2, 3, 4, 5, 15, 16, 34
UK, 51
'Ukāẓ, 63
al-'Ulā', 182, 183
'Umān, 177
'Umar ibn al-Khaṭṭāb, 43, 45, 47, 78, 83, 89, 101, 116, 117, 118, 137, 166, 232, 304, 308
'Umar ibn 'Abd al-'Azīz, 78, 99, 308
Umm Ḥabībah, 80, 83, 162
Umm Kulthūm, 103
Umm Salamah, 4, 19, 43, 54, 55, 79, 83, 85, 162, 291
'Urwah ibn al-Zubayr, 54, 85
'Urwah ibn Mas'ūd, 139
USA, 51, 146
'Uṣayyah, 2
'Uthmān al-Battī, 78
'Uthmān ibn Abī al-'Āṣ, 140
'Uthmān ibn 'Affān, 45, 232
'Uthmānī, Shabbīr Aḥmad, 319, 320, 321

Wādī al-Qurā, 5, 7
Wādī Fāṭimah, 5
Wahb ibn Munabbih, 246
Wāthilah ibn Asqa', 54

Yamnāt, 180
Yarīm, 180
Yarmūk River, 310
Yathrib, 33, 177
Yazīd, 147
Yemen, 129, 139, 174, 175, 176, 177, 179, 180, 181, 182, 183
Yūsuf ibn Mahrān, 305

Ẓafār, 180
al-Zamakhsharī, Abū al-Qāsim Maḥmūd ibn 'Umar ibn Muḥammad, 102, 124, 160, 231
Zayd ibn al-Dathinnah, 2
Zayd ibn Aslam, 305
Zayd ibn Ḥārithah, 16, 17, 19, 22, 25
Zayd ibn Thābit, 47
Zaynab bint Jaḥsh, 1, 16, 17, 19, 20, 22, 30, 43, 61, 62, 63, 64, 65, 66, 67, 79, 80, 85, 89, 103, 111, 112
Zayn al-'Ābidīn 'Alī ibn al-Ḥusayn, 65
Zufar, 78
Zuhrī, 45, 85, 305